MW00466626

15.95

THE GOSPEL
ACCORDING TO LUKE

YOU MAY ORDER FROM:
THE CHRISTIAN GOLDMINE
87 Kight Circle
LaGrange, Ga. 30240
Phone: 404-882-0769
Rev. H. L. Jones

The Gospel According to Luke

By

G. CAMPBELL MORGAN, D.D.

Fleming H. Revell Company
OLD TAPPAN, NEW JERSEY

Dr. Henry Burton says—

"The Beautiful Gate of the Jewish Temple opened into the 'Court of the Women.' . . . As we open the gate of the third Gospel we enter the Court of the Women; for, more than any other evangelist, Luke records their loving and varied ministries."

Fittingly, then, I dedicate this book to my two girls,

KATHLEEN AND RUTH,

who for nine and six years, respectively, and alternately, have become, as Luke's friend, Paul, would say, "Women who have laboured with me in the Gospel," as they have travelled with me from city to city, in a comradeship merry and serious, never failing me in any hour—my Friends.

Foreword

A S in my volumes on Matthew, Mark and Acts, this consists of steno-
graphically reported Lectures.

The Introduction to the Book itself is found in the chapter dealing with
Luke's own Preface.

It goes without saying that these Lectures are not exhaustive. They are
intended to be suggestive, an introduction to a more detailed study of this
wonderful story of Jesus, so scientifically careful in statement, and yet radiant
with artistic form and colour.

Here the sovereignty of the King, and the sacrifice of the Servant, revealed
in Matthew and Mark, are interpreted in the Presentation of the Person of
the Word made flesh, the lonely, unique Being of the cycles of time, of our
very humanity, and yet more, infinitely more.

So I send it forth "at eventide," knowing its imperfections, but praying it
may fulfil some ministry of helpfulness.

G. C. M.

Philadelphia, Pa.

THE GOSPEL
ACCORDING TO LUKE

LUKE I. 1-4

AS introducing the study of the Gospel according to Luke, two matters demand our attention, those namely of the Writer of the book; and his Writing, as he himself introduces it to us in the preface.

Now, when I say that we are going to consider the writer, I do not mean by that I am going to enter into any debate as to who the writer was. We assume at the commencement that Luke wrote the book, and with that assumption today all scholarship agrees. We owe much to Sir William Ramsey for his scholarly examination of the documents, and also to the honesty of Harnack, who admitted the case proven as to the Lucan authorship.

What, then, do we know of Luke? We have no information other than that found in the New Testament. There, the only references to Luke are from the pen of Paul. We will begin by reading those references. The first in order is found at the close of the second of Paul's letters to the Corinthians, and the last chapter. In the King James' Version, we find a subscription, something not part of the letter. In the Revised Version, that subscription is omitted. We may, however, read it.

" The second epistle to the Corinthians was written from Philippi, a city of Macedonia, by Titus and Lucas."

The next reference is found in Colossians, chapter four, verse fourteen:

" Luke, the beloved physician, and Demas salute you."

In Philemon, at verse twenty-four, he is named again.

" Epaphras, my fellow-prisoner in Christ Jesus, saluteth thee; and so do Mark, Aristarchus, Demas, Luke, my fellow-workers."

Once more, II Timothy, chapter four, verses nine to eleven.

" Give diligence to come shortly unto me; for Demas forsook me, having loved this present world, and went to Thessalonica, Crescens to Galatia, Titus to Dalmatia. Only Luke is with me. Take Mark, and bring him with thee; for he is useful to me for ministering."

These are the only direct references which we find to Luke in the New Testament.

His name is suggestive. Loukas is really a pet name for Loukios. We have other illustrations of that nature in the New Testament. Silas is Silvanus; and Prisca is Priscilla; Apollonius is called Apollos; and Antipatris is called Antipas. It is a Greek name, and in the Colossian letter when Paul was ending with salutations, he said of some, these " are of the circumcision;" then he sent other salutations from others not of the circumcision; and Epaphras and Luke are named among those. Luke, then, was a Gentile, and in that the book is peculiar.

Again, he appears in both his books as the friend of Theophilus. His method of addressing Theophilus in the preface to this book, and in the introduction to the Acts, " Most excellent Theophilus," might be accurately rendered, " Your Excellency Theophilus." This whole subject is dealt with fully in a book by Professor Robertson, *Luke the Historian in the Light of Research*. His suggestion is that probably Luke was a freed man, who had been in slavery, and that Theophilus was his patron, who gave him his freedom, and remained his friend after both had become followers of Jesus Christ. What is perfectly clear is that Luke wrote his story for a man whom he calls

9

"Your Excellency," his patron; and also his friend.

There are evidences in the style of Luke that he was a Greek, and an educated Greek. Experts agree that the dialect employed was employed with a literary perfection, which is lacking in the other writings. Dr. Robertson suggests that probably he studied in the Schools of Tarsus, as also did Apollos, and Saul. The suggestion is that all three may have been students there together.

From Paul we learn that Luke was a physician, and in his writings we constantly find medical terms. I believe also that he was a ship's doctor. Read again, merely from the literary standpoint, the account of the long voyage (Acts xxvii). That never could have been written except by a man familiar with a ship, and the methods of the sailor. Now, all this has a bearing on the study of the book. The Divine element in the Bible is never perfectly discovered and realized, until the human element is recognized. These men who wrote these books of the New Testament were not automata. God wrought through the personality, selected by the Holy Spirit. I am prepared to go further. He always selected men who were by natural gifts, when controlled by Divine guidance, fitted for their work.

Let us go a step further at this point. There are those who believe that, even though a Greek, he was a proselyte to the Jewish faith, before he became a Christian. I do not believe it for a moment. I believe he came straight out of paganism to Jesus Christ. I do not think that he passed through the gateway of the Hebrew faith or religion at all. Trained in the Greek school, the university of Greece in Tarsus, or Athens, he had imbibed, from his youth up, all the Greek outlook on life, and that was entirely different from the Hebrew outlook on life. This man Luke, born a Greek, educated in Greek schools, had imbibed the Greek philosophy. The master passion of Greek idealism and Greek philosophy was that of the perfection of personality. The thinking, in those about three centuries of virile thought in Greek history, was not particularly concerned with human inter-relationships, but with personality, and the question of the perfecting of personality. Take the old-fashioned illustration, for it has been used very many times. Compare China with Greece. The history of China stretches back over millenniums. The history of Greece was virile for about three centuries only. In those three centuries, Greece flung up more outstanding personalities than China has in all the millenniums of her history. I am not speaking disrespectfully of China. I am comparing two great, but entirely different outlooks on life. China has stood through all the centuries and millenniums of her history for the solidarity of the race, the worship of ancestors has proved it, and reinforced it; her passion has not been that of the perfecting of individuals, but that of maintaining racial relationship. Greece was not so concerned; she sought for the perfecting of the individual; and she wrought her ideal out into marble, and until this day, the canon and criterion of all accuracy in presentation, and beauty in sculpture is that of Greece.

This, then, is Luke, a man, somewhere, somehow, somewhen,—and none knows when it happened,—was led to Christ, and he found in Jesus—I am taking the human name for a moment resolutely,—he found in Jesus the Personality Who fulfilled all his dreaming, and smashed the mould of Greek thinking by His greatness, for it was too small to hold Him. This Gospel draws the personality of our Lord from that standpoint, as fulfilling the ideal of uttermost and absolute perfection. As far as I am concerned, I say without any hesitation, Matthew could not have written from that standpoint; Mark certainly could not have done so, neither could John. They all had the same material and Person; but differing men, chosen of the Holy Spirit, saw different phases of truth. Here, then, is the writing of a Greek, cultured, educated, refined, with Greek idealism colouring his outlook, coming to Christ, and finding in Christ that which fulfilled the highest in his thinking before he found Christ, and correcting and destroying everything that was false in that thinking. This is the man who writes this story.

Two elements merged in him, which are very rarely found in one person. He was a man of scientific mind. He claims that. This was a scientific treatise, the result of scientific examination of the personality of Jesus. But he is also an artist. There is an old legend of the Church that a painting of the Virgin Mother was found in Jerusalem from the brush of Luke. The early Church writers all spoke of him as an artist. Somebody has said that he was a poet, too, and gives as a proof, that he caught and preserved for us the great songs that burst upon the world with the coming of Jesus into it. Here, then, is a remarkable man, artistic in temperament and scientific in mentality.

And yet once more, and this is of supreme importance. This man was the close friend and fellow-traveller of Paul for years. There is something very beautiful about that. Whether it is true or not, as Dr. Robertson suggests, that they were students together in Tarsus, we do know that Paul was born in Tarsus, and all the early years of his life he lived in Tarsus. Although Paul was a Jew, a Hebrew, and a Jew of Jewry, of the tribe of Benjamin; whereas Paul was all that, and whereas that was the dominant passion in all his mental outlook, he was certainly influenced by those early years and surroundings. Paul, therefore, could sympathize with all the Greek that was in Luke.

We know when he became his companion from Acts xvi.11. He had been recording the work of others in the third person, and suddenly he employs the first person as he said, " We made." Luke joined him just at the beginning of the European campaign. At Philippi he was with him. He was with him, too, in Thessalonica. Then the brethren sent Paul up to Berœa, and presently he went on to Athens. Then Luke was left behind; but he soon joined him again. We pick up the reference in xx.5, 6, and then right on to the end, he was with Paul. He was with him all the two years in Cæsarea, during Paul's imprisonment there. Do not forget here, how near Cæsarea was to Jerusalem. There he was in the neighbourhood of the things which had happened. He was with Paul on the journey and voyage to Rome; and there can be no doubt that some years after he was with him in his last imprisonment; and he certainly passed under the influence of Paul's interpretation of Christ and Christianity. He investigated under that influence.

Here, then, let us turn aside for a moment to consider Paul's interpretation of the humanity of Jesus. There are certain references which we may note. Romans v.15, I Cor. xv.47, Phil. ii.8, I Tim. ii.5. Those are the only places in the writings of Paul where Paul refers to Jesus as a Man, that is, the only places where he names Him Man. If Paul wrote the letter to the Hebrews, then we may add Heb. iii.3, vii.24, viii.3, x.12; but in the Revised Versions, the word " man " is not in either of these references. So I shall, in this connection, leave Hebrews out altogether. Then we have four places where Paul definitely refers to Jesus as Man. If we consider them in their context, we shall find Paul's interpretation of Christ. That is a much larger matter. I refer only to his interpretation of the human in our Lord. There is one pregnant phrase and reference and description in the Corinthian passage, in which Paul called Jesus the " second Man." He also called Him the " last Adam." Do not make the stupid blunder of calling Jesus the second Adam. He called Him the second Man, and the last Adam. If you say second, you postulate a third, fourth, fifth, and a succession. The second Man He was, and from that second Man a whole race of new men has sprung. But He is the last Adam; the race springing from Him will be final, in that it will meet the Divine ideal. Paul saw Jesus as God's second Man, as man's last Adam. Luke's story, the story of a Greek, a physician, educated, trained, of scientific mind, of artistic temperament, and the friend and companion of Paul, sets Jesus forth as being the second Man, the last Adam, fulfilling everything in His idealism, the perfect One, the perfect Personality, and exceeding Greek idealism as revealing Him as Head of a race.

Now let us read the Preface which is contained in the first four verses. A preface is always written to introduce the reader to the book; and the writer always writes it last. There is no question that the first four verses in this Gospel were written last by Luke; the tenses he used prove this. He referred to the writing as completed.

" Forasmuch as many have taken in hand to draw up a narrative concerning those matters which have been fulfilled among us, even as they delivered them unto us, who from the beginning were eyewitnesses and ministers of the Word, it seemed good to me also, having traced the course of all things accurately from the first, to write unto thee in order, most excellent Theophilus; that thou mightest know the certainty concerning the things wherein thou wast instructed."

There are four things Luke tells us in this preface. He names his subject; gives the sources of his information; describes the method of his work; and reveals the purpose of his writing.

He names the subject. " The Word," " eyewitnesses and ministers of the Word." That is his final name for Jesus. He had written his story about Jesus in His human nature and His human life; but when he came to write the preface he summed up, and he does not say, Those who were eyewitnesses and ministers of Jesus of Nazareth, or of the Christ, but " of the Word." That is as definitely a title there, as it is in the Gospel of John.

" In the beginning was the Word, and the Word was with God, and the Word was God. . . . And the Word became flesh and tabernacled among us . . . full of grace and truth."

In reading that, we know John is using a title for Jesus. Translators have always spelled the word " Word " with a capital letter in John, but they have spelled it in Luke with a small letter. Now, there is no reason from the standpoint of translation why *ó logos* in the Gospel of John, and Luke's inflected *tou logou*, should not be treated in the same way. In each case the definite article is used. Dr. Robertson says concerning this book:

" The humanity of Jesus in Luke is not the deity of humanity so much as the humanity of deity."

It is the human we see, but He is here, God manifest in the flesh. When Luke writes, it is the story of the perfect Man, but when the story is finished, he does not talk about Jesus; when he speaks of Him, he calls Him " The Word."

Then he gives us the sources of his information. He tells us that many had taken in hand to write a narrative. The reference may include the story Mark had written, and the story which Matthew had written; but it includes many more. He said many had taken in hand to write. Thus we first see him collecting every such story he could find. But there was another source of information. " Those who from the beginning were eyewitnesses and ministers of the Word "—those who had actually seen Jesus, and served Him in the days of His flesh. To them he talked. His word for these people is arresting: " eyewitnesses," *Autoptai*. This is a medical term. We are familiar with it in its English form, autopsy. What is an autopsy? Strictly it is a personal, first-hand investigation. Autopsy means seeing for yourself. Generally, medical men now use it in connection with post-mortem examinations. But it is personal investigation. Not merely those who had seen Jesus personally, but living ministers to Jesus, who had investigated Jesus for themselves. He got first-hand stories. The word, " ministers," is equally interesting *Uperetai*. It also was a word in medical use. Literally it means underrowers. This word was used for doctors who were in attendance upon the principal physician in any case, internes, as we might call them. Thus this doctor is using medical terms. He said, I obtained my information from those who personally investigated Jesus, those who served Him in the days of His flesh, those under-rowers, who were in attendance upon Him, the Great Physician, as He went out upon His work everywhere.

All this reveals the fact that this book was probably the work of years.

He collected the writings; talked to any one who had first-hand stories to tell him. I have no doubt that somewhere he was introduced to the Mother of Jesus, and from her had the matchless story that he could have gained from none other.

Then he reveals the method of his work. First he says that he traced the course of all things accurately from the beginning. That is an important alteration from the old Version, which makes it look as though Luke meant, he knew all from the beginning. He means the exact opposite. He obtained all the material; and then he traced the course of all things accurately. This was the work of scientific investigation of the whole of the stories he had gathered about Jesus.

In this connection he employed a word which arrests us. He says he traced the course of all things "*anothen.*" We have rendered that, "from the first." Now, that word in Greek use does sometimes mean "from the first," but it also means "from above." In strict etymology, I think the probability is that it means "from above." Note one or two occurrences of the same word. Jesus was talking to Nicodemus, and said: "Ye must be born *anothen.*" The old Version rendered that "again." The Revisers have rendered it, "anew," and "born from above" in the margin. I am quite sure Jesus meant, "from above." Take another illustration. "The wisdom that cometh down *anothen.*" There it must be "from above." My own view is that when Luke says he traced the course of all things accurately "*anothen,*" he meant from above; and that he was claiming that his scientific work was under the guidance of heaven itself, that he not only brought to bear upon his work his own scientific ability to sift and trace; but he sought guidance from heaven. That is how he prepared his material.

And then he says he wrote "in order." This phrase "in order" is one word in the Greek, *Kathexes,* which is the word of the artist. He claims that having obtained his material, and sifted and examined it, and put it in proper relationship, he wrote it in artistic order.

Finally, he reveals the purpose of the writing. "That thou mightest know the certainty concerning the things wherein thou wast instructed." Certainty here means more than intellectual conviction; it signifies safety, security. Then carefully observe the word "instructed," in the phrase "concerning the things wherein thou wast instructed." It should be rendered "instructed by word of mouth." That is very important. Theophilus, his friend, had been instructed, not through writing, but by oral instruction. It is the Greek word from which we derive our word "catechism," which strictly is instruction by word of mouth. Theophilus evidently was not in possession of a writing upon which he could depend. Luke wrote that he might have certainty, safety, that he may know security. That indicates the value of all historic documents. The writing gives fixity to the truth. Oral teaching is never safe for finality. I may tell you the story of Jesus, and I tell it to you honestly as I know it. You repeat it, as the result of your hearing from me, with equal honesty. Inevitably there will be some deflection. By the time this process has gone far enough, the story may not be the same at all. Luke wrote in order that Theophilus might have a document, a writing, giving fixity to the truth, and in it find certainty, certitude. Thus the value of the writing is that it gives the truth in germ and in norm. In germ, that is, it needs development, consideration, amplification. In norm, that is, that in all such processes it is the standard of examination, and the test of accuracy.

Such, in brief, is what we know of the writer, and of the writing. With these things in mind we may go forward with our study of the book.

LUKE I. 5-25

"And he shall go before His face in the spirit and power of Elijah, to turn the hearts of the fathers to the children, and the disobedient to walk in the wisdom of the just; to make ready for the Lord a people prepared."—Luke i.17.

THERE are two more words in our translation, "for Him," but they are supplied. We end where the text really ends, "a people prepared."

This was the statement of the angel Gabriel concerning John. It is central to the paragraph which begins at verse five, and ends at verse twenty-five. Luke begins his story of Jesus with an account of His forerunner. This in itself is immediately arresting and significant; significant of the greatness of John, and of the glory of that for which his ministry prepared. When we read these twenty-five verses we are already standing on the threshold of the most marvellous period in all the history of humanity, that comparatively brief period of a generation, as we measure generations now, of about three and thirty years. The life of Jesus is the central and pivotal generation in human history. There was nothing like it before; and everything before it led up to it. There has been nothing like it since; but everything since has been related to the things that happened then.

This story of John constitutes a link, connecting the work of our Lord with everything that had gone before. The story is the link between the old economy and the new. To use Biblical phrasing, it is the link between that period in human history when in times past God spoke unto the fathers by prophets in divers portions and divers manners, and that period in which God was about to speak to men finally in His Son. The story shows that from the Divine standpoint there is no break, but continuity.

Here we see all the things of the past economy, and this remarkable man, John, linking up that past with that which was to come. The old and the new are seen to be a continuous movement in the programme of God. Sharp the break in many ways between the

old and the new on the level of humanity's experience; but in the economy of God everything moved forward.

The time note is marked in the fifth verse:

"There was in the days of Herod, king of Judæa, a certain priest, named Zacharias."

"In the days of Herod." We read it easily. We have read it all our lives; and reading it easily, and regularly, and persistently, we know what it means; but let us stop and think of its real significance; of the dark, sinister, and terrible condition of things suggested; nay, more than suggested, declared, by this little phrase, "the days of Herod." This is the Herod we commonly call the Great. He was an Idumean. In the twenty-seventh chapter of Genesis, and the forty-first verse we find these words: "And Esau hated Jacob." I need not say more. Herod was an Idumean. Herod did not belong to Jacob. He belonged to Esau; and that long line of continuous hatred had lasted across the centuries. It is an arresting fact, that at that time an Idumean was reigning over the Jewish people. Herod was king. "In the days of Herod, king of Judæa." They had never had a king since the captivity, until this man was king. His title of king was conferred upon him by the Roman Senate, through the influence of Antonius and Octavius. He was a vassal of Rome, and by courtesy was called king. There was no real meaning in his kingship. His authority was only delegated, and the title was the result of his sycophancy with the Roman empire. Herod at this period had done a dastardly thing. He had erected in the land, vast and gorgeous temples for the worship of idols. The Jewish people did not enter these temples; but the land was swarming with Gentiles, and Herod built the temples for them, and the influence reacted upon the Jews. Moreover, he had introduced games which were blasting Rome itself. "In those days," when "Herod was king of

Judæa." That is the time note, and it reveals the condition of the land.

When the declaration came concerning the coming of John, it came to the Temple. The Temple was then in process of building, and had been so for sixteen years. It was not completed when our Lord commenced His ministry. When, thirty years later, they said, "Forty and six years was this Temple in building," they did not say that it took that time, for it was not even then finished. It was of exquisite workmanship, a marvellous structure, a Temple by its very magnificence violating some of the first principles for which these people had stood. Nevertheless, it was the Temple, and when the announcement concerning the birth of John was to be made, it was to the Temple that the angel came, and not to the outer courts. The word translated Temple is *Naos,* which included the Holy place, and the Holy of Holies. The angel appeared in the Holy place, not the Holy of Holies, for the altar of incense stood in front of the veil.

The messenger came to a priest, a priest of the order of Aaron, one in the direct priestly line. The priesthood was still in existence, a Divine institution. But it was to *a* priest, not the high priest, but to a priest in the Temple service. He came on a day when the multitudes were there. They were gathered around the Temple. Luke thus gives us a graphic suggestive picture of the time and the conditions, as he introduces His forerunner. The king is there, degenerate. The Temple is there, desecrated. The priesthood is there, degraded. The people are there, debased. Nevertheless, God proceeds upon the line of His own ordination. He comes to the Temple, though it is desecrated. He comes to the priesthood, though on the whole it is degraded. He did not come to the king. He did not come to the people, save through the appointed channel of the priesthood. In the Divine operation the principle of selection is manifest. The king was passed; he was an Idumean, unrecognized by high heaven. The Temple was desecrated. Presently our Lord said, "Your house is left unto you desolate;" and the desecrating

process was already going forward. Nevertheless, it was the symbol of the Divine presence, successor of the Tabernacle of old, centre of the Divine throne and authority. This principle is manifest again, as God comes to the priest, but not to the high priest, not to the priest degraded and debased by a false thinking about God; but to a priest fulfilling his service. All the old was being linked up to the new. God was not contradicting anything of the past. Everything in the past is seen, moving on towards the fulfilment of the Divine purpose. Jesus is seen coming "in the fulness of time;" the Divine continuity of purpose is at work. And this is the background that we find as we study this particular passage.

So we turn to the declaration of the mission of John by Gabriel:

"He shall be great in the sight of the Lord, and he shall drink no wine nor strong drink; and he shall be filled with the Holy Spirit, even from his mother's womb. And many of the children of Israel shall he turn unto the Lord their God. And he shall go before His face in the spirit and power of Elijah, to turn the hearts of the fathers to the children, and the disobedient to walk in the wisdom of the just; to make ready for the Lord a people prepared."

Gabriel, in declaring what the office of the forerunner was to be, quoted in the listening ear of the priest in the Temple, the very last words of the Nebiim, or Prophets, with which these Hebrews were familiar. Four hundred years before the coming of Messiah, four hundred years before John, Malachi was the last of the great messengers, and these were his final words:

"Remember ye the law of Moses My servant, which I commanded unto him in Horeb for all Israel, even statutes and ordinances. Behold, I will send you Elijah the prophet before the great and terrible day of Jehovah come. And he shall turn the heart of the fathers to the children, and the heart of the children to their fathers; lest I come and smite the earth with a curse."

If we go into any Hebrew synagogue on Sabbath next, and it happens that they are reading that particular passage, you will find the Rabbi never ends with those final words, " Lest I come and smite the earth with a curse." They always go back and read the immediately preceding part of the verse, "And he shall turn the heart of the fathers to the children, and the heart of the children to their fathers." They read the solemn warning, " Lest I come and smite the earth with a curse," but they never end there; they go back and read the words of hope.

It is significant that the angel ended with the last words of hope from the Hebrew prophet. Four hundred years no voice, and then the final words that had come from an authentic prophet, were spoken in the Temple to a listening priest. That prophecy, that final word was now about to be fulfilled, and the mission of the forerunner was declared. He will turn the hearts of the fathers to the children, and the hearts of the children to the fathers. In other words, he will come to restore primal ideals. He will come to turn these renegade people back to the patriarchs, Abraham, Isaac, Jacob, and to the things for which they stood. Thus the angel in the Temple employed the final words of Hebrew prophecy, to show that what was now about to happen was in continuity of a Divine procedure.

A great principle is involved in this. God's work is continuous, but there are often gaps, and the gaps are created for two reasons, first because God never works by almanacks; and secondly because it is possible for men and women, sinning men and women, to postpone His activity, but never ultimately to defeat it. Four hundred years, but now the thing is to go on; and the angel, quoting these final words, declares that the mission of John shall be in fulfilment of that final prediction. One can imagine how, during the dark days of those four hundred years, devout souls would sometimes be tempted to say: God must have forgotten, God must have broken down, God must have failed! Some Christian people so speak today, when things look dark. God has not forgotten, God has not broken down, God has not failed. Malachi, the messenger of the old covenant, closing for

the time being the period of prophetic ministry, declared that the messenger should come, and prepare the way of the Lord, and his mission should be to turn the heart of the fathers to the children, and the heart of the children to the fathers. Four hundred years passed, and suddenly into the Temple, splendid and desecrated; to the priesthood largely degraded, but having its loyal sons within its borders; the angel came, swift from the presence of God, one Gabriel; and he said in effect, if I may change the wording to insist upon the value: God has not forgotten, God has not broken down, God has not failed; the thing predicted is now coming. The continuity of the Divine activity is clearly revealed.

Now we turn to the story itself. With what perfect naturalness and historic simplicity Luke tells it, merging the ordinary and the extraordinary; that is, the natural, and the supernatural.

First, the ordinary or natural things are here. Two people are seen, Zacharias and Elisabeth, both of priestly parentage. I cannot read this story without being arrested by these names. Zacharias means, Jehovah remembers. The father and mother of Zacharias gave the boy a name, and those old Hebrews, when they gave their children names, did not choose them because they thought they were pretty. When this man and this woman chose the name of this boy, and called him Zacharias—not Jehovah, but the shortened form, Jah, Jah, remembers—they had something in their mind concerning the highest things of life. There is in it a sound like a sob of sorrow, a recognition of desolation, but it is a song of assured hope—Jah remembers! Herod was not yet king when that boy was born, but the conditions were leading up to that climax of evil. The darkness of the land was deep, desolation was everywhere; and the man and woman had a laddie born, and they called him, Jah remembers.

Then, in process of time, he married a daughter of Aaron, whose name was Elisabeth. There was another priestly family somewhere, and to that father and mother a girl was born. Perhaps they were a little disappointed that it was not a boy, for such was often the case in Jewish homes in those days; but they gave her a name, a great name. Again in it I think I can find the revelation of a gasp, a hope, an aspiration, a reminder to strengthen faith in dark days. They called her Elisabeth,—the oath of God. These people—Zacharias and Elisabeth, two ordinary people; and yet their very names suggest hope, aspiration, faith, still living in that ancient economy.

Then their character is given in verse six:

"They were both righteous before God, walking in all the commandments and ordinances of the Lord blameless."

That is a wonderful description of these two people. God has always had His elect remnant; and here were two of them unquestionably. "They were both righteous before God, walking in all the commandments"—that is, the moral law—"and ordinances"—that is, the ceremonial law—"of the Lord blameless." That is complete revelation. Nothing need be said about it.

But now observe the next words.

"And they had no child, because that Elisabeth was barren, and they both were now well stricken in years (verse seven).

Once again we must get back into the Jewish atmosphere. That was the tragedy in their home according to their way of thinking; they were childless. Some Jewish writers have told us that the sense of tragedy was not so much that they lacked a child, as that by such lack they were cut off from all relationship to the hope for Messiah. That is something which, I think, we have hardly recognized sometimes, that these people looked upon children as the heritage of the Lord, and were all, the devout ones, hoping that from their loins would spring their long-looked-for Messiah. They were childless, and therefore they had no hope of any living link along the line of the flesh with Messiah. That was the tragedy to the mind of the devout Jew. These two people had desired a son, had prayed

for a son, and had given up praying for that son.

"But the angel said unto him, Fear not, Zacharias; because thy supplication is heard."

Thus it is evident that they had prayed for a son, and the response of Zacharias proves that they had given up hope:

"And Zacharias said unto the angel, Whereby shall I know this? for I am an old man, and my wife well stricken in years."

They had hoped, they had prayed. The answer had not come, and along the line of the ordinary, the natural, there was no hope.

To that man the angel was sent, and the revelation came in the orderly course of his work. But it also is true that it came to him in a great day. It was the day when he passed to the altar of incense, and burnt the incense thereon. That act came to no priest save once in his lifetime. There were at least twenty thousand priests at the time; and every one of them was supposed to have one day when he entered the Holy Place, and standing by the table of incense, he lifted the fire, and caused the incense to rise. It was a great day in the priestly work of Zacharias. It was ordinary, but a great day.

Now let us turn to the extraordinary, or supernatural things. First the appearance of the angel. Luke does not go aside to argue for the existence of angels. He writes it down with perfect naturalness. The supernatural is written down as being natural. The extraordinary is recorded as ordinary. Why? Because Luke was writing from the Divine standpoint; and all the things we call supernatural are only supernatural because they are super, beyond, the reach of our mentality to explain. The angel standing there was supernatural to men, but natural to God.

This was the first angel communication of which we have any authentic record for four hundred years. Its keynote was "Fear not." The outlook was desolate, dark, and an angel came from God. God found His vantage ground in the soul of a man exercising his priestly office; himself righteous before God, walking in all His commandments and ordinances, blameless; and the first words that passed the angelic lips were, " Fear not." Then followed the declaration that to this childless pair, past the years of the possibility of having a son, a son should be born. All the history of the Bible is the history of the extraordinary touching the ordinary, of the supernatural acting upon and beyond the natural. The extraordinary is ordinary to God. The supernatural is natural with God. The son is to be born. Go back to the beginning of the economy. Where did it begin? In Abraham. How did it go on? A supernatural son, Isaac. I can hear Sarah laughing across the centuries. Do you wonder at it? I can see Abraham halting in his belief. Belief had brought him from Ur of the Chaldees; but now he laughed, and Sarah laughed. God is very patient, when unbelief laughs at Him. The son was born!

All this story is background. The light is on the horizon of the coming of Jesus; but this is that which precedes His coming. We are looking at the forerunner, and the supernatural is already seen in the angel's visit, and in the declaration that a son is to be born to Zacharias and Elisabeth, out of the natural order.

The angel tells his name. His name shall be called John. John simply means the grace of God. The father, Zacharias, Jah remembers; the mother, Elisabeth, the oath of God; and now the boy, John, the grace of God. They did not choose the name; the angel declared it as heaven's name for him, the grace of God; the offspring of the remembrance of God and the oath of God.

We turn once more to the ordinary, the natural. Zacharias feared when he saw the angel.

" Zacharias was troubled when he saw him, and fear fell upon him." And he raised the difficulty along the line of the natural, when he heard that the son was to be born. And once again, see the extraordinary, the supernatural, " Fear not," Thy prayer is answered. I am Gabriel. I was sent by God.

In the presence of his fear and doubt, Zacharias was given a sign. What was it? That he should be dumb and deaf. Nine months he could not hear anything, nor speak. Almost all expositors say that this deafness and dumbness was a punishment for unbelief. I do not believe there was any element of punishment in it. He wanted a sign, and God gave him a sign; and it was that he was rendered speechless and deaf. He was plunged into a great silence. He could hear no voices, he could say no word. I do not think it was a punishment. I think it was a sign. He wanted it, and what a gracious sign it was. What a blessed thing to be able for nine months to hear nobody talk, and to talk to nobody! Of course, I mean after a revelation like that. I do not think it was a rebuke. Gabriel did say, " Because thou believedst not my words;" but it does not mean he was being punished. He was plunged into himself with God, for nine months to ponder the thing. When the silence was over, what did he do? He sang the Benedictus, " Blessed be the Lord, the God of Israel." Out of the silence came the song, and in some respects, no greater poem was ever given to the listening ear of humanity.

Thus as we ponder Luke's story of the preparation of the herald of the Lord, we are constrained to exclaim, " Our God is marching on." Human failure everywhere, but the Divine victory is clearly seen. Yet in order to Divine victory, in the midst of human failure, God needed, and He found, loyal souls as His vantage ground. A little group is seen. We shall see more of them anon, Anna, and Simeon, and Mary, and Joseph; all members of an elect remnant, living in the remembrance and truth of the past. There God found vantage ground, set down His foot, and marched on toward the great event; the coming into human life in the Person of His Son, and all that followed thereupon.

Wonderful, wonderful story, the merging of the ordinary and the extraordinary, of the natural and the supernatural; God never defeated, but marching on toward the goal upon which His heart is set.

LUKE I. 26-38

" Now in the sixth month the angel Gabriel was sent from God unto a city of Galilee, named Nazareth. . . . And the angel departed from her."—Luke i.26, 38.

THESE sentences constitute the boundaries of the matchless story of the Annunciation. The story is matchless indeed, mysterious, magnificent, and majestic. It is the story of the coming of the angel Gabriel to Nazareth; the story of a messenger sent from heaven, bringing to earth stupendous tidings. As we approach it, let us do so in the very temper and spirit of the words that were written by the Apostle Paul to Timothy, when he said,

" Without controversy great is the mystery of godliness."

Let us first observe the setting of the event, and then consider the story itself.

In looking at the setting there are two things to be observed; first, the locality; and secondly, the personalities.

" Now in the sixth month the angel Gabriel was sent from God unto a city of Galilee, named Nazareth, to a virgin betrothed to a man whose name was Joseph, of the house of David; and the virgin's name was Mary. And he came in unto her."

As to locality, Galilee, not Judæa; Nazareth, not Jerusalem; the home where Mary dwelt, not the Temple. Judæa was the centre of the land that God had chosen to be the theatre of His operations through the centuries. Jerusalem was—as our Master called it subsequently—the city of the great King. The Temple was at the centre of the city, the very dwelling-place of God, as to His manifestation, and as to His communion with His people.

When this heavenly messenger came to earth with stupendous tidings he passed over Judæa and went to Galilee, Galilee held in contempt, and that for long centuries. We find it existing in the time of Isaiah;

" But there shall be no gloom to her

that was in anguish. In the former time He brought into contempt the land of Zebulun and the land of Naphtali; but in the latter time hath He made it glorious, by the way of the sea, beyond the Jordan, Galilee of the nations" (Isaiah ix.1).

Even then, Galilee had been over-run with Gentiles, and was referred to in contempt. At this time it was the tetrarchy of Herod, in which pagan temples were raised; and in which the games of pagan peoples were demoralizing its people. Therefore Judæa, in her pride of place and power and position, still held it in contempt. To Galilee God's messenger was sent.

Again, he passed by Jerusalem, the city of the great King, and came to Nazareth. This town was situated about seventy miles northeast from Jerusalem, and was a half-way house between that city and Tyre and Sidon in Phœnicia. I want to stay here a moment, because it has a bearing on our study. Nazareth stood on the hillside, and at the foot of the hill ran the great highway between Tyre and Sidon and Jerusalem. Along that highway there passed Roman soldiers, Greek merchants, Greek travellers, Jewish priests. In my boyhood's days Nazareth was thought of as a little village or hamlet of about three thousand souls or less. We know now that Nazareth then had at least fifteen thousand in population, possibly more. It was one of the cities of Galilee; and being where it was geographically, it was the place where Roman soldiers often tarried over-night, and Greek merchantmen put up in the caravansaries. Nazareth was a hotbed of corruption I need not go into details. Your imaginations will help you to see what it could be like under those conditions. When Nathanael said,

" Can any good thing come out of Nazareth?"

he spoke as one familiar with the place. This is one of the popularly misunderstood and misapplied sayings of the Bible. Generally we have imagined that Nathanael was speaking in contempt for its smallness, and relation to Galilee. Do not forget that he belonged to a neighbouring city. He knew Nazareth well; and when he asked the question he was speaking the blunt truth, in the guilelessness of his heart. He said in effect, Can any good thing come out of Nazarath, corrupt as Nazareth is? To Nazareth, perhaps one of the most corrupt towns to be found in all that region at that time, came the messenger.

Notice once more. Passing by Judæa, and going to Galilee; passing over the city of the great King, and going to Nazareth, he passed over the Temple, and entered a home. Something was about to happen on earth which all heaven was watching,—" which things angels desire to look into "—and surely they were watching the hero of God, Gabriel, the messenger going down to earth with a message. They saw him pass the city and the Temple and go into a home.

God, in His actions in human history, is independent of His own institutions, when men degrade them. The land was blighted; the city was blasted; the Temple was degraded; and God's messenger passed them all. God left the land of His own choosing, abandoned the city of His love; and passed the Temple of His own appointment. So much for locality.

Now as to the personalities. There are two; Mary and Joseph. Joseph is named, but we are told nothing about him here. We may go to Matthew, and there we have his description in i.18 and xiii.55. Two things we are told about him. He was "a righteous man;" and he was a carpenter. We speak of the poverty to which our Lord came. Let us not forget that poverty is a relative term. He certainly did not come to wealth, but He certainly did not come to penury. The home of the carpenter in a city like Nazareth was not that of abject poverty. In the book of Proverbs, we have the prayer of Agur,

" Give me neither poverty nor riches;
  Feed me with the food that is needful for me."

Neither too much, nor too little. I think that would describe the home life of Joseph and Mary.

Now let us look at Mary. The Protestant Church has altogether too long wronged the Virgin Mother. Mariolatry is idolatry. But in our rebound from the false position into which the Mother of our Lord has been lifted by the Roman Church, we have too often neglected her, we have been unfair to her, we have consigned her almost to oblivion. Let us therefore look at her as we see her on this page. Gabriel came

" To a virgin betrothed to a man whose name was Joseph, of the house of David; and the virgin's name was Mary. And he came in unto her, and said, Hail, thou that art highly favoured."

That word "Hail" is a greeting, but it is a cognate word of the word favour, or grace. I do not like the rendering "highly favoured," for it suggests that the reference was to the high office which she was to fulfil as Mother of Messiah, whereas it was a description of her character. I am going to change the reading,

" Grace be unto thee, thou art endued with grace, the Lord is with thee."

Thus Mary is revealed to us here. She is declared quite simply to have been a virgin, *parthenos*. There are not two meanings for that word. The meaning is simple and self-evident. But she was a virgin betrothed, not married. Betrothal lasted in those times one year. It was in that period in her life that the angel visited her.

Her character is revealed in the salutation of the angel;

" Grace unto thee, thou who are endued with grace; the Lord is with thee."

This, as I have already pointed out, had no reference to the office she was to fulfil. It had reference to her character, which created her fitness for the office. "Thou art endued with grace, the Lord is with thee." In that salutation we have a portrait of Mary. Living in Nazareth, with the dark and sinister background of its conditions, in the midst of all kinds of impurity and iniquity; she was endued with grace, the Lord was with her. Here we see her, a maiden of the royal line, the blood of David coursing in her veins, in the town, but held from all impurity, endued with grace; living in the fellowship of the God of her fathers, living in quietness and in peace and in purity.

Now notice carefully what happened.

"But she was greatly troubled."

Once again allow me to change the word "troubled." It might mean that she was caused sorrow, or pain. Therefore I am going to substitute another word,—agitated.

"She was greatly agitated at the saying, and cast in her mind what manner of salutation this might be."

She was agitated at the manner of the angel's address. She was not agitated at the fact of an angelic visit. The probability is she had never seen one before; but she believed in them. She undoubtedly belonged to the Pharisaic school as to her philosophy; she was not Sadducean. Of course, it was a wonder when the radiant presence of the angel was discovered in the home; but the thing that agitated her was his salutation. To be told by this bright angelic being that she was endued with grace,—she could not understand it. She did not know that. She was not conscious of the beauty of her character. That is in itself a revelation. Let us go on a little further in order to see her. When presently the angel made to her the great and startling announcement that she was to be the mother of the Messiah, without a moment's hesitation, artlessly and honestly, the transparent simplicity of the woman is revealed when she said to the angel: "How shall this be, seeing I know not a man?" Then, when the angel had answered that inquiry, and more than answered it, as we shall see, look at her once more. That quietly bowed head, and the words that passed her lips are again revealing;

"Behold, the handmaid of the Lord; be it unto me according to thy word."

Have you seen the beauty of that personality? Gabriel Rosetti, in his poem on the Virgin Mother, which he calls "Ave, Hail," has lines in which he describes her imaginatively:

"Work and play,
Things common to the course of day
Awed thee with meanings unfulfilled,
And all through girlhood, something stilled
Thy senses, like the birth of light
When thou hast trimmed thy lamp at night
Or washed thy garments in the stream;
To whose white bed had come the dream
That He was thine, and thou wast His
Who feeds among the lilies.
A solemn shadow of the end
In that wise spirit long contained!
Oh, awful end! And thus unsaid
Long years when it was finished!"

Mary was the elect of God for the fulfilment of that tremendous office, the Mother of Messiah. Behold her, the Virgin Mary; failing, never rightly apprehending the truth about Him until after the day of Pentecost; a sinning soul, needing redemption through her Child, God's Son; and yet radiant in beauty, walking amid the shadows in fellowship with God, in that dark Nazareth; so that when this high messenger came to earth to bring stupendous tidings, he came to God's elect, Mary, endued with grace; and so perfectly endued with it that she was unconscious of the fact, and was strangely startled and agitated at the manner of the salutation.

Now we turn to the story. There are three movements in it. Let me first indicate them. The first, the angelic approach; the second, the angelic annunciation; the third, the angelic interpretation. That covers the ground of the paragraph. The angelic approach, verses twenty-six to twenty-nine. The angelic annunciation, verses thirty to thirty-four. The angelic interpretation in verses thirty-five to thirty-eight. In each case the angel speaks, and Mary answers.

Now as to the first; the angelic salutation.

"Grace unto thee, . . . thou art endued with grace, the Lord is with thee."

Mark the marvel of it. There came this heavenly messenger to this home, to this girl, and so he spoke; heaven sending a stupendous message, and yet so greeting the one to receive it. It is a wonderful revelation of the fact that in any of the darkest days of human history, God has always had His elect remnant. He has always had souls that He could approach, through whom He has been able to move forward. How this gives the lie to the deadly and damnable heresy of Napoleon, that God is on the side of the big battalions. He is always needing vantage ground, and has always found it, and mostly where men would not have sought it. So here the messenger came, not to Judæa, not to Jerusalem; not to the Temple; but to a home, on the level of the ordinary, to a despised town, and rightly despised because of its corruption; and to Galilee, held in contempt by the people of privilege; and to one woman walking in the fellowship of God. There God found His vantage ground.

Such was the angelic approach. I said that in each case we find Mary answering. There is no direct saying recorded here, but the fact is declared that she was troubled at the salutation.

Now come to the annunciation. Think of the world as it then was. Sitting on her seven hills in proud despotism, insolent Rome had bludgeoned a world into submission. But heaven had something to say, and to say it, heaven passed the city on the seven hills, and passed Jerusalem, and came down to a home.

The annunciation commenced;

"Fear not, Mary; for thou hast found grace with God."

When the angel approached, he said "Grace." Now, using the same word, he said, "Fear not, Mary, for thou hast found grace with God." Here we have a new intention in the use of the word grace. This was not a description of her character. This was the description of the high office of that maiden, in human history, in the march of the ages, in the vastness of the economy of God.

When he said "Thou hast found grace *with* God," the preposition is not the same as when he said, "The Lord is *with* thee." In the latter it was *meta,* but this is *para.* Now, that little preposition *para* does not mean merely that God was conferring grace, but she had found grace *by the side* of God, in the fellowship of God. That fact is emphasized as the reason why she was chosen.

"And behold, thou shalt conceive in thy womb and bring forth a Son, and shalt call His name JESUS. He shall be great, and shall be called the Son of the Most High; and the Lord God shall give unto Him the throne of His father David; and He shall reign over the house of Jacob for ever; and of His kingdom there shall be no end."

Thus the Mystery was announced. "Thou shalt conceive in thy womb, and bring forth a Son." That was heaven's declaration to Mary. His name was also announced. We read it with all the radiant glory and beauty of the centuries of interpretation and understanding and experience beating upon it. And yet we may miss something. Thou "shalt call His name JESUS." Jesus is the Greek form of the Hebrew Joshua. What did that name mean to Mary? I wonder if she leapt to its true significance. I but remind you of the fact that there were probably scores of boys in those parts who bore the name; it was one of the commonest names of the time. Where did it come from? The man who first bore that name was the successor of Moses. Where did he get his name? That is not what his father called him. That is not the name his mother gave him. He was born in Egypt, in slavery; and when the baby came, and was preserved, they gave him a name, Hoshea, Salvation! It was a sob and a sigh of people in slavery; yet it was a song of hope, and so in it there merged minor and major notes. He grew up; he became Moses' right-hand man; and when the hour came that Moses knew he was to take up his work and carry it on, Moses changed his name. He took part of the Divine title, Jehovah, and parts of the boy's name, parts of Jehovah and Hoshea, and put them together, and he made a new name for him, Jehoshua, Jehovah-salvation. When this same angel appeared to Joseph in a dream, he said the same thing, but he gave the reason for the name.

"Thou shalt call His name Jesus, for it is *He* that *shall* save His people from their sins."

At last, after the running of the centuries, the One was now coming Who should bear that name perfectly, and fulfil its meaning perfectly; Jehovah-salvation.

His equipment is described in the words,

"He shall be great, and shall be called the Son of the Most High."

It would consist in inherent greatness— "He shall be great;" and in relationship—"the Son of the Most High." His mission is declared,

"The Lord God shall give unto Him the throne of His father David; and He shall reign over the house of Jacob for ever; and of His kingdom there shall be no end."

His Kingship is not to be limited to Jacob; His Kingdom is not to be limited to the nation with which David was associated; His Kingdom shall fulfil everything intended there, and go stretching out and on, having no end.

Then we come to Mary's challenge, and it was the challenge of faith. It was a perfectly natural question which she asked. She did not challenge the fact, but the method. She said;

"How shall this be, seeing that I know not a man?"

I have seen that question translated differently in the interest of softness, and what is falsely called delicacy: "How can this be, seeing that I am an unmarried woman?" I hate this kind

of false delicacy. Leave the question as it is. It is the cold, scientific, biological difficulty, bluntly stated. It is the question being debated hotly today. It is at least interesting, then, to observe that, according to the historic record, the first person to raise the difficulty was Mary herself;

"How shall this be, seeing I know not a man?"

How is it possible for a woman to bear a child, save as the result of the action of a man?

Thus we pass to the third movement, the angel's answer.

"And the angel answered and said unto her, The Holy Spirit shall come upon thee, and the power of the Most High shall overshadow thee."

That is a tremendous word, "overshadow," *episkiazo*, that is, envelope thee in darkness, and it became an enveloping in darkness, which is excess of light. That was the answer of the angel to the question of Mary. I am not attempting any argument as to this answer. I content myself with saying that my philosophy of God, and His relation to the universe makes that answer one which carries the consent of my reason, as the only adequate way of accounting for the Person of Jesus. That is the solution of the biological problem.

But there is another problem. In the light of all human history, there is a moral question. Mary did not raise it. I do not think she realized it. Supposing that it can be that a child can thus be born of a woman, how is that child born of that woman, to escape the constant, continuous sinfulness of humanity? We may quarrel with the old theological terminology, "original sin" and total depravity. I am not fighting for terms, but I am facing facts; and these are historically self-evident. If this Child is to be born of a woman, how is it to be free from, and escape the continuous, persistent contamination which characterizes all human history? There is a moral difficulty here.

Now, it is a wonderful thing that when the angel answered her question, he went on and answered the other, though she did not raise it;

" The Holy Spirit shall come upon thee, and the power of the Most High shall overshadow thee;"

that answered her question; and the angel went on; " Wherefore also—" There is something else, something Mary did not ask;

" Wherefore also the Holy Thing which is begotten shall be called Holy, the Son of God."

The angel answered the biological question, saying: The thing shall be done by the direct act of God, the power of the Most High, the Holy Spirit, wrapping thee round, overshadowing thee, producing in thy womb the Man-child; and *also*, by that same act, by that same energy, by that same force, the Holy Spirit overshadowing, that which is begotten shall be held from contamination with the sin of thy nature, and in human nature. It shail be holy. It shall have being in thy womb by the act of God; and it shall be held from contamination with the sinfulness of thy nature, by the same act of God. The possibility of the Virgin Birth, and the way of the Immaculate Conception were declared by the angel.

Of this power of God, Gabriel gave Mary an illustration, as he said,

"And behold, Elisabeth thy kinswoman, she also hath conceived a son in her old age; and this is the sixth month with her that was called barren."

God is not limited by the ordinary; He can do, and does do, extraordinary

things; God is not imprisoned within that which men call the natural; but for His own purposes, He can act in a way men can only describe as supernatural.

Then he summarized everything as he said,

" For no word from God shall be void of power."

Mary said,

" Behold, the handmaid of the Lord; be it unto me according to thy word."

It was a great act of surrender and submission.

This is the Biblical interpretation of the Person of Jesus. A naturalistic philosophy necessarily cannot accept this as true. Then that philosophy is called upon to account for Jesus in some other way; and the only way to do that, is to do what naturalistic philosophy does; change the Jesus that is presented in this New Testament. To deny the supernatural origin of Jesus, is to make Him natural merely. To do that invalidates the records, not of His Being alone, but of His teaching, and His power in human history. The reason why men reject this story is discovered in their philosophy of God. If He is limited by their knowledge, this thing cannot be. But we are not among the number of those who hold this philosophy of God. We do not think of Him as imprisoned within the laws we have discovered, and the forces we know. Therefore the answer of the angel carries our rational consent; because it is the only accounting for Him, that satisfies our reason.

LUKE I. 39-56

IN this paragraph we have the story of two mothers; and here Motherhood, thus seen, throws a light and a glory upon Motherhood for all time, for here it is seen called by God into cooperation with Him, in His redeeming activity in human history. Here we have reached the point in history, where is fulfilled that Word of God, spoken in the beginning, when the shadows had deepened, and the dark-

ness had fallen because of humanity's revolt from His government; in which He had uttered the promise that one day through Motherhood, victory should be gained over the power of the enemy.

There are two things that demand our attention; first the story, and secondly, the songs.

In approaching the story, we begin with Mary. She had heard the great announcement. She understood, as we

24

were saying in a previous study, that she was to be the Mother of the long-looked-for Messiah. She had with fine honesty challenged the declaration, because she saw the superlative impossibility of it on the human level. She had received the answer from heaven, that the thing should take place by the act and power of God. She had bent her head in reverent and adoring submission, " Be it unto me according to Thy word." The mysterious fact was already accomplished.

Think of her circumstances and consequent consciousness. She was betrothed to a righteous man named Joseph; and there came to him the discovery of the fact that Mary was with child. I know that many suppose that the coming of the angel to Joseph in a dream took place after the return of Mary from her visit to Elisabeth. Personally I believe that, the mighty fact having become a fact by the activity of God, the angel at once visited Joseph. Matthew tells us,

" When His mother Mary had been betrothed to Joseph, before they came together, she was found with child of the Holy Spirit."

This was discovered to Joseph.

"And Joseph, her husband, being a righteous man, and not willing to make her a public example, was minded to put her away privily."

There came to Joseph the knowledge of the fact. He knew nothing of the sacred story. What were the alternatives before him? They are stated quite simply here. He did not desire " to make her a public example." That is a legal phrase; and rather than make her a public example, he decided "to put her away privily." That is also a legal phrase. This was the alternative open to any man under similar conditions. On the one hand he could hand her over to the authorities and make her a public example, which meant that according to the law of Moses she was doomed to be stoned to death. That is what Joseph decided not to do. The other alternative was that he might, to use this technical word, " put her away privily;" that is, grant her a bill of divorcement, cancelling the betrothal.

Betrothal meant among the Jewish people a great deal more than it seems to mean today. In those days a girl was betrothed to a man, and the betrothal was one year before the wedding; and she was as irrevocably bound to him under law, as she was under the marriage ceremony. But the law provided for the sin of infidelity. Instead of committing her to the courts, and bringing about her stoning, and making her a public example, he might give her a bill of divorcement, and cancel the betrothal. Joseph decided to take that course. That was the decision he had made. I think that is a proof that Joseph loved her. You may always be sure that if a person takes action for breach of promise, that person bringing the action does not really love the other. Here was a man, the law on his side; and before he had any interpretation, and although his own heart was breaking, he would cancel the betrothal; rather than make her a public example, he decided to put her away privily.

Then came the angel visit in a dream, declaring to him the mighty secret; and we are told at once that he took her to him. That means that, instead of postponement of the marriage to the end of the legal period of betrothal, he took her at once to his home; and in his own continence, guarded her, by giving to her his name, and the sanctuary of his home. This is a great story of love and faith.

But now go back in imagination to that Nazareth home, that Nazareth society, those Nazareth surroundings; questionings, whisperings, suspicions. Explanation was absolutely impossible. Never forget that when you are thinking of the story. She could not explain. She could tell the story, but would anybody believe it? Now, be quite honest. Would you have believed it? I am quite convinced that part of the sword that pierced the soul of Mary in those earliest days, and I think all through life, was suspicion that rested upon her.

Now we are not surprised to read,

" Mary arose in those days and went into the hill country with haste, into a city of Judah."

The natural humanness of this thing is patent. The mighty secret was with her, she knew it. As she lifted her face toward the God of her fathers, there was no shadow, no cloud; she knew she was the handmaid, the bond-maid of the Lord. But as she looked around in Nazareth, those prying eyes, those whispering voices, and those suspicions! She arose and fled, "in haste." She fled from Nazareth, she fled from Galilee, and she made her way across and down south, until she struck Judæa, and then on to the house of Elisabeth to escape the glances, to escape the whisperings, to find sympathy—I did not say pity, she did not want pity, but she did want sympathy. No one needs pity who is right with God; but if this be so, there still may be circumstances that lead along the pathway of sorrow, and sympathy is needed. She fled for sympathy. I think also that she went to that quiet home, in a priestly city of Judæa, where were Zacharias and Elisabeth, not merely for sympathy, but for time to think.

Now let us go in imagination to that home in Judæa. Elisabeth is there. Six months have passed since the great announcement to Zacharias. Six months since the mystic hour in which supernaturally, in the barren womb, the man-child began to form. Elisabeth was living there, nurturing under her heart that long-hoped-for son. Hope which had perished, had been revived. Nurturing under her heart that son; she was surely brooding over his coming, and over his office; and yet more, over the coming One, of Whose coming her son was to be the herald. Unquestionably Zacharias had written out for Elisabeth the words the angel had uttered to him.

"Thou shalt have joy and gladness; and many shall rejoice at his birth. For he shall be great in the sight of the Lord, and he shall drink no wine nor strong drink; and he shall be filled with the Holy Spirit, even from his mother's womb. And many of the children of Israel shall he turn unto the Lord their God. And he shall go before His face in the spirit and power of Elijah, to turn the hearts of the fathers to the children, and the disobedient to walk in the wisdom of the just; to make ready for the Lord a people prepared."

Elisabeth, in the quietness of that priestly home and city; nurturing under her heart this wonder of a son; pondering his office, was conscious that she was living upon the verge of the dawn of that day for which her people had sighed and suffered through centuries. Then they met. Mary arrived at the house in the priestly city quite unexpectedly. There had been no fore-announcement. When she came in, Elisabeth was filled with surprise to see her. It was a most unusual thing. Elisabeth was not outside, greeting her. She entered the house, and Elisabeth met Mary there. Suddenly they were face to face. And then happened the wonderful thing Luke records, and which Elisabeth herself repeats in the song, that when Mary entered the house, and spoke, the babe leaped in her womb. Elisabeth, in song, says, "the babe leaped in my womb for joy," the word "joy" meaning "exultation."

In this materialistic age, in our materialistic minds, we are inclined to wonder at that story, and even challenge it. Yet what may lie behind this, in the world of spiritual reality. But there is such a world, about which we are singularly ignorant. To me this is very suggestive, that as the Holy Seed within the womb of Mary approached the unborn herald, there was a spiritual consciousness; the babe leapt in her womb for joy. I am not going to debate it, but I often bend over a crib where a baby lies, and watch those baby eyes looking into mine, and wonder how much that child knows. You say, if the child knew, it would tell. Not at all. Wordsworth was not far wrong when he sang,

"Trailing clouds of glory do we come
From God Who is our home;"

and as the years pass, we depart from very real things.

Then Elisabeth was filled with the Holy Spirit, and that means that there came to Elisabeth also something supernatural, an illumination, an understanding. She knew, as Mary came, that

Mary was God's tabernacle, and that dwelling within her was the Lord of life and the Lord of glory.

Directly Mary arrived, Elisabeth broke out into her song. Let me pause for a more general word. Here we approach a matter of arresting interest. Luke is the only one who has recorded for us the outburst of poetry and music in connection with the Incarnation. Matthew does not tell us anything about songs; Mark does not tell us anything about songs; John does not tell us anything about songs; but Luke, the Greek, the artist, himself a poet as well as a scientific man, when he was investigating, and getting these stories, obtained copies of these songs. That is another instance of how the overruling of the Spirit of God allows nothing to be lost. Luke is the instrument, and the right instrument, to give us those early poems and songs. From him we have gained the Beatitude of Elisabeth, the Magnificat of Mary, the Benedictus of Zacharias, and the Nunc Dimittis of Simeon; the Evangel sung by the angel of the Lord over the plains, and the Gloria of the angelic host. Those who love the modes of music will surely linger over these chapters. Luke, the artist, has gathered and collected, under the guidance of the Holy Ghost, the stories which reveal the fact that when Jesus came into the world, poetry expressed itself, and music was reborn.

The Beatitude of Elisabeth was an ode to Mary:

" Blessed art thou among women, and blessed is the fruit of thy womb.
And whence is this to me, that the mother of my Lord should come unto me?
For behold, when the voice of thy salutation came into mine ears, the babe leaped in my womb for joy.
And blessed is she that believed; for there shall be a fulfilment of the things which have been spoken to her from the Lord."

As I have said, this was an ode to Mary, but that is not the deepest truth concerning it. Its deepest note is that of its homage to, and adoration of the Lord. Why did she celebrate Mary? " Blessed art thou among women," why? " Blessed is the fruit of thy womb. And whence is this to me, that the mother of my Lord should come unto me."

It is an ode to Mary, a recognition of the greatness of her office, and the wonder of that office; yes, but her chief glory is that she is the " mother of my Lord." Bengel says not Domina but Mater Domine. The greatness of the Mother was recognized as the greatness of the Child that she bore.

Thus Elisabeth, the daughter of the old economy, was the first singer of the new. Hers was the first song of the Gospel; the first song of the new age that was breaking. All the blessing that she pronounced upon Mary passed through her to the Son in her womb. It was the last poetic voice of the old economy, and it greeted the new; the voice of a daughter of the priestly line, singing of the advent of Him for Whom the old had looked and sighed and sobbed and waited, of Him Whose coming meant the fulfilment of the past, and God's march forward in human history to the accomplishment of the end.

Now let us pass to the Magnificat of Mary. The first thing that impresses us concerning it is that it is wholly Hebrew in thought and expression, in exultation, and in worship. It is almost entirely composed of quotations from the Old Testament psalms. That is interesting in more ways than one. It reveals Mary's acquaintance with that great poetical literature of her people. When she broke out into song, she employed phrases with which she had been familiar through all her years. Yet her understanding of the ultimate value of this poetry is seen in the fact that she wove the scattered phrases from the past into this magnificent song, which today within the Christian Church we call the Magnificat.

Its first movement is a survey of the past. Mary celebrated what God had done. That was the burden of her song. And it was not merely reference to that which God had immediately done; she went back, a true daughter of Abraham, to Abraham; her song was encompassed within the economy of the Hebrew people. But she celebrated in her song what God had done in the past, as it all led to the present. Note that one phrase, "from generation to generation." She was looking back over the history, away back to Abraham; but she saw the activity of God "from generation to generation," and so on to this immediate fact, and stretching away beyond it; "Henceforth all generations shall call me blessed." Burton says the Magnificat is really a Te Deum, "My soul doth magnify the Lord."

It is an arresting fact in her song there is not a single word about the Life mystic and mighty, nestling beneath her heart; and yet the whole song was inspired by that fact. All the past history of her people for Mary in that Magnificat was illuminated by it.

Think of the kind of song a Hebrew maiden might have sung, a devout one, too, in those days. She might have celebrated God, she might have spoken of His might, she might have celebrated His majesty; she might have celebrated His Kingdom; and then all the pæan of praise might have merged into the dirge of disappointment. I think there would have been warrant for any Hebrew maiden in those days to become pessimistic in her poetry. Ah, but Mary could not. At the core and centre of her Mother life, the Holy Thing was enshrined, ratifying all her faith. However dark the outlook, however much the sword was piercing her soul, however much she was entering into fellowship with God as she bore misunderstanding, reproach, suspicion,— the mighty, mighty Secret was there; and Mary could do none other than celebrate God, praise God that He had acted from generation to generation, and for all that He was now doing for coming generations. There is a touch of beautiful naturalness in it when she, looking on to the coming generations, said, "all generations shall call me blessed." Just as Elisabeth had called her blessed, because of the fruit of her womb, so Mary said they shall call me blessed. Her exultation of soul was found in the reason of her blessedness.

Thus while Elisabeth, the daughter of the old, sang the first song of the new, Mary, daughter also of the old, sings of the old; but sings of the old

as ratified, fulfilled, as it moves on to the future, because of the mighty, mystic Mystery that was hidden at the core and the heart of her life.

If we examine the song as to its component parts, we find in it two movements. The first is occupied with her own experience (verses forty-six to forty-nine). In the second, she was celebrating God (verses fifty to fifty-six).

As to her own experience. She begins:

"My soul doth magnify the Lord,
    And my spirit hath rejoiced in God
    my Saviour."

"My soul . . . my spirit." That is not tautology. That is inspired and scientific accuracy. "My soul." The word there is *psuche*, the mind in the full sense. My mind magnifies the Lord. And then "my spirit," *pneuma*, the essential fact of my personality rejoices in God my Saviour. She first speaks of her mind, and then passing behind it, she speaks of the spirit life of her. Her mind was magnifying the Lord, because her spirit life was rejoicing in God her Saviour. The spirit is inspiration; soul or mind is experience and expression, and so she begins her song. The spirit rejoicing in God the Saviour; and therefore the mind grasping the significance of it all, experiencing it, and expressing it, magnifying the Lord. That is pure praise. That is worship on its highest level.

Proceeding, she gives the reason for her rejoicing spirit;

"For He hath looked upon the low
    estate of His handmaid;
For behold, from henceforth all
    generations shall call me blessed.
For He that is mighty hath done
    to me great things."

Then immediately she celebrates God, and there are four clear movements in the celebration;
First,

"Holy is His name."

Second,

"And His mercy is unto generations
    and generations
    On them that fear Him."

Third,

> "He hath showed strength with His arm;
> He hath scattered the proud in the imagination of their heart.
> He hath put down princes from their thrones,
> And hath exalted them of low degree."

Fourth,

> "The hungry He hath filled with good things;
> And the rich He hath sent empty away.
> He hath given help to Israel His servant,
> That He might remember mercy
> (As He spake unto our fathers)
> Toward Abraham and his seed for ever."

Mary thus set forth all the glories of the God of her fathers; His holiness, His mercy, His might, and His faithfulness. By that inward sign, by that sense of the new-born life within her, she knew the holiness of God, she knew the mercy of God, she knew the might of God, and she knew the faithfulness of God.

From Elisabeth we have the first song of the new era; and from Mary, strangely and beautifully crossing hands as it were, we have the last song of the old. I would call Mary's the swan song of the old dispensation. I would call Elisabeth's the birth song of the new.

The last brief statement of the story is that,

> "Mary abode with her about three months."

It is good to think of these two women for three months; Mary in the quietness of the priestly city in Judæa, in the fellowship of Elisabeth. Then she went back to her own house. Six months follow of which we have no account. Yet we know that she lived then in fellowship with the God of her fathers, more wonderful than she had ever known; and that she was guarded from all the bitterness of a town and the stupidity of its idle gossip by Joseph. All the while she was building the body of Jesus! So the mystic story ends.

LUKE I. 57-80

"His name is John."—Luke i.63.

THESE four words constitute the focal point of light in the story contained in the paragraph now under consideration. It commences with the fifty-seventh verse of this chapter and runs to the end (verses 57-80). In it we have the account of the birth of John, and the Benedictus of Zacharias.

We start with the birth of the forerunner. The boy is born. The natural has become active through the supernatural for the fulfilment of the purpose of God. And we need to bear in mind the remarkable declaration made to his father concerning him, when, in the Temple courts, the angel told him that this boy should be born, that he should be filled with the Holy Spirit from his mother's womb. I want to say one thing about that. There is really no article there. It does not read "filled with *the* Holy Spirit." It

is true that in translation we must sometimes supply the article, but here, as in some other cases, the article should not be supplied. The declaration that he was filled with the Holy Spirit must not be taken in the sense in which we speak of the filling of the Holy Spirit today. The declaration is that he was filled with holy spirit. From his mother's womb, this lad was equipped with holy spirit for the ministry to which he was appointed. Here is a case, as in that of Jeremiah, of a prophet known of God from the womb and before his birth, and foreordained to ministry.

The wonder has happened, and we have the picture of his rejoicing kinsfolk;

> "Now Elisabeth's time was fulfilled that she should be delivered; and she brought forth a son. And her neighbours and her kinsfolk heard that the

29

Lord had magnified His mercy towards her; and they rejoiced with her."

Then we have the story of the circumcision, which took place eight days after birth; and we see the family gathering there, neighbours and kinsfolk. In the Hebrew economy, the boy was named on the day of circumcision. These kinsfolk taking for granted, as was so often the case, that he would be called by his father's name, were about to name him Zacharias. Then the mother interfered. She said: "Not so; but he shall be called John." They naturally protested: None of your kinsfolk bears that name. Zacharias, still dumb and deaf, was sitting by, and they made signs to him, and brought him a writing tablet, and he wrote the words, "His name is John." Not, He shall be called John; not, We have decided that he shall be called John; but "His name is John;" the thing is settled. It is not open to discussion. The choice is already made. This is heaven's child, and heaven has chosen his name. "His name is John." His name is the grace of God.

Immediately Zacharias' mouth was opened, and his tongue was loosed. After those months in which in quiet seclusion, shut off very largely from the world, he had brooded on the wonderful thing that was happening to him, forerunner of a yet more wonderful thing;—he broke out into song. It is song, but it is also prophecy; and of him again Luke says that he was filled with, not *the,* but with holy spirit.

Luke tells us that

"Fear came on all that dwelt round about them; and all these sayings were noised abroad throughout all the hill country of Judæa. And all that heard them laid them up in their heart, saying, What then shall this child be? For the hand of the Lord was with him."

Then one stops to wonder, and there is no answer to the wondering; but one is always permitted to wonder, and the question arising is as to how long that lasted. It was thirty years before that boy broke, almost like Elijah, upon the Judæan country with his message.

Doubtless when that time came there would be some who would recall the wonder of his birth.

We have already heard two songs that broke forth in connection with this marvellous event in human history, the coming of God's Son as Son of man. We listened first of all to Elisabeth's Beatitude. Then we heard Mary's answering Magnificat.

Now we come to the third of these songs; the Benedictus of Zacharias. Mary celebrated God in adoration. Zacharias adores God in celebration. Now, if that is apparently a distinction without a difference, let me explain. In Mary's song, she praised the God Who acts. Zacharias' song describes the acts of God. The songs are complementary; the one precedes the other. Mary, in the great Magnificat, was praising God, as we said, making no reference to her own Child. The only personal reference was,

"Henceforth all generations shall call me blessed."

Of course, as we said, the inspiration of her praise was that mystic and mighty Secret that she was nursing under her heart; but she was celebrating and adoring God, the God Who acts. In the song of Zacharias the great musical movement continues, and goes a little further. This song is not in adoration of the God Who acts, but in celebration of the acts of God.

It is arresting to notice the connection between the name of John and the song. All through, the song is celebrating the name. John means the grace of God, and that is what Zacharias was celebrating in this wonderful song-prophecy. He wrote, "His name is John." His song is an interpretation of the name. In the song he celebrates all those activities of God which are the outcome of the fact registered in that name, the grace of God. The theme of the song is salvation, and salvation is the activity of the grace of God.

Notice these lines:

"To show mercy towards our fathers,
And to remember His holy covenant;
The oath which He sware unto
Abraham our father."

I do not think that it is fanciful to say that when he wrote them, he was thinking of his boy; he was thinking of himself; he was thinking of his wife; for the meaning of all the names is there. The boy's name is John, which means, the grace of God. His name was Zacharias, which means, God will remember. His wife's name was Elisabeth, which means, the oath of God. "To show mercy," John's name, the grace of God; "To remember His holy covenant," his own name, God remembers; "The oath which He sware unto Abraham," his wife's name, the oath of God.

What, then, is the theme of the song? I have said the grace of God. That is true. I have said salvation. That is true. I am going to use a word to describe the theme of this song which perhaps has never before been so used. The theme of the Benedictus is the Episcopacy of God. Look at verse 68. "For He hath *visited*." Note that word "visited." Go on to verse 78, "The Dayspring from on high shall *visit* us." Note that word "visit." These are the boundaries of the song. "He hath visited . . . the Dayspring from on high shall visit." The Greek verb in both those cases is the same word, from which we derive our word episcopacy; the Greek verb *episkeptomai*, from which we have derived our words episcopacy, episcopal, and the like, is the word used here. What, then, is the first and simple meaning of episcopacy? Oversight. What is oversight? Government, and government which includes seeing and acting. This song is the celebration of God's government in grace. "He hath visited." Do not read that as though it means only that God had come down to see. It is infinitely more than that. It describes the seeing of God, and the action of God which is in consonance with the seeing of God. When God's ancient people were in slavery, it is said of Him that He declared: "I have surely seen, . . . and I am come down to deliver." That is seeing and action; and that is the idea of the word "visited" here. Whatever is going to happen is thus described as the result of the visitation of God;

the vision of God that leads to the action of God; and the action of God that grows out of His vision. The revelation of the song is that of the nature of the episcopacy of God. "He hath visited . . . the Dayspring from on high shall visit." Notice the change in the tenses. He has visited; He has seen, He has been governing; He is in oversight according to what He is in Himself. And now, as the result, the dawn is coming, the Dayspring shall visit us. The seeing and acting which creates the morning; dawn, resulting from the seeing and the acting of God.

The song falls into three parts. First, it celebrates the action of God out of the past in verses sixty-eight to seventy-five. Then it describes the mission of the child in verses seventy-six and seventy-seven. Finally it declares the action of God in the future in verses seventy-eight and seventy-nine.

As to the first, the action of God out of the past, verses sixty-eight to seventy-five. Notice the references to the past; verse sixty-eight, "Israel," "the God of Israel;" verse sixty-nine, David, "His servant David;" verse seventy, "the holy prophets;" verse seventy-two, "our fathers," and "His holy covenant;" verse seventy-three, "The oath," and "Abraham." The singer was looking back to the old economy, and he celebrated God's action therein.

He started with the source, the origin, the beginning of everything; "Blessed be the Lord, the God of Israel." Then he celebrated the way of the Divine activity, "He hath visited." Continuing, he said, "and wrought redemption." Zacharias was a priest. He employed a Temple word in the Temple sense. And again, "He . . . hath raised up a horn of salvation for us in the house of His servant David." That is the ultimate. There may be differences of opinion, and I am not prepared to be dogmatic, as to the particular significance of the phrase, "a horn of salvation." It may refer to the height and splendour and the dignity and the majesty of the salvation God has provided. It may refer to the completeness and the plentifulness of it. The figure of the horn was em-

ployed in both ways. Then he celebrated the nature of this ultimate
action. "Salvation from our enemies,
and from the hand of all that hate us.
To show mercy towards our fathers,
And to remember His holy covenant."

Some interpreters of this song say
that Zacharias was thinking and speaking in the terms of the narrowness and
selfishness and exclusiveness of the Hebrew people. I do not so read the song.
I believe that already he had seen
God's action for his people, and through
his people, moving out over a larger
area; and with vaster intention. "Salvation from our enemies, and from the
hand of all that hate us." Some say
that he was there expressing the hope
that the coming Deliverer would break
the yoke of Rome. I do not believe it
for a moment. I believe there was a
deeper, spiritual note in the song.
Zacharias was filled with holy spirit,
and there came to him a vision of the
thing that was happening; deliverance
from enemies, and mercy in action, all
this according to the covenant and the
oath, but in the largest sense as for
all men.

Then follows the section in which he
sings of the mission of his son.

" Yea and thou, child, shalt be called
the prophet of the Most High,
For thou shalt go before the face
of the Lord to make ready His
ways;
To give knowledge of salvation
unto His people
In the remission of their sins."

With that we need not tarry.

So we come to the last movement
in which the references are all to the
future.

" Because of the tender mercy of our
God,
Whereby the Dayspring from on
high shall visit us,
To shine upon them that sit in
darkness and the shadow of
death;
To guide our feet into the way of
peace."

In the ninth chapter of the book of
Isaiah we find these words,

" But there shall be no gloom to her
that was in anguish. In the former

time He brought into contempt the land
of Zebulun and the land of Naphtali;
but in the latter time hath He made it
glorious, by the way of the sea, beyond
the Jordan, Galilee of the nations. The
people that walked in darkness have
seen a great light; they that dwelt in
the land of the shadow of death, upon
them hath the light shined."

What did that prophet of the olden
time see when he sang that? He saw
clearly that God's purpose for Israel
was that she was but a medium to an
end, an instrument through which He
would accomplish a larger thing. He
saw away across the centuries the day
coming when the people in darkness
and in the shadow of death should pass
into light. That is what Zacharias
had now clearly seen. He knew the
past and all its glory. But now he saw
away out and beyond. He saw the
fulfilment of the Divine intention in
Israel, because of the tender mercy of
God, whereby the Dayspring from on
high shall visit us, to shine upon them
that sit in darkness and the shadow of
death; to guide our feet into the way
of peace. His very pronouns took on
a new significance. "Shall visit us."
What did he mean by "us"? "To
guide our feet." To whose feet was he
referring? We miss the whole genius
of the song if we say he was thinking
merely of Israel. He answers the questions we have asked;

" Them that sit in darkness and the
shadow of death;"

those great peoples lying out beyond
Israel. He took his place with them,
and used pronouns in the plural number that linked him with all, and all
with him. There had dawned upon
Zacharias, in the gloom and the quietness of those waiting months, the real
significance of the Divine episcopacy or
visitation. The dawn is coming, said
Zacharias, for the dark nations that sit
in the shadow of death. When he gets
thus to this last section of his song, he
indicates the fountain-head of everything anew. At the beginning he had
said,

" Blessed be the Lord, the God of
Israel."

Now he said,

"Because of the tender mercy of our God."

Tender mercy. That expression arrests us. There is a hymn with which we are all familiar. It was written by Isaac Watts, and begins,

"With joy we meditate the grace
Of our High Priest above."

Now I wonder how it goes on in the hymnbook you use. In the great majority of hymnbooks today, it goes on thus,

"His heart is made with tenderness
And overflows with love."

Now, that is very beautiful, but Isaac Watts did not write it that way. When Isaac Watts wrote that hymn, this is what he wrote,

"With joy we meditate the grace
Of our High Priest above.
His heart was filled with tenderness,
His bowels yearned with love."

In nearly all our hymnbooks today we have changed that because we are a delicate people, and we say Isaac Watts was a little vulgar to write it so. As a matter of fact, Isaac Watts was translating literally from the New Testament. The word *splangkna*, literally means "bowels," "the bowels of our God." It is a figure of speech, and in our time, to translate a figure of speech we have done passing well to render it "tender mercies;" and yet I wonder whether we have not sacrificed something. That is the first place in the history of Jesus where the word occurs. Subsequently we find it in many places, but rendered "compassion." It is said over and over again of our blessed Lord that He was moved with compassion. That is the word that Watts had in mind when he said, "His bowels yearned with love." He simply took the Greek word, the figurative word, and rendered it literally. How fine a figure it is! Every strong man or healthy woman knows how under stress of mental suffering, the whole physical nature is ploughed to its very centre. Zacharias, then, used a word that was

so used in that language and in that time; and he dared to use it, and he says, the bowels of God, the tender mercies of our God. The phrase, "tender mercy," lacks the suggestiveness of trouble, and stirring and pain and agony, which are all in the figurative word. It is a very arresting fact that this word is never used in the New Testament of any other except Jesus, or by Jesus.

"Because of the compassion of our God . . . the Dayspring from on high shall visit us."

Zacharias saw the thing that was coming in all its glory; the Dayspring, the morning, the dawn. That sun-rising means light for the darkness, and for those who are sitting in the shadow of death.

The paragraph ends with a brief statement in which, after the manner of Luke, essentials are given rather than incidentals. He passes over thirty years in a verse.

"And the child grew, and waxed strong in spirit, and was in the deserts till the day of his showing unto Israel."

Next time we see John he will be going out, shown to Israel, beginning his mighty ministry.

"The child grew," perfect naturalness; "waxed strong in spirit," that means came to maturity; "and was in the deserts," which does not necessarily mean that he was taken to the wilderness when he was a baby. I think, without any question, John went to the deserts when he was twenty years old. He was a priest; his father was a priest; he was in the priestly line; and in the Hebrew economy the sons of the priests had to take up their courses in the priesthood when they were twenty years of age. I think that he then broke with the priesthood and Temple, under Divine command, and went to the deserts.

Thus we are on the threshold of the greatest hour and event in human history. The herald is prepared; and in the song of Zacharias the progress of God on His pathway out of the old and into the new is celebrated.

LUKE II. 1-20

"There is born . . . a Saviour."
—Luke ii.11.

THAT is the central fact recorded in this paragraph. With reverent reticence, and delicate beauty of diction, the great event was stated by the angel. It was then in the stream of human history that

"Heaven came down our souls to greet,
And glory crowned the mercy-seat."

It was the most stupendous event in all the running decades and centuries and millenniums of the history of man. "There is born a Saviour."

Let us consider the story, noticing first the earthly conditions; secondly, the great fact; and finally, the heavenly activity. The earthly conditions are described in the first five verses. The stupendous fact is declared in verses six and seven; and the heavenly activity in connection with that fact on the earthly level is recorded from the eighth verse to the twentieth.

What were the earthly conditions? The chapter opens,

"Now it came to pass in those days, there went out a decree from Cæsar Augustus."

"In those days"—a "decree from Cæsar Augustus." Cæsar Augustus was the first Roman emperor. His real name was Caius Octavius. He was a great-nephew of Julius Cæsar. The word Augustus is significant. That was his title. He took the name Cæsar by courtesy and by adoption. In process of time the title Augustus was dropped, and the title became Cæsar. When this man became Imperator, and the matter was under discussion as to what title he should assume, he declined to be called Dictator, which suggested a temporary office. He declined also to be called King, as it did not signify enough. In consultation with the Roman Senate, this name was created for him, Augustus, derivable from the word Augur; and consequently indicating a religious sanction. He was moving towards that which happened subsequently, the claim

of deity on the part of the supreme ruler of the Roman Empire. Gradually the power of government had been taken from the people, and vested in military governors; and at last this man, a singularly able man, a singularly astute man, gained the supreme power. He became the first Emperor, the first Imperator, with a capital I. Imperator is a military title. The generals of the Roman republic had all been called Imperators; but at last the plural ended, and the singular marked despotism, autocracy. The Roman republic had passed away, and in its place had emerged the Roman Empire, under Augustus Cæsar.

At the time of this history the doors of the Temple of Janus were closed, had been closed for a decade and more, and remained closed for thirty years. The closed doors of the Temple of Janus meant there was no war. Whenever the Roman republic was at war, the doors of the Temple of Janus were flung open; but in times of universal peace they were shut. "In those days," when the Roman republic had become the Roman Empire, when the Roman people had passed under the despotism of an autocratic ruler; "in those days," when that autocratic ruler and that empire had bludgeoned the world into submission, when the whole world was crushed under the heel of a despot; "in those days," the one period in the history of humanity when power vested in one man, had gained that thing about which we heard a great deal some years ago;—hegemony,—world mastery; "in those days," Jesus was born. Let the hush of it fall upon us. "In those days" Cæsar Augustus issued a decree that all the world should be enrolled, and it was done. There was no appeal. They came, patrician Romans in their purple splendour, and plebians, some in rags; they came, the people came because Cæsar Augustus said they were to be enrolled. It was a period when there was no war. You say that was beautiful. Think again. That was the most damnable condition the world had ever seen. I am not glorifying war;

but when the reason of no war was that the people were bludgeoned into submission, so that no man or woman, boy or girl dare peep, or chirp or mutter, or call his soul his own, or her own, because of the despot on the throne; that was the darkest hour the world has ever seen.

Now, in that Roman Empire, in an outpost, away down in that turbulent little bit of land at the eastern end of the Mediterranean, that little land of Palestine, these things—or rather This Thing happened. There were two people there, a man and a woman, only two individuals amid the multitudes in Judæa and Galilee and that whole region; and amid the massed multitudes of the Roman Empire. Those two people had no more effect upon Cæsar Augustus and upon the Roman Empire than any two of you have upon the President of the United States or the King of England. As to their earthly condition, they were entirely insignificant, and yet touched by the Roman authority. The decree of Cæsar Augustus reached Nazareth. Joseph must bend the neck, even though the royal blood of David is coursing in his veins; he must go up. He cannot enrol by proxy. He must go up to the city of his family and enrol. He went up, and Mary travelled with him; two people. Nobody knew about it, except perhaps the friends of Mary and of Joseph; and they did not know much about it.

But look again. Two individuals marching under the orders of Cæsar Augustus. Look at the woman. Her womb is the tabernacle of the Son of God as she travels. Look at the man. The one passion of his life is to guard that woman. Things are oftentimes not what they seem, if we can only climb high enough to look down on this world from heaven's vantage ground. They were going up to Bethlehem, because Cæsar Augustus had at that psychic moment issued his edict that all the world be enrolled. That edict of Cæsar Augustus rippled across the world, touching everyone. Even Joseph and Mary must go. But in my Bible I find a prophecy written at least six hundred and fifty years before this thing happened;

"But thou, Bethlehem Ephrathah, which art little to be among the thousands of Judah, out of thee shall One come forth unto Me that is to be Ruler in Israel; Whose goings forth are from of old, from everlasting. Therefore will he give them up, until the time that she who travaileth hath brought forth; then the residue of His brethren shall return unto the children of Israel. And He shall stand, and shall feed His flock in the strength of Jehovah, in the majesty of the name of Jehovah His God; and they shall abide; for now shall He be great unto the ends of the earth."

When I read that, uttered six hundred and fifty years before these events, I see that the really insignificant person in the drama is the little puppet in the city on the seven hills, called Cæsar Augustus; and the significant personalities are the woman in whose womb tabernacles the Son of God, and the man who is guarding her. They went up, because Cæsar had issued an edict. Why did he do it? Matthew answers the question. Quoting from the chief priests and scribes in their reply to Herod as to where the Christ should be born, he wrote; "It is written through the prophet." By so doing he declared that this thing happened in fulfilment of prophecy, and so under the government of God. That prophecy declared that this Man to be born in Bethlehem "shall be great unto the ends of the earth." That is hegemony. Cæsar Augustus thought he had gained it, but he never had. Tabernacling in the womb of that woman was the One Who is to have hegemony. Those were the earthly conditions, seen in the light of the heavenly economy.

When they arrived, the stupendous event transpired.

"It came to pass, while they were there, the days were fulfilled that she should be delivered. And she brought forth her firstborn Son; and she wrapped Him in swaddling clothes, and laid Him in a manger, because there was no room for them in the inn."

Once more observe the earthly conditions. "There was no room for them in the inn." What was the inn? When we read that we may think the reference was to a caravansary, a hostel, or in our modern parlance, a hotel. That is not the meaning of "inn." There are two words, both translated "inn" in the New Testament. There is the word *pandocheion,* which does mean a caravansary, a hostelry, a place with a host, and provisions, and apartments. But there is another word, *kataluma,* and it was merely an enclosure, just walls into which travellers might drive their cattle for the night, and in which sometimes there were apartments in which they themselves might rest; but no traveller could obtain food there. There was water, always, water, but no food, no host, no entertainment. There was no room even there. There was no room even in the enclosure for cattle.

What happened then? In the supreme hour which permits of no delay, they had to find some outhouse to a dwelling; and there the Baby was born, and the mother laid It in a manger. No palace, no dwelling-place, no caravansary, no room even in the *kataluma.* He was born outside everything, even the place where cattle might be sheltered through the night. He was born and laid in a manger in some bleak outhouse, outside some dwelling. So He came. The glory of it, the wonder of it. When He came He passed the court, and passed the palace, and passed the dwelling-place, and passed the inn, and passed the *kataluma;* and was born into this world so low down that no baby can ever be born lower.

Then we have the record of the great central fact. Think of the pathos of it. "She brought forth;" "she wrapped Him in swaddling clothes." It is very beautiful, but oh, the pity of it, the tragedy of it, the loneliness of it; that in that hour of all hours, when womanhood should be surrounded by the tenderest care, she was alone. The method of the writer is very distinct. She with her own hands wrapped the Baby round with those swaddling clothes, and laid Him in the manger. There was no one to do it for her. Again I say, the pity of it, and yet the glory of it to the heart of Mary. When I was pondering this matter, there came to me the memory of something Jesus once said, and never before had it occurred to me in

this connection. It will seem to me now, I think, to the end of life, that when Jesus said it to His disciples, He was thinking of His own Mother;

"A woman when she is in travail hath sorrow, because her hour is come; but when she is delivered of the child, she remembereth no more the anguish, for the joy that a man is born into the world."

That surely was the story of Mary.

"She brought forth her firstborn Son."

The simple meaning is that Jesus was her eldest Child, the firstborn Son. But there is in it a larger meaning. Firstborn does not mean only first in time; it means also first in place, first in order, first in importance. In the New Testament He is called "Firstborn of creation." He is called "Firstborn from the dead." He is called "Firstborn among many brethren." And there is yet a profounder note. Who is this Child? The Son of God. That is what happened in that manger. There in that little town of Bethlehem Ephrathah, the Son of God, in human form, had entered the stream of human history. In a wonderful old book called *The Nativity,* written by Isaac Williams, occur these words:

"The unfathomable depths of the Divine counsels were moved; the fountains of the great deep were broken up; the healing of the nations was issuing forth; but nothing was seen on the surface of human society, but this slight rippling of the water."

Lastly let us observe the activity of heaven that day. An angel of the Lord stood by the shepherds, and the glory of the Lord shone round about them. It was night. The shepherds were minding their flocks. I think it is almost generally agreed that in all probability these were temple shepherds, watching flocks intended for sacrifice. Even if they were shepherds engaged in the pursuit of their own calling, they were doing their own work. They were not near to Bethlehem. They said, "Let us now go *even* unto Bethlehem," which shows that they had some way to go. To these shepherds, at night, watching over their flocks, in the discharge of their duty, suddenly the angel of the Lord appeared, and the glory of the Lord shone round about them. He did not appear in Cæsar's palace, nor in the Temple; he came to shepherds. To them came the angel message, and the glory of the Lord; the Shekinah glory shone round about them. These shepherds were filled with fear. So the introductory sentence was, " Be not afraid," immediately followed by the declaration, " I bring you good tidings of great joy which shall be to all people." Hear that message of the angel in the world as it was, a world lacking joy, that had heard no good tidings for generations, that was afraid in its heart of the tyranny of oppression. The world bludgeoned into submission, was filled with sadness and loathing and despair. Then an angel from the presence of God came to shepherds, and he said, " Be not afraid; I bring you good tidings of great joy which shall be to all people." Then the tidings were told,

" There is born to you this day in the city of David a Saviour, Who is Christ the Lord."

So we translate for sake of euphony. As a matter of fact, in the Greek there are no articles at all. The three names were uttered by the angel thus,

" There is born to you this day in the city of David, Saviour, Christ, Lord."

Saviour, Someone confronting all the sin of the world with regal authority, based upon redeeming power. Christ, Someone confronting all the chaos of the world, the Messiah, Who will be able to realize the true hegemony, the Kingdom of God. Lord, the One Who confronts all eternity and all ages; and He is born, He is born today, said the angel. Where shall we find Him? The angel continued;

" And this is the sign unto you; Ye shall find a Babe wrapped in swaddling clothes, and lying in a manger."

Before the shepherds had time to say a word,

" Suddenly there was with the angel a multitude of the heavenly host, praising God."

There one could dream dreams, and let one's imagination take wings. All heaven breaking bounds, sweeping down, and hovering over Bethlehem's plains, with a great Gloria;

" Glory to God in the highest,
And on earth, peace among men
of His good pleasure."

That is the meaning of the coming of this Child. That is the meaning of this Saviour, Christ, Lord. Glory to God in the highest. That phrase, " in the highest," does not mean in the highest degree. It means above. It is a descriptive word of heaven, the dwelling-place of God; " glory to God in the highest." Then on earth, what? Peace. But how? "Among men in whom He is well-pleased." Men everywhere are talking about peace, and they are trying to produce peace; and they are attempting sometimes on the basis of a mistranslation and consequent misunderstanding of this passage. They say that the angels said, " Peace on earth good will to men," and then they say that peace will come by the exercise of good-will. There is no peace for the earth, except among men in whom God is well-pleased. That is the basis of peace, men of His pleasure. Look on for a moment, thirty years from all this. The Boy born, has passed through babyhood and childhood and youth, and stands, thirty years of age, on the verge of His mighty Messianic mission; He goes to baptism, and heaven breaks the silence and says,

" This is My beloved Son; in Thee
I am well-pleased."
" Glory to God in the highest,
And on earth peace among men in
whom He is well pleased."

Mark well the connection. That Baby became the Man in Whom God was pleased. Peace will come to the earth when men are like Him. That is the way of peace, and there is no other way. No discussion concerning disarmament will ever bring peace. Limitation of armaments? Certainly. Scrapping of ships? By all means.

And yet what value is it? All the countries are now multiplying air fleets! We are a mad crowd. Peace will never come that way.

The heavenly host was chanting the anthems of welcome, not merely to that Baby, but to the new race.

" Glory to God in the highest,
And on earth peace among men in whom He is well pleased;"

the race that will spring from that Baby. That Baby is the second Man; that Baby is the last Adam. From that Child, that Son of God, Child of Mary, born and laid in a manger, will spring the race which shall satisfy the Divine demands, and please the heart of God. Peace there is, peace for them.

The old prophetic word rings its minor chord of solemn warning down the ages,

" There is no peace, saith my God, to the wicked."

First pure, and then peaceable.

Let us end where we began. " There is born . . . a Saviour." He has come into the world, in order that the race that is displeasing to God because of its sin, revolt, and pollution, may be made pleasing to God. Let us keep that word Saviour sounding in our souls. Dr. Joseph Parker, of London, preaching on that text, once said:

" ' Unto you is born this day . . . a Saviour.' The world did not want an adviser. The world had advised itself almost into hell. The world did not ask for a speculator. Everything that man could do had been done, and men sat in the darkness of their own wisdom. The world did not want a reformer, a man who could change his outward and transient relations, an engineer that would continually devote his time (for appropriate remuneration) to the readjustment of the wheels and the pulleys and the various mechanical forces of society. The world wanted a Saviour. ' Saviour' is a pathetic name. It is not an official title; it is not an image you could robe in scarlet, and bow down before on account of its majesty and haughtiness; ' Saviour' is an angel with tears in his eyes; arms mighty as the lightnings of God, but a heart all tenderness. ' Saviour' is a complex word. It has in it all human nature, all divine nature, all the past of history, all the possibility of prophecy, all the mystery of apocalypse; the tenderness outvying the love of women, the majesty humbling the haughtiness of kings."

LUKE II. 21-39

THE chief value of this paragraph is the remarkable way in which it places the Child of Mary and the Son of God in relation to the old economy. Throughout this story the goings of God are revealed. He moves forward in spite of all difficulties, in spite of all dangers, and in spite of all oppositions. All history bears witness to the truth, " Our God is marching on." The coming into the world of this Child of Mary and Son of God stands related to everything in the past. His coming was the dawn of a new day, and the commencement of a new movement of God. In this paragraph we see the past as an economy of God; and we see the past as to the people of God, in the little group of expectant and devout souls into whose presence we come. That economy of the past, beginning with Abraham, and moving on down through the centuries, was always prophetic. It existed in the world as God's method of speech to the world; and all within it was predictive; nothing was complete. Abraham was always a pilgrim, always moving towards something not reached. Everything in the ritual, and ceremonial system, and everything in the national life, was moving on towards a goal. When we close our Old Testament we realize that we have followed a magnificent march of majesty and mercy, towards something not yet reached. It ends with a great hiatus, a mighty space. And the people, as distinguished for a moment for the sake of emphasis, from the economy of God, was always in the purpose of God, instrumental, never an end, but a means to an end; ever, in God's purpose, looked upon as the people of His choice, in order that His way and His will might be made known to the world. That did not begin with the coming of Jesus Christ. His coming culminated it, gathered it up, fulfilled it, made it dynamic. God so loved the world, before Christ came, that at last He gave His only begotten Son. He did not then begin to love.

In this paragraph, then, we see that old economy and those people; the economy in the observance of Mosaic rites; and the people, as we listen to the voices of old covenant saints, Simeon and Anna; and see the little group gathered around the Child. Anna arrived at the very moment when Simeon was holding in his arms the new-born Saviour; she blessed God, and spoke of Him to all them that were looking for the redemption of Israel. In that city of Jerusalem there was a company, however large or small we have no means of knowing;—perhaps a very small company,—of devout souls who were looking for the redemption of Israel; and it is evident that they were accustomed to foregather in the Temple courts to pray, and perhaps sing songs of hope, and talk to one another. I never read of Anna speaking to that company without my mind leaping back four hundred years to Malachi's statement;

"Then they that feared Jehovah spake one with another; and Jehovah hearkened and heard, and a book of remembrance was written before Him, for them that feared Jehovah, and that thought upon His name. And they shall be Mine, saith Jehovah of hosts, even Mine own possession, in the day that I act."

Through those four hundred years God had never been without an elect remnant, those who, understanding the meaning of their nationality, were looking for the redemption of Israel; looking on and looking forward. Here, then, we see the old economy, in the observance of the Mosaic rites; and we hear the voices of the saints among the ancient people of God. The Child is thus revealed in relationship with the old by the observance of Mosaic rites, and celebrated by the old in the song and the blessing of Simeon and the prophesying of Anna.

The story of the Mosaic rites is found in the first part of our paragraph; and we should observe carefully that there are two rites here. They are quite distinct and separate. We have first the account of the circumcision and naming of the Child, in verse twenty-one. Then we have the account of the presentation of that Child in the Temple, and His dedication in verses twenty-two and twenty-four. According to the law of Moses, the child was circumcised,—and his name was always given to him at the time of circumcision, and when he was eight days old. The rite of presentation, when the mother came up for purification, took place when the baby was forty days old;

"And when eight days were fulfilled for circumcising Him, His name was called JESUS, which was so called by the angel before He was conceived in the womb."

Here we have two things, the rite of circumcision, and the giving of the name. The rite of circumcision brought every Hebrew boy into relationship with the national life of the people of God. His birth did not do it. No boy born, from the time of Abraham when the rite was instituted, all through the running centuries, was a member of God's nation unless or until he was circumcised. It was God's sign, God's token.

"God said unto Abraham, And as for thee, thou shalt keep My covenant,

thou, and thy seed after thee throughout their generations. This is My covenant, which ye shall keep, between Me and you and thy seed after thee; every male among you shall be circumcised. And ye shall be circumcised in the flesh of your foreskin; and it shall be a token of a covenant betwixt Me and you" (Genesis xvii.9-11).

Circumcision in itself was, as medical science today is recognizing, a great hygienic rite; but it was also made the sign and the token of membership within the covenant of that nation, through which God was moving forward to the accomplishment of His purposes for mankind.

It was by that rite that the Child of Mary, this Son of God, became a member of that nation. He belonged to it; He was of the seed of David, because His Mother was of the line of David; but the fact that He was born of the seed of David did not bring Him into national relationship; the fact of His circumcision did that. He was "born," says Paul, "of a woman, born under the law." By that act of circumcision He was related to the life of the nation which God had made, had sustained, had governed.

Then, as was the custom, still in connection with that rite, they gave Him His name, Jesus. Luke is very careful to draw attention to the fact that the name was chosen, not by Mary, and not by His father by adoption, Joseph; he says,

" Which was so called by the angel, before He was conceived in the womb."

The name was chosen for Him. It was revealed by heaven's messenger; and when He entered into the national life the name was bestowed upon Him. In the Bible we have four boys named by heaven before they were born: Ishmael, Isaac, John, and Jesus.

His name was Jesus. We know that name; and how we love it!

" Jesus, the name high over all,
    In hell, or earth, or sky;
Angels and men before it fall,
    And devils fear and fly.

" Jesus, name of sweetness,
    Jesus, sound of love,
Cheering exiles onward,
    To their rest above.

" Jesus, O the magic,
    Of the soft love sound,
How it thrills and trembles,
    To creation's bound."

We pause to ask, What does the name mean? Where did it come from? Jesus is merely the Anglicising of the Greek name; and the Greek name rendered Jesus is the Greek form of a very well known and common Hebrew name, Joshua; and Joshua is really an abbreviation of the name Jehoshua. I have no doubt that when this Child was born, hundreds of boys bore the name.

It was a common name of the time. The popularity of it was doubtless due to the man in the history of the nation who first bore it. Who was that man? In the book of Numbers, chapter thirteen, and verse sixteen, we read:

"And Moses called Hoshea the son of Nun, Joshua."

That boy, when he was born, was named Hoshea. He was born in Egypt, in slavery, and his father and mother called him Hoshea. That means salvation. Thus the name was a sigh, a sob, and perhaps a song of two people in slavery, looking for deliverance. None but those who had faith would have given a boy that name under those circumstances.

Time passed, and they came out of slavery, and passed through those early wilderness experiences. Then came the day when spies were sent to view the land. Moses evidently had come to know this young man, and then he changed his name. He took letters out of the great name Yahweh, or Jehovah, and he took letters out of the name of the boy, Hoshea, and wove them into one, so that the boy's name now became Yehoshua, Jehovah-salvation. The centuries ran on, and I have no doubt multitudes of people forgot the significance of the name, but they loved to call their boys Joshua, because this man had borne the name. When Jesus was circumcised they called Him Jehoshua, as He was called by the angel. The angel gave that name to Joseph as well as to Mary, as Matthew records. Said the angel to Joseph,

"And thou shalt call *His* name Jehoshua; for it is *He* that *shall* save His people from their sins."

All that was in the name, all that was intended by the name was now coming to culminating realization in the Baby that was born. Jehovah-salvation. That is His name, because that is the meaning of His coming.

So He entered the nation, by the rite of circumcision, and received the heaven-chosen name, which indicated at once the fact of His Being, and the purpose of His coming in that progressive economy of God; Jehovah-salvation.

Then, forty days after His birth, He was brought up again, and here we have a very wonderful thing. Notice very carefully a parenthesis in this passage. It is found in verse twenty-three, and reads,

"As it is written in the law of the Lord, Every male that openeth the womb shall be called holy to the Lord."

In order to understand this, we must see when this was said, and what it meant. In the thirteenth chapter of Exodus, and the second verse in connection with the twelfth, we find the reference,

" Sanctify unto Me all the first-born, whatsoever openeth the womb among the children of Israel, both of man and of beast; it is Mine. . . . That thou shalt set apart unto Jehovah all that openeth the womb, and every firstling which thou hast that cometh of a beast; the males shall be Jehovah's."

If we read it carefully we see that the Divine intention was that in that nation the firstborn male in every family should enter the priesthood.

If we turn from the thirteenth chapter of Exodus to Numbers, chapter three, and verses eleven to thirteen, we find a change in the Divine arrangement.

"And Jehovah spake unto Moses saying, And I, behold I, have taken the Levites, from among the children of Israel; and the Levites shall be Mine; for all the firstborn are Mine; on the day that I smote all the firstborn in the land of Egypt I hallowed unto Me all the firstborn in Israel, both man and beast; Mine they shall be; I am Jehovah."

The tribe of Levi was set apart to priestly function, and a male from the tribe of Levi stood in the place of each firstborn in the families of Israel. The first ideal of God, then, was that the firstborn son should be a priest. One of the most interesting, arresting, and remarkable things in the study of Biblical history is that of God's accommodations to human weakness. Again and again when men could not rise to the heights of His ideals He came down, never in righteousness, but in ritual,

and in ceremony, to their level. God's ideal for the whole nation was that it should be a Kingdom of priests. When they were unable to rise to that height, He gave them Aaron as a representative priest. Aaron was an accommodation. God's ideal for them was that they should be a Theocracy, having no King but Himself; but when they clamoured for a king, He accommodated Himself to them, and gave them a king. We find the same thing here. The Divine ideal was that every firstborn son should be in the priesthood; and the Levitical order, the tribe of Levi, was at last appointed to function; every Levite to represent a firstborn son. Because they were not able to rise to the height of the ideal, the Levites were appointed. When Jesus was taken to the Temple by Mary, it was in fulfilment of the first ideal and purpose of God; He, the firstborn Son, the One that opened the womb, was dedicated to God. Jesus entered the priesthood, not the Levitical, not the priesthood of someone to represent another, but into the priesthood of the firstborn according to the original Divine purpose. So, according to that first ideal of God, this Child not only entered into the nation by the rite of circumcision; He entered into the priesthood by the rite of dedication.

When Mary thus went up, she had to take offerings with her. That was the law. She offered,

"A sacrifice according to that which is said in the law of the Lord, A pair of turtle-doves, or two young pigeons."

In Leviticus, chapter twelve, verse eight, we find the reason for that form of offering;

" If her means suffice not for a lamb, then she shall take two turtle-doves, or two young pigeons; the one for a burnt offering, and the other for a sin offering; and the priest shall make atonement for her, and she shall be clean."

Now when Mary took that Baby and her offerings, she took a pair of turtle-doves. What right had she to do so? The law said if she could not afford a lamb, she might take the turtle-doves or two young pigeons. That is to say,

it was the offering of the poor, and Mary had no wealth. That quaint old commentator, Van Doren, says the Magi had not visited her yet, and she had not gold to buy a lamb! This Baby was dedicated, not by the offering of a lamb that might have been brought by a wealthy woman, but by the offering of the poor. So, as when He was born He passed all palaces and courts and houses, and came to the level of the lowest child, being born in a manger; so when He was dedicated in the Temple to priesthood after the first Divine ideal of dedicated priesthood, the offering of His Mother was the offering of the poor.

Thus the rites have placed Him in the nation, and in the original ideal for the priesthood, within that nation.

Then occurred the beautiful incident of the action and song of Simeon. Luke describes him as " righteous and devout;" the first word, " righteous," describing the relationship he bore to his fellow-men, " righteous;" and the other, " devout," his relation to God. This man is seen in the Temple, waiting, looking for the consolation of Israel, the Holy Spirit resting upon him; and the Holy Spirit had revealed to him that he should not see death until his eyes had seen the Lord's Anointed. We see the old man standing, the Child in his arms, the Child of all the ages. Then there passed his lips the wonderful song, the last of the group that broke out in connection with the Advent.

For the sake of interpretation let me slightly change the rendering of the opening sentence, into a more literal form.

" Now Thou art setting free Thy bond-slave, Despot."

We do not quite like the word despot. It has evil connotations. But that is the actual word which Simeon employed; and it signifies absolute and complete authority. It means one from whom there is no appeal, and to be a bond-servant is to be a slave. The old man said,

" Now Thou art setting free, liberating, Thy bond-slave O Despot, According to Thy saying, in peace."

The Child in his arms, he said in effect: Now Thy bond-slave, held of Thee by the terms of law, and bound to Thy progress in the world, is set free to pass over. To hold that Baby in his arms was to have death revealed to him, not as dissolution, but as emancipation. The great and glorious fact that would emerge presently when this Child had bowed to death, and had broken its power; the fact which presently found expression in apostolic writing, and through the centuries in countless hymns, that He hath abolished death; of this Simeon was already conscious. He held only the Baby in his arms. How dare I say only the Baby! I love George Macdonald's poem about the Baby, but I always feel that it is only perfectly fulfilled in this Baby,

" Where did *You* come from, Baby dear?
Out of the everywhere into the here."

Simeon held that Baby in his arms, as Wesley daringly said, " God contracted to a span;" the little warm Baby, with such dimpled fingers as you see in other babies, lay in his arms, and he sang;

" Now, O Despot, Thy bond-slave Thou art setting free."

And the reason for his confidence he declared;

" For mine eyes have seen Thy salvation,"

"*Thy* salvation,"

" Which Thou hast prepared before the face of all peoples."

There are senses in which Simeon was more clear in his statement of the meaning of that coming of that Child than Elisabeth was in her Beatitude, or Mary in her Magnificat, or even Zacharias in his Benedictus.

" Thy salvation which Thou hast prepared before the face of all peoples;
A light for revelation to the Gentiles."

Think of the Gentile world as it existed then, with its philosophies, seeking to find some solution, gleams breaking through upon sincere souls, and then being lost. Here is the light that is coming to unveiling, the apocalypse and glory of Thy people Israel. This Child, said Simeon in effect, is the Ultimate in all the history of God's ancient people.

And then while Simeon still held the Child, Anna, a prophetess, a Temple dweller, through long long years of widowhood came, and turned and spoke to that little company of faithful souls.

Simeon had said one thing to Mary which we must not overlook. He had told her that a sword should pierce through her own soul; and in connection with that parenthetical word, he said tremendous things about that Child; that His coming should be for the falling and rising of many in Israel, a sign spoken against, One through Whom the thoughts out of many hearts should be revealed. Every one of these predictions was full of meaning, and they have all been fulfilled.

Notice the representatives of that past economy which we have seen. What a wonderful group. Zacharias, the priest; Elisabeth, a daughter of Aaron; Joseph, a son of David; Mary, a daughter of David; Simeon, a citizen of Jerusalem; Anna, a Temple devotee; John, the child of Zacharias and Elisabeth; and now completing the octave, Jesus, the final flower and fruitage of all that Hebrew economy. Gathered round about Him that little group of devout souls. Wonderful ending of the Old, and beginning of the New.

LUKE II. 40-52

THIS paragraph is of very special interest. It is peculiar to Luke. But for this Gospel narrative, we should not have known any of the things that are recorded in these verses. It is part of Luke's scheme of interpretation of the personality of Jesus. After scientific examination of that personality, as he claimed in his preface, Luke produced his remarkable presentation. Nothing we have learned in the last thirty years in the realm of psychology could have taught Luke anything in his method of dealing with his material. With all the light that has come to us in the last generation in our study of psychology, when a delineation of personality is attempted, we begin with the pre-natal facts. That is exactly what Luke did when he began to investigate the personality of Jesus. And so we have the story, which he could have gained from none save Mary; the story of the Virgin Birth.

When the pre-natal facts are discovered, what is the next fact of importance? According to modern psychology, the next point of interest is adolescence, which begins somewhere around twelve or thirteen years. To that hour Luke takes us next. He gives us this illuminative portrayal of the Boy at twelve years of age.

The next point in the development of personality is that of maturity. To that Luke passes as he reveals Jesus at thirty years of age.

Our present paragraph reveals the Boy as He came to adolescence. But this is prefaced with a brief but complete account of the first twelve years of His life;

" The Child grew, and waxed strong, becoming filled with wisdom; and the grace of God was upon Him."

Then Luke gives an equally brief but complete account of the eighteen years between boyhood and maturity;

"And Jesus advanced in wisdom and stature, and in favour with God and man."

Now let us look first at the account of the first twelve years; the period of growth. He grew for twelve years. Then for eighteen years He advanced. There is a distinct difference. The King James renders the second word "increased." That just misses the idea, because increase may be growth, but advancement is growth controlled. To which we will return presently.

In the first twelve years He grew. Growth, whenever it is used in the realm of life, indicates an activity of life. In growth there is no responsibility in the realm of will. In growth, pure and simple growth, will has no place and no power. None grows by trying to grow. Growth is life without responsibility. Do not miss that, because while we are looking at this one lonely supernal Person in all history, God's second Man, we have a wonderful sidelight on our own children. The one business of every child from birth until twelve or somewhere around there, until the period of adolescence, is to grow, and nothing else. The child should grow without any sense of responsibility except obedience to authority; and obedience in the case of the child is always in order to give the child perfect freedom from everything else, without any sense of responsibility. That is the story of Jesus; He grew!

Luke describes that growth. He "waxed strong." That is physical. We may reverently imagine it all. That Baby that had nestled in the arms of Mary, learning to walk, learning to pick things up, and put them down; and so on. Jesus went through all that. For twelve years He grew, waxing stronger physically all the way.

Then, "Becoming filled with wisdom;" not "filled with wisdom," as though through childhood He was replete with wisdom. Apocryphal literature has described Him as full of wisdom from babyhood up. Luke's statement is that He was gaining knowledge by observation, and by asking questions, and by receiving instruction.

And then that last beautiful touch, in which we reach the climax in the description of the personality of the growing child. "The grace of God was upon Him." Grace is first, that which delights and charms. Grace secondly, is desire to impart to others the things that make them happy. Grace finally is the activity that does this at all costs. The grace of God was upon the Child. In the Apocrypha, in the book of Ecclesiasticus, there is a description of an ideal child, and I never read it without thinking how it must have applied to this Child;

" Hearken unto me, ye holy children,
    And bud forth as a rose growing
        by a brook of water;
And give ye a sweet savour as
        frankincense,
And put forth flowers as a lily,
    Spread forth a sweet smell, and
        sing a song of praise."

Thus Luke, in describing those twelve years, has taken the essential things and not the incidental. That is to say, Jesus is presented in the things that are common to all childhood, and not in the things which separate one child from another. There are children in one home and district, and there are children in another home in another district; and in all the incidentals of their lives they are entirely separated from each other; but in essential things, all children are alike. This Child grew, physically, mentally, spiritually; waxing strong, becoming filled with wisdom; and all the while the grace of God was upon Him in spirit. I do not say that all children grow perfectly physically. Alas it is not so. But all have the physical. I do not say that all children have the same mentality. But all have mentality. As to spiritual life, all children are spiritual in essence. The grace of God resting upon the child does not depend at first upon the child, but upon the father and the mother and the home and the surroundings. Here, however, we are looking at the ideal Child.

Now let us examine the picture of the Boy in the Temple. Here we notice at once that the designation is changed. "The Child grew," and the Greek word means the little child, the undeveloped child. Now Luke speaks of "the Boy." The two words have entirely different significance. He is no longer the little Child. He is now "the Boy." The Jewish boy of devout parents at that period comes to his *Barmitzvah*. *Barmitzvah*; *bar*, son; *mitzvah*, commandment; that is, son of the law. It may be that Jesus precipitated His own *barmitzvah* when He went into the Temple, or possibly He had already passed through the ceremony in the synagogue at Nazareth. This, however, is certain, when He went into the Temple His right of entry was that He went as a Son of the law. Until that time a boy's father and mother were responsible for him religiously. From that time he assumed responsibility himself. Here Jesus, as we have said, either precipitated His own *barmitzvah* by going to the *didaskaloi*, the teachers; or else He went in as a Disciple, already a Son of the law.

He tarried behind in Jerusalem. That was an act of personal volition. He was now acting for Himself. So acting, He went into the Temple of God, and sat as a Disciple at the feet of the rabbis, more accurately the *didaskaloi*, teachers. He ranked Himself a Disciple by His own volition.

He sat down as a Disciple. They talked to Him, and taught Him, and asked Him questions. He answered them, and they listened in amazement. Then He did what every disciple had the right to do; asked them questions, questions arising out of the religious training He had received at home; and still they were amazed. The thing that amazed the teachers was that this Boy, simple, artless, the grace of God resting upon Him, revealed in the answers He gave and the questions He asked, such clarity of apprehension, and insight of mind. They had never had a Boy like that before.

Then came Mary and Joseph. They had travelled a whole day before they missed Him. Undoubtedly they started in the early morning, and never till evening did they look for Him, "supposing Him to be in the company." Some people think that to be a reflection on them. My view is that they had such perfect confidence in the Boy that they did not ask where He was; they were sure He was where He ought to be. But when eventide came, of course the mother looked for the lad, and He was not there. Then they left that travelling company and went back. They were a day's journey away, and that meant a day's journey back to Jerusalem, and accounts for the fact that they found Him on the third day. They found Him in the Temple, and

they were astonished as they listened. Then his mother spoke to Him, and she said, "Child." This is another word altogether. It is not the "child" of the fortieth verse, and it is not the "Boy" of the forty-third. It is a tender Mother word. It is a word that has exactly the value of the Scotch word, "*bairn*." When a Scotch-woman talks of her bairn, she means the child she has borne. The Greek word has exactly that significance, and Mary used it, and she said, "Child, *Bairn* of mine, why hast Thou thus dealt with us? behold, Thy father and I sought Thee sorrowing." Then we have the first words from the lips of the Boy, beautiful words, simple, artless, natural, true. He said,

"How is it that ye sought Me? knew ye not that I must be in the things of My Father?"

He said in effect: But, Mother, surely you understood; how is it that you sought Me? And then the central thing of the Boy life;

"I must be in the things of My Father."

"*I must.*" In those words the Boy expressed His sense of relationship to God, of responsibility to God, and of response to that responsibility. The perfect Boy is revealed by that "I must."

In this connection there is a simple matter to be noted, which is nevertheless arresting. In the Greek the statement of Jesus takes this form:

"I must be in the things of the Father of Me."

That, of course, may mean, and in some senses does mean, "My Father." But it is at least worthy of note that whenever Christ spoke of God as His Father, He used the definite article; and He never used the definite article before Father when He was speaking of God as the Father of anybody but Himself. In the twentieth chapter of John He said, in our translation,

"I am not yet ascended unto the Father; but go unto My brethren, and say unto them, I ascend unto My Father and your Father."

In the Greek New Testament, the form is different;

"I ascend unto the Father of Me, and Father of you."

Now, that means hardly anything to an English reader, but it means everything to an interpreter of the Bible, and to one familiar with the idiom of the Greek language. God was in a special sense His Father, and the special relationship is suggested in the method of reference—"The Father of Me." He had that consciousness even as a Boy, "I must be in the things of the Father of Me."

Then Luke tells us that,

"He went down with them (His parents), and came to Nazareth; and He was subject unto them."

The ideal Boy, His volition poised to the will of God, expressed it in subjection to His parents. That is to say, the perfect response of the Boy to the will of God meant for Him natural correspondence to ordinary conditions. It did not set Him free from responsibilities to the home in which He had been brought up; but under the mastery of the will of His one Father, He submitted His life to the authority of the home.

Then Luke gives us the account of eighteen years in brief but pregnant sentences.

"And Jesus advanced in wisdom and stature, and in favour with God and men."

The whole fact is declared in the statement that "He advanced." This is an entirely different word from the one used of the first twelve years—"He grew." Dean Farrar says of this word:

"The word used here is derived from pioneers, cutting down trees in the pathway of an advancing army."

Thayer, that great master of words and phrases, says *Prokopto*

"Means to lengthen out by hammering as a smith forges metals."

I am not going to decide between these two authorities as to the etymological origin of a word. Either of these definitions gives the same idea. If we examine the make-up of the word, it means to chop forward, to beat forward, to hack on. The idea of the word, then, is that of strenuous activity rather than passive development. The Child grew for twelve years, passive development, no volitional responsibility; but He was now a Son of the law, and had to hack His own way on. Life now became responsible. For the future, development must be not merely the passive growth that answers life, but the bringing of all life under control. "He advanced."

How did He advance? First, "In wisdom." He had to face problems, He had to seek for information; He had to find out. From Boyhood up to thirty years of age, we see a perfectly natural and beautiful process of mental life, not growing merely, but as all mental growth is under the control of will, He is seen having to hack His own way on. We may reverently say of Him, He advanced in wisdom, having the loins of His mind girt up.

Then the physical. The order is now changed. In the Child the first thing was the physical, "waxing strong;" and that is always the first thing with the child. But now the mental is first. The physical, however, is not excluded. He advanced in stature. Not merely grew; He advanced, practising the culture of the body, and the restraint of the body, holding passion under the mastery of principle.

And finally, "He advanced" spiritually, "in grace." As a Child the grace of God was *on* Him. Now He is living *in* grace. He advanced in grace with God and men. Here I submit that the translation, "grew in favour," is faulty and misleading. It has constantly been taken to mean that *as* He grew up, He became more and more a favourite with God and men. The preposition here rendered "with" reveals the true meaning of the statement. It is the Greek preposition *Para*, by the side of. He advanced in grace by the side of God and men. He lived in all the years of development, maintaining His fellowship with

God, and His fellowship with men; by the side of God, and by the side of men. Thus, abiding in grace, He advanced. Thus we see the spiritual development of Jesus from Boyhood to Manhood under the constraint of a will submitted to God.

Here, again, as in the verse about the Child, Luke has recorded essential and not incidental things; things common to humanity, the mental, the physical, the spiritual. Incidental things which divide are not referred to.

This, then, is God's second Man. In this whole paragraph we see His growth from Babyhood to Boyhood; the Boy coming to adolescence, becoming the Son of the law; everything poised to the will of His Father; and then for eighteen years advancing. We shall see Him next in this narrative, when He is thirty years of age.

LUKE III. 1-20

THE focal point of light of this paragraph is found in the words:

"The word of God came unto John."

In it we have Luke's account of the ministry of John. It is a condensed account. Other particulars are given by Matthew, and by Mark.

Our previous glimpse of John was in the final verse of chapter one;

"And the child grew, and waxed strong in spirit, and was in the deserts till the day of his showing unto Israel."

Now we reach the account of the day of his showing unto Israel. We find him in the wilderness, the district described by Moses as "the great and terrible wilderness." How long he had been there is a matter of conjecture. There are those who believe he had been there from childhood. I believe he went into the wilderness when at twenty years of age. He should then have taken up his course as a priest. But knowing the work to which God had called him, he passed into the wilderness to prepare for his prophetic work. If that be so, he had been there at least ten years. Luke tells of his ministry, and then runs ahead historically for at least a year, as he records the fact that Herod the tetrarch being reproved of him, shut up John in prison.

Describing the beginning of his ministry, Luke says,

"The Word of God came unto John."

This is an old Hebrew formula. We find it in the prophetic books again and again. It should, however, be understood that the term here is not *logos*, but *rhema*. The significance of the Greek word *rhema* is that of a distinct message. It was not the whole of truth that came to him; but a particular message from God, which he was charged to deliver. That does not minimize the value or importance of the statement. It rather accentuates it. John in the wilderness received a message from God, and whatever that message was, that was the burden of his preaching. There can be no doubt that during those ten years this man had meditated and pondered upon the condition of his times. He was certainly familiar with the darkness of the age. The iron of it had surely entered into his soul; he knew the sin of his people, and the condition in which they were living. But his message did not come out of his own pondering. His message was a word from God. His pondering was part of the preparation for delivering the message, for there is always perfect harmony in the elections of God, between the fitness of the instrument and the work to be done. But when John left the wilderness to preach, he did not come out to discuss with his age the situation as he saw it, even as the result of his own devout observation. The word came to him from God, and came to him there in the wilderness.

In this translation I do not like that preposition "unto." The Greek preposition is *epi;* and it ought to be rendered, "The word of God came *upon* John." The force of the preposition is that of pressure from above. The word of the Lord came upon him, pressed down upon him from above. Here is the qualification for preaching. The message of God comes upon a man. It is a great thing that he be prepared in every way; but preparation leaves a man unable to preach until the word of the Lord falls upon him. That is the keynote to the marvel of this ministry.

As we consider the story of this ministry there are three things to notice; the date of its exercising; the call as it came to him; and the exercise that followed the call.

First, then, as to the date. It is an arresting thing, and not to be lightly passed over, the remarkable way in which Luke dates the fact that the word of God came to John. In order to do it he made use of one emperor, one governor, three tetrarchs, and two high-priests. The whole world is referred to. The thing that happened when the word of the Lord came to John, happened in the wilderness, and its influence was felt presently in Judæa; but Luke shows that it was a thing of world significance; as he presses into the service of marking the hour, the emperor, Tiberius Cæsar; one governor, the governor of that immediate district, Pontius Pilate; three tetrarchs, Herod, and Philip, and Lysanias, the region lying round about Judæa; and two high priests, Annas and Caiphas.

Let us glance at the conditions revealed by this list of names of august personages. He says that it was in the fifteenth year of the reign of Tiberius Cæsar. Van Doren, referring to him, has thus described him:

"Tiberius Cæsar was talented, ambitious, cruel, licentious, infamous, inhuman."

That was the man. Luke says, "In the reign . . . of Tiberius Cæsar." The word there rendered reign is an arresting one. It is the word *Hegemonia*. It was in the *hegemony* of Tiberius Cæsar. During the war we heard much about *hegemony*. It was said—whether rightly or wrongly I am not now discussing—that it was the passion of the Kaiser to gain *hegemony*. What, then, is *hegemony?* World mas-

tery, world dominion. Now, here is the arresting fact. Luke uses that very word; and thus we have a picture of the world immediately before our eyes. Tiberius Cæsar, the licentious, who at last retired to the island of Capreæ, and there lived in such lustful excesses that they thought he had killed himself; and when the false rumour came that he had done so, they announced Caligula his successor while he was yet living; with the result that with great brutality he retaliated, until at last the men of Rome, seeking to rid themselves of him, smothered him. Yet at the time he had world authority. And while that was so, the word of God came to John, and nobody knew about it, and if they had known about it, they would have counted it of no importance.

Then glance at the others named. Pilate was governor. He represented the *hegemony*. The power of life and death for that district was in his hands, as the representative of the Roman Empire. The tetrarchs named were all vassals of Rome. There were two high priests. That was not according to the Divine economy. Neither of them had any right to the high-priestly office. Annas was the high priest. Rome objected to him; therefore he was set on one side, and Caiphas was put in his place. Annas was allowed to remain and retain the name and be president of the Sanhedrim. Thus Rome is seen arranging the priesthood of God's ancient people!

From that world outlook suggested by those earlier names, turn to the outlook upon God's people, the commonwealth of Israel. They were divided, and ruled by vassal rulers, and blighted by a degenerate priesthood.

Now, under those conditions, the word of the Lord came. Where did it alight? Not in Rome, sitting in her proud insolence upon her seven hills; not in Jerusalem, sitting amid the spiritual and moral ruin that characterized the age, the appalling disaster of the rebellious people of God. The word of God passed the emperor, passed the governor, passed the tetrarchs, passed the priests, and lighted upon a man, a man prepared of God; lighted upon him in the wilderness. To me there is great significance in that. There is suggestiveness even in the geographical statement. Where will the word of God find a place? Where can it find vantage ground? Not in Rome. We hardly expected it would there. Not in Jerusalem. We might have expected it there. It went outside everything, to that tract of country geographically a symbol of the world's spiritual and moral condition at that time, the wilderness. Nineteen hundred years have gone and more; and now we know that the most important event in the world's history at that moment was the coming of the word of God to that man. When it happened, it did not create a ripple on the surface of things apparently. As he went on with his mighty work, it created more than a ripple in that neighbourhood; but do you suppose for a moment that in imperial Rome they knew anything about it. The world went on its own blind way in rebellion. Yet there was God's vantage ground. A man who had been in that desert land for at least ten years, roused himself one day under the mastery of a pressure upon him from above, of the message of the living God, and he passed from the wilderness out to proclaim that message.

The story of the exercise of his ministry follows:

"He came into all the region round about the Jordan, preaching the baptism of repentance unto remission of sins."

In that sentence we have the burden of his message. He was

"preaching the baptism of repentance unto the remission of sins."

John, the voice crying in the wilderness, and preparing the way of the Lord, was dealing with sins, and the need of the hour, the remission of sins. He was calling men to repentance unto the remission of sins. The rite of baptism in John's ministry was the outward confession of repentance unto the remission of sins. It never brought the remission of sins. It only indicated the fact of a mental attitude that would make possible the remission of sins, and that is where he ended. His

ministry never went beyond that. The ministry of John was incomplete; gloriously complete, as fulfilling a Divine purpose, and delivering a Divine message; but the whole message of John was a message declaring a completeness to come through the Messiah;

"I indeed baptize you with water; but there cometh He that is mightier than I."

He was not the Word of God. He was not even delivering the word of God in its fulness. He was a voice, and a messenger, preparing the way for the Word, and the final speech of God to men in His Son. Remission of sins can only come through Him.

The method of his preaching was that of a terrific severity.

"Ye offspring of vipers, who warned you to flee from the wrath to come?"

Matthew tells us that John said this when he saw Sadducees and Pharisees in the crowd. It was to the men who supremely felt that they needed no repentance, that he addressed the stinging, biting, sarcastic words that called them an offspring of vipers.

Moreover, as he called them to repentance, he declared that it must be a real repentance; "bring forth therefore fruits worthy of repentance." He told them that they were trusting in their relation in the flesh to Abraham; and declared that God could raise up children of stones unto Abraham.

In his ministry he talked to inquirers, and we have an account of some of the things he said. The multitudes said, What shall we do? That was the question asked in conversations, resulting from the appeal of his prophetic ministry. His answer to that is very arresting. He said,

"He that hath two coats, let him impart to him that hath none; and he that hath food, let him do likewise."

He told them that their activity was to be love-inspired. Give, is the word. If you have two coats, give one to the man who has none. If you have food, and another man is hungry, give him food. There, before the Sermon on the Mount, before the teaching of Jesus, before all the marvel of that teaching, revealing the fact that the height of morality is the love-mastered life, John said the same thing. He was the forerunner of the King.

Then the publicans also came to him, perhaps a deputation of them, representing their order, and they said, "Teacher, what must we do?" To them he replied:

"Extort no more than that which is appointed you."

Here is the same law of love, governing them in their gathering of the Roman taxes. And soldiers came, and the Greek word means soldiers on active service, and they said, "And we, what must we do?" And he said,

"Extort from no man by violence, neither accuse any one wrongfully, and be content with your wages."

Thus the law of love was enforced in every answer he gave to personal inquiry.

And so we reach the final note, as Luke records it. One result of his mission was that a false impression was being created concerning him.

"As the people were in expectation, and all men reasoned in their hearts concerning John, whether haply he were the Christ."

This shows that the false impression was gaining ground, that he was himself the Messiah. Then John came out with the clearest statement, and so fulfilled his function of forerunner. He said,

"I indeed baptize you with water; but there cometh He that is mightier than I, the latchet of Whose shoes I am not worthy to unloose; He shall baptize you in the Holy Spirit and fire; Whose fan is in His hand, thoroughly to cleanse His threshing-floor, and to gather the wheat into His garner; but the chaff He will burn up with un-quenchable fire."

Mark the contrast, "I," "He." I, said John, have my ministry; I have my message, the word I received from

God; and all the meaning of my message may be gathered up by what I can do; I baptize you in water, a symbol, indicating a change of mind; that is my limit. But He that cometh shall baptize you in fire, not a symbol but a fact, and a fact that produces not merely a change of mind, but a change of nature. I baptize you with water, and my baptism in water is symbolic of the cleansing of your thinking; but if that is all, you are still helpless and hopeless. He that cometh after me shall baptize you with the Spirit and fire, producing a change in nature. A change of mind is necessary, or there never can be a change in nature. Until man changes his mind, there can be no baptism of the Spirit that changes his nature.

It is the record of a marvellous and a mighty ministry. It touched all classes, all sorts and conditions of men. All Judæa went out to him. He gathered them around him. Even Herod went to him; and we have that tremendously significant declaration that there was a time when Herod heard him gladly, so gladly, that even when he turned back to his wallowing in the mire, he still held John in such respect that he tried to save him from the anger of a wanton woman, and put him in prison, not because he was opposed to him, but to try and keep him safe. His was the authentic voice of a prophet for the first time for four hundred years, reverberating over the hills and along the valleys, and from everywhere they went out to hear him. But the ultimate marvel of it was that it was but a preparatory ministry for something mightier than itself. Luke points out that it was in fulfilment of the prophecy of Isaiah, and there is tremendous significance in that. Matthew refers to it, and Mark notices it. As also does John. Thus each of the evangelists links up the ministry of John with the prophetic movement in the book of Isaiah. If we turn back to Isaiah, beginning at the fortieth chapter and running on, we shall read of the way by which the wilderness is to be made to blossom as the rose. It is by the coming of the Servant of the Lord, through travail to triumph. John was the forerunner of the Servant of the Lord, himself exercising a mighty ministry, its mightiest fact being that it was preparatory for something greater.

As we come to the end of this meditation on the ministry of John, there are questions that beat in upon the mind. I wonder whether we do not need a ministry of this kind now. I sometimes wonder whether Christ does not still need John the Baptist to prepare His way. I wonder it, in these days when I consider some types of evangelistic work, from which the note of stern demand upon men seems entirely absent. I wonder whether the message of the Christ can ever prevail until the message of John has gone before it. If someone objects to that way of putting it, I will put it in another way. Let us say the forerunner and the necessity for him have gone. What, then, is the message of Christ? The first note in the message

of Christ as recorded, is the whole message of John. Go back and read it.

" From that time began Jesus to preach, and to say, Repent ye; for the Kingdom of heaven is at hand."

That is where He began; and He never departed from it. But someone says, There was more tenderness in Jesus. Think again. John said, " Ye offspring of vipers." Listen to Jesus when that same crowd of Pharisees and Sadducees were opposing Him, and saying that He was in league with the devil. Or again when denunciations were falling from His holy lips, He also said, " Ye offspring of vipers," more than that, He said, " Ye serpents." The note of severity was there. Somehow we are missing a vital element in our message from Christ if we fail to understand that the call to repentance must always precede the call to confidence in the redeeming Lord.

LUKE III. 21-38

" Now it came to pass, when all the people were baptized, that, Jesus also having been baptized, and praying, the heaven was opened, and the Holy Spirit descended in a bodily form, as a dove, upon Him, and a voice came out of heaven, Thou art My beloved Son; in Thee I am well pleased. . . . And Jesus Himself, when He began, was about thirty years of age, being the Son (as was supposed) of Joseph, . . . the son of Enos, the Son of Seth, the son of Adam, the son of God."—Luke iii.21-23 and 38.

HERE we reach the culminating point in Luke's delineation of the personality of our Lord. He does what no other evangelist does—mentions His age when He began. The words " to teach " are not in the Greek text. They have been supplied by translators, to make smooth reading. I am not quarrelling with them; but I remember that when Luke began his second treatise for his friend Theophilus, the book of the Acts, he said, " The former treatise I made, O Theophilus, concerning all that Jesus began both to do and to teach." There we have Luke's own words, " He began

to do and teach," and I think if we want to supply anything here, we had better take Luke's words, and say, " Jesus Himself, when He began to do and teach."

I say he names His age, about thirty. If the Bible is to be trusted in this incidental revelation, thirty years is the age when human personality reaches maturity. Joseph was thirty years of age when standing before Pharaoh he began his great work. By the Mosaic law the Levites, whereas they entered upon priestly courses at twenty, were not allowed to take full work until they were thirty. King David came to the throne when he was thirty years of age. The order of the scribes began their work, receiving their insignia when they were thirty years of age. Luke says that in the development of His perfect personality, Jesus came to full maturity about thirty years of age.

Here it may be well to recapitulate the facts concerning the Person of our Lord as we have seen it in Luke's delineation. This man, as we said in our very first study, of the scientific method, has traced all things accurately, and of the artistic temperament, has set them in order. He first of all went behind the birth of the Baby to discover pre-natal facts; and we have the account of His conception in the womb of the virgin by the power of the Most High. He then shows us the Baby born; no room for Him in the inn, passing all palaces, and all homes, and all houses, and even the caravansaries, or hotels; born in a manger. He then tells of this Child of eight days of age being circumcised, and thus coming into relationship with that nation which God had created. He then presents this Child at forty days old, presented in the Temple; the firstborn according to the original Divine provision, taking up the position of the priest. Then He tells of His growth in the home, shows Him at twelve years of age, a Son of the law, the Boy dedicated completely to one thing, His Father's business. He then records that for the next eighteen years He advanced; His life now under the mastery of will, and perfectly poised to the will of God. There are sidelights on those eighteen years in other narratives. Matthew and Mark in slightly different ways tell us the same thing; Matthew in his thirteenth chapter records the fact that men said of Him, "Is not this the carpenter's son?" Mark, giving us the record in his sixth chapter, says that men said of Him, "Is not this the carpenter?" Both tell us that men said that they knew Joseph, and they knew Mary; and that the brothers of Jesus, James, and Joses, and Judas, and Simon were with them, and sisters. The family life of Jesus is there revealed during all those years. His occupation, a carpenter, technically an artificer, a labourer in wood, a producer, a builder. Presently when He began to preach, His daily calling served Him. He talked about yokes, He had made them; He talked about ploughs, He had made them; He talked of building houses on rock or sand, He knew the work exactly, for He had done it. In this Gospel of Luke, in the next chapter, we find another sidelight. We read He went into the synagogue, "as His custom was." All this gives us a picture of those

eighteen years; a family life, His mother and her husband, the father of Jesus by adoption; four brothers, their names given; sisters, the number not given; and during all the time He worked in the carpenter's shop, learning the use of the tools of His craft, making Himself acquainted with wood, forming yokes and ploughs, and building houses; and always on the Sabbath day in the synagogue, listening to the reading of the Law and the Rolls, and the teaching of the rulers.

Now those years were over, and He came to maturity; and entered upon His Messianic mission. He did not then begin to be Messiah, as to personality, but His mission began.

Luke first records the fact of His beginning, the anointing of the Spirit, and the attestation of His Father as He entered upon His Messianic work; and then goes back, and places Him by giving His genealogy. We will reverse the order of our consideration. We will begin where Luke ends, with this genealogy, and then we will consider the account of the beginning of His Messianic mission.

Luke uses a phrase in referring to our Lord which is arresting. He says, "And Jesus Himself." Why did he use the word "Himself" there? It would have been quite simple to say,

"Jesus, when He began, was about thirty years of age,"

but he does not write it so. He says, "Jesus Himself." He was thus laying emphasis upon the personality which he has already described. In chapter one, verse thirty-one, I read,

"Behold, thou shalt conceive in thy womb, and bring forth a Son, and shalt call His name JESUS."

There the name first occurs, in the great annunciation. In chapter two, verse twenty-one, I read,

"When eight days were fulfilled for circumcising Him, His name was called JESUS, which was so called by the angel before He was conceived in the womb."

Again in the same chapter, verse twenty-seven, I read,

"He came in the Spirit into the Temple; and when the parents brought in the Child Jesus."

He was then forty days old. In the same chapter and the forty-third verse I read,

"And when they had fulfilled the days, as they were returning, the Boy Jesus tarried behind in Jerusalem."

Twelve years had now passed. Once more in that chapter, verse fifty-two, I read,

"And Jesus advanced in wisdom and stature, and in favour with God and men."

In chapter three, verse twenty-one, I read,

"Jesus also having been baptized;"

and now finally in verse twenty-three,

"And Jesus Himself."

The angel said, You shall call His name JESUS. They called His name *Jesus*, as the angel had said. Then the Child *Jesus* grew. Twelve years passed, and we see the Boy *Jesus*. From that moment *Jesus* advanced. Eighteen years went by, and *Jesus* was baptized. Now, says Luke, that Jesus, Jesus *Himself*, and none other. So that little word *"Himself"* insists upon the personality as described.

Thus identifying Him, Luke says of Him, "being the Son (as was supposed) of Joseph." To the ordinary reader that phrase may suggest that everyone supposed, in our sense of the word, that He was the son of Joseph. It means nothing of the kind. The word so rendered literally means, " according to law." Jesus was the Son, according to law, of Joseph; that is, not the actual Son, but the adopted Son. The genealogy begins in that way, and then moving on, refers to Joseph as "the son of Heli." Now Matthew says that Joseph was the son of Jacob. Joseph was the son of Heli, by marriage with Mary; and the line here is Mary's line. If we compare the genealogy in Luke with that in Matthew, we find that from Abraham to David the names are the same.

But in Matthew, when we reach David, the line continues through Solomon. But in Luke, when we reach David, the line continues through Nathan. Jesus was born of Mary in the line from David through Nathan.

Thus Luke passed back along the true line, the royal line from David, the national line from Abraham; but he did not finish there; he looked upon Jesus as infinitely more than of the line of David, and Son of Abraham; he went back, until he said at last that stupendous thing, " Seth, the son of Adam, the son of God." That is Luke's interpretation of humanity, and of Jesus as fulfilling the first Divine ideal of God in the creation of man. Jesus was the Son of God in His human nature, as well as in the profounder and eternal sense of His Divine nature.

Pause here for a moment and observe the beacon lights of personality; Adam, Seth, not Cain; Enoch, not Lamech; Noah; Shem, not Japheth or Ham. Abraham; Isaac, not Ishmael; Jacob, not Esau; David; Nathan, not Solomon. The Divine procedure is seen overriding and setting aside things that man makes supreme. The old law of primogeniture is ruled out when God begins to deal with men. If the firstborn son fails, he is set on one side, and another man is taken; but the line of Divine purpose continues.

Here is seen at work the great principle to the recognition of which Peter had come when he said,

" I perceive that God is no Respecter of persons."

God never has respect for any of the accidental things.

" But in every nation," again to quote Peter, " he that feareth Him and worketh righteousness is acceptable to Him."

Now let us go back to the marvellous story of the commencement of the Messianic mission of our Lord.

" Now it came to pass, when all the people were baptized, that, Jesus also having been baptized, and praying, the heaven was opened, and the Holy Spirit descended in a bodily form, as a dove, upon Him, and a voice came out of heaven, Thou art My beloved Son; in Thee I am well pleased."

Luke recognizes the baptism by reference to it as accomplished; and then records events immediately following it. Here let us carefully mark the attitude of our Lord. He was praying. Luke, portraying the personality of the Lord, is careful to say that He was praying. There are eight or nine different Greek words in the New Testament used to express the activities of prayer. The word used here is the word which includes them all. The word *proseuchomai* literally means to wish forward. That covers the whole fact of prayer in the New Testament, wishing forward, desiring onward. That is prayer. It has many activities. There is petition, there is thanksgiving, there is supplication; but this describes the whole attitude, the attitude of a worshipping and adoring soul in the presence of God. He was praying. He had submitted to the rite of baptism, numbering Himself with transgressors. And now He was in the attitude of adoration and worship.

That is an arresting characteristic of Luke's story. That is the first mention of the fact of our Lord's praying. In the fifth chapter, verse sixteen, when we are told that His fame was growing, we are told that He went apart to pray. In that same chapter we are told that when He chose the twelve, before He did it, He went apart to pray. In chapter nine, when He was about to challenge His disciples at Cæsarea Philippi as to what men said about Him, before He did it, He went apart to pray. Luke tells us, too, in that chapter that He was transfigured when He was praying. In the eleventh chapter he tells us that when His disciples said to Him, "Lord, teach us to pray," they had been watching Him pray. Luke, moreover, tells us in the twenty-second chapter that He went into Gethsemane to pray. Thus we have seven occasions in the course of the book when Luke uses this very word to describe the attitude and activity of this Man.

Born, grown, advanced, mature, committing Himself to Messianic office by His baptism, He is seen praying! To return. The significant thing here is that Luke emphasizes the fact that having been baptized, He was praying; He is seen in the attitude of adoration, the attitude of worship, the attitude of submission to God, the attitude of dependence upon God.

We turn, then, to the happenings as recorded. "The heaven was opened." Observe, not "the heavens," but "the heaven." Luke was a Greek, but here is writing a Hebrew story. The Hebrew spoke of the heavens; and when he did so, he had a clearly defined philosophy. The first heaven was the atmosphere round the world. To that Jesus referred when He said, "Behold the birds of the heaven." The second heaven was that of the stellar spaces. The third heaven was the dwelling-place of angels and of the spirits of the just made perfect, and the place of the supreme manifestation of God in the universe. When our Lord taught His disciples to pray, He used the word "heaven" the first time in the plural, and then in the singular.

"Our Father, Who art in the heavens (plural, all heavens), . . . Thy will be done on earth as in heaven" (one only, the principal heaven, the central heaven).

Now, "the heaven was opened." The reference patently is to the third heaven. Then the Holy Spirit descended in a bodily form as a dove upon Him. Here is a case in which, if I were translating, I would bring over into our language the very idiom of the Greek. It says, "The Spirit, the Holy," the definite article before "Spirit," and before "Holy." The emphasis there is placed upon the holiness of the Spirit. "The Spirit, the Holy" descended upon Him. The Spirit of God did no violence to holiness when He descended upon Him. There are men in this world upon whom the Spirit cannot descend. The Spirit only descends upon us, enters into us, and dwells in us, through Jesus Christ the Holy One. Our reception of the Spirit is a miracle of redeeming grace. The Spirit, the Holy, descended upon Him from the opened heaven, having found in Him vantage-ground; in perfect accord with the Holiness of God.

Then we come to that very arresting thing about which I am always inclined to speak with some reticence, the Spirit descended in a bodily form as a dove. Bodily form; the word form there means appearance, bodily appearance. When Paul spoke of Christ later, he said,

" In Him dwelleth all the fulness of the Godhead bodily,"

that is, corporeally; the same word. The Spirit took bodily form, like a dove. That is the only place in the Bible when the Spirit is referred to under the figure of the dove. In Talmudic literature we have a reference to such a thing. It says about Genesis i.2:

" The Spirit of God moved on the face of the waters like a dove."

That is peculiarly interesting. Milton evidently was familiar with that Talmudic literature, because he says,

"And with mighty wings outspread, Dove-like sat brooding on the vast dark abyss."

One reverently asks, What was the significance of that? And just as reverently a man has to say, at least I have to say, I cannot possibly answer the inquiry dogmatically. I do remember, however, that Jesus used a remarkable word one day about a dove. He told His disciples in a world like this they would have to be as " wise as serpents, and as harmless as doves." Harmless, and the meaning of the word is unmixed, sincere, simple, no guile, no deceit; and therefore harmless in effect. The dove is the symbol of harmlessness. And yet again, I cannot read that without my mind reverting to the ancient economy, and the whole sacrificial system; and to the fact that the offering of the poor was two doves. The dove stood surely for sacrifice. The Spirit that brooded over the chaotic earth before humanity came into existence, and held it until God restored the earth for the new thing in the universe; that spirit in this

Man has found vantage ground, the Spirit, the Holy; and in coming upon Him took the form of a dove, harmless, and sacrificial.

Then came the voice; a voice came out of heaven. Three times in the course of our Lord's ministry do we read of that happening. Here first, then on the mount of transfiguration, a voice out of the cloud that came upon Him; and then in the twelfth chapter of John, when the Greeks had come, a voice out of heaven. A voice out of heaven at His baptism, a voice out of the heavenly cloud at His transfiguration; a voice under the very shadow of the Cross. Three occasions, and in each case we are in the realm of the Cross. He had just consented to be baptized with a baptism of sinners, numbering Himself with transgressors, and thus foreshadowing His passion baptism; and the voice out of heaven spoke. On the mount of transfiguration, He talked with heavenly visitors, about the exodus He was about to accomplish, the Cross; and the voice out of heaven spoke. In the last day in Jerusalem, with the Greeks waiting to see Him, He talked of His Cross, the grain of wheat falling into the ground and dying. He said,

" Now is My soul troubled; and what shall I say? Father, save Me from this hour?"

But He did not say that.

" But for this cause came I unto this hour. Father, glorify Thy name."

Then came the voice out of heaven.

The voice uttered a double affirmation. First as to the Person of Jesus; " Thou art My beloved Son." Let me again give that in the idiom of the language in which it was written;

" Thou art the Son of Me, the Beloved."

That little article in front of " Beloved " makes it emphatic, and gives emphasis to this word of heaven. There He was, a perfect Man, praying. The heaven opened; the Spirit descended upon Him—a vantage ground for a new and redeeming activity, in the form of a dove—and a voice said,

"Thou art the Son of Me, the Beloved."

Then the second thing;

"In Thee I have found delight."

That was heaven's estimate of Him. Mark the value of that second word, "In Thee I am well pleased." First of all it flashes light backwards upon the thirty years; God's approval of the thirty years. Thirty years in which there had been no deflection from the straight path of obedience to the will of God. Thirty years; nothing in the life, nothing in thought, nothing in speech, nothing in deed, nothing in work, that had not filled the heart of God with satisfaction. In Thee I have found delight.

But there is something more. It was not only the approving of the thirty years now passed; it was also the accepting of the three and a half years to come, the direction and purpose of which had been indicated by the baptism of this Man in Jordan. "Thou art the Son of Me, the Beloved; in Thee I have found My delight."

Thus has Luke set before us the Person of the Word made flesh. In that Person all human history is re-born. That is God's new starting-point for the human race. There we see the Second Man, as Paul says, or as Luke says, "Jesus Himself." From this point on through the Gospel we shall see Him doing and teaching in the line of the Divine programme.

LUKE IV. 1-13

HERE we have Luke's record of the first activity of our Lord after dedication and consecration, the activity of temptation. It is important to realize that this threefold temptation was wholly Messianic. I am not saying that there are not personal values in it. We have in the study a revelation of the processes of the evil one, as he attempts to seduce Mansoul from loyalty to God. But it is of vital importance that we should understand that the temptation recorded here was directed not so much against the personality of our Lord, as against His Messianic office. Matthew and Luke both give the account of it. Mark refers to it in that one brief paragraph (i.9-13), into which he condensed so much; viz., that Jesus came from Nazareth, and was baptized and anointed, that He was attested, and that He was tempted. Thus each evangelist reveals the same order; the dedication of our Lord to His great mission, and then the temptation. The personal temptation of Jesus did not begin here. That had gone on through all His life. Through childhood and youth, and in all the years of His advance, He was tempted;

"Tempted in all points like as we

are, sin apart."

And before the great climacteric attack of the enemy, He was tempted all the forty days. Here we have the story of hell's attempt to thwart heaven's purpose. This is not so much Satan attacking the Person of our Lord, as attacking the purpose of God Almighty as it was to be realized by our Lord. It was an attack upon Him as the Messiah. He was the Anointed One of high heaven, confronting the whole empire of evil and of darkness, in the person of its over-lord, Satan; and confronting that underworld, and that central personality, as King and as Priest, the two offices merging in Messiahship. Matthew shows Him confronting the empire of evil as God's anointed King. He gives first the bread temptation, then the temptation to cast Himself from the pinnacle of the Temple; and then the temptation which confronted Him, as Satan asked for His homage, in order to gain the kingdoms. Matthew is showing the three ways in which man has attempted to set up world-kingdoms. All human governments and all human empires have been built up on one of three false foundations; the bread basis, caring only for the physical; the false religious basis, emphasizing the spectacular; and a compromise basis. Luke, who is dealing with the personality of our Lord, and with His redeeming mission, records the same temptations, but he puts them in another order, and in doing so, another aspect of them is brought before us. It is still Messianic, but here particular emphasis is upon the fact that our Lord was tempted as Redeemer. Here we have false conceptions of humanity.

First, Luke describes how He was tempted as Man personally; then as Man socially, the whole social order of the world, the kingdoms of the world, the orders of life in the world; and then as Man spiritually. Here we are looking at the Person from the standpoint of the redeeming Kinsman, the Man of our humanity, but acting on behalf of others—the Priest,—the other office in the Messianic mission.

In this paragraph there are three parts. In the first two verses we have the Person of our Lord revealed as He faced the devil. In verses three to twelve we have the process of that temptation described; and in verse thirteen we have a postlude.

Notice with what care and accuracy, and yet with what brevity and completeness, Luke describes Jesus as He faced temptation.

"And Jesus full of the Holy Spirit."

"Full of the Holy Spirit." There the emphasis is not upon the fact that He was anointed by the Holy Spirit. That was true. He had been specifically and specially anointed for His holy work; but here Luke shows you God's Man, His adult Man, thirty years of age, His mature Man, anointed of the Spirit for Messianic work, but in the perfection of His humanity going into the wilderness, "Full of the Holy Spirit." That is normal human life. That is not normal human life as the world knows it today; but the world does not know what normal human life is. That is the trouble with the world. The world is less than human. To me the idea that man has ascended from the ape is ridiculous when I think of what man really is. I am very much more inclined to think sometimes that he is descending to the ape! Men

and women who have been born again are admitted into normal human life, according to the Divine ideal and purpose. This is God's Man, full of the Holy Spirit. God never intended man to live in his own strength, and walk alone. The original creation of man was the creation of a being, the secret of whose mental and spiritual power, in order to complete realization of personality, was that he should be full of the Holy Spirit. God never intended man to face temptation in his own strength. God's second Man passed down to face it, full of the Holy Spirit, and therefore perfectly equipped in His fellowship with God, through the Holy Ghost, for everything that lay ahead. He was confident, not in the ability of His human life divorced from God, but in His humanity in fellowship with God, because He was filled with the Holy Spirit.

There is another statement. He

"Returned from the Jordan, and was led in the Spirit in the wilderness during forty days, being tempted of the devil."

Look at His two environments; "in the Spirit," "in the wilderness." He went to the wilderness. He certainly did, and the first phase of the temptation took place there. The wilderness was real, definite, acute, positive. But He was in the Spirit, and that environment was closer to Him than the wilderness and its desolation. It was the environment of the Holy Spirit.

Notice again. "Led in the Spirit," which means that He was submitted to the Spirit, under the mastery of the Spirit, obedient to the Spirit. Matthew and Mark, as well as Luke, emphasize this. Matthew says He was "led up of the Spirit" into the wilderness. He did not go there of His own volition. He went in obedience to the leading of the Spirit. Mark, who is brief in his story, is nevertheless most remarkably blunt in his description of it. He says, "The Spirit driveth Him." The Greek word *ek ballo* means, cast Him out there. "The Spirit drove Him into the wilderness," so says Mark. "The Spirit led Him up into the wilderness," says Matthew. Luke says, "The Spirit led Him in the wilderness." Thus the same thing is said by each, but in different ways. Our Lord is seen here then, going to the wilderness to be tempted under the guidance of the Holy Ghost. Normal humanity can only come to its perfection, because of the nature of its being, as it faces temptation; and it can only be victorious over temptation by the guidance of the Holy Ghost. It is when man faces temptation in his own strength that the devil is victorious. When man or woman, youth or maiden, boy or girl, stands up against temptation under the mastery of the Spirit of God, that man or woman, youth or maiden, boy or girl, feels the impact of it, but there is no need for defeat. In fellowship with God, man is mightier than Hell.

"During forty days." All the forty days tempted; through all the forty days led. I cannot ponder this story without seeing that this temptation of our Lord was a part of a larger purpose than His own mere living. Here was a definite action of the Holy Ghost, calling Messiah to face the underworld of evil. I see Him, led of the Spirit, confronting that underworld, challenging that underworld, and presently conquering that underworld. Jesus was led there to confront Satan, and compel him to come into the open. My philosophy of the universe does not conceive of the devil as a free agent, outside the government of God. Even though he is in revolt against God, he is still within the grasp of the Divine compulsion. This, then, was more than the temptation of an individual. An individual He surely was, but representative, the Messiah. In the wilderness He, compelled by the Spirit, forced the enemy into the open.

During forty days He did eat nothing. Temptation was no child's play, even though He was led of the Spirit to be tempted; and was led of the Spirit while tempted; and faced temptation in the fulness of the Holy Ghost. Forty days, He did eat nothing. All the forces of His holy personality were gathered up, and focussed upon the meeting of the foe. Forty days He did eat nothing. Then

afterwards He was hungry. That is a sign of perfect physical health.

Then came the great offensive. The devil, completely defeated in the Person of Jesus through thirty years; the devil, completely defeated in the Person of Jesus through forty days, now came up with all the forces of his subtlety against Jesus in His redeeming office. He attacked the purpose. He proceeded against Him in those three temptations in His representative capacity as the Redeemer.

There are three places referred to; the wilderness; Luke does not name the mountain, but he says He was led up, and that has the same significance; and the Temple. The first, in the desolate loneliness of the wilderness. The second, on some great mountain height, from which suggestively the whole known world would pass in panoramic view before the vision of Jesus. The third, in the Temple.

The first of these temptations was an attack on man, but upon this Man in a representative capacity. The Divine purpose of human redemption could only be fulfilled by a Person representing humanity. The first appeal of Satan was worded thus:

"If Thou art the Son of God, command this stone that it become bread."

What was the suggestion? Even admitting that man is son of God, bread is necessary to life. Nothing else matters. Sonship, valuable as it is, is valuable principally as a means of supply for the physical. Secure the physical, supply what is necessary in spite of the fact that, led of the Spirit, Thou hast taken nothing, and art hungry. If Thou art the Son of God, whatever that may mean, use the Sonship for the supply of the one necessity of Thy life, which is bread. The attack was made upon man personally, and so upon the unit which makes up the human race. It was an attack upon man generically.

The force of the temptation merges in the answer.

"Jesus answered unto him, It is written, Man shall not live by bread alone."

Our Lord thus told Satan that in his suggestion that the physical was everything, he was slandering humanity. He said to him in effect, Thy estimate of humanity is false. The suggestion behind the temptation is that all that humanity needs is the physical, and the material supply of that. " Man shall not live by bread alone." Bread without God is not life at all. The physical is incomplete humanity. Standing there as a Person, as the unit of the race, as the second Man, in Him all the race was attacked. The suggestion was made to the whole race that all that man needs is bread.

We hear voices round us today saying,

" What shall we eat? What shall we drink? Wherewithal shall we be clothed? "

Hear the startling yet healthy satire of Paul:

" Whose god is their belly."

The devil's suggestion to humanity is that all that it needs is the physical. Thus the whole race was slandered and attacked in Jesus; and He, God's Man, standing for the race, refused the lie and the suggestion; and declared that such is not life at all; that man does not live by bread alone. The completion of the sentence is found in Matthew,

" But by every word that proceedeth out of the mouth of God.'

Said the devil: Man is only an animal, highly developed possibly; but bread is the one thing necessary; and whatever may be meant by being the Son of God, its value is that it is a means by which to satisfy the physical.

Said Jesus: Man is not an animal. He does not live as animals live. His life cannot be sustained on that level. Man doth not live by bread alone. Away there in the wilderness this was the voice of God's Man, answering for the ideal race according to the purpose of God; and refusing the slander on humanity, which the devil uttered then, and utters still, when he suggests that the physical is the supreme.

The second temptation recorded by Luke opens with the statement:

" He led Him up, and showed Him all the kingdoms of the world in a moment of time."

Here a slight difference in the records of Luke and Matthew is suggestive. Matthew says that he showed Him all the kingdoms of the world. Luke says so, too, but they use different words. The same truth is put in two ways. Matthew says he showed Him all the kingdoms of the world, the *cosmos*. Luke does not use the word *cosmos*. The Revised Version in the margin draws attention to the difference. In that margin you will find this note: " Gr., the inhabited earth." Such a rendering misses the thought, as surely as does the word " world." The Greek word does not mean the inhabited earth. It is the word *oikoumene*. Our English word " economy " is the transliteration of this Greek word *oikoumene*. Now, says Luke, he showed Him all the kingdoms of the economy. It is the same thing as Matthew's " world," or " *cosmos*," but with a different emphasis. At that time the word *oikoumene* was synonymous with the Roman Empire. It was constantly called by this word.

Notice yet more carefully how Luke puts it:

" He showed Him all the kingdoms (plural) of the *oikoumene*."

For a moment think of the world as it was then. The economy of the world was that of the Roman Empire. What kingdoms were in it? Greece, Pergamos, Bithynia, Bosphorus, Syria, Pontus, Egypt, Judæa. Those were the kingdoms within the Roman Empire. The devil showed Jesus the thing as it was then. It may have been that, pointing to the north and south, and to the east and west, he brought to the mind, if not to the actual vision of Jesus, the kingdoms of the economy. He said in effect: There is the economy of the world, under the Roman Empire, and all the kingdoms within it.

" To Thee will I give all this authority, and the glory of them; for it hath been delivered unto me."

That does not mean that God had delivered it unto him, but that men had yielded it to him. "Prince of the world," Jesus called him, and so he was by the world's choice.

"It hath been delivered unto me; and to whomsoever I will I give it."

When the devil tells the truth, we may know he is in hard straits. He said,

"All *this* authority, and the glory of them, . . . hath been delivered unto me."

That was true. But it was not all the truth when he said, "To whomsoever I will I give it." His gift of anything to men is only transitory; he can give nothing to men with the right of eternal possession. He gives for the time being.

This, then, was the economy of the world at that time. Rome was mistress of the world under Tiberius, under the devil! Any knowledge of world conditions then compels us to say that it was a damnable world, mastered by fiends. And Satan said to Jesus,

"To Thee will I give all this authority. . . . If Thou therefore wilt worship before me, it shall all be Thine."

He was offering Him authority by the policy of compromise. In effect He said: Look out over the world. The kingdoms are all in my authority. The authority has been delivered to me. I am mastering Tiberius. I am master of the Roman Empire. I am ruling over all these kingdoms; and if Thou wilt give me one moment's homage, I will transfer all to Thee.

There is only one word that can possibly describe the devil then and now, and the one word is "liar." Jesus knew perfectly well, His baptism in the Jordan was the symbolic proof that He knew, that His way to the possession of the Kingdom was a way through death, the way of the Cross, the way of travail. Satan said: Do not take that way; here is a short cut, use this method. This was an attack, not merely upon the generic man; but

upon society, a world order, an economy, an established order on earth, all human inter-relationships.

What was the answer?

"It is written, Thou shalt worship the Lord thy God, and Him only shalt thou serve."

Observe at once that here are two things about which the devil had said nothing. He had said nothing about God, and he had said nothing about serving. In the temptation of Satan, God is not referred to except in the use of the word "if" in regard to the sonship of Jesus. For all practical purposes God was banished and the devil claimed that he was in authority. God is dismissed by the devil as though there were no God; or as though, if there be a God, He were powerless in the economy.

Again, he did not say anything about serving. He said, Worship me; but made no reference to the fact that worship always issues in service.

When our Lord answered, the complete philosophy of human society was revealed.

"It is written, Thou shalt worship the Lord thy God, and Him only shalt thou serve."

There is one Throne to be considered, one King to Whom submission is to be rendered; worship, homage, to Him is the only worship and homage of a human life. Our Lord added what Satan had omitted, "and serve." I cannot read that, solemn and tremendous as the hour was, without believing that if I could have looked into those wonderful eyes of Jesus, I should have seen in them a gleam of satire. As though He had said, Thou hast asked Me for My worship. Why didst thou not name what that would mean? If I should worship thee, I should serve thee. God is the only One to be worshipped. God is the only One to be served. Thus, the devil's temptation against human inter-relationships, against society and nationality, and inter-nationality; against the setting up of an economy according to the Divine plan; was hurled to hell, as Jesus reaffirmed the sovereignty of God, and the fact that man can only worship Him and serve Him if he is to live.

Once more, he led Him to Jerusalem, and set Him on a pinnacle of the Temple and said to Him,

"If Thou art the Son of God, cast Thyself down from hence, for it is written."

Twice over our Lord had said, "It is written." Now Satan adopted the same method, and quoted what "is written." Observe that in so doing he admitted relationship, and revelation. Then he asked Him to use His relationship to God, and to act upon the revelation that God had made to Him, on His own initiative. He said in effect: Do something daring, venturesome, splendid, spectacular. Cast Thyself off this wing of the Temple,

"For it is written, He shall give His angels charge concerning Thee, to guard Thee."

Mark the subtlety of it, the devilishness of it. Satan was manipulating Scripture. He said,

"It is written, He shall give His angels charge concerning Thee, to guard Thee."

Nothing of the kind is written. What is written is,

"He will give His angels charge over Thee,
To keep Thee *in all Thy ways*."

He missed out the defining phrase, and he asked this Man to fling Himself out of the Divine arrangement, and do the spectacular thing, to traffic with His spiritual nature. Thus the last attack was on man spiritually, in his relationship to God.

In the answer of our Lord we have a faithful and complete and full philosophy of spiritual life.

"Jesus answering said unto him, It is said, Thou shalt not make trial of the Lord thy God."

Satan asked Him to prove His relationship, and His belief in the revelation, by doing something spectacular.

The reply of Jesus shows that to do so would be to prove that His trust in God was not perfect. That is always so. The moment we do something to prove God, we are proving that we are not sure of God. Trust never employs tricks to find out whether the one trusted is trustworthy. That is the philosophy of spiritual life.

And so at last He stood erect, Victor over the attack upon man generically, the attack upon man socially; and the attack upon man spiritually.

A closing word concerning the postlude. All the anthems of victory are ringing through this thirteenth verse.

"And when the devil had completed every temptation, he departed from Him for a season."

"The devil had completed every temptation." It is a tremendous word, that Greek verb *sunteleo*. He had carried out to definite completion every temptation. Every avenue of attack he had moved along, every means of reaching Christ he had employed; he had completed every temptation. There was nothing else he could do. Hell had exhausted itself.

What did he do then? "He departed from Him;" and again I like the more blunt Greek word there; he stood off—that is the word—he stood off. And then that sharp little word, "for a season." Here the margin says, "until a season." What season? In Luke's story in chapter twenty-two, we see Jesus in the garden; and Luke tells how Judas came, and how the rest came; and Jesus said,

"This is your hour, and the power of darkness."

If we examine the record from this hour of temptation until the hour of Gethsemane and the Cross, we shall find that Christ never addressed any member of the underworld of evil save in the tones of absolute authority over them.

Then hell gathered itself for a final attack upon Him under the shadow of the Cross. Having completed every temptation, the devil left Him until that season, "the hour and the power of darkness."

Later in the New Testament we are told the issue of that final attack; He

"put off from Himself the principalities and the powers"

of evil that were in the heavenly places. He was again and finally Victor in the Cross.

Thus we see the Messiah, the Kinsman Redeemer, victorious, not for Himself alone, but—as representing God's purpose and ideal in human history and human nature,—in representative capacity. Because of His victory He will become, not merely the second Man, but the last Adam through Whom shall come the race of men and women who are victors over evil, and realize the Divine purpose.

LUKE IV. 14-30

LUKE having completed his delineation of the Person of the Word made flesh, and having recorded His Messianic dedication, consecration, attestation, temptation; proceeded now to tell the story of all He "began both to do and teach," to take his own description of His work as found in Acts i.1. We are entering now on that part of the book where Luke is no longer showing us the Person, but the Messiah at work. The word "began" in this connection is very suggestive. All the Gospel narratives which we are to examine are concerned with beginnings. The double work of doing and teaching continues until this day. Christ has not given up His doing and teaching. The nature of the doing and teaching of the Christ of God today is the same as it was in the days of His flesh. Thus, speaking of commencement in that way, we postulate continuity, and point to consummation. The work of the Son of God, the Son of man, the Word made flesh, had a commencement, it has a course, it will have a consummation. The course and the consummation are involved in the commencement. I am saying all that to emphasize the tremendous importance of what we now begin in our study of Luke. We shall watch Him at His work, and listen to His teaching, in order to understand the continuity of both to the consummation.

In this paragraph we have two parts. First, in verses fourteen and fifteen, a summary; and then Luke records the inauguration of His intentionally public ministry.

Between the Temptation and the point where Luke takes up his narrative, a whole year elapsed, of which he gives no account. There is a gap in the record. In Dr. Stalker's *Life of Christ* he divides the ministry of our Lord into four parts: The year of obscurity; The year of public favour; The year of opposition; and The end. Now neither Matthew, nor Mark, nor Luke tell you anything about that first year. We should have known nothing of it if we had not had the Gospel of John. Matthew and Mark both tell us that Jesus began to preach when John was put in prison; and Luke begins his story at the same point. Many speculations have been indulged in about that first year, as to why He did not sooner begin His more definitely public propaganda. I do not think that anything can be said dogmatically on the subject. The fact, however, is patent that after His dedication, consecration, attestation, and temptation, when He seemed ready for His work, He did not begin that public ministry which immediately drew widespread attention to Himself. There was a quiet year in which He waited, as I think, for John to round out his ministry. One thing about it is certainly impressive, that of the freedom from haste which characterized the method. "He that believeth shall not make haste."

Let us first notice what Luke tells us in the opening summary. He says, He

"returned in the power of the Spirit into Galilee."

The use of the word "returned" here unquestionably is a reference to His visits to Galilee during the first year.

and to His own early years spent there. Matthew says, "He departed into Galilee." Mark says, "He came into Galilee." Luke says, "He returned into Galilee." Herod had silenced the voice of John. He had put him in prison. Directly the voice of John was silenced, Jesus moved into Herod's tetrarchy; and made it the base of His mighty work for the coming months.

He returned, says Luke, "in the power of the Spirit." A simple statement, but we link it up at once with things already considered. "Full of the Spirit" He went into the wilderness. He was "led of the Spirit" in the experiences of temptation. Now we see Him coming to His ministry in "the power of the Spirit."

Then Luke tells us that "a fame went out concerning Him." Let us glance on for a moment in this same chapter to verse thirty-seven;

"There went forth a rumour concerning Him, into every place of the region round about."

And once more, on to the next chapter, chapter five, and there at the fifteenth verse we read,

"But so much the more went abroad the report concerning Him."

The fame of Him, a rumour concerning Him, the report concerning Him. I frankly confess that I do not like the words *fame* and *rumour* and *report*, as they are placed in this translation. The word "fame" is unfortunate; it certainly ought to be "rumour," for that is what the Greek word *pheme* really signifies. It was not fame; it was a rumour. That rumour spread over all the district very speedily; and so rumour became a roar, for that is the meaning of the Greek word *echos*. The word suggests a stir everywhere. That which was first a rumour had become a roar, the whole countryside was talking about Him. There to translate *echos* "rumour" does not give the true gradation. Now, when we get to verse fifteen in chapter five, we read,

"So much the more went abroad the report of Him."

The word there rendered "report" is *logos*, which means an intelligent apprehension; people began to understand. Thus again, the word "report" seems to me inadequate there, as a rendering of *logos*. Stages are thus marked. First a rumour of Him began to spread everywhere; in a little time a rumour became a roar, the whole countryside was moved; and at last the thing became intelligent; it became a *logos*, a word, a distinct message.

Then Luke records an arresting fact. He says,

"A rumour went out concerning Him through all the region round about;"

and He

"taught in their synagogues, being glorified of all."

In the Greek New Testament the word *He* is emphatic; as though he had written, "He Himself." A contrast is suggested. Everybody was beginning to talk about Him; there was a rumour; but He Himself went into the synagogues and taught. We have a revelation of the method of Jesus there. He was not swept away by the rumour; He went into the synagogues and taught. Those synagogues originated in the time of Babylonish captivity, and they were the gathering places of the Jewish people who could not go to the Temple. By this time they were scattered everywhere. In any little town where there were ten Jews, they could have their synagogue. They were gathering places, the rallying centres of the religious life of the people. Jesus went up and down, here and there, in and out, into their synagogues, and taught.

To this Luke adds, "Being glorified of all." I do not like the word "glorified" there. The word, as used here, does not at all mean that they glorified Him in the sense in which we glorify Him, who trust and worship Him. There came a day when He said,

"If any man thirst, let him come unto Me and drink. He that believeth on Me, as the scripture hath said, from within him shall flow rivers of living water;"

and John made a comment on that and said,

"But this spake He of the Spirit, which they that believed on Him were to receive; for the Spirit was not yet given; because Jesus was not yet glorified."

There "glorified" has its full meaning. Here it has not. It is the same word, but I would like to change it in translation here. It is the Greek word *doxazo*, from which we get our word doxology. Here it is used in the sense of praise, and so I would render it, "being praised of all." It is a solemn consideration that men can praise Jesus and never glorify Him in the full sense of the word. Luke is not saying here that His ministry was being completely victorious. He does say that it was well received, and people praised Him.

Now we come to the account of the inauguration of the public ministry, His intentionally public propaganda. He had not commenced that until now. Here we have the account of the beginning, the inauguration.

It is important that we should not confuse this story in the fourth chapter of Luke with the story found in the thirteenth chapter of Matthew and in the sixth chapter of Mark. In those chapters we have the story of His going to Nazareth, and of His being rejected there. In some of the Harmonies of the Gospel, these three passages are placed side by side. They say that Luke put the visit to Nazareth early, and the others put it much later. Nothing of the kind. He went twice. Just as one cleansing of the Temple took place in the first year of the ministry, and another at the very end; so there was a second visit to Nazareth, the account of which we have in Matthew thirteen and Mark six. That must not be confused with this. There are many points of similarity, but there are points of very distinct difference. This was the first visit.

When He would begin His definite and intentionally public propaganda, in which He intended to draw attention to Himself and His message, He went up to Nazareth where He had been brought up,

"And He entered, as His custom was, into the synagogue."

He went to the place where He had lived as a Boy, where He had been brought up through youth. He went to the place where they all knew Him as the carpenter. He was about to begin His great Messianic ministry, and He went to the little synagogue to which He had so often gone,—"as His custom was." What emotions must have filled His heart as He remembered the earliest times, when with faltering footsteps He had gone as a Child, and listened to the reading of the law.

Having come into the synagogue, to use a term of modern times, He "read Himself in" to His Messianic mission. He stood up to read. That was permitted, not only to priests and scribes, but to any who had a prophetic word. They either read the portion from the Law, from the Prophets, or from the Writings. There is no doubt that on that particular day, the portion from the Law had already been read; and now the time had come for the portion from the Prophets. The attendant, seeing Him rise, handed Him the roll for the day. It was a perfectly orderly and natural procedure. The prophetic reading for the day was from the prophecy of Isaiah, and He found the place where it was written. I do not think that this was an independent finding, because in the synagogues the readings for the day were appointed.

The reading was from that part of the prophecy which deals with the Servant of Jehovah. If we read in Isaiah, we find the words,

"To bind up the broken-hearted;"

and these are absent from our Versions. If we read what Jesus says, we find these words,

"Recovering of sight to the blind."

That is not in Isaiah. The quotation was evidently taken from the Septuagint, from the Greek Version, and it was freely given. Taking it as we find it in Luke, we read;

" The Spirit of the Lord is upon Me,
  Because He anointed Me to preach
    good tidings to the poor;
  He hath sent Me to proclaim release
    to the captives,
  And recovering of sight to the blind,
  To set at liberty them that are
    bruised,
  To proclaim the acceptable year of
    the Lord."

" The Spirit of the Lord is upon Me,"
epi, upon, pressing down upon Me;
the idea being that of the Spirit as a
holy unction from on high, an anointing for work. The rest of the quotation describes that work.

When He reached the words,

" To proclaim the acceptable year of
the Lord,"

He stopped. If we look back to our
Old Testament, the only stop we see
is a comma. The thing runs right on:

"And the day of vengeance of our
God; to comfort all that mourn; to appoint unto them that mourn in Zion, to
give unto them a garland for ashes, the
oil of joy for mourning, the garment of
praise for the spirit of heaviness; that
they may be called trees of righteousness, the planting of Jehovah, that He
may be glorified."

He did not read that. He stopped,
rolled up the scroll, and gave it back
to the attendant. Then He said to
those in the synagogue,

" Today hath this Scripture been fulfilled in your ears."

Is all that in Isaiah which comes
after unimportant? By no means. He
stopped where His then present mission in the world was to end. That
mission was to proclaim "the acceptable year of the Lord," and so to usher
it in. The next phrase is, "The day
of vengeance of our God." He was
not in the world for that then. He
was not anointed for that, at that time.
What comes after the day of vengeance
of our God? To comfort all that
mourn. That is something beyond the
day of vengeance. In Luke we have
the record of all He began to do and
teach. His work was not finished.
His atoning work was finished on Calvary. But He has other work. His

work is going on still; and His work
in this world will never be finished
until He come again. The first Advent demands the second. The day of
vengeance of our God must come, and
He will be the Instrument of it; but
only in order that beyond it He may
comfort all that mourn. Vengeance in
order to comfort! Dr. Burton has
very beautifully said that as He stood
before the people in the synagogue that
day, He stood before the world as *the*
Evangelist, *the* Healer, *the* Emanci-
pator. Beginning His public ministry,
in these terms He indicated its meaning, its method, its movement, and its
message.

The story ends with what happened
in the synagogue. First they admitted
the grace of what He said, and they
wondered as they listened to Him.
Then somebody said, " Is not this
Joseph's son?" That was the excuse
of unbelief. They were not prepared
to yield to the claim He had set up.
They had felt the wonder of His
words; they were strangely moved by
them; but they must find a way out;
and so they adopted the mean despicable method of discounting His claim
by accounting for Him on a low level.
They thought they knew everything
about Him, and they did not know
anything. No, He was not Joseph's
Son.

He interpreted their thinking, and
He said,

" Doubtless ye will say unto Me this
parable, Physician, heal Thyself; whatsoever we have heard done at Capernaum, do also here in Thine own
country."

Then He uttered that tremendous
word,

" No prophet is acceptable in his own
country;"

and turned on them in a very remarkable way. He gave them two illustrations of how the power and the blessing
of God had gone outside their nation.
He went back to Elijah and He went
back to Elisha; and He said, There
were many widows there in Israel in
the days of Elijah; but it was not a
widow of Israel to whom the prophet

was sent, but a widow in Sidon. And there were many lepers in the time of Elisha, but only Naaman was healed, and he belonged not to Israel, but to Syria. Thus He declared to them that the benefits and the blessings of the Divine Kingdom were coming in answer to faith, and not in answer to racial relationship.

Then they were filled with wrath, and excluded Him from the city. They took Him to the brow of the hill to cast Him down headlong. Hostility thus broke out there at the beginning; but hostility had absolutely no power,

" He passing through the midst of them, went His way."

Thus began the public ministry of the Man of Nazareth, of Jesus, of the Word made flesh; and that ministry stands in the annals of propaganda lonely, and unique. The Lord thus dedicated, consecrated, attested, tempted and victorious, Messiah, moved out along the pathway of His public ministry. Thus Luke, having ended his delineation of the Personality of the Word made flesh, shows Him entering on the central phase of His ministry by solemn inauguration.

LUKE IV. 31-44

LUKE begins his story of the more definitely public ministry of our Lord with the account of a Sabbath day in Galilee. He came down to Capernaum, a city of Galilee. Capernaum was about twenty miles northeast from Nazareth. It was situated on the northern shores of the Sea of Galilee; and at that time, to quote the words of Josephus, was the centre of the manufacturing district. Galilee was a crowded area. Again, Josephus tells us that in the time of our Lord's ministry, in that small area of Galilee, there were at least two hundred and forty towns and villages; and Capernaum was the centre of activity. It was a great centre, too. Three of the highways along which traffic was always moving, centred there. From Capernaum ran the highway up to Tyre and Sidon; from Capernaum ran another highway across to Damascus; and from Capernaum ran the main highway down to Jerusalem. Luke says He came down to Capernaum, a city of Galilee. Matthew, at that point in the ministry of our Lord, says,

" Leaving Nazareth, He came and dwelt in Capernaum."

Luke simply tells us He came from Nazareth to Capernaum; Matthew says He went to live there; and later on, Matthew, in the ninth chapter, refers to it in a passing reference, and calls it " His own city." At this moment, when our Lord began this public ministry, He made Capernaum His base of operations. To Capernaum He constantly returned. From Capernaum He went out on those varied and wonderful journeys. Surely there was significance in it; and perhaps more than one line of significance. First of all, it was in Galilee, and Isaiah revealed the contempt in which Galilee would be held by Judæa. " Galilee of the Gentiles," which, of course, did not mean that Galilee was populated by Gentiles, but that it had passed under the influence of the Gentile nations; and therefore Judæa held it in contempt. Our Lord went into Galilee, and made it the base of His operations for at least two years of public ministry.

Another significant fact, to which I have made reference before, is that all this happened when Herod had put John in prison. Then it was our Lord began this distinctly and intentionally public propaganda. He went down to Herod's tetrarchy, and in one of the principal cities of that tetrarchy He found His base of operations.

In this story of a Sabbath day, we see Jesus in four different places; first in the synagogue, then in the home of Simon, then in the street at eventide, when the crowds gathered about Him for healing; and then alone. Some time after midnight, He escaped from the crowds, and went out into the desert.

In the morning He was found in the

synagogue. In the afternoon He went to Simon's house in Bethsaida. Then at eventide we see Him in the streets. Then presently we see Him breaking away, and getting out into the desert, alone. In the morning in the synagogue, the scene of religion. In the afternoon in the home, the great circle of God for the creation of a true society, the family, the place of the family. In the evening in the streets, confronting all massed humanity with its sorrows and its suffering. And then when the day was done, between the stroke of midnight and the blush of dawn, alone in the desert with God.

In the morning He was found in the synagogue in Capernaum. That was an interesting synagogue. It had been built by a Gentile. A centurion had built it for them. It was interesting for another reason. One of its rulers was Jairus. These synagogues were scattered all over the land, and were assembling places for men for religious purposes, who were unable to get to the Temple by reason of geographical distances. They sprang up after the return from captivity. Jesus observed the Sabbath, and observed it religiously. It was His custom to go to the synagogue.

Now, what happened there? The first thing we are told is that,

"He was teaching them on the Sabbath day."

He taught them. What did He teach them? In the course of His great ethical Manifesto, He said this:

"Whosoever therefore shall break one of these least commandments, and shall teach men so, shall be called least in the Kingdom of heaven; but whosoever shall do and teach them, he shall be called great in the Kingdom of heaven" (Matthew v.19).

That is only a sidelight, but I am quite sure He was teaching them the law. Some people seem to think He came to set people free from the law. Indeed, we have a hymn which says,

"Free from the law, O happy condition,
Jesus hath bled, and there is remission."

Very true, if we know what we are singing. If we think it means that we are free from the moral obligation of the law, let us give up singing it. It means nothing of the kind. In the fifteenth chapter of Matthew something appears that is worth looking at in this connection. He was talking to the rulers,

"Ye hypocrites, well did Isaiah
    prophesy of you, saying,
This people honoureth Me with
    their lips;
But their heart is far from Me.
But in vain do they worship Me,
Teaching as their doctrines the
    precepts of men" (Matthew
    xv.7-9).

He was denouncing men for teaching tradition, instead of truth, for superadding to the law the traditions of men. Negatively, then, I know He did not do that.

There is another word on this subject in Luke. Jesus had been to the Cross, and was alive from the dead, and He was talking to His disciples. He tells us there what He was teaching:

"He said unto them, These are My words which I spake unto you, while I was yet with you, that all things must needs be fulfilled, which are written in the law of Moses, and the prophets, and the Psalms concerning Me" (Luke xxiv.44).

I know from that, what He taught in the synagogues. He took the whole of the Hebrew Scriptures, for He named the three divisions of them; the Law, and the Prophets, and the Psalms; and taught them that all the things in these Scriptures must be fulfilled in Him. He was not denouncing the Law, and laughing at the Prophets as obsolete, and dismissing all the rest of the literature as out of date! He was showing that everything in that literature was moving on towards the climax and fulfilment; and it was His claim that He had come to fulfil the law and prophets and psalms.

Observe carefully here what Luke tells us.

"They were astonished at His teaching; for His word was with authority."

Matthew tells us that when the multitudes heard His ethical Manifesto, they were astonished by His authority. He says,

"He taught them as One having authority, and not as their scribes."

What does that mean? Does that mean the scribes had no authority? Certainly not. They were the authoritative teachers, and they were the men to whose authority all the people were submitting. But when they listened to Jesus, they said: This Man speaks as having authority, and it is not the same sort of authority to which we are accustomed. It is different. What was the difference? The scribe was the official teacher. The scribe sat "in Moses' seat"—I am quoting Jesus—and the authority of the scribe depended upon the authority of Moses. They said, Now listen to this Man; no official position gives Him authority. He is not a scribe, He is not sitting in Moses' seat, but the thing He says carries conviction. It is not the authority of an official position. They did not recognize that He had one. We know He had, an eternal position, but they did not. When men listened to Him, they said: Yes, He is right, that is so. The truth He uttered was authoritative, and men knew it. That is still true. Take the New Testament, and out of the New Testament take any word Jesus uttered, any word from His discourses, from His discussions, or from those scattered sayings that fell from His lips, as He passed on His way; take any word of Jesus, and proclaim it, and the common consciousness of humanity knows the thing He said is true. The authority of Jesus was the authority of absolute truth.

Suddenly in the synagogue there was a startling interruption. A man was there, possessed of an unclean demon; and his voice was suddenly heard crying out. The Old Version says that he said, "Let us alone." The Revised Version renders it, "Ah!" All scholarly opinion agrees that the word here is part of a Greek verb that marks terror; and the word there is not an appeal to be let alone; it is the cry of terror. Suddenly that evil spirit knew Who was in that synagogue; and the first cry is terror, "Ah!" Luke is very careful to tell us that this was an unclean demon. There were demons not characterized by uncleanness in this particular way; but this man was in the grip of filth and beastliness, and suddenly the demon knew Who was there in that synagogue; and there escaped from the man, the demon speaking through the man, the cry of terror, "Ah!" Then he raised a protest,

"What have we to do with Thee, Jesus Thou Nazarene?"

One is tempted to answer him, and say, Nothing; you have nothing to do with Him, but He has everything to do with you. He is Master of the underworld.

"What have we to do with Thee, Jesus Thou Nazarene? art Thou come to destroy us?"

Then that gasp of confession, that marvellous word,

"I know Thee Who Thou art, the Holy One of God."

From that demon, that kind of confession was one of absolute defeat. A holy man is a man who has mastered every attack of evil; and the voice of the demon is heard in terror, in protest, and in confession concerning Christ.

What happened? "And Jesus rebuked him." Keep your mind on that word "rebuked." We shall find it again before we are through. What did He say?

"Hold thy peace, and come out of him."

I suppose that our translators are anxious to be euphemistic in rendering; and "hold thy peace" is perfectly correct; but really I would like to see that translated literally. I think we would gain a little of the force if we did. What does the Greek word mean? "Be muzzled." Literally that is what He said; "Be muzzled." Christ refused here, and refused always to accept the testimony of demons. They knew Him, and He refused their testimony. Paul took up the same attitude. When the girl with the spirit of divination went out proclaiming to all that he was really a servant of God, Paul silenced her. Christ needs no testimony from the underworld. He silenced him, and commanded the demon to come out. The arresting thing is the immediate obedience of the demon.

What happened then? Luke says, "Amazement came upon all." That is another word. When they listened to His teaching, it was astonishment. Now it is amazement. Astonishment was surprise. Here, if you want to get it into good colloquial English, they were dumbfounded. They first felt the moral impact of His authoritative teaching, and now they saw that He did something, that He had an authority beyond that of moral interpretation. He had authority which relieved humanity from its demon possession; it was an authority of power. They were amazed, they were dumbfounded; surprised at the authority of the teaching; dumbfounded when they saw the same voice that had spoken truth to them in His teaching, now address itself to an evil spirit, and at once the spirit was subjected, and came out.

Then they recovered their speech, and held a consultation. What is this word? They were greatly impressed that He only spoke. There were no tricks of the professional exorcist, no incantations over the man; a word, and the demon was out. They said, "What is this word?" What is the nature of the word, "for with authority and power"—authority plus dynamic—"He commandeth the unclean spirits, and they come out."

That was the Sabbath morning in Capernaum, in the synagogue, teaching; so teaching that He gripped the reason and the conscience of them, and they knew the thing He said was so, the authority of truth; and suddenly breaking in upon the religious exercises of the hour, the cry of a demon through a man possessed; and the Teacher Who had carried conviction by the moral authority of His teaching, is seen Master of that whole underworld, for at His command the demon came out.

Then comes the verse we referred to in our previous study;

"There went forth a rumour concerning Him into every place of the region round about."

I think that word "rumour" is very weak there. The Greek word is *pheme* in the other case in iv.14; but here the Greek word is *echos*. It was more than a rumour, it was an uproar. It means that from that happening in that synagogue, a report of Him spread over the countryside which became tumultuous. Everybody began to talk about Him. He became the centre of discussion after the Sabbath morning in the synagogue.

What next?

"He rose up from the synagogue, and entered into the house of Simon."

He went quietly home, and He went with Simon. There was a sick woman in that home, and Luke, the doctor, says she was "holden with a great fever." This was a medical term of the times. In those times fevers were divided into two classes, little fevers and great fevers. They would have called malaria a little fever, and typhus a great fever. This woman was suffering from something virulent and dangerous. "They besought Him for her," which does not suggest that they had to persuade Him to act. The Aorist tense means that they made one request. Again Luke uses a strictly medical term. "He stood over her." This Jesus went in as another doctor would, and stood over her; only He did what no other doctor could do, "He rebuked the fever"—the same word employed previously concerning the demon. He rebuked the demon. He rebuked the fever. I wonder how He did it. I do not know. I wonder if He said, "Be muzzled," as He did to the demon, as He did to the winds and the waves. I think the devil was behind the storm. The devil may have been behind the fever; I do not know; but He rebuked it in the home, and the fever left her. His healing was always perfect. When He healed somebody, that person did not have to be helped out of the synagogue, or off the platform. This woman was perfectly healed; and the proof of it is very interesting, and very beautiful;

"Immediately she rose up and ministered unto them."

Fever does not ordinarily leave us quite equal to doing that. I had some experience of it some years ago. I know after I had months in a nursing home, when the fever left me, I did not get up and minister to anybody immediately. Among other things, I found I had forgotten how to walk. I had lost my power of co-ordination. When Jesus healed from a great fever, the woman got up, and went about her household work, and she ministered unto them. That was the afternoon of this Sabbath day. Jesus in the home as Healer.

Then we have no further particulars about the afternoon. At last the sun was westering, and the shadows lengthening, and there was a commotion outside. What was happening?

"And when the sun was setting, all they that had any sick with divers diseases brought them unto Him."

The events in the synagogue in the morning had started a roar; and the result was that they were gathering people to Him,

"all they that had any sick with divers diseases."

Now we may read the next sentence quickly, and be on to something else. But let us halt a moment;

"He laid His hands on every one of them, and healed them."

I can read that in seconds, but it took a long time to do. The sun set, and the Syrian sky became bright with stars; and still He moved amongst that derelict company, laying His healing hands on them. He

"laid His hands on every one of them, and healed them."

The argument from silence may be a dangerous argument, I know, and yet I have no hesitation in saying that He laid His hands on them, going from one to the next, and that is all He did. He imposed no condition upon them. He did not inquire about their family life. He asked nothing about their past history. He healed without any reference to anything in them but need. I certainly am not told that He looked at them and said, The condition of your healing is your faith, and if you have faith enough you can be healed. He put His hands on them, and healed them. That was His healing ministry. There were some of those people demon-possessed, and there also His power was operative,

"Demons also came out from many,"

and they came out crying,

"Thou art the Son of God. And rebuking them"—

the third time we get the word, rebuke—

"Rebuking them, He suffered them not to speak."

Why not?

"Because they knew that He was the Christ."

He was seeking no credentials from the underworld, even though the thing they said might be the true thing. He had authority over them, but would have no patronage from them. The attitude of our Lord is very marked on these two occasions.

The story of that healing ministry is a very great one. One would like to dwell upon it. Luke leaves it there. Matthew makes a comment upon it. Telling us the same story, he says:

"When even was come, they brought unto Him many possessed with demons; and He cast out the spirits with a word, and healed all that were sick; that it might be fulfilled which was spoken through Isaiah the prophet saying, Himself took our infirmities, and bare our diseases."

Matthew has given us the inspirational secret for the activity of Jesus as He laid His hands on all that multitude. His quotation was from Isaiah, chapter fifty-three, and verse four. Let us read it as we find it there:

"Surely He hath borne our griefs, and carried our sorrows."

The Hebrew which is here rendered "griefs" is sicknesses; Surely He hath borne our sicknesses and carried our sorrows. I would ask you to notice carefully that saying has nothing of atonement in it. "He hath borne our sicknesses," that is not atonement. "He hath carried our sorrows," that is not atonement. If you will go on,

"Yet we did esteem Him stricken, smitten of God, and afflicted,"

in spite of the fact that He bore our sicknesses, bare them sympathetically, carried our sorrows sympathetically; that is how we esteemed Him. Now,

"He was wounded for our transgressions, He was bruised for our iniquities; the chastisement of our peace was upon Him; and with His stripes we are healed;"

that is atonement. That is in verse five. Atonement is not in verse four. Verse four is the public ministry of sympathy. He did not atone for sickness. He atoned for sin; and the healing of the body is not guaranteed in atonement in this life, any more than exemption from death is guaranteed. Sickness He can heal, and He often does heal today without any human means; but far more often He heals through means. I have no quarrel with the man who tells me he is healed by the Lord, providing he does not say he has been healed by his faith. Divine healing, yes; and there is no healing that is not Divine. God is able, if that be His will, to heal without means; but in the great majority of cases He uses means, and blesses means.

Notice the word Matthew used in quoting Isaiah.

"Himself . . . bare our diseases."

Please remember the word "bare" there does not mean atonement. The writer of the letter to the Hebrews says,

"He was offered to bear the sins of many."

Peter says, "He bare our sins," but that is not the same word at all. In these cases an entirely different word is employed. The word, "bare our sicknesses" is the word that you get when Paul says,

"Bear the infirmities of the weak,"

or,

"Bear ye one another's burdens."

Jesus went forth, "bearing His Cross." Bearing our sicknesses is the Greek word *bastazo*, which means He gets under them with us in love, sympathy, and help. The word "*bare*," in reference to atonement, is *anaphero*, which means to lift up and carry away. He did that with sin; He did not do that with sicknesses. Out of the sympathy of His heart He bare the sicknesses, and He took them away, not by virtue of His atonement, but by virtue of His infinite compassion and Almighty power. Then beyond that, came the hour when He got down deeper, to the profound cause of all suffering and all sorrow, sin; then He bare sin in a new sense. He did not get under it merely, to carry it with us; He took it upon Himself, and bore it into the land of eternal forgetfulness and extinction. That is atonement.

What next? Between midnight and morning, at the beginning of day, a long while before it was day, Mark says He went into the desert. He wanted solitude. He wanted loneliness. How constantly we find Him doing it. It would be irreverent to follow Him with any investigation, because investigation could only be speculative. Yet we are warranted in saying He escaped for a little to be alone with God. Do not pity Him, that rough road to the desert. For Him in the desert was the hour of perfect peace and perfect quietness and perfect joy. He communed with His Father; and as the hours went on, these people naturally came, and wanted Him to stay, and He said, I cannot stay. I must preach

"to other cities also; for therefore was I sent."

Acting under authority, and therefore

in authority, both as to His teaching and as to His power to deliver man.

Then Luke adds that little last word that summarizes His ministry.

"And He was preaching in the synagogues of Galilee."

We thank God for Luke's first picture of a Sabbath day. Mark the sequence. The synagogue, the place of religion; the home, the place of the family; the street, the place of crowding necessity; and the desert, the place of quietness with God. We have seen His authority, ethical authority, and executive authority, which is power; power over disease, power over demons, power sufficient to set men free from the trammels of false teaching, and from the bondage of evil. Such is the picture of the Lord on that first Sabbath day in Galilee.

LUKE V. 1-16

IN his account of the public ministry of the Word, Luke, having described a Sabbath in Galilee, and having recorded the declaration of the Lord that He must go to other cities, tells us that "He was preaching in Galilee."

Having done that, he proceeded to give incidents of that ministry; and in the paragraph before us we have two such incidents. Let us spend a moment or two relating these to the procedure of His ministry.

We need to be very careful not to confuse this story of the draught of fishes, and the words which our Lord spoke to the disciples, with the call of the four to leave their nets. I say that emphatically, because almost constantly it is done; I mean by those who harmonize these stories. The calling of the four recorded by Matthew in chapter four, and Mark in chapter one, to leave their nets, is confused with this. There is a very distinct difference between the occasions. In Matthew four and Mark one, we have the account of our Lord calling these men to leave their fishing nets, and go with Him. When He did that, they were fishing; Matthew and Mark distinctly telling us that they were at the moment casting their nets. Here they were not casting their nets. They were washing them. As the story goes on we find that they had been fishing all night, and had had a bad night. The boats were standing empty, and the men were washing their nets. That first call to leave their nets came between the inauguration in Nazareth and the arrival at Capernaum when He made it His base of operations. On His way, passing the lake, seeing these men, He called them to leave their nets and come after Him, and they went, Matthew and Mark being witness. These four men became disciples immediately after the baptism of our Lord, and then evidently went back home after a time. I think He sent them back. Then when He began His public ministry, He called them to leave the nets, and they left them. Here, they had gone back to the nets, they had gone back to fishing. Not many weeks had passed since they had left all to follow Him, and now we find them back at the business again. This has an important bearing on this story.

The other preliminary thing I desire to point out is that the next incident, that of the cleansing of the leper, followed the sermon on the mount immediately. Matthew gives us that story. Luke does not record the sermon on the mount. Mark only gives parts. The Harmonies almost invariably give the sermon on the mount, as being recorded in Luke six. That is not the sermon on the mount. Our Lord repeated parts of the sermon on the mount with changed emphases, and added things He did not say before. It is well for us to understand this, because it has a bearing on our consideration of the healing of the leper. This leper came to Jesus when He left the mount of ethical enunciation, where the multitudes had been astonished at His teaching. I am rather inclined to think that the leper had been on the outskirts of the crowd, listening to

Jesus; and I have a conviction in my own mind that it was listening to, and looking at Jesus, then, that made him come to Him as he came.

Now let us look at these two incidents. First the story in the first eleven verses.

"Now it came to pass, while the multitude pressed upon Him and heard the word of God, that He was standing by the lake of Gennesaret; and He saw two boats standing by the lake."

They were empty;

"but the fishermen had gone out of them, and were washing their nets. And He entered into one of the boats, which was Simon's, and asked him to put out a little from the land."

I have no doubt the fishermen were close there, because He spoke to Simon. Observe the significance of His act. These men had gone back to the boats they had left, and that particular night they had been out fishing, and they had taken nothing; a night of failure, and the washing of the nets followed that night of failure. Get it sharply in your mind, for it is significant. A few weeks before, certainly not more than a few weeks, He had called these men to follow, and they had left boats, nets, and fathers and mothers, kith and kin, and had gone. Now we have no details, but we have the fact, that they were back at the business again. Notice what the Lord did. We have no record that He rebuked them. I think, however, that we see the underlying criticism of their action as we follow the story through. He went on board one of those boats, and took command. He did not ask that the boat might be lent Him. He did presently ask Simon to put out a little way, but He assumed command. I do not know why they went back. I could speculate upon that, of course. I have done the same fool thing more than once in the life of my discipleship. They had left the fishing and nets, to go when He called them; but they had gone back, and now they had been out fishing, and failed; and the Lord came, and He quietly got on board one of the boats, and took command. If we let our

imagination help us, and keep our eye on Simon, Andrew, James, and John, I am quite certain we shall see them looking at Him, and wondering what He was going to do now.

Then what happened? He called Simon, and asked 'im to put out a little way, and ..on did so, without a question. When the boat was resting a little way from the shore, Jesus sat in it and taught the multitudes. That is a great scene. It is a great theme for an artist, that little boat riding on the waves quite gently, with Simon sitting in the boat listening and watching.

What happened next is significant. Luke gives us no account of what He said that day, but he gives the narrative to lead to the incident.

"When He had left speaking, He said unto Simon, Put out into the deep, and let down your nets for a draught."

He finished teaching, and now positively, He was going into the fishing business with them! He had called them to leave those fishing boats and fishing nets, and they had done it: but they had gone back, and now He had come, and taken possession of a boat, and taught out of it; and when He had done, He said, Get back to your business; put out into the deep, and let down your nets. He was going fishing, too.

Then a beautiful thing happened. Simon made a fisherman's protest. He said,

"Master, we toiled all night, and took nothing, but at Thy word I will let down the nets."

Watch the movement in the mind of Simon. After his protest, quickly, before any word could possibly be spoken, he said, Nevertheless, and called Jesus *Epistates*, Master. This does not mean Teacher; it really means Master in the sense of Captain, captain of the boat. Over went the nets, and it was not long before they were so full that they had to beckon for help, for the boats were in danger of going down. Then Peter fell on his knees; and he said,

"Depart from me; for I am a sinful man, O Lord."

What did he mean? He meant, Oh, give me up; You called me some weeks ago to follow Thee, and I am back at this business of fishing; give me up, depart from me; am a sinful man. That was his confession of wrong in going back to fishing. I am a sinful man, O Lord, depart, give me up. You saw me over a year ago, and looked into my eyes, and told me I should be Rock. I have been back home in between, and I have been going on with my fishing, because You did not ask me to give it up; but a few weeks ago, You asked me, and I did it; and here I am again, I am back; there is no Rock in me; give me up; I am a sinful man.

Now what did Jesus say? Oh, the infinite music of it. He first said, "Fear not." He said it to that man, that elemental man, great emotional soul; the man who did not seem to have strength to arrive anywhere; and He said it to him, conscious of his failure. When he said,

"Depart from me; for I am a sinful man,"

Jesus said, "Fear not."
Then what?

"From henceforth thou shalt catch men alive."

That is the Greek verb; it is peculiar. It only occurs in one other place in the New Testament. When Paul was writing his second letter to Timothy, in chapter two, he said,

"The Lord's servant must not strive, but be gentle,"

and so on, and so on; but he must correct

"them that oppose themselves; if peradventure God may give them repentance unto the knowledge of the truth, that they may recover themselves out of the snare of the devil, having been taken captive by him unto his will."

It is at least suggestive that the only two places where the word is used are

when the Lord said, "catch-men-alive;" and where it speaks of the fact that the devil catches-men-alive.

"Fear not; from henceforth."

That is a great word, "henceforth." It breaks with the past; it changes everything. Simon said, I have played the fool again; I have gone back to fishing, after You called me to be with You;

"Depart from me, for I am a sinful man, O Lord."

Jesus said to him, Don't be afraid, fear not; that is all over. You will not do it again;

"From henceforth thou shalt catch men alive."

He revealed Himself to that little group of fishermen as Supreme in the realm with which they were familiar, fishing. By doing so, He revealed to them that He was Supreme in the unfamiliar realm to them, of the work He was in the world to do, and the work He wanted their help in doing: catching men alive. In all the toil of the coming years, when they were out upon the tumultuous and tempest-tossed seas of human life, catching men alive, they would never forget the hour when He came back to them, and went fishing with them, and showed them that He was Master there.

This story has abiding values. That draught of fishes was intended by Jesus to reveal to these men exactly what He wanted them to do, when He asked them to leave their fishing nets.

What does it teach us? First of all, that Christ calls men into His service, and asks them to consecrate to His service the gifts they have; and that He can take every capacity of life, the capacity of the fisherman, and turn it into the very capacity for doing His work. I never heard Christ say to me, Come ye after Me, and I will make you a fisher of men. Why not? Because I am not a fisherman. I never was a fisherman. I never earned my living fishing; and—some of you may pity me if you like—I never got any fun out of fishing. I always agree with Charles Lamb, about a man and a line with a worm at one end; and I am not going to finish the quotation! These men were fishermen. In the year 1886 I sat at my desk teaching, with boys around me, and I loved my work, and I would love it still. I was trained to teach. But there came the hour when my Master passed by, and He said, Follow Me, and I will make you a teacher of men. The capacity that one has is what He wants to use in His Kingdom. That is the philosophy of the story.

Now go back and take the fishing illustration. Here we learn that He appropriates our boats and our nets. It is our business to provide the boat, the bait, and the nets, as well as the fishers; the organizations as well as the men. Then all He asks is that we submit to His mastery, that we really and sincerely call Him in this regard, *Epistates*, Master. That means that we yield not the boat merely, but ourselves.

Then I look again, and learn that if He gets our boats and our nets, He will make our work so mighty that it will break our nets and swamp our boats. If we have got an organization in our church which never gives way, under the pressure of His power, we may know He is not on board. He will break our nets.

Again, it is when our nets are breaking, and our boat is swamped because of success, that we call to our partners in the other boats. That is the only basis of Church union that is worth anything.

Now let us turn to the second incident, that of the cleansing of the leper. Luke says,

" It came to pass, while He was in one of the cities."

The city is not named. Dean Farrar suggested that the city was probably the city known at the time as Hattin, which was right at the foot of the mountain, on which Jesus had uttered the Manifesto. Luke does not merely say a leper; he tells us the case was as bad as it could be: "full of lep-rosy," a medical term. That leper came to Jesus, and he said,

" Lord, if Thou wilt, Thou canst make me clean."

He did not ask Him to cleanse him, and yet everybody knows that such was the desire in his heart. " Full of leprosy," absolutely beyond the reach of all human aid; so far gone that if we are to trust the Levitic code, the chance of contagion was passed. Amelioration was out of the question here. He said,

" Lord, if Thou wilt, Thou canst make me clean."

There was a time when I criticized him for coming in that particular way. Here was a man, knowing the ability of Christ, but not sure of the will of Christ. Is it not more true to say that this man was sure of His ability, " Thou canst;" but was submissive; recognized the sovereignty of Jesus, " Lord, if Thou wilt." He desired cleansing, but he did not ask for it. He linked up with the sovereignty of One, Whom he knew could cleanse him. I am more and more inclined to think the " If Thou wilt " of the leper was a remarkable revelation of the fact that he stood in the presence of One Whose ability he knew perfectly well, and his desire was for cleansing; but he conditioned it by the one phrase that ought to condition my prayer and your prayer at all times, " If Thou wilt."

What happened? Again let us look carefully. Luke says,

" And He stretched forth His hand, and touched him, saying."

Now when you get a participle like that, it shows there was simultaneous action of word and work. It does not mean He touched him and then spoke. As the words were spoken, the act was performed. The thing was quicker than the lightning's flash, quicker than the twinkling of the eye; before the hand reached him, before the full sentence was over, the leper was clean. He touched him, saying,—the word and work synchronizing; and Luke says,

" Straightway the leprosy departed from him."

The word of Christ was—

" I will ; be thou made clean."

" I will." As though He had said, Thou hast obeyed the highest law of life, preferring thy desire, not as a demand or request, but in submission to My will, recognizing My ability, knowing that I can make you clean,

" I will ; be thou made clean."

He touched him, and the leprosy left him.

There is an old question, and there has been a good deal of debate concerning it. It has been said when the Lord touched the leper He broke the Mosaic law. The Mosaic law demanded that no leper should be touched. I give it to you as my profound conviction, that He did not break that law; and that He did not touch the leper, He touched a cleansed man. Word and work synchronizing; " I will," and as soon as the " I will " was across the lips of Jesus, His cleansing power had operated, and as I read it, He touched him to show that he was clean. " I will ; be thou made clean." and the touch demonstrated the cleanness, because Jesus did not break a yod or tittle of the law of Moses.

Now look at the story, and mark the attitude of Jesus. What is His attitude to leprosy? He is against it. It is not His will that any man should be a leper; there is no leper on the earth today, a leper within the will of God. God overrules, God permits, but He is against all leprosy. His attitude towards faith when it is submissive, is that of quick and ready and immediate response; " I will ; be clean."

But no one can read that narrative without seeing in it a revelation of our Lord's dealing with the deep moral malady, the leprosy of sin. It has been said, and perchance it is true, that nowhere in the Bible is leprosy named as the type of sin. If that be so, it is none the less true that the common consciousness of men and women who have believed in God for ages, the Hebrew expositors, and theologians, and the Christian expositors and theologians, have all seen in leprosy, even though the statement is not made in the Bible, the most revealing symbol in the material, of what sin is in the spiritual. It is suggestive that we never read in the New Testament that Christ healed a leper. He cleansed the leper. Leprosy is on the material level, the most perfect symbol of sin in its insidious beginning, in its paralyzing and blasting and damning growth and advancement. Here, then, was a supreme case. The man was full of leprosy, and Christ had absolute power to cleanse the man, a symbol for evermore, of what Christ can do for the leprosy of sin in the soul of man.

How does it end? He charged him to tell no man; but to go his way, and to fulfil the requirement of the law, and show himself to the priest, and make an offering, and He added the significant thing,

"According as Moses commanded, for a testimony unto them."

Those very priests, spiritual rulers, already manifesting hostility to Him; He said, Go to them, and let your cleansing witness to them.

Then Luke tells us that "the report concerning Him" spread through all the district. That is the third of the three statements we referred to in a previous study. The first was that there was a fame of Him; then a rumour; now a report;—so said our translation. As a matter of fact, the first word is the Greek word pheme, which means a rumour; the second was echos, which suggests rather a roar, a disturbance. Here Luke used the word logos, which means not merely that a rumour was spreading concerning Him; not merely that it was a rumour that caused a noise, an uproar, almost consternation; but that the people were beginning to understand Him, an intellectual appreciation. This came after the cleansing of the leper.

One thing more that needs very little said about it, but it is a wonderful thing;

" But He withdrew Himself in the deserts, and prayed."

He left the leper, left the crowds, all the thronging and pressing multitudes, and went to the desert and prayed. The word for "prayed" there is the word that means far more than that He asked for things. It is the word that means He worshipped. He left men, for communion with God.

LUKE V. 17-28

IN this paragraph the opposition of the rulers begins to be definite.

This hostility had already shown itself in the first year in Jerusalem. We know that from the story in John, of how He went through Bethesda's porches, and healed the derelict. Hostility manifested itself then, first because as they said, He had caused a man to break the Sabbath; and secondly, and principally, because He claimed equality with God. Luke so far had not referred to it. He had recorded the terrified protest of demons; and the attitude of His own townspeople in Nazareth; but this is the first occasion upon which he records this hostility on the part of the rulers.

As we saw in our previous study, Luke says that a "report" of Him was being spread abroad; people were now beginning to understand; and it was at this point that the definitely hostile attitude and activity of the rulers began more patently to manifest itself. It never abated. As we go on from here, in this Gospel or in the others, we shall find the hostility being manifested all the way; and we shall see our Lord quietly going on with His work, but constantly encountering this opposition; never ignoring it, but dealing with it in quiet dignity.

This paragraph falls into two parts. In verses seventeen to twenty-six, we have the account of a day of paradoxes. Then in two verses, twenty-seven and twenty-eight, we have the account of the call of Levi.

I have said that in verses seventeen to twenty-six we have the account of a day of paradoxes. My reason for the use of the word "paradoxes" is found in the text.

"And amazement took hold on all, and they glorified God; and they were filled with fear, saying, We have seen strange things today."

The Greek word there rendered "strange things" is the word *paradoxa*. They said: We have seen paradoxes today. "Strange things" is an excellent translation of the Greek word, and yet there is a quality in the word paradox, as we use it, which helps us. These people said, We have seen paradoxes; *para*, against; *doxa*, opinion; that is to say, things we do not understand; strange things, apparently contradictory things; and yet they were things that made them glorify God, and filled them with fear.

Now, what had they seen? The first thing we are told is that He was teaching, and that the power of the Lord was with Him to heal. There were Pharisees and doctors of the law present, who were come out of every village of Galilee and Judæa and Jerusalem. Thus it is seen that Christ was becoming an increasing problem to the teachers of the law, the spiritual rulers. It was a very remarkable assembly. They were "sitting by." They were watching Him.

Suddenly something happened, there was a startling interruption. The roof over the court in which they were gathered was broken through, and a man was lowered into the midst of the assembly. He was sick of a palsy. I need not stop describing the physical malady. In this man's case it resulted from a moral malady. That is not always so. There is a good deal of sickness that is not the result of the sin of the persons who are sick. Here was a clear case of a man suffering from moral malady, and so from physical disability. His palsy was due to his immorality. That we know, by the way our Lord dealt with him. Such an interruption was startling, but more startling things happened.

There he lay, shaking in every limb; and in his own soul the consciousness that all his physical suffering was the result of his moral uncleanness. Jesus looked at him, and said,

" Man, thy sins are forgiven."

One of the other evangelists tells us that Jesus said,

" Be of good cheer."

He did not heal him, He did not begin with the physical malady. He first went to the thing that had caused the physical malady. He said, " Man, thy sins are forgiven."

Straightway that company of Pharisees and teachers of the law began to criticize. They were sitting by, they were watching. The suggestion is they had found nothing in His teaching with which they could take issue; but now He had said something. He had said to that man, " Thy sins are forgiven thee." They reasoned about it, they discussed it. With what result? What was their finding? What was the problem? That Jesus had said to a man, " Thy sins are forgiven thee;" and the finding of the doctors of the law was that this was blasphemy. That was their decision. It was blasphemy. But why was it blasphemy? They gave the reason; because

" None can forgive sins but God only."

These doctors of the law said, This teacher has invaded the prerogative of God, and has spoken words that none but God can speak. Blasphemy, was their finding. The invasion of the prerogative of God, was the reason for the finding.

Let us stop there for a moment. Were they right? Let us pause with their reason. The reason for their finding was that none can forgive sins but God. Were they right? Perfectly right. When they said therefore it was blasphemy, were they right? If He were no more than a human teacher, they were right. Thus immediately I am arrested. I want to see how He dealt with it. He said to them,

" Which is easier, to say, Thy sins are forgiven thee; or to say, Arise and walk? "

Supposing we had a record of what they said. They did not say anything, because He went on; but supposing they had answered, I think I know how they would have done it. I will imagine I am one of them. I am a doctor of the law; and Christ has said to me, Which is easier? I would have said to Him, From the standpoint of their philosophy;—Of course, it is not easier to say, Arise and walk, because that, also, is possible only to God. That is why Christ challenged them in this way.

Then continuing, without waiting for their answer, He said:

" But that ye may know that the Son of man hath authority on earth to forgive sins,"

and He did not finish the sentence to them; the finish of the statement was an act, preceded by a word to the man;—

" Rise, take up thy bed, and go to thy house."

In a moment the man was on his feet, and he left them, glorifying God, Who only forgives sins, and Who only heals. The thing that halted them was the word of authority in the moral realm. He was teaching them that the word of authority in the moral realm is proved by the word of power in the physical realm. God forgives sins. God heals; and in this case the two things were identical. He demonstrated His authority to forgive sins, by His power to deal with the issue of sin in the physical disability of the man. The proof of moral authority was found in the physical healing; and the man departed. He glorified God. For his healing? Yes, but I think far more for that his sins were forgiven.

Then one pauses, and wonders what they had to say. I have no record of anything they did say, unless perhaps "Amazement took hold on all." I think we may take that " all " as including the doctors, as well as the people listening.

Luke next records the call of Matthew.

" He went forth, and beheld a publican, named Levi."

Matthew, Mark, and Luke all tell the story of his calling. Luke says,

"He went forth, and beheld a publican, named Levi."

Luke, writing from a distance, having examined and sifted the accounts, gives the fact, and so names him as a publican. Mark, who unquestionably told the story from the standpoint of Peter, says,

"As He passed by, He saw Levi the son of Alphæus, sitting at the place of toll."

Mark does not call him by the objectionable name, publican, but records the fact. Matthew himself says,

"As Jesus passed by from thence He saw a man called Matthew, sitting at the place of toll."

He does not name himself a publican. He is careful to do so later when he puts his own name in the list of Apostles. He says, He beheld a man. That is what Jesus always does see, a man.

He was collecting tolls from the boats on the seashore. Matthew in all probability, almost certainly, was a servant of Herod, a vassal of Rome. He would probably pay an annual sum to

Rome, and put the toll in his pocket. I have no doubt it was a lucrative business. He was a rich man. Jesus passing by, looked at him, and said, "Follow Me." He said literally: Join Me in the way, and travel with Me. He asked for complete submission, but He asked for it, in fellowship. Come and travel with Me; take My road, be My friend, be My companion.

Then the record says:

"He forsook all, and rose up, and followed Him."

I do not like the word "forsook." We have the idea far more simply and accurately in the old rendering, "He left everything." There was immediacy; there was a sudden call, and in response to it, a sudden act. Jesus left the house, and walking by the shore of the lake, there was this man sitting, collecting the toll of the Capernaum boats coming in; and Jesus quietly said, Come and travel with Me, and he dropped everything, and went.

"He left all, and followed Him."

The result was ultimately that he became the King's recorder, and when the Gospel was to be written that shows the Kingliness of Jesus, this is the man who wrote it.

LUKE V. 29-39

HERE we have the sequel to the call of Matthew. It is the story of the great feast in his house. Luke says,

"And Levi made Him a great feast in his house; and there was a great multitude of publicans and of others."

This man celebrated his renunciation with a feast. He had renounced everything. He had left his toll, left his calling, broken with Herod, and abandoned the Roman Empire. He cut himself adrift, but he did not call his friends together and emphasize his sacrifice. He made a feast in honour of the renunciation.

Luke says, "He made Him a feast." It was in honour of Jesus, and it is

wonderful to see how this man understood Jesus. He knew the sort of people Jesus desired to meet. He knew He would rather sit down with a crowd of publicans than any others. Is there not more significance in it than that? I think there is. He was eager that the men of his own class, and his own order, should be brought into touch with Jesus. He knew the people Jesus would like to meet, and he knew that these men supremely needed to meet Jesus. Jesus accepted the invitation. Jesus accepted the honour as Matthew intended it should be when he made Him a great feast. He went to the feast. He sat down with them, and He ate with them. The rulers could not understand this. When we get to chapter fifteen, when He came out of the house, we find that the Pharisees were watching Him, and they criticized Him for His attitude towards the unwashed crowd. They said,

"This Man receiveth sinners, and eateth with them."

It was an unpardonable thing in their view. Now let us keep our eye upon our Lord, and see Him flung up into clear and sharp relief, in His majesty, and in His dignity, and in all the compassion of His heart, against the background of the hostility of the rulers. The story of the feast is the story of two criticisms levelled against Him.

The first was an oblique attack upon Jesus, through the disciples.

"The Pharisees and their scribes murmured against His disciples, saying, Why do ye eat and drink with the publicans and sinners? And Jesus answering said."

It is a great thing to have Him on hand to answer when we are attacked for His sake. He answered, and He said,

"They that are in health have no need of a physician; but they that are sick. I am not come to call the righteous but sinners to repentance."

The charge was that He and His disciples were consorting with sinners; and if we consider it, it really was a startling thing. One thing that constantly puzzled these men, these religious rulers, these scribes and these Pharisees, these men who were custodians of morality and uprightness, as they understood it, was the attitude of Jesus towards these notoriously sinning folk. There is a sense in which their criticism was justified. There are people from whom you dare not accept an invitation to dinner; people notoriously corrupt. In a high and fine sense, it simply is not done. That is what these men meant. The first criticism of our Lord, then, the oblique attack upon Him through His disciples, was that He consorted with sinners.

How did He answer it? He said, "They that are in health"—He granted the malady; He did not quarrel with

them when they described these people as sinners. He said in effect, They are sinners. You are quite right about that. I am not denying that; but they that are whole are the people who do not need the physician. The implicate of that was that He went and sat with those people because He was the Physician. He went on, and said,

"I am not come to call the righteous but sinners to repentance."

These men said, Why do You do this? His answer was: Why do I do it? Because the sinners are the very people I want to reach, and I want to reach them because they are sinners, because the malady of sin saturates them. I am here as the great Physician to deal with that very malady.

Now, I said a moment ago that we cannot consort with sinners. Let me qualify that statement. We can do so if we go in His company, with His passion in our heart to reach them, and heal them by bringing them to God. One of the most difficult things today that a minister has to do with true spiritual success, is to accept invitations to dinner. I have been at this work now for over half a century. I have seen more prophets spoiled dining out than in any other way. It takes more courage to talk to a man across his table than it does to stand here, and tell you the truth. Let us go back and watch Him, and God bring us into fellowship with Him. Yes, He said, I will sit and eat with them, because I am after them. You are quite right; they are sinners. You are quite right, they are suffering and dying from the malady of sin,

"I am not come to call the righteous but sinners to repentance."

That is what I am in the world for. He is after the men and women who need Him, the sinning crowd. Their first criticism that He was consorting with sinners is answered. He was consorting with them, to cure them of the malady that excluded them from the company of righteous souls.

Then His enemies approached Him in another way. This time they talked to Him, and it was a direct attack;

but it concerned His disciples. They had no more to say when He said that He had come to call sinners to repentance; but now they were troubled about the disciples;

"They said unto Him, The disciples of John fast often, and make supplications; likewise also the disciples of the Pharisees; but Thine eat and drink."

They were now complaining that the attitude of His disciples was characterized by an absence of ascetic practices. They were complaining that their outlook on life was too cheerful. They said: The disciples of John, and the disciples of the Pharisees fast, and they make supplications. They are attempting to realize spiritual strength by ascetic practices. Look at Your disciples; they are eating and drinking. The contrast was that between the ascetic and the human way of living. They said, These disciples of John and our disciples, practise fasting; practise the ascetic life; they maintain the attitude of serious solemnity in the presence of life, for the creation of the sanctity of their own souls. Your disciples are eating and drinking, on the level of the ordinary and the everyday and the human.

The answer of our Lord to that is full of vital importance. He answered it first with a statement that was local and transitory. Then He gave an answer that was parabolic and abiding. I want the division to be clear. The first answer was local and transitory. It has no application to us at all. They said, Your disciples are going about eating and drinking, observing no fasts. They are characterized by merriment and hilarity. They are a happy crowd. We do not see signs of sanctity, signs of grim solemnity, and the ascetic attitude towards life. He said,

"Can ye make the sons of the bridechamber (that is, the companions of the bridegroom) fast while the bridegroom is with them?"

He said in effect, How can these men be other than merry while I am with them? Their gladness is caused by their companionship with Me.

"But," He said, "the days will come

when the bridegroom shall be taken away from them."

The verb there arrests, if we are reading the Greek New Testament, *apairo,* which was a suggestion 'hat He would be taken away violently. He had not told them yet about the Cross, but the suggestion of a violent end was in the verb. The days are coming when these men will fast. The days did come, and they did fast. That was local and transitory. That has no application to us. Why? Because He is with us. He is not taken away. That only applied to the few days between the Cross and the resurrection, and in a lesser degree to the period between resurrection and Pentecost. When He came back by the Spirit to abide with them, the need for fasting passed. He was simply looking at the facts of the case. You criticize My disciples for living the life of merriment, of joy; they cannot help it, they are with Me; we are together; but the days will come when the Bridegroom shall be violently taken away, then they will fast.

Now, what was His second answer, the parabolic, the abiding?

"And He spake also a parable unto them; No man rendeth a piece from a new garment and putteth it upon an old garment; else he will rend the new, and also the piece from the new will not agree with the old."

He said,

"No man rendeth a piece from a new garment and putteth it upon an old garment."

Well, if he did, what then? He will rend the new; he will spoil the new in an attempt to mend the old. And what else? The piece from the new put upon the old, will spoil the old, too.

But again;

"And no man putteth new wine into old wine-skins; else the new wine will burst the skins, and itself will be spilled, and the skins will perish. But new wine must be put into fresh wine-skins."

Here let us carefully observe one or two very simple things, often lost sight of when studying this passage. First, wine, after fermentation, when it is completely fermented, can be put into any bottles, old or new, and it will not burst them. Do not forget that. Secondly, wine in process of fermentation, that is, that which is intended to become fermented, would burst any bottles, old or new, in the process. Wine unfermented can only be kept in new bottles. If we put the unfermented wine into the old, where the fermented has been, it will be infected by the old, and will burst them.

Our Lord here was talking about new wine, the new wine of the Kingdom, unfermented, pure wine. He said: You cannot put that back into your old bottles, that have had in them fermented juices. He was saying in effect, You cannot put My new wine, the unfermented wine of the Kingdom, into these old bottles, because if you do, it will

become fermented, and break the bottles, and everything be lost.

What is the great teaching here? It is that He did not come to mend, but to end the past and start the new; and that the things of His Kingdom, the things He had come to initiate, cannot be contained within the formulæ of the past. It requires new forms, new methods, new laws, new rules, new wine-skins for the new wine.

When He had said that, He added,

" No man having drunk old wine desireth new; for he saith, The old is good."

It was a satirical condemnation of these men. You are satisfied with this old; you have been drinking the old, and you are drunk; and you are saying, We like the old best! That is why they crucified Him!

LUKE VI. 1-11

WE are still in the atmosphere of hostility to our Lord, on the part of the rulers. Here we have two incidents, in which the opposition of the religious rulers is seen, and in each of them the question is that of the Sabbath. One incident is in the grain-fields. The other is in the synagogue.

What were these disciples doing that raised the hostility in the grain-fields? We are told that,

" His disciples plucked the ears, and did eat, rubbing them in their hands."

Evidently they were walking through the corn-fields, and as they walked, they plucked some of the ears, and rubbed them, and ate them. They were hungry, so they ate.

Was there anything wrong about that? Let us turn to Deuteronomy, twenty-three, verse twenty-five.

" When thou comest into thy neighbour's standing grain, then thou mayest pluck the ears with thy hand; but thou shalt not move a sickle unto thy neighbour's standing grain."

That was the law. They were per-

mitted to do exactly what they were doing. They were not breaking law.

What, then, was the trouble? The trouble was that they did it on the Sabbath day. Our Lord, in the course of His ministry, continually denounced these rulers for being anxious about their own traditions, rather than the commandments of God. He was constantly protesting against adding human tradition to the law. That is exactly what they had been doing. The order of scribes had their origin in the time of Ezra; and then a little later on, in the time of the Maccabees, the order of Pharisees sprang up. When it began, it was a mighty movement. But gradually, in the process of the intervening years, these men, in order to insist on the law of God, began interpreting the law; and in order to guard it, they superimposed upon it interpretations and applications of it. About two hundred years before Christ there arose what was known as the Great Synagogue. The first reference we have to it in the Mishnah is so dated. That Synagogue took the ten commandments of the law, and the whole law of Moses, and added interpretations. This they did, not by teaching the inner spirit of them, but by adding to them other commandments.

Take this Sabbath question. The Great Synagogue had given thirty-nine prohibitions, to interpret that one word of the law, "Thou shalt do no manner of work." Those prohibitions were called *Abhoth*, which meant fathers. Then they added what they called *Toldoth;* the word *toldoth* meaning descendants, that is, descendants of *abhoth*. *Abhoth* were fathers; *Toldoth* were descendants of fathers.

One of the *Abhoth,* the Synagogue prohibitions, said, Reaping is work; threshing is work. Those were named among the thirty-nine prohibitions; therefore you must not reap and thresh on the Sabbath. Then came the *Toldoth,* the rules to help you to carry out the idea; and in the *Toldoth* it distinctly said plucking the ears of corn is equal to reaping, and rubbing in the hands is equal to threshing!

The disciples of Jesus, as they walked on that Sabbath day through the grain, were hungry, and they did what the law said they might do, they

"plucked the ears, and did eat, rubbing them in their hands."

But they were breaking *Toldoth,* and by breaking *Toldoth* they were breaking *Abhoth,* and by breaking *Abhoth* they were breaking the law! So argued the Pharisees. They were not breaking the law. They were violating the traditions of men. Always, and at all times, Jesus is seen trampling roughshod over all human traditions; but never violating the law of God, or lowering its standard of requirement.

When the Pharisees criticized the disciples for doing it, Jesus answered for them. He said,

"Have ye not read even this?"

He did not say, Have ye not read this? He said,

"Have ye not read *even* this?"

The satire in that "even" is patent. These men were fighting for the law, these men knew all about the law; these men boasted themselves in their knowledge of their Old Testament Scriptures. These men could tell how many letters there were in the Pentateuch, where the middle letter was, were careful about the *yod* and tittle. To them He said,

"Have ye not read *even* this?"

Of course they had read it. Of course they knew what

"David did, when he was hungry,"

how he went

"Into the house of God, and took and ate the shewbread, and gave also to them that were with him; which it is not lawful to eat save for the priests alone?"

Yet, that was His first answer, an answer vibrant with sarcasm. Of course they had read it. No, they had not. They had never read it. They had constantly read it. They had never read it at all. They knew all about it. They did not. They missed the significance of what David did. Christ said in effect: You would say it is not lawful to eat the holy bread; remember David did eat. Did he then violate the law? He did not.

Our Lord was thus attempting to show them that life is the supreme thing, and that for the sustenance of life it is perfectly proper to do things that otherwise might be illegal. Mark tells us that He said,

"The Sabbath was made for man, and not man for the Sabbath."

No, said Christ, God's Sabbath fits the need of man perfectly. All that is intended in the Divine economy by the Sabbath, stands. David, when he was hungry, had a perfect right to eat the shewbread. The sustenance of life is the supreme thing, and the Sabbath was never created to do anything that should harm life. As though He had said, These disciples of Mine, travelling with Me, were hungry, and when they plucked these ears of corn, and rubbed them and ate that corn, they were strengthening life.

Having thus revealed the principle by illustration, our Lord said:

"The Son of man is Lord of the Sabbath."

He did not abrogate the Sabbath. He did not come to set the Sabbath aside; but He did come to interpret its meaning, and to safeguard it from misinterpretation.

The doing of anything that is really necessary for the sustenance of life does not violate the command that there shall be no work done on the Sabbath. Of course, it must be really *necessary*. There is a quaint story told in England of a farmer who was given to making use of the Sabbath for getting hay in. A godly old man, a farm labourer, simple and uneducated, went to work for that particular farmer. Soon there came hay time, and one Saturday the farmer said to him: "We must get this hay up to-morrow." The old man said, "I cannot come tomorrow, it is Sunday." "But," the farmer said, "this is a work of necessity, and it must be done. Your Master said if an ass or an ox fell into a pit on the Sabbath day you were to get it out." "Yes, sir," he replied, "but not if you put it in on Saturday night!" No work is permissible, if it can be done on another day.

The Sabbath principle is far older than Judaism. It is as old as humanity. It is rooted in the inherent necessity of human nature. Go back to Genesis, and there you find it. There the Sabbath of man was the seventh day in the creative process; but it was the first in human existence, because the seventh day of creation was man's first day of life. Thus originally man's first day was his Sabbath day, it was not the seventh day. It was God's seventh day of work, and His seventh day of work was man's first day of life, and was his Sabbath. Out of the first day of rest, man went to his work. Under the Hebrew economy it was the seventh day; man worked his way into rest. The resurrection changed everything, and men of the new race went back to the original ideal of the first day. We are no longer working into rest. We are resting and working as the result of our perpetual rest. But the principle of the Sabbath abides;

and our Lord has revealed here the fact that the principle of the Sabbath day is certainly a provision for rest, but principally for worship. That is the profound underlying meaning of the Sabbath. It is not indolence; it is not doing nothing; but it is ceasing all the work necessary for the here and the now, for the temporal and the material, in order that we may enter into His courts, that we may hold fellowship with Him. Christ has not violated that. He says He is Lord of that; but He broke through the super-added traditions that made the Sabbath a burden that could not be borne.

Now as to the second incident. Here we have the same thing, but with something added, which is very arresting. Jesus went into the synagogue, and Luke tells us that there was a man there, and his right hand was withered. The scribes and Pharisees were watching to see whether He would heal on the Sabbath day;

"That they might find how to accuse Him."

Their watching was malicious. That is granted. They were expecting He would heal that man. That expectation was an unconscious compliment to Jesus. All sorts of people were in the synagogue, and a man with a withered hand. He was the one derelict there, and these malicious watchers knew Jesus well enough to know that this cripple was the man who would appeal to Jesus. He is always after the derelict.

Christ knew their thoughts, and He acted at once. He said to the man:

"Rise up, and stand forth in the midst."

Now look at Him; that withered arm, that useless member, affecting all his powers and marring all his life. Here is a Sabbath question. Will He heal that man on the Sabbath? Jesus spoke to them; He pulled them sharply up. He said, "I ask you." He appealed to them.

"I ask you, Is it lawful on the Sabbath to do good, or to do harm? to save a life, or to destroy it?"

It was a most startling question. Might they not have said: Teacher, is that quite fair? We don't wish to harm that man; we are not thinking of destroying him; but cannot he be let alone until tomorrow? The startling nature of His question is found in His statement of alternatives. He said in effect: In the presence of a man like that, you do one thing or another; you either do him good, or harm; you either save him or destroy him. You are either acting for his recovery; or you are acting for the perpetuation of his misery. That is the startling contrast of alternatives. Christ sharply challenged them by the questions He asked. In the presence of human misery and dereliction, we cannot be neutral. We must either do something to save, or we are destroying. We must do good, or we are harming humanity.

All their traditions, if they could but have understood, were shrivelling up like the leaves of trees, struck by the lightnings of God. That is our test of work. We cannot stand in the presence of a man like that, and be neutral. We must either do good if we can, and if we do not, when we can, we are harming him. Those are the violators of the Sabbath, who are content to leave a man like that on the Sabbath day, when he might be healed.

The necessity for sustenance is revealed in the first incident; the necessity for the alleviation of suffering is revealed in the second. If there is suffering, any work that goes to heal, to bless, to relieve, to lift is no violation of the Sabbath.

In both these cases our blessed Lord ran counter to religious scruples which were not founded on true sanctions. He violated tradition in the interest of truth. There was no abrogation of the Sabbath in either case, but the restoring of it to the high level of the Divine intention. Life must be sustained if necessary, by going into the Holy, and eating the shewbread; certainly by plucking the ears of corn and rubbing in their hands. Suffering must be alleviated whether on the Sabbath day or not; for to stand neutral at any time in the presence of agony, when we could alleviate it, is blasphemy against humanity, and that is always blasphemy against God.

LUKE VI. 12-16

"And it came to pass in these days."

WHAT days? Days in the ministry of our Lord characterized by growing popularity and growing hostility.

These things have been self-evident in our preceding studies. The hostility to our Lord on the part of the rulers was becoming more and more manifest, and more and more bitter. It is equally true that His fame was spreading, that it had become a report, and in measure an understanding.

That statement introduces the section beginning at the twelfth verse, and ending at the forty-ninth. In this section there are two movements closely related.

The first begins in verse twelve:

"And it came to pass in these days, that He went out into the mountain to pray; and He continued all night in prayer to God."

The second commences at verse seventeen:

"And He came down with them, and stood on a level place."

He went into the mountain. He came down to the plain. These two statements break this section up into two parts. We may name them thus: His ascent to the mountain, and the events on the mountain; His descent to the plain, and the events that took place there. Our present study is concerned with the first of these.

In these days, days of growing hostility and days of growing popularity, Jesus went into a mountain, and something took place in the mountain. When it had taken place, He came down from the mountain, to the plain, and something took place on the plain. On the mountain He elected His twelve apostles. On the plain He talked to the twelve apostles, in the hearing of the other disciples and the multitude.

Here our Lord began to arrange for the carrying on of His emprise by others. The whole history of the service of the Christian Church is rooted in this little paragraph. If we are Christians in very deed, we are all in apostolic succession. This does not mean that we are called to the specific ministry, either of apostles, or of prophets, or of evangelists, or of pastors and teachers. But, even though we may not have received any of these gifts, we are all in apostolic succession. In the passage in the Ephesian letter, which speaks of the very gifts I have named, Paul points out what is the use of these gifts within the Church;

"He gave some apostles; and some prophets; and some evangelists; and some pastors and teachers, for the perfecting of the saints, unto the work of ministering."

This means that all the saints are in the work of the ministry. No man or woman can become a member of Christ, and a member of His Church, without having personal and first-hand responsibility in the world for carrying on the work of Jesus Christ. We are all His witnesses. We are all called into the ministry of witness, and the ministry of service; and that because we are members of the Christ, and of His mystical Body. The Church is the Body of Christ, through which today He is operating in the world, as He did operate through that Body prepared for Him in the days of His flesh.

Now, while as I say, the whole Christian service is rooted here, this story has a special application to such as may be called by specific gift, into what we usually describe as the regular ministry, to the apostles and prophets, to the evangelists and pastors and teachers.

Is it not an amazing thing that He committed His emprise to us? Angels would surely have been glad to carry on His work. But they could not have done it. There was an inherent necessity that His work should be carried on by men and women. Nevertheless, the amazement of the fact that He has entrusted His emprise to us, grows.

Here we have two things; night and morning. He went up to the mountain. He was there all night; that is night. When it was day, that is, at the dawning, He called His disciples. Is there anything more arresting, is there anything more wonderful, is there anything more beautiful, than this story of that night in the mountain, before Jesus selected from the first company of His disciples, these twelve men?

"He went out into the mountain to pray; and He continued all night in prayer to God."

I would like to read that in churches where they are going to elect deacons and officers. Ballots and elections, and so often candidating for votes, even for bishops! Before Christ chose the first twelve, He spent a whole night alone in the mountain, and in prayer.

We have noted in previous studies, how at critical occasions, Luke draws attention to this place of worship in the life of our Lord as neither Matthew, Mark, nor John does. We have seen two such already. After His baptism He prayed; and then the Holy Ghost fell upon Him. When the fame of Him was spreading through the countryside, He went to prayer. Here we find it again. He went to spend the night in communion with God. The form of statement in the Greek is arresting; He continued all night in the prayer of God. The word *proseuche* came to mean a house of prayer, an oratory. I cannot help believing, when I read it there in the Greek New Testament, that it means, He continued all night in the house of prayer of God. The house of God, what a great phrase it is. I love it, and I love it still as a phrase descriptive of our places of worship; His house, where we go on the first day of the week. Where does this phrase, "house of God," first occur in the Bible? Jacob, waking at Luz, said,

"This is none other than the house of God, and this is the gate of heaven."

86

There was no temple there. The temple was not built. There was no tabernacle there. The tabernacle was not built. There was no altar there. He had left the altar at home. He was at the place called Luz. There was no place of worship there, using the phrase as we usually use it. He had only a stone for a pillow that night. He lay down at the foot of the mountain, sloping up in terraces; and in his dream, the terraces of the mountain were translated into the ladder. This is the house of God.

In the first year of our Lord's ministry, in Samaria, talking to a woman, He said:

"Woman, believe Me, the hour cometh, when neither in this mountain nor in Jerusalem, shall ye worship the Father. . . . God is a Spirit; and they that worship Him must worship in spirit and truth."

He said in effect, The house of God is where the soul seeks God, anywhere! He went into the mountain to pray, and He continued all night in the prayer house of God.

Next day He was to make a selection of twelve men, through whom to carry on His work over a wider area, twelve men to whom presently there should follow the long succession through the centuries, of His witnesses to the world. He was about to select those twelve men, and He went up into the mountain, and He communed with God. In the seventeenth chapter of John, we have the account of the prayer that He prayed when His earthly mission, except for the Cross, was already completed. In that prayer He said:

"I manifested Thy name unto the men whom Thou gavest Me out of the world."

These were the very twelve men who were selected by Him, after that night on the mountain. About them He said, "The men whom Thou gavest Me." In that night of communion with God, He made the selection of the twelve, and He made the selection in the prayer house of God. In His worship He is revealed, not beseeching, begging, asking; but communing with His Father; His will so yielded to the will of God, that God made known to Him His thought, His mind. He went and communed with God through the livelong night, before He indicated the twelve. Our Lord, beginning His organization, the whole night was spent in fellowship, holy fellowship; yes, I dare say it, happy fellowship, free fellowship, unbroken fellowship with God. Then when the sun rose, when the day was come, right at the dawn, He knew whom He would appoint, because the selection had been made in communion with God.

"When it was day, He called His disciples;" that is, all of them, and there was a great company; for the seventeenth verse distinctly says, "and a great multitude of His disciples." He called them all. They had left Him alone through the night; but when the day broke, He called them. When He had called them, He chose from them, twelve. That was election. That was selection. This was the action of absolute sovereignty. He did not call all His disciples and take them into consultation. He made His own selection, and it was the selection of eternal wisdom. He chose the right men. A number of years ago I read a statement on this subject from which I differ absolutely. The writer said that the reason He chose only Galileans, and plebians, was that Jesus found "none other available;" and that "if there had been a disciple like Paul in the ranks," or "Nicodemus had been bold enough," or "Joseph of Arimathæa developed earlier," He would have included them "in the roll." All which I believe to be gratuitous and mistaken. Our Lord knew exactly what He was doing, and I think had Saul of Tarsus been available at the time, he would not have been chosen. He chose the twelve men after communion with God. It was a choice of infinite wisdom.

What do we know about these twelve men? I wonder how many people could give their names quickly, without consulting the records, or taking time to think? We should all make a splendid beginning, quite courageously, Peter and James and John; and perhaps one or two others, and then we should have to pause to think. What does this mean? That we have no record of what they did. It looks as though two or three were successful, and the rest were not. Let us not make any mistake. The Biblical literature gives us one flaming light upon the magnificence of their service, without any details. The seer of Patmos had a vision of the city of God, and the ultimate victory, and he says that on the twelve foundations were the names of the twelve apostles of the Lamb. In order to get at what I am after, I will be almost grotesque. When we see those stones one day, and find the names inscribed, we shall find that Peter has no larger foundation stone than the others, whose names we have forgotten! That is really a profound truth. The ultimate reward of service will never depend upon notoriety, but upon fidelity. There is a day coming when some of us, whose names unsought, have been blazoned round the world; will have to give place to perhaps a wee bit of a woman, our mother, our fellow-helper, who has rendered just as much service to the Kingdom of God as we, whose names are known.

But there is another matter here of vital value. I never read this story without gathering a great deal of comfort from it. When He chose these men, the responsibility of the choice rested on Him, and not on them. Now, supposing I had been one of the twelve. From that day forward, and growingly, as the years passed, I should have wondered why He chose me. I wonder at the fact as it is. But He did choose me, and that is enough for me; the responsibility is on Him. Oh, the comfort of it. Oh, the strength of it. If a man hold any office in the Christian Church, whether preacher, elder, or deacon, and God did not choose him, God pity him. If He did, and the man knows it in his deepest soul, that is the secret of courage, that is the secret of strength. He chose me. I am not speaking for effect. I am saying the deepest thing in my soul. I wonder, I wonder many, many a time, when I am alone, why He ever chose

me; but He did it! Hallelujah! I am not responsible. If there was any blunder, He made it! He will forgive me for making such a suggestion, for there was no blunder in choosing the twelve. He makes no blunders.

There is one solemn and amazing thing in this story. "Judas Iscariot, who became a traitor." Let no one say that is not a difficult thing to read; but it is there. I am not going to say very much about it. If we are to get any light on it, we shall have to get it from Him. In the sixth chapter of John, at verse seventy, I read this—He was speaking—

" Did not I choose you the twelve, and one of you is a devil? "

He did not say demon. Again in this Gospel of John, in that great prayer, where He spoke of the fact that God gave Him these men, He said,

" While I was with them, I kept them in Thy name; . . . and I guarded them, and not one of them perished, but the son of perdition; that the scripture might be fulfilled."

He chose Judas. What does He say about it? I chose you, and one " is a devil;" and later on, He used another description, equally startling, " the son of perdition." Those are the only references explanatory of the fact. He chose Judas. I do not believe Judas was a man in the ordinary sense of the word. I believe that he was a devil incarnate, created in history for the nefarious work that was hell's work. I cannot number Judas among other men, any more than I can number Jesus among other men. Among the twelve He chose and included that dark and sinister and terrible personality; that upon no human soul should fall the curse of being a traitor. I leave it there. I have no more to say about it. I have honestly given my profound conviction about Judas. For me, that explains the mystery of the choosing of Judas the traitor.

Once again, He not only elected, He named them. That is interesting. Apostles was His name for them. We all know an apostle means a messenger; but there is a value in the word which we may miss. The Greek word *apostello* is formed of two words; *apo,* apart; *stello,* set fast. The first meaning of *apostello* is one set apart. The second meaning, the meaning it gained in use, is delegated messenger, representative. The word came to indicate ministration, service; but its root significance is set apart. Mark, in his Gospel, tells the story of this election in an arresting way. He says that Jesus appointed the twelve to be with Him, and to go. First to be with Him, then to go. Never to go until they had been with Him. He set them apart, to be with Him, and then to go and to represent Him.

Such was the event of the morning, after the night of prayer; and there began everything of true organization, everything of true ecclesiastical value, in the history of the Church. There began the arrangements for the mighty service to be rendered to the Lord of the Church. He communed with God; He called all His disciples; He chose twelve; He named them apostles; and presently He sent them forth.

LUKE VI. 17-49

DESCENDING from the mount of election, our Lord exercised a marvellous ministry of healing, and then addressed His disciples in the hearing of the crowd. It is important that we observe the distinct difference between this discourse of our Lord and the Sermon on the Mount. Many Harmonies of the Testament put these two things together, the Sermon on the Mount in Matthew five, six, and seven, and this account of our Lord's discourse in Luke six. This is a mistake. The occasions were different; the places were different. In this discourse He repeated things He said in the Sermon on the Mount, but it is characterized by remarkable omissions; and things are found in it that are not found in the Sermon on the Mount. He was speaking, not to the twelve only, but to "a great multitude of His disciples." Moreover, others were there, for Luke says, "a great number of the people," from all Judæa and Jerusalem, and from the coast of Tyre and Sidon were there. I think we are justified in concluding that in that promiscuous crowd, there would be, as at that time was constantly the case, a number of the rulers. Although the fact is not named here, it is evident from some of the things He said, that those rulers were there, and He had them in mind.

But once more, that being said, let this be added, there is no doubt that all through this discourse, the twelve were principally in His mind. He had elected His apostles; and then He addressed them, so that the crowd could listen, and all the other disciples also.

Glancing first over the discourse as a whole, we see that it falls into four parts. First He instituted a contrast between prophets in verses twenty to twenty-six. Then He declared love to be the law of life, and illustrated His statements in verses twenty-seven to thirty-eight. Next He revealed the reason why He was giving this kind of teaching, in verses thirty-nine to forty-five. Finally He uttered His superlative claims in verses forty-six to forty-nine.

My reason for referring to the first movement, verses twenty to twenty-six, as "a contrast between prophets" is found in the paragraph itself. At the end of verse twenty-three we read,

"In the same manner did their fathers unto the prophets;"

and then in verse twenty-six,

"In the same manner did their fathers to the false prophets."

In the mind of our Lord, addressing that company that day, with His mind certainly upon the twelve, was the whole business of prophesying, in the full sense of the word. The prophet is the man who speaks forth the Word of God.

Notice, then, His contrast. In the first section, beginning in the middle of verse twenty and running to the middle of verse twenty-three, what is the key word? "Blessed." Then from verse twenty-four to twenty-six, what is the key word? "Woe." "Blessed," the word applied to some prophets; "Woe," the word applied to other prophets.

"Blessed are ye poor; for yours is the kingdom of God. Blessed are ye that hunger now; for ye shall be filled. Blessed are ye that weep now; for ye shall laugh. Blessed are ye, when men shall hate you, and when they shall separate you from their company, and reproach you, and cast out your name as evil, for the Son of man's sake. Rejoice in that day, and leap for joy; for behold, your reward is great in heaven; for in the same manner did their fathers unto the prophets."

There He had in mind that long and illustrious line of men in the history of God's ancient people, who had spoken forth the Word of God. They had been persecuted, the true prophets had been persecuted.

Now take the second section,

"But woe unto you that are rich! for ye have received your consolation. Woe unto you, ye that are full now! for ye shall hunger. Woe unto you, ye that laugh now! for ye shall mourn and weep. Woe unto you, when all men shall speak well of you! for in the same manner did their fathers to the false prophets."

The first group, prophets persecuted; the second group, prophets patronized. To the persecuted, Blessed; to the patronized, Woe.

Does that mean that a prophet of God is always to be so angular and peculiar that nobody loves him? It certainly does not. Does it mean that a false prophet is always to be so smooth and pleasant that everybody loves him? It certainly does not. We have not touched the deepest note until we have examined the reasons for the blessedness, and the reason for the woe.

Now look at them. "Blessed are ye poor." If we go back to Matthew, we find that in the Manifesto He said, "Blessed are the poor in spirit." There He was stating the principle fully. Here He was addressing Himself to certain men, "Blessed are ye

poor," and He certainly meant the same thing, poor in spirit. There is no man we naturally dislike more than the man we call a poor-spirited man. If we think of poor-spirited as meaning weak, vacillating, without conviction or courage, that certainly is not what Jesus meant. That is not the poverty of spirit upon which He pronounced His beatitude. The poor in spirit are the men and the women who are supremely conscious of their own poverty, of their own unworthiness; who are mastered by a great humility, characterized by a genuine modesty, as distinguished from a mock modesty. We get the idea exactly in another word; meekness. Jesus said, "I am meek and lowly;" that is poverty of spirit in the sense in which He used it; no vacillation, no lack of courage, no lack of conviction, but self-emptied. It is ever the man who is poor in spirit in his own self-consciousness, who is mighty in spirit, when he stands in front of men, to speak for God.

"Blessed are ye that hunger now; for ye shall be filled. Blessed are ye that weep now; for ye shall laugh."

Again we must interpret by the longer statement in Matthew.

"Blessed are they that hunger and thirst after righteousness; for they shall be filled."

Hunger after righteousness is an essential condition of prevailing prophesying. It is only when a man is poor in spirit, and yet in his heart and soul there burns a consuming passion for righteousness, that he is ready for the work of prophesying.

"Blessed are ye that weep now; for ye shall laugh."

There is no interpretation of that in Matthew. We must interpret by the progressive idea. The man poor in spirit, the man meek and lowly, the man with no consciousness of his own value or importance, but with his heart burning with a passion for righteousness, steeped with hunger for it in himself, and in the world everywhere; that is the man who knows what it is to weep. There is an old prophetic picture of a man with an ink-horn, who set a mark upon the foreheads of those who sigh and cry. Every man who is a prophet for God knows what it is to sigh and cry, to mourn, to weep.

"Blessed are ye, when men shall hate you, and when they shall separate you from their company, and reproach you, and cast out your name as evil, for the Son of man's sake."

We live in the year of our Lord, 1931, and this does not seem applicable to us, but the principles abide. When Jesus uttered these words, He was giving an exact description of what His disciples and apostles were really to go through. They will shun you for a time to see if you change your mind and method. They will slander you. They will cast out your name; that is final excommunication. He was showing these men what they would have to go through. Then He added that wonderful thing.

"Rejoice in that day, and leap for joy; for behold, your reward is great in heaven."

The words "for joy" are not in the Greek text.

"Rejoice in that day, and leap; for behold, your reward is great in heaven; for in the same manner did their fathers unto the prophets."

Men are in the true prophetic succession when these marks are upon them. Poor in spirit, hungry for righteousness, mourning over the sins of the world, hated, persecuted; these are the hall-marks of prophetic ministry in a world like this.

Then He said—and now He was not talking to His disciples; they were listening, but He was talking to others whom He saw in the crowd;

"Woe unto you, ye that are rich! for ye have received your consolation."

In the teaching of Jesus sometimes there was a vein of just, but of very definite scorn and satire. It was so here. "Ye have received your consolation." But there is more to be said.

"Woe unto you, ye that are full now! for ye shall hunger. Woe unto you, ye that laugh now! for ye shall mourn and weep."

And finally,—

"Woe unto you, when all men shall speak well of you! for in the same manner did their fathers to the false prophets."

Observe the perfect balance of all this. Blessed, woe; poverty, riches; hunger, repletion; mourning, laughter; persecution, popularity.

In these days we know little of persecution. Men today do not seem to be inclined to treat the prophets of God this way. They do not seem to hate us, they do not want to separate from us; they do not slander us; they do not excommunicate us. Why not? There may be two reasons. One reason may be found in the fact that the world is indifferent, rather than serious. Or, I wonder if there is not something lacking in our prophetic note. I am not saying it is so. I am wondering about my own soul.

Then passing on, we come to the second movement, verses twenty-seven to thirty-eight. It reveals the law of love, operating as against hatred. He had spoken of the prophets who would be hated. Now He declared how such are to behave themselves when they are hated. Look at the positive things there. Love, do good, bless, pray. Whom am I to love? "Your enemies." To whom am I to do good? "To them that hate you." Whom am I to bless? The man who is cursing you. For whom am I to pray? The man who is despitefully using you. The law of love as against hatred. That is active. The other part is passive. If a man smites you on the cheek, offer him the other. If a man takes away your cloak, let him have your coat, too. Give to every one that asks you, and do not wait for the charity commissioners to investigate. We say these are counsels of perfection. Such action is not practicable. The only reply is that these were the words of our Lord to His own, and any criticism of them must be referred to Him! Only, let it also be remembered that He Who called men to such impossible heights, in redeeming grace provided power to obey.

In verses thirty-one to thirty-four we have the revelation of the method of all action under the law of love. The Golden Rule from the Sermon on the Mount was repeated. We can never obey that, save as we are love-mastered. He then gave illustrative application of the rule, and in connection therewith, thrice asked the question, "What thank have ye?" The Greek word there rendered "thank" is *charis*, grace,— "What grace have ye?" If you love them that love you, what grace have you? If you do good to those that do good to you, what grace have you? for even sinners do the same. And if you lend to them of whom you hope to receive, what grace have you? even sinners lend to sinners. It is grace which outstrips every demand of mere righteousness, and of mere justice, and of mere equity. That is what He is looking for in His own, and especially in His prophets.

The way to overcome hatred is with love (verses thirty-five to thirty-eight); and if we only love well enough, and actively enough, with grace enough, and abide in the fellowship of God Who is our Father, the very people who hate us will presently come back to us with their gifts and their blessings. He loved His enemies. He did good to them that hated Him. He blessed them that cursed Him. He prayed for those that despitefully used Him. When they smote Him on the cheek, He turned the other. When they tore away His coat and gambled for it, He made no protest. The Master is the Revelation and the Interpretation of His own law. I cannot live there, save in the measure in which my life is His life, interpreted to me, realized within me, manifested through me, by the ministry of the Holy Spirit.

The third movement is contained in verses thirty-nine to forty-five. In that our Lord gave the reason why He was saying these things. The parable about the blind guiding the blind is explained by what He said concerning the beam and the mote. The blind cannot lead other blind people. Neither can the faulty sight of a man with a mote in his eye, be corrected by a man with a beam in his own eye.

But again. The test of goodness is fruit, and the purpose of goodness is fruit. The apostles, as His witnesses, were all the time in His mind.

Thus we reach the last movement, verses forty-six to forty-nine, in which He uttered His final claims. First He gave them a solemn warning, Why do you call Me Lord, Lord, and do not the things which I say? Here evidently He was speaking, not so much to the twelve, or the disciples, as to the crowd. To them He declared the conditions of relationship with Himself.

"Every one that cometh unto Me, and heareth My words, and doeth them."

Such a person is digging deep to rock foundation, and when the storm comes, his building stands. What are the conditions? He that cometh, that is surrender; he that heareth, that is discipleship; he that obeyeth, that is obedience.

Now observe the sharp contrast.

"But he that heareth, and doeth not, is like a man that built a house upon the earth without a foundation."

The building of such a person is destroyed in the day of storm. Who, then, is this man who never digs deep, gets down to rock? He that heareth and doeth not. The conditions of building, so that the storms cannot destroy; he that cometh, he that heareth, he that doeth. The conditions of building so that the first storm will wreck the building; he that heareth, and *doeth not.*

Are we among the number of His disciples? Are we among the number of those chosen from the disciples for specific work? Let us ponder all this, the contrast between the prophets; the law of love; the reason of these sayings, we are to guide the blind, we are to bear fruit; the rock foundation on which we may build, so that no storm can destroy our building, coming to Him, hearing Him, obeying Him.

LUKE VII. 1-17

FROM the hour when He chose His twelve, and named them apostles, to the critical hour of Cæsarea Philippi, the days were crowded days in the ministry of our Lord. Luke by no means gives us a full account of those days, but he illuminates the period by incidents and illustrations.

Following that election, and the discourse on the plain, He entered Capernaum. There the centurion approached Him. Then Luke says,

"And it came to pass soon afterwards,"

and many of the old manuscripts read,

"And it came to pass on the next day."

Evidently very soon afterwards, perhaps on the next day, the next incident that Luke has recorded took place. He came to Nain, twenty-five miles away from Capernaum, and there He met the funeral procession at the gates. We have, then, in this paragraph, two incidents; the healing of the centurion's slave, and the raising of the widow's son.

This story of the centurion is recorded by Matthew in the eighth chapter, verses five to thirteen. I refer to it because there is a notable difference between the two stories; and I can understand that they might appear to be contradictory. The story in Matthew certainly suggests that this centurion came to Jesus personally. From Luke's account we gather that he first sent the elders of the Jews. They would be the rulers of the synagogue. Then he sent some of his friends to Him. As we read it in Luke we find that Jesus never met this man. There is no contradiction in the stories. Matthew simply tells you the centurion came to Him, approached Him; and to express it simply, what others do for one, one does for himself. The "cometh" of Matthew does not necessarily mean that he came personally, but that he came through representatives. Luke, in my understanding of the story, makes it plain that the man and Jesus did not meet on that day.

He was a centurion, and that means that he was living a military life, within the Roman system of government. We find three opinions concerning him, in the reading of the paragraph. The first is in verse four. It was the opinion of his fellow-townspeople; and moreover, of the elders of the Jews. When they came to Jesus they said of him,

"He is worthy that Thou shouldest do this for him; for he loveth our nation, and himself built us our synagogue."

Another opinion of him, his opinion of himself, is found in verse six;

"I am not worthy that Thou shouldest come under my roof."

The word "worthy" there is not the same word that the rulers had used of him. His word meant sufficient; I am not sufficient that Thou shouldest come under my roof; that is to say, he was expressing his sense that he could not entertain Jesus as Jesus ought to be entertained. Continuing, however, he said:

"Neither thought I myself worthy."

There he did use the word they had used.

"Neither thought I myself worthy to come unto Thee."

His townsmen said, He is worthy. He said to Jesus: I am not competent, I am not sufficient to entertain Thee, and I do not think I am worthy to come to Thee myself. That was his own opinion of himself.

A third opinion of him is found in the ninth verse; it is Christ's opinion. He said,

"I have not found so great faith, no, not in Israel."

Christ's opinion of the man was that he was a man of remarkable faith.

Three opinions. His fellow-townsmen, and they Jews, and he a Gentile, said, "He is worthy." He said, I am not sufficient to entertain Jesus, and I am not worthy to come to Him myself. Christ said He had not found in all Israel such remarkable, such great faith, as he manifested.

Let us watch this man's approach to Jesus. Why did he approach Him at all? Because he had a slave that was sick unto death. It is an arresting story, this, of a Roman centurion caring about his slave, loving him, and so loving him as to approach Jesus, on his behalf.

But what made this man approach Jesus? What had he seen in Jesus that made him go to Him? He was evidently perfectly certain that Christ could heal his slave. He said distinctly, Speak the word only, and my servant shall be healed. How did he know that? What had he seen that made him act as he did? In the words this man uttered, he showed he had a remarkable spiritual apprehension of the philosophy of the life of Jesus. He said,

"I also am a man set under authority."

What does the "also" mean? Why did he say "also"? He revealed, in connection with the statement, the order of his own life;

"I also am a man set under authority, having under myself soldiers; and I say to this one, Go, and he goeth; and to another, Come, and he cometh; and to my servant, Do this, and he doeth it."

That is how he lived. He said, I am under authority, and therefore I am in authority. I am set under authority, and I have men under me; I am under authority, and therefore I am fitted to be over men. I am submitting to rule, and therefore I am exercising rule.

Above me is my superior officer; and above my superior is the Roman Emperor. I live under authority, and because I am under authority I am in authority. I can say to the soldiers who are under me, Go, Come, and Do this, and they obey. And he said to Jesus, Speak the word and my servant shall be healed; for Thou art living by the same philosophy. I *also* am a man under authority. This man saw that Jesus was under authority, and therefore in authority. He had a marvellous conception of the truth of the philosophy of the life of Jesus. Said the centurion, in effect, Just as I am under authority and therefore in authority, just as I exercise the authority I am under, and apply it to those who are under me; so art Thou under authority, and because Thou art under the authority which is the ultimate, and final authority, Thou art in authority.

Nothing more remarkable was ever said to Jesus than that. He said, I am not sufficient to entertain Thee, and yet he knew He was a Galilean peasant, so far as earthly position was concerned. Still this man said, I have nothing in my house that is worthy; I am not sufficient to entertain Him. I would be almost afraid to have Him come across my threshold; and I am not worthy to come near Him. What a vision he had of the glory of Christ. Remember he lived in Capernaum, and almost certainly had seen Jesus, and heard Him. He recognized that under the authority of God, He was completely in authority over all the things of life. His venture of faith was made upon the basis of that understanding. I think it is fair to surmise that he knew by experience that Christ could heal, without going. It had been done in that very city. In the fourth chapter of John, we have the story of a nobleman who sent to Jesus about his boy, and Christ had healed that boy without going to him.

What was the action of our Lord in response? When the elders came and asked Him to go, He went at once, readily consenting. When the friends met Him, before He arrived, and asked Him not to enter the house, He agreed again; He did not go. He healed without a word or an act; the omnipotence of the will of Christ is seen perfectly poised to the will of God. Under the authority of the Divine will, He was in complete authority, there was no need to go. He did not even utter a word, but when they got back, they found the boy made whole.

Then Luke says:

" When Jesus heard these things, He marvelled at him."

Jesus " marvelled," and turning, said unto the multitudes that followed Him,

" I say unto you, I have not found so great faith, no, not in all Israel."

In Mark's Gospel, and in chapter six, we have the account of His coming to His own country, and in verse six we read:

"And He marvelled because of their unbelief."

These are the only two occasions on which we have the statement that Jesus marvelled. Once at unbelief, and once at belief, He marvelled. The statement that He marvelled does not mean that He was ignorant, but rather that He had clear comprehension of that man's faith, of the majesty of it, of the sweep of it, of the grasp of it, of the marvel of it.

Now we pass to the next incident, so full of beauty that much in the way of exposition is not necessary. He came to Nain. I wonder whether I am foolish, but I wish I could paint pictures. I have an artist's sympathy, but I cannot draw anything; but I can see these pictures. This is one of the meeting of two processions at a city gate; one approaching the gate, the other emerging from the gate.

Look at this procession coming up the narrow road that led to Nain. The central Figure was Jesus. Round Him were His disciples; and Luke says a great multitude. They had travelled, some of them I have no doubt from Capernaum with Him; others joining with Him from everywhere. I think I am warranted in saying that if you could have looked into those faces the dominant colour would have been a colour of joy and gladness; and a scowling face or two perhaps, on some of the rulers that were watching Him.

Look now at this procession going out. What is the central figure there? A corpse, " One that was dead." And then, his mother; Oh, the pathos of it, " his mother," and he her only son, and she a widow. All the tragedy of life is in that procession coming out, sombre, sad, sorrowful; the central figure dead, and the mother walking in desolation. Luke says,

" Much people of the city was with her;"

so a crowd was coming that way, too. Look at their faces. No smiles there.

These two processions met. The two central figures are at once connected in Luke's narrative. He says, " When the Lord saw her," the Lord saw her. That is where His eyes went. He always has eyes for the broken-hearted. Then what? " He had compassion on her." He said, " Weep not." Then the action.

" He came nigh and touched the bier, and the bearers stood still."

Then He said,

" Young man, I say unto thee, Arise."

He talked to him as though he could hear Him. So he could hear Him! He talked to him as though he was alive. He was alive! The body was dead. The man was not dead. No man is ever dead when his body lies dead! There is dissolution between the spirit and the body, but not death. Three times our Lord raised the dead, and every time he did it in exactly the same way, talking to the dead as though they could hear Him. The lassie in Jairus' home, that sweet twelve-year-old lassie dead. He bent over her, and touched her, and He talked to her. He said to her, " Talitha cumi," in the soft mother tongue, " Little lamb, arise." He spoke as though she could hear Him, and she did hear Him, and back she came. Then there came another day when He stood by a sepulchre in which a man had lain four days; and when He dealt with Martha and Mary, He talked as though the man could hear Him, " Lazarus, come forth," and Lazarus heard Him, and came forth.

That is the central flashing wonder of this story. It reveals Christ's power over the spirit world that lies beyond our ken. I have no power there. When my lassie lay dead in my home long years ago, I talked to her as she lay there, but I knew she could not hear me; and I have never been fool enough to try to talk to her since, either through spiritual mediums, or any other foolhardiness. But they are alive, and He can speak to them so that they hear. Notice the fitness and intimacy of it in each case; to the lassie, "Little lamb;" to His friend, "Lazarus;" to this son of his mother, "Young man." In every case a familiar earthly designation, addressed to the living.

The final touch is full of beauty;

"He gave him back to his mother."

What pictures of joy that statement inspires.

A funeral procession had become a march of life. A bier had become empty. A desolate mother had been turned into a singing mother. A public highway had been a highway of glory when Jesus passed along. They were filled with awe,

"and they glorified God, saying, A great prophet is arisen among us; and, God hath visited His people."

They were quite right, and yet how little they knew. How true, and yet how little they knew. A prophet, yes. God has visited. Yes. That is God incarnate; God has indeed visited His people. Luke ends the story by saying,

"And this report went forth concerning Him in the whole of Judæa, and all the region round about."

"Report," and once again the word is *logos*. Certainty it means a report, but it means an understanding of the report. He had done things that brought conviction, marvellous and mysterious, about Him.

LUKE VII. 18-35

OUR previous study ended with the declaration that a report went forth concerning Him in the whole of Judæa, and all the region round about, and the word thus rendered "report" is "*logos,*" that is, intelligent information. Men were beginning to understand.

That statement is immediately followed by a story which shows how imperfect was that understanding. The story falls into two parts; first, that revealing the perplexity of John; and then, that in which our Lord declared the unreasonableness of the generation. The story of John is told in verses eighteen to thirty. In verses thirty-one to thirty-five we have our Lord's interpretation of the generation.

This story of the coming of the deputation from John is very full of interest and of value. Let us notice first the coming of the deputation; and then the answer of Jesus to these men sent from John.

What was the occasion of this deputation? John was in prison. It has been said that his question was the result of his imprisonment, that is to say, that at the close of that marvellous ministry he was suffering from physical and mental reaction; and that he was somewhat like Elijah under the juniper tree. I do not believe it for a minute. I do not think John's question was the outcome of any depression. I believe that he was as keen, as alive, as alert, as passionately devoted as ever to his mighty ministry and mission. How, then, are we going to understand his question? Luke says,

"The disciples of John told him of all these things."

What things? They told him all that Jesus was doing, told him how the fame of Him had gone out, until it had become a roar, and that there was manifested some intelligent apprehension of what He was doing. They would tell him also of the growing hostility of the rulers. And when he heard these things, he called to him two of his disciples, and said: Go to

Him, and tell Him I have sent you,
and ask Him,

"Art Thou He that cometh, or look
we for another?"

As John heard of what Jesus was
doing, the thing that amazed him was
not what He was doing, but the things
He was not doing. John could not
understand the method of Jesus. He
was perplexed beyond measure at the
very reports they brought. He had
spoken in marvellous terms, Divinely
inspired terms, of the coming of Jesus.
He had declared that He would come
with the fan and with the fire, that He
would come to depress mountains and
exalt valleys. Now at least eighteen
months had gone, and it seemed to
John that He was doing nothing likely
to bring in the Kingdom. He had
raised no standard of revolt against the
tyranny under which men were living.
He had issued no political programme.
He seemed to be quite careless about
organization. This great soul in prison
was saying to himself: How is the
Kingdom of God to be set up unless
there be revolt from the tyranny under
which men are living today? How is
a new order to be established in the
world, unless there shall be a political
platform? How is it ever going to be
possible to accomplish the best things,
and establish the Kingdom without an
organization? Moreover, He is an-
tagonizing the rulers. Go and ask
Him, Was I mistaken when I identi-
fied Him as the Messiah? It was the
question of a keen, honest, puzzled
soul, perplexed at the methods that
Christ was adopting.

The same thing is puzzling people
today. They cannot understand the
method of Christ. We are being told
that the Church of God has failed, and
that the only way in which we can
ever be successful is that of raising a
standard, and issuing a programme,
and highly organizing of our forces.
An attempt was made awhile ago in
America, with the backing of a million,
to organize the forces of God, and put
them on a commercial basis. God
smashed the whole business, and so left
His Church free to do her work in
His way.

Let us now consider Christ's answer
to the inquiry.

"In that hour He cured many of
diseases and plagues and evil spirits;
and on many that were blind He bestowed sight."

Observe the repetition of the word
"many." That was not done quickly.
Time was taken. When they came
with the question to Jesus, the first
thing that He did was to keep them
waiting, while He went on doing the
very things that had puzzled John.
Mark the weight of that. I am certain that what Livingstone said once
was true, "My Lord is a perfect Gen-
tleman." He would receive the disciples of John courteously. Then He
turned from them, and went round all
the crowds of people, healing them.
He had just raised the son of the
widow of Nain, and they were there
with sick folk, and diseased folk, and
blind folk; and He quietly went on
with His work. That was the first line
of His answer.

Then He turned to them, and spoke
to them. He said,

"Go and tell John the things which
ye have seen and heard."

Then He described His work. There
is a threefold movement in that description. He stated it in an ascending
scale of values. He first said,

"The blind receive their sight, the
lame walk, the lepers are cleansed, and
the deaf hear."

That is one line. Go and tell John I
am doing that. Go and tell John I am
not proceeding through this countryside with a mailed fist in order to raise
a standard of revolt, and break a
tyranny. Tell John I am going in and
out among the people, and I am re-
moving disability wherever I meet it.
Blind eyes are looking at things they
have never seen. Cripples are leaping
and walking with strength and with
gladness. The lepers, shut out from
everything, are being cleansed, and restored. Ears that have heard no song
of bird, or music, are listening.
Then He said, "The dead are raised
up." The ultimate dereliction of hu-

manity is death. Death is the last enemy. Death is the issue of everything else, of sin, and of sickness, and of sorrow. Go and tell John I am Master there.

Then the great climax was reached. Tell John that the poor have the Gospel, the good tidings preached to them. The relief of disability was introductory. The raising of the dead was the supreme manifestation of His power in all the realm of human dereliction. But His principal work was not the relief of disability, was not the raising of the dead, but that of preaching the Gospel to the poor. The word "poor" here does not mean people without money; any more than when our Lord said,

"Blessed are the poor in spirit."

Sometimes the wealthiest people as to this world's goods are the poorest; and the poorest are the wealthiest. The poor are those who lack the true wealth, those who have no soul wealth; those who are not rich towards God.

What Gospel was He preaching? The Gospel of the Kingdom. He was declaring the fact of the Kingship of God; and announcing its availability to man, with the consequent right of man to deal directly with God. Go and tell John that while I have raised no standard of revolt against the tyranny of the Roman yoke, have issued no political programme, and am not careful about organization, I am relating the souls of men to God, so that they may have the franchise of eternity. When a man is right with God, Cæsar cannot tyrannize over him. Thus, all the meaning of the mission of Christ flashes out. Go and tell John I am relieving disability. Go and tell John I have the last and ultimate power to raise the dead when necessary. But tell him that as I walk over the Judæan hills and along the valleys, and out through the towns and villages among the people, I am preaching the good news to the poor, of the Kingship of God. I am bringing men into right relationship with God; and when they are brought there, every other relationship is changed. That was Christ's answer to John.

He completed His answer as He warned John by a beatitude.

"Blessed is he, whosoever shall find no occasion of stumbling in Me."

Very gentle, very beautiful; but a definite warning. He was saying in effect, John, if you cannot understand My method, I ask you to trust Me; and when you are unable to see why I am doing, what I am doing; or why I am not doing what you think I ought to be doing, all I ask is that you follow and trust.

What a wonderful revelation we have of our Lord in all this. First of all we see that need appealed to Him more than intellectual difficulty, even of the loyal-hearted. John was in trouble, and he sent a deputation. Christ let that deputation wait while He went on with His ministry of tender dealing with human need. This He will always do. That is a microcosm of the whole story of Christianity. He is still keeping the intellectual crowd waiting for interpretation; but He is eager to reach, and help, and lift, and save, and bless derelict humanity.

We also see that His work is the final answer to perplexity. Are we perplexed about Him? Are we wondering at His methods? He says to us: See what I am doing. Examine what I am doing. Really understand it. Do not measure the method of Christ by the wisdom of the world. If we do so, we shall for evermore feel that it is at fault. Paul understood that when he said: God has chosen the foolish things of the world to confound the wise, and the weak things to bring to naught the mighty, and the things that are not to bring to naught the things that are. The method of Christ remains an enigma to men. It always has been so, and we have never more hindered Christ than when we have tried to adopt the methods of worldly policy and worldly cleverness in the carrying on of His enterprises.

Is the Church of God being criticized for her failure? How is she to answer her critics? She is first to go on with her work. Then she has the right to point to the things He has done through her. Her first ministry is the ministry of alleviation. All the hospitals in the world are in the world today as the result of the coming of the Christ, in His Church, to the world. There were no hospitals until Christ came. Do we realize that? I do not know any organization in the world today that fills my heart with greater satisfaction in certain senses than the Red Cross Society. It rendered marvellous service in the War, and has gone on doing wonderful work since. But do not forget the sign, the Red Cross! That is how the thing began. The work of the Church is the work of alleviating human suffering.

But that is not her final work, and that is not her principal work. What about raising the dead? She cannot do it. He has not given her that work to do. Her principal work is that of relating the souls of men to God, so that they may have the franchise of eternity, and the fellowship of God, and thus be set free from all tyranny. That is her work, as it was His work. He has opened the Kingdom of heaven to all believers. He preached the fact of it; and by His Cross we declare its availibility to men everywhere, and in all power. When we bring men into living relationship with God, we are doing Christ's work.

When the deputation had left Him, the Lord did a wonderful thing, a gracious and beautiful thing. He did not allow that crowd, who had heard the question asked, and heard His answer, to think unworthily of John. It is a wonderful testimony that He bore to him. First by questions He revealed the true meaning of the mission of John.

"What went ye out in the wilderness to behold? A reed shaken with the wind?"

Is that your view of him? What did you go to see?

"A man clothed in soft raiment?"

And with a touch of sarcasm,

"Behold, they that are gorgeously apparelled, and live delicately, are in kings' courts."

If John had been careful about the softness and the ease and the luxury of life, he would not have been in prison; he would have been in the palace. Then again,

"But what went ye out for to see? A prophet?"

They claimed that John was a prophet. He said, You have missed it; "Much more than a prophet." Then He took them back to their own scriptures, the voice of Malachi. Malachi had written,

"Behold, I send My messenger before Thy face,
Who shall prepare Thy way before Thee."

That, said the Lord, is the one to whom you have been listening; the man who links the old with the new. No reed shaken with the wind, no man seeking for softness and ease. A prophet, yes, but much more; the messenger, foretelling the advent of Messiah Himself.

Then He paid a marvellous tribute to the natural greatness of John.

"Among them that are born of women there is none greater than John."

When Jesus said this, "born of women," He did not use the word Paul used when he said of Christ, "born of a woman." They are two different words, having relationship, but with an entirely different significance. *Gennetos,* said Jesus of John. *Ginomai,* said Paul of Jesus. The first simply means, Born. The other means, Become of a woman, made of a woman, no man in the transaction. Paul is perfectly clear about the virgin birth, by that very reference. Jesus did not use that word. He used the common word, and He said, No man born of women is greater than John. It was a tribute to his natural greatness; a great man, in intellect, in emotion, in volition. He towers above the rank and file in the greatness of his natural being. Nevertheless, He said,

"He that is but little in the Kingdom of God is greater than he."

That does not shut John out of the Kingdom. When John entered into the

Kingdom of heaven, he became greater than he was outside it, though he was greatest born of women.

And so we come to the second part of our consideration, that of Christ's complaint as to the unreasonableness of the generation. He said:

"Whereunto then shall I liken the men of this generation, and to what are they like?"

Then came His parable; shall I dare to say a playful parable? A parable of play certainly, and with a playfulness that is full of light, a parable of children, playing in the market-place. Children do play at strange things. I have no doubt our Lord had watched them. They played first at a wedding, and then they played at a funeral. Some of them would not play at either. Those playing said to these dissatisfied children, "We piped unto you," we played wedding, "and ye did not dance." And then "we wailed," we played funeral, and you would not mourn. You would not play wedding or funeral. There, said Christ, is the picture of this generation. Those children that will neither play wedding nor funeral are like the generation. What did He mean? He went on and told them what He meant.

"John the Baptist is come eating no bread nor drinking wine; and ye say, He hath a demon."

John came, refusing absolutely to dance to the piping of his day. He would not dance. He would not enter into all that which was the cause of merriment in his day. He was an ascetic. Jesus said, You say he has a demon. You are not satisfied.

"The Son of Man is come eating and drinking; and ye say, Behold, a gluttonous Man, and a winebibber, a Friend of publicans and sinners!"

The Son of man came, and there was nothing of the ascetic in His manner of life. The Son of man came, and the disciples that gathered round Him were happy souls. They did not even fast. The Son of man came, and wherever He came there was the note of gladness and joy and merriment. John came, and he would not dance to the piping of his age. Jesus came and refused to be melancholy for the reasons that made men mournful. John would have nothing to do with their piping. Jesus would have nothing to do with their mourning. What made men merry in those days? What made people sad in those days? John would not dance to their piping. Jesus would not weep to their mourning. The unreasonableness of the generation was revealed in that it was neither satisfied with the ascetic note of John, nor with the human note of Jesus.

That is where the Church of God ever stands. She refuses to dance to the piping of the age, and she refuses to mourn at the things that make men sad. Jesus summed it all up when He said,

"Wisdom is justified of all her children."

Which simply means that the results vindicate the method. The sternness of John, and the humanness of Jesus are not contradictory; they are complementary. The two things are needed. Wisdom, the wisdom that is from above, that is first pure and then peaceable, and easy to be entreated, for evermore declines to dance to the piping of the age. That wisdom refuses to bow its head and be overcome with melancholy for the reasons that are filling men with sadness. Wisdom is justified, vindicated, in her children; in those that hear the voice of God and obey it, that learn the true asceticism, the refusal to dance to a piping which in itself is inspired of destruction; and refusing to be overburdened and crushed by sorrows that are transient and will pass. Wisdom is justified in her children.

LUKE VII. 36-50

IN our last study we considered the
account of the deputation that came
from John to our Lord, and our Lord's
dealing with that deputation, followed
by His criticism of His age for its
unreasonableness.

Matthew gives us the same story of
the coming of that deputation, but adds
something to Luke's account of the
things immediately following. He tells
us that after complaining of the unreasonableness of the generation, He
went straight on, and

" began to upbraid the cities wherein
most of His mighty works were done."

Then Matthew tells us that, continuing, Jesus ceased speaking to the
crowd, but in the hearing of the crowd
spoke to His Father,

" I thank Thee, O Father, Lord of
heaven and earth, that Thou didst hide
these things from the wise and understanding, and didst reveal them unto
babes; yea, Father, for so it was well-
pleasing in Thy sight."

Then again, speaking to the crowd, He
said :

"All things have been delivered unto
Me of My Father ; and no one knoweth
the Son, save the Father ; neither doth
any know the Father, save the Son, and
he to whomsoever the Son willeth to
reveal Him. Come unto Me, all ye that
labour and are heavy laden, and I will
give you rest. Take My yoke upon
you, and learn of Me ; for I am meek
and lowly in heart: and ye shall find
rest unto your souls. For My yoke is
easy, and My burden is light."

Now we have gone back to Matthew
because it helps us here in Luke. In
that connection, then, we take up the
story in Luke.

"And one of the Pharisees desired
Him that He would eat with him."

The city where this happened is not
named. The last city named by Luke
in the sequence we are following is
the city of Nain, that little city about
twenty-five miles from Capernaum.
The next place reference in Luke is in
the first verse of chapter eight:

"And it came to pass soon afterwards, that He went about through
cities and villages."

I am inclined to think that, having
completed His discourse, and uttered
His great call, our Lord returned to
Capernaum, the place which He had
made the base of His operations. This
is not vital. The story is vivid; and
its chief attraction and value is that
it brings two human beings into the
light of our Lord's presence. The
contrasts are very sharp in every way.

Let us, then, examine it, noticing
the occasion, and the persons, and the
happenings.

First the occasion. Simon gave
Jesus an invitation to eat in his house,
and our Lord accepted it. The invitation was not cordial, but uncouth.
We should not have known that if it
had not been for things that happened
afterwards. Presently our Lord pointed
out to Simon that when He entered
his house, he neglected the common
courtesies of an Eastern home. In an
Eastern home the first thing on the
arrival of the guest is the bringing of
water to wash the feet; the first mark
of welcome and salutation is the kiss
implanted upon the cheek; and the
guest is offered oil for his head. Simon
did none of these things. It was an
uncouth invitation, lacking all cordial-
ity. Then why did he ask Him to go
to his house? There can be only one
answer. I have seen it suggested that
he asked Him out of curiosity. I do
not think so. Curiosity is usually polite. It was hostility that prompted the
invitation. He wanted to watch Him,
to see if anything happened in his
house upon which he could fasten, and
he found it. It seems an amazing
thing that Christ accepted such an invitation. But when I have said that,
the saying reacts upon my own soul.
I am judging my Lord by myself, and
it is a condemnation of myself. Jesus
loved Simon just as much as He loved
that woman. In Simon's house He
sought to open Simon's eyes, and lead
him into the light, just as surely as

He had been a blessing to that woman who came there. That is why He accepted the invitation. It was an amazing thing that He should accept an invitation from a man like that, but I will tell you something more amazing. It is that He ever came to a world like this. Going to Simon's house was part of that greater thing. He loved Simon as much as He loved the woman. The atmosphere of Simon's house, the atmosphere of Simon's smug self-complacency, was just as repugnant to the soul of Christ as the atmosphere of a brothel. But He went.

Let us, then, look at these two persons who are brought out into sharp contrast in the story. Luke simply says that Simon was one of the Pharisees. That puts him in a class, and puts him in an atmosphere, and puts him in an ethical and a theological position. At once we know the sort of man he was. The word Pharisee is a revealing one. It is not a Greek word. It is in the Greek New Testament, the adaptation of the Jewish name for these men. The name came from the Hebrew word which means separation. Their history was a fine history. The order arose in the period between the close of our Bible history in Malachi, and the opening of it in Matthew, the Maccabean period. The order of the Pharisees was an order of men committed to hold the people from mixture with idolatrous peoples. In process of time they had become satisfied with externality and ritualism and creed, until the very word Pharisaic for us today has come to describe an attitude of complacent self-satisfaction. Their hostility to Christ is marked. Luke names them twenty-eight times in the course of his Gospel, and every time they are seen in hostility to Jesus. Simon belonged to them; perfectly satisfied with himself, perfectly satisfied with observing the tradition of the elders, and the ritual of ceremonial ablutions, and so forth.

With great delicacy, which is characteristic of the method of Luke, he tells the story of the woman.

" Behold, a woman who was in the city, a sinner."

The word used in that way was the equivalent for harlot. That is the woman; and she is seen in the Pharisee's house. Immediately the story becomes arresting. These two were the extreme representatives of the social scale, at the poles asunder. I do not know, I cannot tell you the name of the street in which Simon lived, or the place where the woman had had what she had perhaps called her home; but I am perfectly certain that they were at the extreme ends of the city. Here was a man out of the suburbs, and a woman out of the slum. Or, perhaps we can make it a little more vivid in America, by saying here was a man representing the boulevards, and a woman representing the red light district. They were in the same house; and the reason for their being there was Jesus.

Now let us look at the story from the standpoint of the things that happened. The coming of the woman is a most arresting thing. What brought her into that house? Edersheim suggests that it may have been that Simon had had illicit dealings with that woman, and she knew her way about his house. I do not believe it for a moment. I think Simon was far removed from any possibility of that kind; and to him the amazing thing was that she should enter his house at all. If a man belong to the tribe of Simon, this sort of woman is not going to call on him. He never need be anxious. She is not coming his way. If Simon objects to the idea of getting near a woman of that kind, she just as much objects to have Simon come near her. Now look at the facts. Why did she go?

" When she knew that He was sitting at meat in the Pharisee's house."

That is why she went. That is what took her in. She violated all her own prejudices, the old prejudices, the wrong prejudices if you like, the scorn in her heart for the cold moralist. She knew perfectly well with what scorn that sort of man would look on her, but she was blind to everything. Jesus was in the house, and into the house she went.

Now the narrative makes it certain that before that, she had received the forgiveness of sins. The parable Jesus used makes that clear. It means, She loved much because she was forgiven. It was not the first meeting between the woman and Jesus. If it was, then do not forget that that day she had probably heard Him say,

"Come unto Me, all ye that labour, and are heavy laden, and I will give you rest."

It may be that in that restless crowd that listened to the great call, she was one and heard it, and understood it, and responded to it. It may be so; for had He not already said,

"I thank Thee, O Father, Lord of heaven and earth, that Thou didst hide these things from the wise and understanding; and didst reveal them unto babes."

Possibly then the crushed, broken heart of the sinning woman in the crowd had heard Him, went to Him spiritually, found His rest.

When she came in, passing swiftly behind the guests, she came to where the feet of Jesus were exposed, and bending over them, she wet His feet with her tears, then seeing her tears, she loosed the tresses of her hair, and wiped them dry, and bending over, she kissed His feet. The Greek word is kissed repeatedly, and I think we get in our Anglo-Saxon speech the value of that if we render it, smothered them with kisses. Then she broke that alabaster cruse of perfume, and poured it out.

Now turn from the woman and look at Simon. We are told what he was thinking. He said within himself,

"This man, if He were a prophet, would have perceived."

What did Simon see that day? He saw the strange thing, the amazing thing, the shocking thing;—I am talking out of Simon's consciousness;—he saw a fallen woman fondling Jesus; a harlot pouring upon Him all the tender expressions of the devotion of love. Simon, watching it, said, This man, if he were a prophet—notice this—the

Old Version reads, "would have known." There is a great advantage in the Revised,

"He would have perceived who and what manner of woman this is that toucheth Him, that she is a sinner."

He quite made up his mind now that Jesus was no prophet. Therefore, in his thinking, one of two things was true; either there was some guilty secret lying behind this, or else He was careless of His moral nature.

Now watch our Lord dealing with him. He said to him,

"Simon, I have somewhat to say unto thee;"

and Simon's answer surely had in it the touch of superciliousness as he said, "Teacher, say on." Then the Lord gave him that exquisite little parable. It is full of playful irony. He said,

"A certain lender had two debtors; the one owed five hundred shillings, and the other fifty."

One owed him ten times as much as the other; but both were debtors. The creditor forgave them both. He forgave the five hundred debtor, and the fifty debtor. Simon, which of them would love him the most? The Lord was saying in effect to Simon, Simon, I know how you are looking at this woman. You say she is a sinner, and you mean she is a great sinner. Well, Simon, are you prepared to say you are not a sinner? Simon would have said, Certainly, I am not prepared to say that. I am a sinner, but I am not like that woman. There was another of his clan who said, I thank Thee that I am not as other men, not even as this publican; I fast and give tithes. That was Simon's attitude. He would have admitted he was a sinner, but he was congratulating himself that he was not a great sinner—like that woman. The Lord knew his attitude of mind, and I am going to dare to use my word again, with playful irony He said, I will take you on your own showing. You are thinking about this woman; a great sinner, five hundred; and yourself as a less sinner, to about fifty.

In the economy of God, and by the provision of redemption, there is forgiveness for both. Which, from your standpoint of observation, is going to love the one who forgives most? Simon said,

" I suppose, to whom he forgave the most;"

and swiftly our Lord said no more than, " Thou hast rightly judged." By which He meant to say: Simon, all the love that you see being lavished on Me, comes out of the fact that this woman is a forgiven woman. Moral rectitude has opened up the fountains of adoration. She is a cleansed soul, she is forgiven. The things that you do not understand, Simon, come out of other things that you do not understand.

He had not done with Simon, and Luke, who is an artist, says,

" And turning to the woman, He said unto Simon."

That means He talked to Simon over His shoulder. We know what He said. Let me tell it in a slightly different way. He said,

" Simon, seest *thou* this woman? "

What was Simon saying in his soul just now? Simon

" spake within himself, saying, This Man, if He were a prophet, would have perceived who and what manner of woman this is that toucheth Him, that she is a sinner."

And Jesus said, Simon, you are thinking if I were a prophet, I should be able to see her, to perceive her. Simon, can you see her? Simon might have replied: " Oh, yes, I can see her. I have seen her for a good many years. I know all about her." Hold, Simon, can you see her? Said Jesus in effect, You cannot see her, Simon. You are blind, you cannot see this woman as she *is* for looking at her as she *used to be*. Then said our Lord, in effect, Simon, I will help you to see her, and I will help you to see her by putting her into contrast with you. He did not put her into contrast with Simon

on the high level of spiritual condition. He did not contrast her even on the level of morality. He put this woman into contrast with Simon on the level of common everyday courtesy. He left the height of the spiritual. He even went below the level of the moral. He said, Simon, now look at this woman. Let Me help you to see her. I came into your house. You neglected the common courtesies of an Eastern home. She has remedied your boorishness. You brought Me no water for My feet. She has bathed them with her tears. You gave Me not the ordinary kiss of polite salutation. She has smothered My feet with kisses. You did not even bring oil, the coarser material, for My head, the supreme member of My body. She has brought ointment, the finer material, and poured it out upon My feet. Simon, you said, if I were a prophet I could see her. Can *you* see her, Simon? I have put you side by side, and by comparison you are as coarse as sackcloth, and she is as fine as finely spun silk!

Then He spoke to the woman, and He said, " Thy sins are forgiven;" not that they were then forgiven, but that they were already forgiven. The thing had happened, perhaps in a private interview, I do not know; perhaps out there in the crowd when He said, " Come unto Me," and she came spiritually. She was a free woman, and her moral regeneration had restored to her the grace and the beauty of the fineness of her woman nature.

That is the trouble with Simon, and with all the tribe of Simon. They cannot see. Thinking they see everything, they see nothing. Simon could not see that woman as she then was, for looking at her as she had been. There are members of the Christian Church, today, who look at that woman as she used to be, and never see her as Christ made her. The eyes that are Christ-anointed eyes will see her as she is, and be blind to what she was. The eyes of Simon see only what she was, and are blind to what she is.

It is evident all the way through that our Lord was dealing with Simon. I do not know anything about Simon, but I tell you, honestly, I should not be surprised to meet him in heaven, I should not be surprised to find out that his eyes were opened. I am perfectly certain our Lord was after him in love, to attempt to get him to see things. He is the same Christ for Simon, and for the woman. Simon needed Him, and He tried to win Simon.

Now, what made that woman what she was, as Jesus revealed her in all the fineness and delicacy and beauty of her attitude to Christ? What lay behind it? The only true nobility is the nobility of birth, and that of the new birth. It is the soul born again that catches the refinements of life, and becomes mastered by them. Sins forgiven, the soul loosed from them, that soul passes into the realm of great and beautiful refinement. That is what this story teaches.

It teaches yet one other thing. It shows me that Christ does notice neglect, and He does appreciate devo-tion. He notices it. Simon did not bring Him water for His feet. Simon gave Him no kiss. Simon did not put oil upon His head. He did not say anything. He went in, and took the invitation, the uncouth welcome as it came, but He noticed it; and under stress of circumstances, He revealed the fact He noticed it.

Are we giving Him a cordial or an uncouth reception? He notices neglect, and He values adoration. There is another scene and a different one, which reveals the same truth. When Mary of Bethany anointed His feet under the shadow of His Cross, Judas said, Why was not this ointment sold for three hundred pence, and given to the poor? All said the same thing. It was unanimous. Christ sharply rebuked them. Let her alone, for My burying she did it. He valued it. The aroma of the nard that filled the house this day, and again when Mary brought it later on, was a sweet thing to the heart of Jesus Christ.

LUKE VIII. 1-18

WE have in this paragraph a summary, and a general description of the work of the Lord as it grew in public influence. That is found in the first three verses. Then, beginning at verse four, and running to the end of the eighteenth verse, Luke records two parables of our Lord, given unquestionably, as the result of this increase in popular attention.

In the first paragraph Luke describes our Lord's work, and tells us of the company that travelled with Him; and how He and the band of twelve that He had called to Him, were supported. As to our Lord's work, he says,

" He went about through cities and villages, preaching and bringing the good tidings of the Kingdom of God."

In the Old Version it reads,

" preaching and shewing the glad tidings of the Kingdom of God."

The Revisers have changed the word " shewing " into the word " bringing." Either word will do, and neither word is necessary; the word is simply evangelizing.

" Preaching." That word gives clearly the method of our Lord, His style and manner. " Evangelizing." That reveals the content of His preaching. Whenever He proclaimed the evangel, He was preaching. Whenever He preached, He was proclaiming the evangel. He did not preach one day, and evangelize the next. Whenever He preached, the content of His preaching was the evangel, the good news of the Kingdom of God.

The word " preaching " shows the style, the method. It is the Greek verb *kerusso,* which means to proclaim as a herald. Preaching is proclaiming as a herald, and when a herald proclaims, he is representing a King, and therefore there is authority in his message. Preaching is proclaiming with authority in the name of a King.

The word " evangelizing " reveals the content of the preaching. What was it? Telling good news. What good news? The good news of the

Kingdom of God. That was the content of the preaching of our Lord.

A question is often asked as to what is the difference between the Kingdom of heaven and the Kingdom of God. The answer is perfectly plain. They are the same. The phrase, the Kingdom of heaven, is peculiar to Matthew; and you will find that the other evangelists use the phrase, "the Kingdom of God." When Matthew uses the phrase, the Kingdom of heaven, he is not shutting out the idea of the Kingdom of God; and when Luke uses the phrase, the Kingdom of God, he is not excluding the Kingdom of heaven. The Kingdom of heaven always refers to the establishment of the reign of God on this earth ultimately. To that Matthew was forever looking forward. The Kingdom of God means that, but it means more. It means that God is King now, and always. The Kingdom of God is in existence. God has never been dethroned; and this is what Jesus preached. Sometimes it is good to change a word. Instead of Kingdom, suppose we read Kingship. There is no reason why we should not. Indeed, that is the first meaning of the word, its application to territory being secondary. He was proclaiming the Kingship of God, the rule of God, the fact that the Lord reigneth. That was the good news that Jesus preached to men. He came to tell men, moreover, that this Kingdom was available to the human soul through grace. He was Himself the King, acting in grace, and declaring that the King eternal, immortal, invisible, had made a way by which those in revolt might be reconciled. Thus the good news was that of the Kingship of God, existing and available.

That is the Gospel. God reigns, and He has provided a way by which banished ones may return. He went everywhere, not submitting a Gospel to the consideration of the crowd, but heralding it, declaring it, God's message to men, good news. He went through the cities and the villages, heralding the good news of the Kingdom of God.

At this time He was not travelling alone. The twelve were with Him, and more than the twelve, for there accompanied Him a band of women who had received from Him healing and blessing; evidently a goodly company of them. Three of them are named here, but Luke says, "and many others." The three named stand out. "Mary that was called Magdalene," which simply means, Mary of Magdala; and we are told one thing about her, "from whom seven demons had gone out." "Joanna the wife of Chuzas, Herod's steward," a woman belonging to the official class; we meet her once again in this Gospel, among the company of those who were present on the resurrection morning. That is all we know about her. There is one other name here, "Susanna," and that is all we know of her. She is never referred to anywhere else. They "ministered to them of their substance."

During these years of public ministry, our Lord had no visible means of support. He had been a carpenter in Nazareth, living by His own toil; and if legendary lore is correct, Joseph had died early, and Jesus had held that household together. When He left it, He had no accumulation of wealth. And that little group of men, the twelve that were with Him, were not wealthy men. They were for the most part in the fishing business. John had a private house in Jerusalem, but, as a rule, there was little money among the fishermen. So we have this picture of a little company of women of wealth, taking care of the group. It is full of beauty. I always see here for myself the grace of Christ, that He was content to be supported in that way, while He carried on His work. It is more blessed to give than to receive, and it takes more grace to receive than it does to give. He was content to live on charity, while He carried on His mighty ministry. It seems to me as though that little group of women will always have an honoured place in the Glory Land, because they took care of the Lord of glory during those years of earthly ministry. Christ had first ministered to them, and then they ministered to Him; and let me say very reverently, but with profound conviction, He would not have accepted their material aid, unless they had yielded allegiance to His message and to God.

It is at least worth noticing that we have no record of any woman hostile to Jesus in these Gospel narratives.

Now we pass to the two parables. Luke says,

"And when a great multitude came together, and they of every city resorted to Him, He spake by a parable; The sower went forth to sow his seed,"

and so on. We have here either a part of the great parabolic discourse recorded in Matthew thirteen, or else we have the account of another occasion upon which Jesus used the parable of the sower and the seed. The general time notes show the same period in the ministry of our Lord, but there are notable differences between the parable of the sower in Matthew, and the parable of the sower here. As we find it in Matthew, it has a different emphasis from that which we find here. In Matthew we have the parable of the sower, and then the parable of the darnel, generally called the parable of the tares and the wheat. In the first there is a sowing of a field, and the results are described. In the next we have again the sowing of the field, but there are two sowings, that of the wheat, and that of the darnel. Our Lord explained the second parable, the parable of the darnel, and in doing so, He said distinctly,

"The good seed, these are the sons of the Kingdom."

So also in Matthew, in the parable of the sower, He does not talk about the word being the seed, but of individuals being the seed, "He that is sown." It is always personality in Matthew. Here in Luke He distinctly says,

"The seed is the Word of God."

There is no contradiction. In Matthew, the "sons of the Kingdom" constitute the seed. Who are the sons of the Kingdom? They that have received the Word, and are incarnating the Word. So the Word is still the seed. There, our Lord shows that the seed becomes propagative in living men and women. That is the emphasis in Matthew. It does not contradict this.

Here, there is no reference to individuals as constituting the seed, but

"The seed is the Word of God."

The implanted Word, in a man, in a woman, in an individual, becomes the seed of the Kingdom.

Then He goes on, and changes the figure, from the sowing of the seed to the lighting of the lamp. We find something about that lamp in Matthew. Not in the parabolic discourse, but in the ethical Manifesto, the Sermon on the Mount. I am convinced that it was at that time that He used the figure of the sower as Luke records it; but He used it again later, not contradicting, but complementing; carrying the teaching a little further on, and showing how the seed of the Word is rendered propagative through living men.

Let us glance at these parables. First the public utterance of the parable of the sower, and then the private explanation. The public utterance is found in verses four to eight. Notice carefully when He uttered this parable He said,

"The sower went forth to sow his seed."

He does not say, A sower, but "The sower." He does not name the sower, but He fastens their attention upon an illustration in a way which shows He has one thing in mind.

In his *Land and the Book,* Dr. Thomson describes what he actually saw of a sower at work. He says:

"'Behold, a sower went forth to sow.' There is a nice and close adherence to actual life in this form of expression. These people have actually *come forth* all the way from June to this place. The expression implies that the sower, in the days of our Saviour, lived in a hamlet, or village, as all these farmers now do; that he did not sow near his own house, or in a garden fenced or walled, for such a field does not furnish all the basis of the parable. There are neither *roads,* nor thorns, nor stony places in such lots. He must go forth into the open country as these have done, where there are no fences; where the path passes through the cultivated land; where thorns grow in clumps all around; where the rocks

107

peep out in places through the scanty soil; and where also, hard by, are patches extremely fertile. Now here we have the whole four within a dozen rods of us. Our horses are actually trampling down some seeds which have fallen by this wayside, and larks and sparrows are busy picking them up. That man, with his mattock, is digging about places where the rock is too near the surface for the plough; and much that is sown there will wither away, because it has no deepness of earth. And not a few seeds have fallen among this *bellan*, and will be effectually choked by this most tangled of thorn bushes. But a large portion, after all, falls into really good ground, and four months hence will exhibit every variety of crop."

That helps us to see the picture vividly as those disciples were familiar with it.

Now the disciples asked Him, What this parable might mean? He answered them by first declaring the principle upon which He was using the parabolic method. He said,

"Unto you it is given to know the mysteries of the Kingdom of God; but to the rest in parables; that seeing they may not see, and hearing they may not understand."

Now, there is one of the most difficult things to be found in our New Testament. It looks as though Jesus said, Unto you it is given to know the mysteries of the Kingdom of God, but to the rest these mysteries are given in parables in order that they may not understand. Now, let me speak with perfect frankness. Years ago, when I was beginning more earnestly to study, I came across that, and it pulled me up. I said in my soul, It cannot mean that. Jesus did not go on preaching, and adopting a method in order to prevent people understanding Him. When I find expositors, and some of the most orthodox expositors, trying to persuade me that is what He meant, I deny it emphatically. At your leisure, read it in Matthew, and when you read it in Matthew, you find His explanation in full. He is quoting from Isaiah. There we find that the people referred to had hardened their own hearts, lest they should understand. That is the ultimate. Luke has recorded the words

of our Lord without any doubt; but here He states a principle, and then makes an elliptical quotation; and you must fill in an ellipsis if you want to understand it. Now, listen to it again. He said,

"Unto you it is given to know the mysteries of the Kingdom of God; but to the rest in parables."

What? It is given to you to know it at first hand. You are with Me, you can have these interpreted to you without parables; but to the rest in parables. His declaration is not that He is using a parable to hide, but to reveal. Then the elliptical quotation, and if we go to Isaiah we find the explanation. The people had hardened their hearts, they had blinded their eyes, in order that they might not hear or see; and the Lord now lured them from their blindness by employing the parabolic and the pictorial method. To them who would not listen to the plain declaration, who were in revolt against it, He adopted the parabolic method.* Now, when He had uttered a parable, He said, He that has ears to hear, let him hear. Does someone suggest that He was mocking them; that He had said something they could not understand, and then told them to hear? Never! His parable was intended to arrest, and lure by the picture method, by the story method, those people who had steeled their hearts against Him. That is the meaning of the parabolic method.

Having given them the principle, He then went on to explain. Here I need not stay. This is familiar ground. On the wayside; people hard, there was no result. They heard, but they did not heed in any sense; and consequently the seed that fell was plucked up; the birds of the heaven came, the devil snatched it away. People still hear like that. They hear, but there is no intention in their hearing, no heeding in their hearing. Those on the rock. They hear, listen, and with joy receive; but there is no root, conse-

---

* In my volume on the Gospel of Mark, I have dealt with this matter at greater length.

quently they fall away, apostatize. They heard, they believed; but there was no root, no depth of earth; and they apostatized.

"Other fell amidst the thorns; and the thorns grew with it, and choked it."

He described the thorns. The cares of this life, the riches of this life, the pleasures of this life. The arresting things are the first two, the cares and riches, which stand exactly opposite to each other. Cares, poverty, with the anxiety which it creates. Riches, wealth, with the ennui it creates. People hear, people receive, but the carking cares of life spring up and choke the seed. People hear, and receive, but the wealth of life ministers to everything that is earthly, and the seed is choked. Or the pleasures of life, the application of which is self-evident.

And He went straight on, but with the disciples specially in view. When He said, You are to proclaim from the housetop, He was talking to His disciples. He said, You do not take a lamp and hide it, you do not cover it, you do not put it under a bed; but you put it on a stand that its light may be seen.

"There is nothing hidden that shall not be made manifest; nor anything secret, that shall not be known and come to light."

That cuts clean across the idea that His parables were intended to hide. He was telling the disciples that He was there to make things known, and that their business was to go out and make things known.

"Take heed therefore how ye hear; for whosoever hath, to him shall be given; and whosoever hath not, from him shall be taken away even that which he thinketh he hath."

Observe the value of this paragraph as a whole. To the twelve, the parable of the sower would illustrate what was then going on, in the crowd listening, and what would always go on, when they preached; and what always goes on, whenever His messengers preach.

We scatter the seed, proclaiming the Word of God. It falls on the highway, on the rock, amid thorns, on good ground.

To the listening crowd it created an opportunity to test their own hearing.

"And other fell into the good ground, and grew, and brought forth fruit a hundredfold. As He said these things, He cried, He that hath ears to hear, let him hear."

That is the application to the hearers. How does He end the other?

"Take heed therefore how ye hear."

The appeal to the insensate people, to quote the Old Testament, who having ears hear nothing, having eyes, are blind, He that hath ears, hear. Then when He suddenly turned from them to the parable of the lamp and its application of shedding light, He said, Take heed how ye hear. Which means, You hear in order that you may proclaim. You hear in order that the word may be in you a light shining.

Three sorts of ground were disappointing; the wayside, trampled; the rock, no depth of earth; the thorns, choking. Are they all quite hopeless? Dr. Burton, of England, in a volume he wrote on Luke, said something about that, that when I read it, I made a note of. Let me quote it;—

"Oh, no, that kind of soil is not ultimately necessarily hopeless. The fallow ground can be broken up; the rock can be shattered; the thorns can be uprooted; the desert may blossom as the rose."

So those who go out, bearing precious seed, shall come again, bringing their sheaves with them; and they go out, knowing that there will be all kinds of hearers, but they are never to speak of any as hopeless. The fallow ground can be broken up The hard and flinty rock can be shattered. The thorns that choke can be uprooted. The appeal of the Gospel is an appeal that we are called upon to make to all sorts and conditions of souls; and we may ever do it in hope, as well as in faith, and in love.

LUKE VIII. 19-39

CONTINUING the story of the ministry of our Lord in the crowded
days, in this paragraph Luke records
three incidents. He gives us first the
account of the visit of the Mother and
the brethren of our Lord, verses nineteen, twenty and twenty-one. Then the
wonderful incident of the stilling of
the storm, verses twenty-two to twenty-
five. The third incident, beginning at
verse twenty-six and running to the
thirty-ninth, is that of the saving of
the Gerasene demoniac.

Luke has given us a condensed and
yet very succinct account of the coming to Him of His Mother and brethren. We are now moving on, in the
ministry of our Lord, towards the end
of the third year, towards the crisis at
Cæsarea Philippi; and in that period
this thing occurred. In the third chapter of Mark the account is found more
fully. At the end of verse nineteen in
that chapter we read,

"And He cometh into a house. And
the multitude cometh together again, so
that they could not so much as eat
bread. And when His friends heard of
it, they went out to lay hold on Him."

"His friends" there means His kinsfolk, His Mother and His brothers.

"When His friends heard it, they
went out to lay hold on Him; for they
said, He is beside Himself."

That was not an unkind speech. That
was not hostile criticism. That was
simply the conviction of those who
loved Him, that He was putting His
mental balance in danger. That has
been said over and over again to men
and women who follow Jesus Christ,
when they overstep the bounds of supposed propriety in service. Let such
be comforted. They said it of Jesus.
They loved Him, and they said, "He is
beside Himself." The story in Mark
goes on. The scribes came down from
Jerusalem, and things were happening
there in the house. At verse thirty-one
we are told that His Mother and His
brethren arrived;

"There came His Mother and His
brethren; and standing without, they
sent unto Him, calling Him."

What did they want with Him?
Surely they wanted to save Him from
Himself, from His unutterable folly in
spending Himself in the way He was
doing; pouring out His strength in
such ceaseless service that He hardly
had time to eat; making Himself, on
the human level, so tired out that
presently when this scene was over, He
had to ask His disciples to let Him
get to the boat, and go to the other
side, that He could have the chance
to rest. His Mother thought He was
imperilling His sanity. I am perhaps
interpreting by my own experience of
a mother. Dear heart, she thought I
would kill myself before I was forty.
I did not. I want us to see the tenderness and the beauty of it. She got
those younger boys to go with her.
She said, Let us stop Him; He is going
mad, He is killing Himself. It was
the language of a fine human affection;
and away they went in order to try to
persuade Him to stop and come home.
When they arrived, they found the
throng there, and they could not get
near Him, but they got a message to
Him. Then our Lord said that wonderful thing;

"My Mother and My brethren are
these that hear the Word of God, and
do it."

To whom was He referring? Matthew
tells us that He pointed to His disciples, and said,

"Behold, My Mother and My brethren! For whosoever shall do the will
of My Father Who is in heaven, he is
My brother, and sister, and Mother."

Love that wanted to help Him was
acting in such wise that if He allowed
it to prevail, He would be hindered.
The subtlest peril we have to face, if
we are Christian workers, is not the
peril of the man who fights us. We
rather enjoy that. If a man is going

to attack me, I am braced up. My lover and my friend, who, not quite understanding the meaning and the reason of things, dissuades me from service in the interest of self-preservation, is my graver peril. That is what His Mother was doing. Then it was He gave utterance to this remarkable word, declaring that His next of kin was not the Mother of His body, were not the brethren of the flesh; but those spiritual souls who were devoted to His own reason and passion for everything; the will of God. Fleshly relationship, high and tender and beautiful as it is, is lower than the kinship of souls devoted to the will of God. This has a bearing on the whole interpretation of Scripture. Jesus once told the men who were boasting that they were Abraham's seed; they were Abraham's seed, but not his children. If they had been the children of Abraham they would have done as Abraham did. They had no spiritual kinship with Abraham, even though they had a fleshly relationship. Paul wrote later on,

" They are not all Israel that are of Israel. "

The highest kinship with Christ is that of the spiritual affinity which comes when His passion, the will of God, becomes ours.

The next incident took place in close connection with the coming of His Mother and His brethren. Luke says that it was " on one of those days." This voyage across the lake was taken at His request. Mark tells us that they took Him into the boat, " as He was;" and that directly He went into the boat He went to the hinder part of the vessel, and lay down and went to sleep, the sleep of a tired Man. But the sleep of a tired man is Nature's provision, which is only another way of saying God's provision, for the saving of that man from the peril of insanity, the very thing they feared. A man who can sleep will not lose his reason. As we watch this, the thing that arrests us is that the storm did not wake Him, did not disturb Him at all. It was no ordinary storm. Luke uses a little expression which is true to the geographical situation. The storm " came down." On that lake the habit of storms is that of coming from the mountains, almost without notice they sweep down upon the sea. One moment that Sea of Galilee will be calm as a mirror, and then in ten or fifteen minutes, lashed into fury by the swift descent of the storm from the mountains upon its unruffled surface. The storm was so fierce that Luke says they were " filling with water;" so fierce that " they were . . . in jeopardy." But He did not wake. He still slept.

The next thing that we observe is the concern of the disciples. They did everything they could before they woke Him, and do not forget they were not novices. They knew how to navigate that boat. When they were beaten, were completely at their wits' end, and when they saw they could do nothing else, and saw the boat was nearly filling, and they were in jeopardy, then they woke Him. Now I think we had better get bluntly to the point at once, they made a mistake. It is very easy for me to say that. I would not dare say it except upon a certain basis. If I know myself, I would have wakened Him before they did. I think I would. I would have got after Him before they did, but I would have been wrong, as they were. " He awoke," and stilled the storm. He pronounced the word, He brought about peace; exactly what they wanted; and the moment He had done it He turned to them, and said, " Where is your faith ? " Matthew, Mark and Luke all record that, in different phrasing. They do not give you exactly the same words. They all declare when Christ had stilled the storm, He criticized the men who woke Him; and the reason of His criticism was that their action demonstrated their lack of faith. They made the mistake of waking Him. It is a hard thing to say to my own soul. They made a mistake because there was no need to wake Him. Why? Do you think any boat can go down if Christ is on board? That is the whole question. We have a hymn, " Master, the tempest is raging." In it occur these words:

"No waters can swallow the ship,
    where lies
The Master of ocean, and earth,
    and skies."

They did not understand that; they did not feel that. He said, "Where is your faith?" What were they concerned about? They said, "Master, Master, we perish." When they said "We," what did the "we" stand for? Themselves and Jesus. If you look at the story you will see that personal pronoun in the plural, in the objective case; then you find it in the nominative case. Jesus had said, "Let us go over." "Let us," and Luke is careful to tell us that Jesus "Himself and His disciples" went. When they came to Him they said, Don't You care that we perish; not merely we disciples, but the whole of us are going down. I do not believe those men were frightened of death. I do not think that such an idea touches the deepest note. They were afraid they would be drowned, and they were afraid He would be drowned. Well, what of it? Is that all that troubled them? Not at all. They felt that if that boat went down, everything He stood for was going to fail. They had heard Him preach for nearly three years now. They had heard Him teach. They had been with Him. They had seen the glory of the Kingdom of God as He had interpreted it. They had seen the breadth and beauty and beneficence of the ideal. They saw the glory of the thing towards which He was moving. They felt that all that was imperilled. Don't You care that we are perishing; and that if we perish in this boat, the Kingdom of God is going to fail. That was the trouble of the disciples. Master, how can You sleep here. The boat is going down, and what about those parables concerning the coming of the Kingdom?

There are many Christians today who seem to think the boat is going down! I am tired of the wailing of some of my friends who take that view. The boat cannot go down. Jesus is on board.

The storm could not disturb Him, but the unbelief of His disciples did.

The rush of the waters and the sweep of Euroclydon as it tossed them with fury did not wake Him; but that little group of frightened souls woke Him. Disturbed by the unbelief of His own; and yet how patient He was, how tender, how strong, how beautifully He came to the side of the boat, and He looked at those tossing waters. Mark tells us what He said. Luke does not. He said, "Peace, be still." To translate that a little more bluntly, this is what He said to the waters, "Hush, be muzzled." "Be muzzled." That is interesting, that is arresting. I find that He used that word when talking to demons. He now said it to the waters. I am not going to dwell there, but I will tell you why I think He said it. I think He knew that the devil was at the back of the storm; for I still believe in the book of Job, that Satan gets the mastery of the elements, and attempts to make them hinder the purpose of the God of the elements. I think the devil thought he had the chance of ending the whole enterprise. What a fool the devil is! He was when he first rebelled against heaven's high decree. That is the story of Lucifer, son of the morning.

Then He addressed His own, asking them, "Where is your faith?" They were filled with fear, and they said, "Who, then, is this," what manner of man is this, "that He commandeth even the winds and the water, and they obey Him?" They came through that experience to a further conviction of the mystery and the marvel of His personality. That was great gain. Read the story again, and look at the world today, tempest-tossed and in the storm, and it does look now and then as though the enterprise of God is in danger. Christ seems to be asleep. Well, don't wake Him. Don't be panicky. Don't imagine that God wants your hands or mine to keep the ark safe, or the boat up. He does not. Hear again the lines:

"No waters can swallow the ship,
    where lies
The Master of ocean, and earth,
    and skies."

We pass now to the third of the incidents, the longest as to words, and a very remarkable one. It begins, "And they arrived." I like that, after the other story. "They arrived." We always arrive, if we have Christ on board. "They arrived," but it was a strange place at which they arrived, and a wonderful thing happened.

Matthew, Mark, and Luke all tell this story. There has been difficulty about it. I am inclined to think the difficulty was first raised by Huxley. He and Gladstone had a long controversy on the difficulty of this story. The difficulty as raised by Huxley, and raised by a great many people, is that of the destruction of the swine. It has been said that Christ had no right to destroy property. It may be well to say here that there are only two occasions in the ministry of our Lord when any act of His power was along the line of destruction. One was the withering of the fig tree, and the other was this of the swine. So far as I am concerned, the matter needs no debate. I have three things to say. First, the fact that He did it, is its justification. I never question anything Jesus did. If you say that is not enough for you, then I ask you to remember that you have got to put over against two thousand pigs, one man. But that is not the final answer. The final answer is the simplest. These people were living on Jewish territory. They belonged to the Jewish nation. They had no right to have pigs. He was there as Jewish Messiah, and when He permitted the demons to enter the pigs, He swept out a forbidden traffic. The people who had vested interest in pigs, were just as mad with Him as some people are with most of you decent folk who believe in prohibition! It is the same thing! Touch vested interests; interfere there, and they tell you you are kill-joys. The moral issue is not considered. They are simply in succession to these pig-dealers.

Three worlds meet in this story; the underworld of evil spirits, the world of human experience, and the overworld of Divine control. The underworld of evil spirits is seen here. It is a great subject. These demons are revealed as desiring a material or physical contact, getting hold of human beings to enter in and master them; and when they are cast out of a human being, they would rather go into swine than be left without contact with something material. Jesus said,

" The unclean spirit, when he is gone out of the man, passeth through waterless places, seeking rest, and findeth it not."

An unclean spirit coming to a man has found a place of rest. When turned out of a man it has no rest. " Then he," the unclean spirit, " says, I will return into my house." Demons are ever seeking some material or physical contact. Why? It is the restlessness of evil purpose; seeking some material or physical contact. Demons can only blight the work of God, in the creation and in this world, as they find vantage ground in the physical in man; and if not in man, then with some lower form of physical life. It is an arresting revelation.

But there is something else. They fear the abyss. That is merely the English form of the Greek word. It only occurs nine times in the New Testament, once here, once in the letter to the Romans, and all the rest in Revelation. Whenever we find it in Revelation, the reference is to the bottomless pit. These evil spirits dreaded that. Thus these demons are seen, fearing the abyss, and desiring some physical contact through which they could express their evil purpose, and fight against humanity and against God.

But look again, and note the authority of Jesus. How that blazes in this story.

" What have I to do with Thee, Jesus Thou Son of the Most High God? I beseech Thee, torment me not."

They besought Him that they might not go to the abyss, and that if they left the man, they might enter into the swine. The underworld of spirits stands revealed, fearing the abyss, desiring physical contact that they may carry out their evil purpose, and recognizing the authority of Jesus.

Now, with the story in mind, look

at the world of human experience as you see it here. Men in the grip of demons; a terrible thing. That one man;—there were two of them, but one was superlative, and Luke only names one,—in the grip of demons. And in that city, others in the grip of greed, which is worse, infinitely worse, more difficult to deal with.

Look again. A man is delivered from the demons by Jesus; and a community is delivered over to its greed by Jesus, because it refused Him. He left them. That man lived among the tombs. Today, in that particular district, you will find people called Troglodites, which being interpreted means, Dwellers among tombs. A community that rejected Him, He left it, and that is the issue in the long centuries.

That leads us to the third thing, the overworld of Divine control. Christ had complete authority over the underworld. He had complete authority over the world of men to deliver from Satan, or to deliver to Satan. The nature of the exercise of His control depended upon the attitude of men towards Himself. If the city does not want Him, He will not force Himself upon it. He entered into the boat, and left them. He trod upon their shores, strong to deliver, mighty to save. He gave them one illustration of what He could do in the case of the man. No, they said, we are not prepared for this. We can hardly see the man because we have lost our pigs. Oh, the terror of the picture, and yet how up-to-date it is. If the minute He lands, He rebukes our iniquity and our traffic, and sweeps out our pigs, supposing we let Him come up, what will He do in the city? What changes will He want to make? Send Him away. And He went, He turned His back upon them. The sentence of His back turned on them was as authoritative as the sentence of His face when He looked into the mad eyes of the man, and freed him from his madness, by casting the demons out.

Thus three worlds are seen; and high over all of them in authority as Lord and Master, our Saviour and Redeemer,

" Jesus, the name high over all,
In hell, and earth, and sky.
Angels and men before Him fall,
And devils fear and fly."

LUKE VIII. 40-56

"And as Jesus returned."

THAT sentence links this story with the previous one. He had been in the country of the Gerasenes, and they asked Him to depart out of their coasts, and He did so.

"And as Jesus returned, the multitude welcomed Him; for they were all waiting for Him."

This statement shows the popularity of Jesus in Galilee at that time. Then Luke gives the story of Jairus and the woman. The story of Jairus is broken in upon by the story of the woman. They are interlaced. They belong to each other. There is a singular beauty in them, because there are remarkable contrasts between the two stories, and yet a wonderful harmony of revelation. We begin with Jairus. The background of that picture is full of sunshine. This man Jairus was a ruler in the synagogue. He was known there. Probably it was the very synagogue built for the people by the centurion for whom they urged Jesus to do something, when they said,

" He is worthy . . . for he himself built us our synagogue."

Jairus evidently knew Jesus, and had seen Him work wonders before. He had a daughter, an only daughter, and she was twelve years old. For Jairus, twelve years of sunshine, twelve years of music, the music of the prattle of her tongue and the patter of her feet, twelve years of the sunshine of her eyes, of the joy of the girlie in the home.

The foreground of the picture is a foreground of darkness. " She was dying." Some grim disease possessing her, some fierce fever burning up her vitality; dying! And Jairus left her, and found his way to Jesus with his story of sorrow.

"He fell down at Jesus' feet, and besought Him to come into his house."

Driven by agony, driven by that terrible darkness, the insufferable fact that his girlie was dying, he besought Jesus to come into his house. The faith of Jairus was not equal to the faith of the centurion. The centurion had said to Him,

"I am not worthy that Thou shouldest come under my roof . . . but say the word, and my servant shall be healed."

It was that faith that amazed Jesus, and He said He had

"not found so great faith, no, not in Israel."

This man's faith did not rise to that level. He asked Jesus into his house. I refer to it in order to observe that Jesus went. He went immediately. He did not stand for any particular type of faith. If faith is there, He will respond to it. If faith says there is no need for You to come to my house, Jesus stands amazed, and says,

"I have not found so great faith, no, not in Israel."

This man believed that if Jesus came, there would be help. Christ immediately went.

Luke is careful to tell us at the end of the first stage in the story, that "the multitudes thronged Him." He used a singularly strong word. Mark tells you the same thing, and uses a word that means the same thing, but is not quite so strong as Luke's. I think it is good to notice the two of them, the verb that Luke used is a verb which means to strangle. Luke, who was an artist in the use of words, evidently wanted to impress upon the mind of his reader Theophilus, for whom he wrote the story, how great and eager the crowd was that day. He says, It strangled Jesus, that is, they so pressed upon Him that it was difficult for Him to get forward. Mark uses another verb, with the same idea, but not quite so strong, which means to press in on every side. The welcoming crowd was so great and so eager that Jesus, on the physical plane, could hardly move along the road.

This brings us to the story of the woman. A woman, having an issue of blood for twelve years. That is a background of darkness and of suffering. In the house of Jairus twelve years of sunshine and song and music and joy; and this woman suffering through all those years. This was a very remarkable and interesting case. We must not interpret it by our attitude towards disease today. We must get back into those times in order to understand it. By the law of Moses this woman was not allowed to touch any human being, and no human being was allowed to touch her. The law demanded that a woman suffering in this way should be segregated. Here is a case in which tradition had superadded to the hygiene of the law, a positive brutality. It was believed that any woman suffering from a hæmorrhage (as a matter of fact that is the Greek word employed here), suffered as the result of personal immorality. It was an absolutely false conception. The Levitical code did not teach that, but it was the belief of the time. Tradition had superimposed upon the hygienic requirement of the Levitical code, that any woman so suffering should be segregated, with other restrictions. For twelve years this woman had been excommunicated from the Temple and from the synagogue, from every religious place of assembly. Now, that may have been in harmony with the requirement of the Levitical law, but by the interpretation of the time, she was excommunicated, upon the supposition that her disease proved her immorality. The segregation of this woman, or any woman or man so suffering, according to the Mosaic law, was hygienic; but a false conception of the nature of the disease had created a tradition by which she was divorced from her husband, shut out from her family, ostracized by society, and treated as a pariah. Excommunicated, divorced, ostracized; and all on the basis of a false view of her disease. Twelve years of this, twelve years of struggle to regain health, and to find some way for the staunching of that flux. She had spent all her living. She was down in the depths. What a contrast to the twelve years of sunshine in the house of Jairus. Twelve years of darkness, and of shadow for this woman.

But today there was hope in her heart. Why? Jesus was passing by. She had heard of Him, and she heard He was there. I never read the story either in Matthew, Mark, or Luke, without some amazement as to how she managed to get near Him. It is very wonderful how strong need becomes in its weakness.

What did she do? We have read it all our lives, that she touched the hem of His garment. Now, as a matter of fact, the word "touched" does not convey accurately the thought of the Greek verb; neither does the word "hem" or "border" give us the true idea of the Greek noun.

She did more than touch. She fastened upon. We get nearer to the meaning of the verb if we use the word, clutched. She did not merely put her hand out, and touch. She grasped something.

What? She fastened upon the *kraspedon*. Now, what was the *kraspedon?* The tassel. In these Eastern garments were four tassels, one at each wing, or corner. In the book of Numbers, in the fifteenth chapter, verses thirty-seven to forty-one, we read:

"And Jehovah spake unto Moses, saying, Speak unto the children of Israel, and bid them that they make them fringes."

The margin says, "Or tassels in the corners." Let us begin again, and so read it:

"And Jehovah spake unto Moses, saying, Speak unto the children of Israel, and bid them that they make them tassels in the corners of their garments throughout their generations, and that they put upon the fringe of each border a cord of blue; and it shall be unto you for a fringe (a tassel), that ye may look upon it, and remember all the commandments of Jehovah, and do them; and that ye follow not after your own heart and your own eyes, after which ye use to play the harlot; that ye may remember and do all My commandments, and be holy unto your God. I am Jehovah your God, Who brought you out of the land of Egypt, to be your God; I am Jehovah your God."

That was a Divine enactment. That was not a piece of ritual superimposed by tradition. There is no doubt that Jesus kept that commandment, and wore a garment that had those tassels, and into the tassels was woven the thread of blue. Now, the Eastern robe was put on, so that one end being flung over the shoulder, one of the tassels was always upon the back of the wearer as he walked along. That is what the woman fastened on. She got her way through the crowd, and there she saw, at one corner of the robe, the *kraspedon*, the tassel. She got through the crowd, and put out her hand, and she fastened on that; she clutched at it as He passed by. It was a daring and a desperate venture. The law said she was not to touch, but in her agony, her helplessness, she had become a veritable outcaste in every way, her strength ebbing away, she thought, Jesus is there. If I can make contact with Him, I shall get help.

It was a clandestine act of faith, and superstitious withal. Dean Farrar says,

"She fancied that Christ's miracles were a matter of nature, and not of will and power."

That is very illuminative, and it is very true. She thought if she could get near Him, something in Him would automatically help her. But there was faith, also; faith working through superstition. In the book of Acts, chapter nineteen, and verses eleven and twelve, we read,

"And God wrought special miracles by the hands of Paul; insomuch that unto the sick were carried away from his body handkerchiefs"—sweat-cloths —"and the diseases departed from them."

That, again, was superstition with faith behind it. Their faith expressed itself superstitiously. But they were healed. So with this woman. All of which is very revealing.

If there be faith, even though the faith of Jairus is not the faith of the centurion, even though faith act superstitiously, the superstition is ignored, the faith is honoured. That is what our Lord meant.

She had gained her healing; but it was necessary that she should come into the light herself; and that her witness should help Jairus. That is why Christ stopped and said, Who is it that fastened upon Me? Peter made protest against the question in view of the crush of the people. According to Luke's account, it was the unanimous opinion of the disciples, but unanimity is not always a proof of accuracy. He knew the difference between the crush of the curious crowd, and the contact of a soul in need and in faith. Said He,

" Someone did fasten on Me, for I perceived that power had gone forth from Me."

Thus He brought the woman before Him, and when she came, she told Him all the truth. Then He looked at her, and said,

" Daughter, thy faith hath made thee whole."

Thy faith, not thy superstition. You were not made whole because you touched a tassel; but the faith that made you act, even though superstitiously, made contact with Me, and so came the healing.

Then He gave her the programme for the future. " Go," not " in," but " into peace."

All this while Jairus was waiting. Think of the suspense of the delay to him. I am certain when Jesus stopped and asked that question, and they had to make way for that woman, Jairus was impatient. Jesus delayed, while the child was dying. And yet, in the delay, however impatient Jairus may have felt, he heard that this woman had been completely healed by making contact with Jesus. This must have had its effect on what immediately followed.

Then came to Jairus the crash of doom, a messenger breaking through the crowd from his house, saying: Do not trouble the Teacher; she is gone, she is dead. Faith shaken, love wounded, hope destroyed. Jesus, says Luke, heard the message and straightway turning to Jairus, said,

" Fear not, only believe, and she shall be made whole."

Made whole? Jairus had heard Jesus say that word a moment or two before to the woman. He had heard Him say,

" Thy faith hath made thee whole;"

and now he heard Jesus say to him,

" Only believe, and she shall be made whole."

Then let imagination help us. They went the rest of the journey until the house of Jairus was reached. I do not know how far. Can you travel that distance with Jairus? He went in faith. Faith does not necessarily mean that he went, sure he would get his lassie back. His was perhaps wistful faith, possibly wavering faith, but certainly hopeful faith. On the rest of the journey he was facing the future with Jesus. They arrived, and our Lord first excluded the curious. If we fill up the story there from the other evangelists, we find that they laughed Him to scorn, but He put them all out. He said,

" She is not dead, but sleepeth."

Now, she certainly was dead in the sense in which we use the word. He said about Lazarus,

" This sickness is not unto death,"

but Lazarus died! From Christ's viewpoint that is not death which we call death. When the spirit has left the body, that is not death. Death is a deeper thing than that.

Then, as Luke tells us, He took the hand of the child and, bending over, said to her,—Mark gives us His actual words; one of those occasions when He dropped into His mother tongue, Aramaic—"*Talitha cumi;*" which means, Little lamb, arise! Then her spirit returned. Her spirit had never been dead. The essential part of her still lived, when the body was lifeless.

Now, do not miss the last thing in the story.

"He commanded that something be given her to eat."

Oh, the beauty of it, the tender touch of it. He knew what she needed. She has resumed the earthly level; now give her something to eat. The philosophy of that simple thing is very profound, and far-reaching in its application. Those who have sanctified humour will grasp it.

LUKE IX. 1-17

CONTINUING his narrative of our Lord's ministry, Luke now gives salient features of the closing part of what is usually called the Galilean ministry, that is, the period of public favour and popularity. In this particular paragraph we have the account of the first mission of the twelve. In every way, to the end of the age, this story must be full of interest and of value. Here is the account of the first time that He sent men out to represent Him. The whole Church is in apostolic succession in the great work of witnessing for Jesus Christ, and going forth for Him.

The story falls into three parts. In verses one to five, we have the account of their sending out; in verses six to nine, that of the work they did when they were sent out; and in verses ten to seventeen, that of their return, and the things that happened in connection with that return.

This was the last tour of our Lord in Galilee. In the next six months He went into Galilee, but He did not stay there. He was mainly on the other side Jordan, in Peræa, in the neglected area. Jesus had made two great tours in Galilee. On the first of them He was accompanied by four disciples. On the second He was accompanied by twelve. During that first period He gained many disciples; and at the close of it, He selected twelve; and as Mark tells us with care, having selected them, He appointed them to two things; first to be with Him, and then to go for Him. During the second great tour in Galilee, the twelve were with Him travelling everywhere. Now this is the third and the last tour

in Galilee. It occurred unquestionably during the third year, perhaps towards the end of it. Quite probably it occupied most of the year, because it is said that they "went throughout the villages," and that was not done quickly.

On this third occasion the twelve went alone. He was not with them. He went alone, too. The tenth chapter in Matthew gives the full account of the charge He laid upon them; and then of their going forth; and Matthew tells us in the eleventh chapter that when He had completed all the sayings, and laid the charge upon the twelve as they went, *He* went to *their* cities, that is, the cities from which the twelve had come. He sent them to the villages and to other cities; and then He went to their home towns, and went on with the work while they were away.

The first thing that arrests me as I read the story of the sending out of the twelve, is the wealth of these men; and the second thing that impresses me is the work to which He sent them; and the third thing is that of their poverty in going. Their wealth, their work, their poverty.

What was their wealth? Power and authority over demons, and to cure diseases. Here are two words which are sometimes confused.

He gave them power. Power is *dunamis*. Power is energy, it is force, it is dynamite. He gave them power, but He gave them more; He gave them authority. Authority means a right, the right to exercise power. Power is capacity. Authority is the right to use it. So He sent these men out, and He gave them authority, and He gave them power.

What, then, was their work? Was it to cast out demons, and to heal the sick? By no means. All that was incidental. The power was to be used by way of illustration, in order to arrest. He did not send them out to cast out demons, and He did not send them out to heal disease. He sent them out to preach the Kingdom of God. He did not send them forth for the specific purpose of casting out demons, or healing the sick; the great work of the twelve was " to preach the Kingdom of God."

The question is often asked as to what is the difference between the Kingdom of heaven and the Kingdom of God. There are some people who make a very clear and sharp distinction between the two. Matthew almost invariably uses the term " the Kingdom of heaven." The other evangelists almost invariably use the term " the Kingdom of God." Sometimes when Matthew reports Jesus as saying " the Kingdom of heaven," at the very same place, Luke reports Him as saying " the Kingdom of God." In the last analysis there is no difference at all between the Kingdom of heaven and the Kingdom of God. There is no doubt that when Matthew used that phrase in writing of the Jewish Messiah, and looking out upon the Theocracy, he used it with reference to the establishment on this earth of the Divine order, and the Divine Kingship. The Kingdom of God is larger than that. It has to do with the universal fact, with the fact that the Lord reigneth everywhere. Here the greater includes the less.

We get to the heart of the matter if we change the word Kingdom, and read the Kingship of God. People talk about the Kingdom of God sometimes, and the Kingdom of heaven, and they think of a territory. It has territorial application. I am not denying that. Some people talk about the Kingdom of God, and the Kingdom of heaven, and they apply it to a period. It has application in that way, but it is bigger than that. What Jesus sent these men to preach was what He preached, and

what John the Baptist had preached. John the Baptist began his ministry on this note,

" Repent, for the Kingdom of heaven is at hand."

Jesus began His ministry by saying,

" Repent, for the Kingdom of heaven is at hand."

The great message that these men were sent to deliver was the message of the fact of the Kingship of God. Some of us are in danger of getting away from the vastness and the impact of the whole, because we are occupied with some partial application. We talk about the Kingdom of God, and Kingdom of heaven, and we say they are synonymous terms, and refer to the order to be set up on the earth. We are not wrong. The view is not inaccurate, but it is absolutely inadequate. The Kingdom of God is the Kingship of God, the Sovereignty of God. That is what He sent them to preach. What this age needs is the proclamation of the sovereignty of God, the Kingship of God, the Kingdom of God. This Kingdom is not postponed. He reigns now, and our business is not to tell men that He is going to reign by and by. God has not handed the world over to the devil. He has the devil and the world in His grasp today. He is making evil express itself in order to its exhaustion. These men were sent to preach the Kingdom of God, and to declare its availability to all men, to tell men that they were in it, and that they could come into it; to tell men they existed in it, but they could not realize its benefits unless they became as little children, and turned back to God in repentance. Man cannot put himself outside the Kingship of God, but what does he know of its beauty and breadth and beneficence? Thus He sent them to preach what He preached. God reigns, and He is available to the human soul. When a man yields himself up to that sovereignty, nobody can tyrannize over him. He has the franchise of eternity, the freedom of the ages, eternal life. He said, Go and preach the Kingdom of God.

I want to emphasize another word in the sentence. He sent them forth to *preach* the Kingdom of God. The Greek word is *kerusso,* which means to herald. A herald is always a representative of a king. The verb means to deliver a message authoritatively. The business of a herald is not to discuss difficulties. He sent them to herald the Kingdom of God, to proclaim it with authority.

And now the local has its undercurrent of perpetual application. He said to them,

" Take nothing for your journey; neither staff, nor wallet, nor bread, nor money; neither have two coats."

That, of course, is purely Eastern in detail, but the principle abides. It is that of a splendid poverty; their only wealth was their message, their power, their authority; and the fact that they represented Him.

Then His sense of the vital, tremendous majesty and dignity of the mission emerges. He says, When you leave a house, if they will not receive you, shake the dust off your sandals for a testimony against them.

Then follows the account of their going. Verses six to nine. Here occurs the word, " evangelizing." There are two great words in the New Testament to describe the function of preaching. There are about eight different Greek words, but two principal ones. One is *kerusso,* and the other is *euaggelizo,* proclaiming good tidings. As they went, heralding the Kingdom of God, they were evangelizing. That is all we are told of their work. If that had happened in these days, there would have been voluminous reports issued; but that is how it is dismissed here, and Matthew dismisses it in the same way, and so does Mark.

The details are unimportant, but the great fact is that they went, and as they went, they evangelized. But we are told one result of their going.

" Now Herod the tetrarch heard of all that was done; and he was much perplexed, because that it was said by some that John was risen from the dead; and by some, that Elijah had appeared; and by others, that one of the old prophets was risen again. And Herod said, John I beheaded; but who is this, about whom I hear such things? And he sought to see Him."

Everything centres there in the Lord Himself. It was the fame of Jesus which produced these different opinions concerning Him, every one of them having in it the touch of the supernatural; John risen, Elijah appeared, one of the old prophets alive! The result of the apostolic work was that attention was drawn to their Lord. This was the result of their work. We have no other details. There are no statistics; which is significant!

Finally we have the story of their return. They reported to Him all they had done. What a wonderful thing it would be if the Church returned to this apostolic method. If it should say: We are not going to publish any report of what we are doing; all reports shall be given to Jesus, and not to the world. I think we are hindered by our reports and our statistics.

Then what did He do? He took them across the sea to Bethsaida. He said,

" Come ye yourselves apart into a desert place, and rest awhile."

They were tired, and He knew it. When He had received their report, He said, Come away with Me, to a desert place and rest. They reached the desert place, but when they arrived the multitude was already there.

Now mark what happened. The crowds were there, and we have that significant statement, " and He welcomed them." He

" spake to them of the Kingdom of God; and them that had need of healing He cured."

He went on doing what these twelve men had been doing.

The sun was setting. Evening was coming on, and it was desert; and those careful disciples, who would have been excellent men to put on a committee of finance for management, said. Master, send the multitude away, that they may go and get provisions. He said, "Give ye them to eat." They said, We have no more than five loaves and two fishes, except we go and buy for them. They evidently had a consultation, and Philip made a calculation. He said, Two hundred denarius' worth of bread would not do it. That was their calculation. Jesus said, Make them sit down; and He took those five loaves and, looking up to heaven, He blessed. He did not bless the loaves. He blessed heaven; He gave thanks. Then He put His hands on those five loaves.

"'Twas spring-time when He blessed
    the bread,
'Twas harvest when He brake."

Luke, Mark, and Matthew do not tell us, but John tells us that the next day Jesus interpreted His miracle of feeding on the spiritual level, and rebuked the crowd because they were interested in the material, and not in the spiritual. He said, You have not sought Me because you understood the sign, you sought Me because you ate and were filled. You are impressed with the material. I had a spiritual intention in what I did. What He said to the twelve on the level of the material, He said to them on the level of the spiritual. He is saying it to the Church today. "Give ye them to eat." The hungry massed multitudes are dying of starvation because they lack the bread of life. That is His command to His own; "Give ye them to eat."

Now mark His method. He took what they had. It was their loaves and fishes that fed that crowd; their loaves through His hands. We say, What can we do to feed the hungry world? We have nothing except—and then we name the things which mark our poverty. The answer is that He takes these very things, and makes them the media of supply. Forty years ago, in a little town in England, I went to conduct some special Evangelistic Services. I preached on the first Sunday morning to the church, trying to get it into line for our work, and my text was, "Give ye them to eat."

What I asked was that the church members would consecrate to the great business whatever they had. At the end of the morning service a good woman came up to me, and said, "I have heard you, and I would like to have some part, but what can I do? I cannot do anything." I looked at her, and I said, "Can you sing?" "Oh, yes," she said, "I sing." "Have you ever sung in public?" "Oh, yes, I have helped sometimes at church concerts." "Well," I said, "be here in the vestry with me before the service this evening, and come and sit in the pulpit with me and sing a Gospel song." "Oh, no," she said, "I never sang anything like that." I said to her, "I thought you wanted to help." She said, "Do you really mean it? What shall I sing?" I said, "Get some simple message of the Gospel, and sing that." In the evening she was there. She was a magnificent singer, but she had never sung a song for Jesus. She sang her Gospel message, just a little song; she did not think there was anything in it. That night there sat at the back of the church a farmer, a prosperous man. As he told me afterwards, he was so glad the Mission was in March, because he knew he would be so busy in the lambing season that he could not come. But that was Sunday night, and so he came. The first man to come out in the after-meeting was this man. He gave himself to God. "Yes," he said, "it is done, but you know, it was not your sermon. I don't even know what you said." I said to him, "What was it?" He said, "The message of that woman's song." I went out into the church, and said to the woman, "Come back here, and shake hands with this man." She knew him, and said, "Certainly, but why?" I said, "There is your soul won for Christ because you gave Him your voice." That man became a mighty power in all that district.

Let us bring Him our five loaves. It is no good our trying to feed a crowd with our loaves. It is good bread, wholesome bread, but it is no use our trying to feed the crowds with it. Give it to Christ. He will take the worthless things of our poverty, and He will multiply them to the feeding of the crowd.

Finally, when "they were all filled," every one of the twelve had his wicker basket full of bread for himself. That was the overplusage; more than enough for the crowd when Jesus blesses the bread, and something left for me, more than I had when I started.

LUKE IX. 18-27

LEAVING out many incidents, touching only on the salient facts, Luke follows his account of the mission of the twelve, with the record of the crisis in the ministry of our Lord at Cæsarea Philippi. Matthew gives the story with greater detail. Luke's account is more condensed. Matthew gives the formula of Simon's words when he made the confession,

"Thou art the Christ, the Son of the living God."

Luke records the fact that he confessed; and he puts the confession in condensed, sharp, brief form: "The Christ of God."

In this connection Matthew shows that in immediate succession to this confession of Simon, our Lord revealed three secrets He had never revealed before; the secret of the Church, the secret of the Cross, and the secret of the second Advent. Luke, in his record, makes no reference to the revelation of the secret of the Church, but he does show that our Lord then revealed three things: His Messiahship, His Cross, and His crowning.

Now let us follow these lines; first of all considering the method of the revelation, and then glancing at the threefold revelation.

In considering the method of it, we note Luke's statement,

"And it came to pass, as He was praying."

Matthew does not tell us that. Neither does Mark. Luke alone draws attention, and evidently with intention, to the fact that this occasion was introduced in the life and ministry of our Lord, by His own praying. This revelation of our Lord is peculiar to Luke. There are seven points where Luke shows Him praying, and the others do not record the fact. Luke tells us that before His baptism, He was praying. He tells us that when His fame was growing abroad, He retired to pray. He tells us that before He chose the twelve He was praying. Here, again, at Cæsarea Philippi, He is seen first praying. We find again in connection with the transfiguration, that Luke says He was praying. And He was praying, before He gave His disciples instructions on prayer. Finally, in Gethsemane, we find He was praying. Thus Luke ever shows the Son of man, the Word incarnate, the Human, living the life of prayer.

There is, however, an arresting statement here. Luke says

"As He was praying apart, the disciples were with Him."

Does that look like a contradiction? The Old Version had it,

"As He was alone praying, His disciples were with Him."

I like that better than the new. Let us read it so;

"He was alone praying, the disciples were with Him."

That is an incidental revelation of the plane of the prayer-life of our Lord. There is a sense in which it is true that our Lord always prayed alone; He always prayed apart, He never really prayed in the fellowship of His disciples. They never moved on His level of prayer. He prayed on a different level. We never pray without having to come to God recognizing our need of some mediation that will admit us to Him. We never pray without a deep sense that we must come on the basis of His mercy, pity, and compassion. Jesus never came that way. He never came in prayer to God needing a mediator between Himself and God. He never came in prayer to God on the basis of Divine mercy or pity. He talked with God familiarly. His was the praying of perfect fellowship. That is what Luke means, "He was alone praying." He was with His disciples; they were there, but He was praying in separation, He was alone praying.

If here we follow the story geographically, we find that He had been leading these disciples for some time towards the northeast region, toward the extreme confine of Jewish territory. If they had gone a little further, they would have been over the line into another land. He led them up into the rocky fastnesses of Cæsarea Philippi. Evidently He had been leading this group of His disciples away from the crowds.

Then, one day, when they were alone, He asked them a question,

"Who do the multitudes say that I am?"

He did not ask them to tell Him what the rulers were saying about Him. He did not ask them to tell Him what the priests were saying about Him. He did not ask them to tell Him the opinion of kings or procurators or imperators concerning Him. There is a sense in which He ignored all the things that gave men prestige or privilege. He was not concerned. He was concerned about the people. A little more than fifty years ago there was a movement in England. It was supposed to be political. As a matter of fact, it was profoundly religious. I refer to the Chartist movement. It was so called because a body of men drew up a charter, demanding from the Government certain rights and privileges for the people. Many of those Chartists were put in prison. One of their number, Ebenezer Eliott, was a poet, and he wrote,

"When wilt Thou save the people?
  O God of mercy, when?
Not kings and lords, but nations!
  Not thrones and crowns, but men!
Flowers of Thy heart, O God, are they;

Let them not pass, like weeds away—
Their heritage a sunless day—
  God save the people!"

That is what Jesus felt.

"Who do the multitudes say that I am?"

Then they told Him, and they only told Him the best things they had heard. Some said He was John. But John was beheaded and dead. Others said He was Elijah. They had been looking for some coming of Elijah. Others, one of the old prophets. It was remarkable testimony. In every case the things said, revealed the fact that men had discovered in Him something supernatural. Then He brought the great crisis, as He said,

"But who say ye that I am?"

Are you agreeing with these reports, you men who have been with Me through these three years, twelve of you, in intimate companionship, My chosen men, the men I selected to be with Me, and whom I have sent out. What do you say about Me? Do you agree with these views? Who do you say that I am? Simon, the representative, spokesman for the rest, then declared that He was "The Christ of God."

Then the threefold revelation. We have the first in the confession made that He was "The Christ of God." The very simplicity of Luke's statement shows the value of the confession. The great fact is crystallized into sharp declaration, "The Christ of God." We can only understand what that meant when we remember that the confession came from a Hebrew. Christ is merely the Anglicized form of the Greek word, and the Greek word is the equivalent of the Hebrew word, Messiah. The Hebrew nation, through all its history, whether on the heights or in the depths, through the shadows or in the sunlight, had looked for the coming of Messiah. To them the Messianic hope had a threefold significance. Messiah to the Hebrew meant the Prophet Who should bring forth a full and final revelation. Messiah to the Hebrew meant the Priest Who should exercise a redeeming mediation. Messiah to the Hebrew meant the King, Who should rule and reign, as absolute Monarch. Sometimes the emphasis was on the prophetic ministry of Messiah, sometimes on the priestly ministry, sometimes on the kingly. In the time of our Lord they had almost forgotten the priestly and the prophetic, and the emphasis was on the kingly. Here, then, was a man, blunt of speech, of that nation, saying to Jesus, Thou art the Prophet, the Priest, the King, promised, looked for, waited for, now come from God. Thou art the Revealer; Thou art the Redeemer; Thou art the Ruler.

Now put the confession into comparison with other opinions.

"Who do men say that I am?"

Some say John; some Elijah; some, one of the prophets; but this Hebrew said, Thou art not one among others; Thou art *the* One to Whom all the others looked; "The Christ of God." That was the confession. That was the great revelation.

If we ever consent to place Him in the company of others, we insult Him, and degrade Him. The Christ of God is out of the realm of comparison with all others. *The* Prophet, bringing the final revelation; *the* Priest, providing perfect redemption; *the* King, ruling absolutely. Jesus immediately charged them, commanded them to tell this to no man. Did you ever wonder at that? Why did He tell them not to tell that to any man? I think there were two reasons. First because, even though the confession was complete, they did not then understand it, they did not know all that it meant. They had no full apprehension of how that Prophet would reveal the truth, of how that Priest would become Redeemer; of how that King would rule. They were not ready. They had an incomplete understanding. To proclaim Him as the Messiah, Prophet, Redeemer, Ruler, apart from the Cross was to break down. They had to wait. They were not ready.

I think the other reason was that the fact that He is the Messiah can never

be proven by dialectics. No clever argument can bring conviction worth while. Matthew tells us that when Peter made the confession, Jesus said, " Blessed art thou, Simon Bar-Jonah ; for flesh and blood hath not revealed it unto thee, but My Father Who is in heaven."

Conviction of His Messiahship can only come by direct Divine revelation. We get nowhere along the line of the dialectician, nowhere along the line of argument. What we have to do is to bring men to Him, get them face to face with Him, and then the conviction will come from God through Him, as to Who He really is.

Having come to this great revelation of the lonely superlative nature of the Person and of the office of our Lord, He told them that He must

" suffer many things, and be rejected of the elders and chief priests and scribes, and be killed, and the third day be raised up."

This Christ of God must suffer, must be killed, must be raised up. A great " must."

Then He told them how they could be His disciples, and what it involved ; that they had not merely to know the truth about His Messiahship, but they had to conform to His programme.

" If any man would come after Me, let him deny himself, and take up his cross daily, and follow Me."

Continuing, His Messiahship confessed, His Cross declared as absolutely central and necessary, He went on to the inevitable issue and sequence. He said,

" Whosoever shall be ashamed of Me and of My words, of him shall the Son of man be ashamed, when He cometh in His own glory, and the glory of the Father, and of the holy angels."

That was the third element in the revelation. He is coming in His glory, and He is coming in the glory of His Father with the holy angels. That Person, not John, not Elijah, or one of the prophets, but the Christ of God must go by the way of suffering and the Cross and the resurrection, and therefore He must come in His glory. The inevitability of this is patent. He said, If any man shall feel himself disgraced by Me and My words, of him shall the Son of man feel disgraced in the day of His glory. That is the testing day, and if I am ashamed of Him today, He will be ashamed of me then. Why? Because of inherent necessity. If I am ashamed of Him I am ashamed of everything pure, high, noble, beautiful. If I am ashamed of these, then I descend to the low, to the ignoble, the beastly, and He will be ashamed of me in that day of His glory. To that hour we are all moving. Shall we in that hour be among the number of those of whom He is ashamed? That is a question to be answered not in public, but in private. Finally He said,

"I tell you of a truth, There are some of them that stand here, who shall in no wise taste of death, till they see the Kingdom of God."

That is often taken to refer to the transfiguration. I do not so understand it. They did not see the Kingdom of God then. One of the evangelists adds, "coming in power." They did not see it coming in power at the transfiguration. They saw a picture of it; there was a revelation of the order to be set up, but they did not see the Kingdom coming in power when they saw the manifestation of it in the glory of the mount. When did they see the Kingdom of God come? When they saw Him on the Cross, and when they saw Him risen from the dead; then the Kingdom of God had come in power. Not in finality, not in completeness. That will be when He comes in His glory, but it came in power then. They saw it come, when they thought it was all over, and ended. When they saw Him despised and rejected, and spit upon, and put on His bitter Cross, and they thought everything was gone, they saw it come. Presently they knew they had seen it come, when they saw Him alive from the dead, the risen Saviour.

LUKE IX. 28-50

"And it came to pass about eight days after these sayings."

THE time note here is important. "About eight days after." After what? "After these sayings." After what sayings? The sayings that we were considering together in our last study. We shall best be prepared for this particular study, if we at once put ourselves into the place of the disciples.

What had just happened? The Christ had been confessed, and the confession had been confirmed by Jesus. The great hour had come, and Simon, spokesman of the little band of disciples, had declared the tremendous truth that Jesus was "the Christ of God." That must have been an hour of joy to the disciples. Then immediately the Lord had declared to them for the first time in the process of His teaching, that He must go to the Cross, and they were at once unutterably bewildered. They could not understand how the Messiah could carry out His great Messianic mission, if He should be put to death. They were bewildered, and in connection with those sayings our Lord had indicated to them parenthetically, but none the less definitely, that He was coming into His Kingdom, that He was coming to His crowning, and that He Himself would come with the holy angels. We can understand their bewilderment.

Now, "After about eight days." We have no record in either of the Gospel stories of what happened during those intervening days. This silence is very suggestive. Remember where they were, at Cæsarea Philippi, amid its rocky fastnesses; and assuming that the transfiguration took place not at Tabor, but on Mount Hermon, it looks as though during those six days, they stayed up there quietly, and I cannot help believing that they were six days in which these men were strangely bewildered, six days perhaps, of silence six intervening days, in which our blessed Lord gave Himself to quietness. So in close connection as to the event, but separated by a week of time, we come to the narrative.

In it there are four movements, marked by four localities. First we see the mountain, verses twenty-eight to thirty-six. Then we are in the valley at the foot of the mountain, verses thirty-seven to forty-three. Then we are travelling along the highway, verses forty-three to forty-five. Finally we are in Capernaum, the base of His operations, verses forty-six to fifty.

Now let us take the first; on the mount, verses twenty-eight to thirty-six. He

" went up into the mountain to pray."

He went into solitude, and while He was in communion with God in the loneliness of the mountain, He was transfigured. Worship is the highest function of human nature. Here, then, was the perfect Man, God's second Man, praying. That was His occupation.

As to what took place, Luke does not use the word which Matthew uses and Mark uses. Luke describes an effect, without using the word which reveals the cause. Luke says, "As He was praying," the appearance of His face, "the fashion of His countenance" became other, it was changed. He does not give any description beyond that, but he adds this remarkable thing,

" His raiment became white and dazzling."

We have a fine word there, " dazzling." The old word was " glistering." Now, the word that really helps us, because it baffles us, is lightning. His raiment became white and lightning, flashing with splendour. His raiment took on the appearance of lightning.

Now, whereas the word is not in Luke, we turn to Matthew and Mark. They say He was transfigured. If we take the Greek word there, and instead of translating it, transliterate it, that is, put into English letters instead of the Greek letters, what do we get? Metamorphosed. That is the actual

word. He was metamorphosed. A metamorphosis is a complete change of form and of appearance. When the chrysallis becomes a butterfly, that is a metamorphosis; the same essential life was in the chrysallis, but in the butterfly the form is changed.

Now mark the significance of it. He was metamorphosed. The thing that happened was not that a light fell on Him, out of heaven, irradiating Him. Neither is it correct to say that on that mount there shone forth His Deity. Deity has no earthly spectacular form of manifestation. What, then, did happen? He came to the completion of His human life, on the level of the earthly, and the beginning of it on the level of the heavenly. The change took place in Him, which prepared Him to leave the world, and pass out into the infinite wonder of the life that lies beyond. He was God's second Man, that is, God's man, realizing God's ideal when He said, " Let Us make man." We do not really know what God meant when He said that, until we have seen Jesus. We go back into Genesis, and read the account of the creation of man, but before we have time to see what man is, man has broken the relationship, the relationship is ruptured, he is a wreck and a ruin. We come down all through the Old Testament, and look at the beacon lights of personality, great men, towering men, splendid men, but not one of them is what God meant when He said, " Let Us make man." We never understand what God meant, until we see this Man. Now, here on the mount, if His only mission in the world is that of realizing and revealing the meaning of humanity, He has done His work. There is no more to do. On the mount He came to the climax, the completion of His own personal, individual, human life. There was no need for Him to die. He was metamorphosed. He might have left the world without dying, so far as He Himself was personally concerned. Death is not the Divine ideal for the consummation of the earthly life of a man. Death is the wage of sin. Death is the result of rupture. If the first man had not sinned, would he have stayed for ever on the earth? Certainly not. Earth is the sphere of probation. If Adam had not sinned, when his earthly career was over, he would have been transfigured, metamorphosed, and by that metamorphosis would have left the world without dying. That is what happened on the holy mount. Jesus was metamorphosed. Here was a Man, God's Man, coming to the true ending of probationary life.

Supposing He had gone out from earth, into the vast amplitudes of those worlds beyond, to which He might have passed then, what then? If I had had the record up to this point, and no more, I should have understood the meaning of human nature, and for evermore have been filled with despair, because I am not that, and I cannot be that. But I should have seen what God meant when He said, " Let Us make man."

Now, what happened? Two men were seen with Him, from the heavenly world, Moses and Elijah, the great lawgiver, and the mighty reforming prophet. They are there. It is very interesting to notice that they were still alive, and still conscious.

What was the subject of their converse? Were they talking about the glory to which by virtue of the sinless perfection and obedience of His life, He had won His way? Were they talking about the metamorphosis that prepared Him for entering upon that life without death? They spake with Him of His decease. What does decease mean? It is an arresting fact that as a result of Christianity, we now use this word of death. Because we use the word decease of death, we are inclined to say they were talking about His death. Yes, but infinitely more than that. Decease is the Anglicized form of a Latin word, *decessus,* which means a going out, a going away from. *Decessus* is the Latin equivalent of the Greek word here used, *Exodos.* Now, they spake with Him of the *exodos;* and for our purpose we can change *o* into *u;* they spake with H'm of the exodus which He was about to accomplish at Jerusalem.

Take one other look at the mount.

We are told of the disciples that they " were heavy with sleep." I can understand it. It was night. They were tired. That heavy sleep was possibly the reaction from the six days of mental strain, in which they could not understand what He had been saying about going to Jerusalem to die. Then they awoke, and Luke says, " when they were fully awake," they became conscious of another voice and voices. Then Peter said,

" Master, it is good for us to be here."

What did he mean by that? The last time we heard him say anything was at Cæsarea Philippi; God help You, not that; pity Yourself, not that. He was angry, and Jesus sternly rebuked him. This is the next thing on record that he said;

" Master, it is good for us to be here."

Master, this is how we want to see Thee, in Thy glory, conversing with these heavenly visitors, coming in Thy power and beauty; it is good to be here. Let us stop here. I must not put too much emphasis upon what he said, because Luke says he did not know what he said. Yet the *here* is certainly emphatic.

Then there came a cloud and overshadowed them; and

" they feared as they entered into the cloud."

What made them fear as they entered into the cloud? I think that demands another question. What sort of cloud was it that overshadowed them? We often imagine the cloud that overshadowed them on Hermon, was one of the clouds with which we are familiar. It was not so. It was a cloud of angels, a bright cloud, the same kind of cloud that greeted Him when presently He ascended; a bright cloud of angelic hosts appeared; and they feared as they entered the cloud.

Then they heard a voice, and with the sounding of the voice the cloud passed, the angels went back, Moses and Elijah went back; but the Voice said:

"This is My Son, My Chosen; hear ye Him."

Peter had just said, It is good to be here on the mount, in the glory, not going to Jerusalem to suffer and die. Jesus had said He must go to Jerusalem. He had talked about going with Moses and Elijah. Simon said, No, let us stay here. God said, This is My Son, My Chosen, hear Him. Do we wonder that when they came down from the mountain,

"they held their peace, and told no man in those days any of the things which they had seen"?

And now we see this Man, fulfilling the Divine ideal, passing not out to the worlds beyond, but going down into the valley of earth. The only One Who realized the Divine ideal, has left the mount for the valley. What is that which confronts Him down there in the valley? A laddie, twisted, distorted, writhing, foaming at his mouth. What is the matter with him? He is demon-possessed. Who is that boy? It is very interesting, it is more than interesting, it is arresting, that his father said, "He is mine only child," or to translate literally, "an only-begotten he is to me." Mark the vividness of this fact of contrast. In the valley an only-begotten son of a man, demon-possessed. Coming down from the mount the Only-begotten Son of God. If He had never come down from the mountain that boy would have remained in that condition. But He came down. "Being found in fashion as a man," on the mount of transfiguration, He has humbled Himself and come down; and in coming down has power that enables Him to deal with that boy, to cast the demon out.

Having given the boy back to his father, Jesus and His disciples travelled back south towards Capernaum. As they journeyed,

"He said unto His disciples, Let these words sink into your ears; for the Son of man shall be delivered up into the hands of men. But they understood not this saying, and it was concealed from them, that they should not perceive it; and they were afraid to ask Him about this saying."

He was insisting again upon the necessity for the Cross. He had talked to them about it at Cæsarea Philippi eight days before, and they were afraid. They went to the mount; they heard Moses and Elijah talk about it. They heard the voice of God saying, This is My Son, hear Him; and now they had seen that demon cast out; and as they travelled, He again told them that He must be delivered up into the hands of men, and charged them to let the words "sink into their ears."

They arrived, and came into the house. They had been through all these experiences, and yet when they came back into the house they were reasoning and questioning among themselves, as to who was the greatest. Then He took a child and set him in the midst, and He said in effect: If you receive that child, you receive Me, he is My ambassador. If you receive Me, you receive God. I am God's Ambassador. The man among you that is the least, that is the great man.

And then John was seeing things. He saw that act, and heard what Jesus said; and he saw that he had done something wrong. John said in effect, I have played the fool; there was a man, and he did a thing, and he did it in Thy name, but because he was not with us, we forbad him.

"Jesus said unto him, Forbid him not; for he that is not against you is for you."

He may not follow with us, he may not say shibboleth as I say it, siboleth; his accent may not be your accent; his method may not be your method; but if in the name of Christ he is casting the demon out, don't forbid him. He that is not against you is for you.

So ends the story as Luke tells it of the great central period in the ministry of our Lord.

LUKE IX. 51-62

WE now commence the third and final movement in the Gospel according to Luke. Hence, we follow our Lord through the last six months of His earthly life, to the Cross, and beyond the Cross, until we see Him in resurrection power and glory. Thus we shall see Him proceeding to the accomplishment of that redeeming work through which He, the perfect Man, is able to perfect many sons, and bring them to glory.

In this paragraph we have a revelation of His attitude, the attitude through the whole of this period; and we have illustrations of the principle involved. The revelation of His attitude is found in verse fifty-one; and the illustrations of the principle in verses fifty-two to sixty-two.

We begin, then, with verse fifty-one,

"And it came to pass, when the days were well-nigh come that He should be received up."

In this connection there is a marginal reading. "Gr., were being fulfilled." The Old Version reads,

"And it came to pass when the time was come that He should be received up."

That is infinitely better than the Revised. The translators of the Revised say, "The days were well nigh come," and they tell you in the margin that the Greek is, "were being fulfilled." That is correct, but what it means is not that they had nearly come to the time, but they had actually come to the time, the days were come. The way the Authorized Version has it, interprets the thought of the Greek more accurately than the Revised does. Dr. Moffatt renders it,

"The time for His assumption was now due."

That is excellent interpretation, because "assumption" is a fine translation of the Greek word analepsis;

"The time of His assumption was now due."

I pause with that, because it is important that we should understand what it means. It is often interpreted as referring to our Lord's ascension after His resurrection. Now, as a matter of fact, this does not refer to the ascension at all. The time was not come for the ascension. There was six months before the Cross. What, then, does Luke mean here by His analepsis, His taking up? Not His ascension after the Cross and the resurrection, but His transfiguration. That was the time for His taking up, the time for His assumption was now due. This word analepsis occurs nowhere else in the New Testament. In the Septuagint, the word is used of Elijah's translation, when he was taken up, it is called his analepsis. Now the time for His analepsis was come, an analepsis by metamorphosis.

All we are now to consider depends upon an accurate understanding of this tremendous statement. Our Lord came to the natural ending, that is, the consummation of His sinless life, upon the Mount. If He had no mission in this world other than that of living a perfect human life, and revealing to humanity a perfect ideal, He never need have come back from the Mount. There He was metamorphosed, and the time of His assumption was come.

Now complete the statement. He was not received up.

"He stedfastly set His face to go to Jerusalem."

It was an hour of crisis in which, having realized all that God meant when He said, "Let Us make man," having come to the completion of the ideal, having done with the transient, the earthly, the probationary, He might have been received up; but instead,

"He stedfastly set His face to go to Jerusalem."

The words reveal the attitude of Christ, the mind of Christ, the will of Christ, the consecration of the personality of Christ to something other than that which He had already done.

What, then, was the goal towards which He set His face? Jerusalem. How did He see Jerusalem? What did Jerusalem mean to Him? In the thirteenth chapter, and in verse thirty-four, we find His words:

"O Jerusalem, Jerusalem, that killeth the prophets, and stoneth them that are sent unto her! how often would I have gathered thy children together, even as a hen gathereth her own brood under her wings, and ye would not!"

That is how He saw Jerusalem. He saw Jerusalem hostile to Him. It was hostile to Him in all the elements of its authority, in all the elements of its policies. He had already told His disciples that "He must go to Jerusalem, and suffer many things of the elders," civil rulers; "and chief priests," religious rulers; "and scribes," the moral rulers. The Sanhedrim was made up of elders and priests and scribes, the civic and spiritual and moral rulers. They were all against Him. The whole city in the realm of its authority was hostile to Him, and the people were following their rulers. He knew it. He told His disciples before transfiguration the condition; He told them He must go, and suffer, and be killed. He saw Jerusalem was hostile. What, then? He stedfastly set His face to go to Jerusalem, hostile.

Is that all He saw? In chapter twenty-one, and in verse twenty, He said,

"But when ye see Jerusalem compassed with armies, then know that her desolation is at hand."

And again in verse twenty-four:

"They shall fall by the edge of the sword, and shall be led captive into all the nations; and Jerusalem shall be trodden down of the Gentiles until the times of the Gentiles be fulfilled."

That is how He saw it. I did not finish the reading in chapter thirteen. I read so far as the revelation of what He saw,

"I would have gathered thy children together, even as a hen gathereth her own brood under her wings, and ye would not!"

How did He go on there?

"Behold, your house is left unto you desolate."

"When ye see Jerusalem compassed about with armies, then know that her desolation is at hand."

So that if He saw Jerusalem hostile He saw Jerusalem doomed, and literally doomed, not merely figuratively but actually. He saw what happened actually within a generation, the city encompassed with armies, the Roman eagles passing through, the streets running rivers of blood. The thing happened, and He saw it. When the time was come that He should be received up, He stedfastly set His face to go to Jerusalem, Jerusalem hostile, Jerusalem doomed.

Is that all He saw? No. In Patmos John saw Jerusalem.

"And I saw the holy city, new Jerusalem, coming down out of heaven from God, made ready as a bride adorned for her husband" (Revelation xxi.2).

"And he carried me away in the Spirit to a mountain great and high, and showed me the holy city Jerusalem coming down out of heaven from God" (Revelation xxi.10).

Jesus had that vision long before John had it. Jesus saw Jerusalem rebuilt. He saw that heavenly Jerusalem.

"He stedfastly set His face to go to Jerusalem."

Hostile, doomed, but through the murk and the gloom and the muck and the misery, resulting from their rejection of Him, He saw it rebuilt. He saw the triumph beyond the travail, the victory beyond the apparent defeat.

In this revelation of the attitude of our Lord we see perfect humanity acting in complete union with Deity. Let Paul interpret the thing we are looking at. In that great Philippian passage on the *Kenosis,* when dealing with the Person of our Lord, speaking of His essential Deity, He says, "He emptied Himself." Then when he comes to His perfect humanity, he

says, "He humbled Himself." Watch
the process;

"Who, existing in the form of God,
counted not the being on an equality
with God a thing to be grasped, but
emptied Himself."

That was action wholly within Deity.
Then he told the result;

"taking the form of a Servant, being
made in the likeness of men."

Once more:

"And being found in fashion as a
man."

When was that? When He was born?
No, He was a Baby then. Was it when
He was twelve years of age? No, He
was a Lad then. At thirty years of
age? No, He was mature then. When
He came to the Mount, then He was
" found in fashion as a man." Then
He filled to the full the Divine ideal
of humanity not only as to personal-
ty, but as to perfect functioning.
Then

"He humbled Himself, becoming
obedient unto death, yea, the death of
the Cross."

Thus perfect Humanity is seen *syner-
gic,*—acting together—with God. Here
was perfect harmony between the activity of Deity in the Self-emptying, and
the activity of humanity, "He humbled
Himself." When the time was come
that He should be received up, He
stedfastly set His face to go to Jerusalem, hostile, doomed, rebuilt; in order
that by His going He might perfect
many sons and bring them to glory.
Having thus revealed the attitude of
the Lord, Luke gives three illustrations
of the principle applied. The first was
immediate. When coming back from
the mountain, His face being set towards Jerusalem, a Samaritan village
refused Him; and we find out how
James and John felt; and we hear
what the Lord had to say to them
about their feeling. That is in verses
fifty-two to fifty-six. In verses fifty-
seven to sixty-two we have three men
presented to us. Luke's story is not
in strict chronology. Quite evidently

here he was intending to illustrate, and
so selected three incidents.
First, then, as to the immediate
Samaritan incident. He " sent messengers before His face," and they
went "into a village of the Samaritans, to make ready for Him." When
these Samaritans saw that He was on
His way to Jerusalem, they would not
receive Him. James and John were
true Boanerges, sons of thunder; and
as a quaint old Puritan writer said:

"What wonder the sons of thunder
wanted lightning out of heaven to burn
up the village."

They said,

"Lord, wilt Thou that we bid fire
to come down from heaven, and con-
sume them?"

The Revisers, both English and
American, in giving the reply of our
Lord, relegated some sentences to the
margin which, I think, should be retained in the text. Four of the Codices
omit these things; and there are those
who think that to be sufficient warrant for omitting them in the Revised
Version. I do not agree. Canon Farrar, when it was done, said;

"It is impossible to doubt the genu-
ineness of these things that are now
omitted, because the things omitted
breathe a spirit which is exactly in
accord with the Spirit of Christ, and
it is almost impossible to believe that
Luke wrote no more than that, 'He
rebuked them.'"

They said,

"Lord, wilt Thou that we bid fire
to come down from heaven, and con-
sume them even as Elijah did?"

That was perfectly natural.
He said,

"Ye know not what manner of spirit
ye are of. For the Son of man came
not to destroy men's lives, but to save
them."

His disciples in loyalty, went to a
Samaritan village; and in loyalty,
when the Samaritans would not receive
Him, would have destroyed the Samaritans by fire. It was loyalty, but it was

loyalty out of harmony with the spirit of the Master, and out of harmony with the method of the Master. It is possible to be zealous for the honour of God in a spirit which puts us out of fellowship with God. That is what kept Moses out of the promised land. Loyalty in a wrong spirit. He spake unadvisedly with his lips when he went to the people clamouring for water, and grumbling against God. He smote the rock, and he showed an angry spirit; and God excluded him from the promised land.

Well, what is the true spirit? What did Jesus do?

" They went to another village."

To destroy by fire in loyalty to Him would manifest a spirit contrary to the Cross. His face was towards Jerusalem. That revealed His spirit. That revealed His attitude. He was led as a lamb to the slaughter, as a sheep before her shearers is dumb, so He opened not His mouth. When He was reviled, He reviled not again. That is the spirit of the Cross. The spirit that wants to call down fire upon those that are refusing Jesus Christ is not Christ's spirit, in that it lacks the principle of the Cross. Are we with James and John, loyal, passionately devoted, wanting to destroy men by fire? Our loyalty, because it is in a wrong spirit, puts us out of fellowship with Jesus Christ. Fellowship with Christ means going all the way to Calvary, bearing shame and scoffing rude, with no anger, and no desire to call down fire.

Let us glance at the other three incidents. Three types of men are seen in the presence of the enterprise of Jesus, attracted by Him, wanting to be loyal to Him, desiring to be enrolled under Him, wanting to serve Him, making their suggestions, or stating their difficulties.

The first was a man attracted by Him. The second was a man whom He called to certain and definite relationship with Himself. The third was a man wanting to serve Him, but postponing his service.

The first man came to Jesus.

"A certain man said unto Him, I will follow Thee whithersoever Thou goest."

That was splendid. Don't speak disrespectfully of that man. It was a great outburst. Christ had the man captured at least in the realm of his admiration, admiration expressing itself in devotion. Many commentators criticize him for being impulsive. Is there anything wrong in being impulsive? I love him for it. The Church is starved today for lack of impulsive men who dare say great things like this to Jesus.

What did the Lord say to him? Yet, I do not think I am so concerned with what the Lord said, as with how He said it. He looked at that man and He said,

" Foxes have holes, and the birds of the heaven have nests; but the Son of man hath not where to lay His head."

He said in effect, If you are coming after Me, that is the condition; you have to share that kind of attitude towards the world; the attitude of detachment from all that prevents progress towards Jerusalem. For years I had an idea that there was a sort of sad note in His voice as He said,

" The foxes have holes, and the birds of the heaven have nests; but the Son of man hath not where to lay His head."

I do not think so, now. I believe He was jubilant. I have nothing that holds Me back from My progress to Jerusalem. The Son of man had no anchorage in the world that for a single moment prevented His progress towards the hostile, doomed city, that it might be rebuilt, and become the city of God. When next you quote these words as the words of Jesus, don't pity Him. He does not need your pity. Pity yourself rather if you have a home that holds you back, when Christ wants you out upon the high places of the world. That is the principle. Pity yourself if you are rooted anywhere, when He would have you move to some other place in your pilgrimage.

grimage with Him towards the Cross, and for human redemption. That is the first condition, detachment from everything that prevents progress towards God's ultimate.

Next we have the man to whom Jesus said, "Follow Me." Matthew tells us that this man was a disciple, so the Lord was calling him, not to become a disciple, but to join Him in His enterprises; and he said,

"Lord, suffer me first to go and bury my father."

I think it is very important we should understand what that meant. Some years ago when I had been out in this country, visiting the Northfield Conferences, I had the privilege of travelling back across the Atlantic with Sir George Adam Smith. He told me, once when he was in Palestine, he wanted to get off the beaten track, into an unfamiliar area, and he wanted a guide. He had a young friend, an Arab sheik, and he tried to persuade him to go on the journey to guide him; but he refused. As he was talking to him, the sheik's father was sitting in the door of the tent, hale and hearty, but venerable; and the young Arab said to Sir George,

"Sir, suffer me first to go and bury my father."

His father was not dead, but he was expressing devotion to his father; saying that he could not possibly go away as long as his father was alive. That is what this man said to Jesus. He meant, I want to come, I would like to come, but I have home ties and responsibilities that hold me. I cannot come while my father is living. I will have to stay until he has passed over, and then I will make the great adventure. Quick, sharp, definite, the Lord's word, ringing across the centuries,

"Leave the dead to bury their own dead; but go thou and publish abroad the Kingdom of God."

What did He mean by this? Remember, He had called that man. There was some peculiar quality that made Him want that man immediately.

Therefore His demand was that the man must abandon his nearest and highest earthly tie. Christ's call is superior to the highest and the most beautiful of earth's obligations. That is the Cross. Christ had flashed upon him the light of a tremendous enterprise, the enterprise of preaching the Kingdom of God; and that demanded the abandonment of the earthly tie, when it conflicted with the call of his Lord.

The last example is that of a man who said,

"I will follow Thee, Lord; but first suffer me to bid farewell to them that are at my house."

Thou hast captured me, and all Thy purposes appeal to me; I will follow Thee, but suffer me first to bid farewell to them that are at my house. What did Christ say to that man?

"No man, having put his hand to the plow, and looking back, is fit for the Kingdom of God."

Again quick, sharp as a knife, decisive, what is this? The same principle of the Cross. Fidelity to Him through all the processes, allowing nothing to hinder them for a moment.

Group the three illustrations, and we find His threefold demand. Detachment from all that hinders progress, no anchorage that holds me back, when He wants me to be marching with Him. When the highest earthly love and obligation comes into conflict with my loyalty to Him, then let the dead bury their own dead; I am to go for Him and upon His business. When the hand is upon the plow, to look back, is to be unfit for the Kingdom of God.

Observe carefully that everything that our Lord demanded here, He was Himself already doing. In the demands He made upon these men, we have an interpretation of His face set to Jerusalem. The first is self-evident. He named Himself. If you are coming after Me, here is the way I am travelling. Foxes have holes, and the birds of the heaven have nests; but the Son of man has no shelter from the storms, no place to lay His head:

nothing that hinders Him for a single moment in the onward progress.

Let the dead bury their dead; abandonment of the nearest earthly tie, when it conflicts with the purpose and the passion that moves toward Jerusalem. That was His attitude. One day Mary, who loved Him with a great love, was somewhere in the neighbourhood of Nazareth, and she heard He was tiring Himself out, and wearing Himself out; and she thought He was going to kill Himself, and that He was beside Himself; and she took a long journey to try and stop Him; and when she arrived, He was still in the house, and the crowds were about Him, so that He had no time to eat. She got a message in to Him, and they said, Your Mother and brethren are outside, wanting to see You. Tender, beautiful words; He knew why she was there; and He said, Who is My Mother, and who are My brethren? They that do the will of My Father. Even the sweet and beautiful kinship on the earthly level, that of His Mother, so tender

that in the agony of the Cross He thought of her, and provided for her; yet when out of affection she would hinder Him, He swept all aside, and said, Nearer of kin to Me than the Mother of My flesh, are the men who do the will of God, who fulfil the purpose of God.

" No man, having put his hand to the plow, and looking back, is fit for the Kingdom of God."

Don't you see Him? Take the first verse of this paragraph, and take the last. Put them together.

" He stedfastly set His face to go to Jerusalem."

" No man, . . . looking back, is fit for the Kingdom."

He was not looking back. He never looked back. He set His face to go until He came to hostility, to doom to death; and through all to the travail that makes the Kingdom sure.

LUKE X. 1-24

HERE we begin a section of the Gospel according to Luke which is peculiar to that Gospel. From chapter ten to chapter eighteen, as far as verse fourteen, we have material not found in Matthew, Mark, or John, except for the paragraph xi.14-32, in which, for purposes of illustration, Luke goes back in chronological sequence to something which Matthew and Mark show had taken place earlier in Galilee. Most of the ministry of our Lord at this time was being conducted in the country on " the other side Jordan," which now we usually call Peræa. Jerusalem and Judæa constituted the centre; that was the land of pride, and prejudice, and supposed privilege. To the north was Samaria, the region toward which Judæa felt perpetual hostility. Further north was Galilee. " Galilee of the Gentiles " was a term of contempt. Judæa held Galilee in contempt. There was a third region. It lay on the " other side Jordan," and the attitude of Judæa to

it was not that of hostility, nor yet that of contempt, it was that rather of indifference. Peræa was the most neglected area, from the standpoint of the religious ministry emanating from Jerusalem and Judæa. Samaria hated, Galilee held in contempt, Peræa neglected.

If that be understood, we at once see the suggestiveness of the fact that most of the last six months in the ministry of our Lord was spent over Jordan, in the neglected area. Luke has told us in this section, chapters ten to eighteen, verse fourteen, largely about that ministry. Matthew and Mark tell us nothing of the period. John does record some incidents that took place then, two visits our Lord paid to Jerusalem, a time of quiet retirement in Bethabara beyond Jordan, and the raising of Lazarus. John, however, tells us nothing that Luke does, and Luke tells us nothing that John does.

In the paragraph now under consideration (x.1-24), we have the account of the mission of the seventy. That mission was something quite new in the method of Jesus. It was a planned campaign. In the first three years of His ministry there seems to have been an absence of what we should call organization. Here, on the contrary, is the account of carefully organized work. He

" appointed seventy others, and sent them two and two before His face into every city and place, whither He Himself was about to come."

It was the last movement in His public ministry, and He planned, what we should be inclined to call today, an intensive campaign. He intended to visit a great many places, and He had selected the places. They were in this neglected area, on the other side of the Jordan. To those selected cities He sent the seventy men, two by two; thirty-five teams to cover the ground, in preparation for His last personal intensive campaign; not in Judæa, the land of privilege; not in Samaria, the country hated by Judæa; not in Galilee, held in contempt by Judæa; but in the neglected area of Peræa.

The story falls into three parts; first, the charge He laid upon the seventy, verses two to sixteen; secondly, their report of their work, verse seventeen; and finally, what He said to them about their report, verses eighteen to twenty-four.

The charge to the seventy is characterized by similarity to that delivered to the twelve as recorded in the tenth chapter of the Gospel according to Matthew; but there are differences. When He sent these men out, He gave them no charge to cast out demons, or to raise the dead. They did cast out demons, as we shall see. I merely point out now that He did not tell them to do so. This was evidently a hurried and temporary piece of work.

What, then, were they to do? Two things,

" Heal the sick; . . . and say . . . The Kingdom of God is come nigh unto you " (verse nine).

He gave them authority and power to heal the sick, but their main business was to say,

" The Kingdom of God is come nigh unto you."

That, in essence, is the exact equivalent of the declaration that

" The Kingdom of heaven is at hand."

Now, what was the inspiration of that planned campaign in the heart of our blessed Lord? What did He see, that made Him select those seventy men, and send them out two by two? The answer to that question is found in the first thing He said.

" The harvest is plenteous, but the labourers are few."

He saw harvest. What, then, did our Lord see that He described as harvest? There are three occasions on record upon which He used that figure of speech, to describe what He saw; and seeing which, His compassion was moved. The first time in chronological sequence is recorded by John. When He was in Samaria He said,

" Say not ye, There are yet four months, and then cometh the harvest? behold, I say unto you, Lift up your eyes, and look on the fields, that they are white already unto harvest."

If the disciples had been constituted a committee to investigate the condition of Samaria as a field of operations for the Christian enterprise, I know exactly what their findings would have been. They would have examined the country, and the people, and would have gone back into the history, and they would have said: Without any doubt, Samaria needs the Gospel of Christ; but it is a terribly hard field, there is a great deal to be done before we can hope to see any results. We shall have to plough up the fallow ground, and sow the seed, and wait patiently for the harvest; " four months, and then cometh the harvest." That was their outlook, but He said:

" I say unto you, Lift up your eyes

and look on the fields, that they are white already to harvest."

They would postpone harvest. He said harvest was ready. But it was a desolate country. The Samaritans were dark and benighted. Exactly, said Christ, and that constitutes harvest for Me!

The second time He used the figure of harvest was in Galilee. Matthew tells us in the ninth chapter that He

"went about all the cities and villages teaching, . . . preaching . . . and healing. But when He saw the multitudes, He was moved with compassion for them, because they were distressed and scattered, as sheep not having a shepherd. Then saith He unto His disciples, The harvest indeed is plenteous."

He saw the multitudes distressed, scattered, fleeced, harried by wolves, fainting, dying, and He said, that is harvest.

This story of the sending out of the seventy records the third time of His using the figure. He was now in the neglected area. First in the hated country; secondly in the country held in contempt; and finally in the neglected country. That reveals the inspiration of this campaign. If you know of any country that is more difficult than another, anywhere, submerged in the darkness of a false form of religion, that is harvest. Wherever there is dereliction and desolation on earth, Christ says that is where our harvest is.

In the charge, two commands were given these men; first, pray; secondly, go. Pray.

"Pray ye therefore the Lord of the harvest;"

and when you have prayed, that is not enough;

"Go your ways; behold, I send you."

All their authority is found in those four words; "Behold, I send you." Where shall we place the emphasis in that sentence? Not on the "you." "I send *you*." Put it on the "*I*." "*I* send you," so that when they went.

they knew they went under His charge, and the responsibility of their selection and sending rested on Him.

He called them to poverty. As they went,

"Carry no purse, no wallet, no shoes."

The purse was for money, the wallet was for food, the shoes were for change for ease.

There was to be no delay.

"Salute no man on the way."

Salutations in the East take up much time. No such waste of time was to be permitted.

He then gave them the manner of salutation they were to employ;

"Into whatsoever house ye shall enter, first say, Peace to this house."

As a matter of fact, He told them, When you enter the house, adopt the ordinary salutation, the thing you are constantly saying, Peace be unto you; but in their case it would have a new and richer content and significance;

"And if a son of peace be there, your peace shall rest upon him; but if not, it shall turn to you again."

Observe the next thing:

"In that same house remain, eating and drinking such things as they give; for the labourer is worthy of his hire. . . . Go not from house to house."

The last thing He told them was,

"He that heareth you heareth Me; and he that rejecteth you rejecteth Me; and he that rejecteth Me rejecteth Him that sent Me."

Those seventy men were sent out to represent Him, and to represent God. Therefore those men representing God, came with one great message,

"The Kingdom of God is come nigh unto you."

Then follows the account of their return and report.

"And the seventy returned with joy, saying, Lord, even the demons are subject unto us in Thy name."

He did not send them to cast out demons. When they came back, they had had so successful a time, that they said to Him in effect: "We have delivered the message; we have done what we were told; and more, *even* the demons, that Thou didst not mention, are subject to us in Thy name." That was their report. They reported success in excess.

It is significant that when they came back, they reported to Him. I sometimes think that one of the things that has hindered Christian work has been reports made in public meetings, and printed. It would be a great thing if we only reported to Jesus. That was true, also, of the twelve. We should like to know more about those cities they visited; the names of them, and the sizes of the congregations, and the numbers of the sons of peace they found, and the centres where they did their best work. But why do we hanker after such particulars? Our passion for statistics is self-centred, and of the flesh, and not of the Spirit.

Finally, let us examine what He had to say to them. What were His comments on their report? He said first;

"I beheld Satan fallen as lightning from heaven."

That is the whole story of Satan, from His view-point. "I beheld Satan fallen;" that is the origin of him, that is how he came to be what he is. "I beheld Satan fallen;" that is the history of him. "I beheld Satan fallen;" that is the destiny of him. They came back, and were a little astonished that the demons had been subject unto them. In effect He said that they need not be. He knew the truth about Satan; the initial truth, the abiding truth, the universal truth; truth from the standpoint of the government and authority of God; "I beheld Satan fallen." "Behold, I have given you authority." "I beheld Satan fallen," "I send you," "I have given you authority." That accounted for the victories they had gained.

Therefore He said more;—

"Nevertheless in this rejoice not, that the spirits are subject unto *you*."

Here the emphasis was surely on the "you." He was criticizing them, He was reproving them. But there is a wonderfully beautiful touch to finish with. He said:

"Rejoice that your names are written in heaven."

Link that up with the thing already said. "I beheld Satan fallen from heaven," "your names are written in heaven." You are burgesses of heaven from which Satan has fallen. In your relationship with Me, you are living in that realm that is higher than Satan, and master of Satan. Your names are written in heaven. Do not rejoice in that which is personal, in your success. Rejoice for evermore in the fact that you belong to the heaven, and the throne, and the God, and the Kingdom, which are victorious over all the power of the enemy.

Carefully observe the end of the story.

"In that same hour He rejoiced in the Holy Spirit."

There was no depression in His mind. The word "rejoiced" here means He exulted in the Spirit. Why this exultation? The answer is found in what He said to His Father.

"I thank Thee, O Father, Lord of heaven and earth, that Thou didst hide these things from the wise and understanding"—

that is, the clever people, who put two and two together, and say they are four, and see no more, the mathematicians. The more is hidden from them, but revealed to babes. Christ rejoiced in the fact that the deep and profound things of the Kingdom of God are clear to babes, even though they are hidden from clever people.

"Yea, Father; for so it was well-pleasing in Thy sight."

Then addressing Himself again to the seventy, He said things that on another occasion Matthew records Him saying;

"All things have been delivered unto Me of My Father; and no one knoweth

Who the Son is, save the Father; and Who the Father is, save the Son, and he to whomsoever the Son willeth to reveal Him."

Then turning to His disciples, He said privately; not to the crowd:

" Blessed are the eyes which see the things that ye see; for I say unto you, that many prophets and kings desired to see the things which ye see, and saw them not; and to hear the things which ye hear, and heard them not."

That reveals Christ's consciousness of the greatness of His own mission.

The story of the seventy is a wonderful story, telling of an intensively planned campaign in the neglected area; the things that happened, the teaching that emerged; and the instruction of a group of men for their work. The principles underlying it abide for all time, and it has its living message for us.

LUKE X. 25-42

IN this paragraph we have two incidents in the ministry of our Lord, full of light and full of colour. The first is that of the question of the lawyer, which called forth the parable of the Good Samaritan. That occupies verses twenty-five through thirty-seven. The second is that of a glimpse of the home at Bethany. That is found in verses thirty-eight to forty-two.

The story of the lawyer begins;

"And behold, a certain lawyer stood up and made trial of Him, saying, Teacher, what shall I do to inherit eternal life?"

The Authorized Version read, "tempted;" the Revisers have changed it to "made trial of." The word Luke employed is a singularly strong verb. It is an intensive form of the ordinary word. We only find it in two other connections in the New Testament. The evangelists who record the temptation of our Lord do not use the word concerning His temptation; but they do use the word when they are reporting what Jesus said to the devil;

" Thou shalt not tempt the Lord thy God."

The only other place we find it is in I Corinthians, ten, nine, where Paul is warning men against tempting Jesus Christ. The word may be rendered thus;

"A certain lawyer stood up and put Him thoroughly to the test."

This man may have been asking a very genuine question. I am rather inclined to think this lawyer had listened to Him, and now stood up, and put a question to Him which, in his view, would put Jesus thoroughly to the test. On the other hand, it may have been a malicious question. In either case it was a supreme question;

" What shall I do to inherit eternal life?"

There is no greater question than that. For us, this phrase " eternal life " is baptized and suffused with redeeming grace, but as the lawyer used it, it was not so. The phrase was a common one in the theology of the times. We find it occurring in the Rabbinical writings. Hillel said this, " He that gets to himself words of Torah "—that is, the Law—" gets to himself eternal life." By the phrase these men meant life, not merely that lasts, but that is full, complete, full-orbed, a life that is life indeed. This lawyer said, Teacher, what shall I do to gain eternal life? It was a great question, and he asked Him the question, putting Him thoroughly to the test.

The Lord replied:

" What is written in the law? how readest thou?"

He sent this man back to law, and he was a lawyer. Christ said to him in effect, You are asking a question, but you have your answer. Your answer is in the realm in which you are a specialist, an expert. You ask Me how you are to gain life, eternal life, fullorbed life; well, what is written in the law, how do you read it? " He answering said," evidently quickly, confidently, without hesitation,

"Thou shalt love the Lord thy God with all thy heart, and with all thy soul, and with all thy strength, and with all thy mind; and thy neighbour as thyself."

Jesus said,

"Thou hast answered right; this do, and thou shalt live."

That is very arresting. Later on, in the history of Jesus, as Matthew tells us in the twenty-second chapter, He was in the Temple, and we read in verse thirty-four:

"But the Pharisees, when they heard that He had put the Sadducees to silence, gathered themselves together. And one of them, a lawyer, asked Him a question, trying Him,"—

that is not the same word there for trying, it is a weaker word,—

"Teacher, which is the great commandment in the law? And He said unto him, Thou shalt love the Lord thy God with all thy heart, and with all thy soul, and with all thy mind. This is the great and first commandment. And a second like unto it is this, Thou shalt love thy neighbour as thyself. On these two commandments the whole law hangeth, and the prophets."

Thus, later on, when Christ was asked for the great commandment, which had in it the content of everything in the law, He quoted exactly what the ruler had quoted to Him. That is the secret of eternal life.

The next thing we read is:

"But he, desiring to justify himself, said unto Jesus."

This does not prove that he was not sincere at the beginning; but he had been brought crash up against something which he knew; and now he wanted to justify himself. He said to Jesus,

"And who is my neighbour?"

He had been hard hit. He had to find some way out. He knew he had not eternal life, and he wanted an excuse for not having it. He wanted to jus-

tify himself for breaking law, so he raised the question, "Who is my neighbour?"

For answer, Christ told him a story, asked him a question about it, and said, "Go, and do thou likewise."

The first thing which arrests me in reading the story is that Christ never answered the question the lawyer asked. In His reply He changed the whole emphasis of the man's question. The man said, I am, according to law, to love my neighbour; who is my neighbour? Christ's answer did not tell him who was his neighbour. The whole point of Christ's answer is this: The question is not who your neighbour is, but are you a neighbour? The Samaritan was neighbour to the man; the priest was not a neighbour, the Levite was not a neighbour. The Samaritan was the man who came into his neighbourhood. He came over to him, and bound up his wounds, and put him on his own beast, and brought him to the inn, and took care of him. The lawyer said, Who is my neighbour? Christ replied: Be a neighbour, and the moment you are a neighbourly man, you will find your neighbour in the man that needs your help. He said, Who is my neighbour? Who am I to love? Christ said in effect, It you are what you ought to be, if you really love God, then you will love man; and you will find your neighbour in the man that otherwise you would not look at. The priest and the Levite passed by, because there was no compassion in them. There was no compassion, because they were not loving God, and therefore they had not made the road safe originally, and, when they saw the man who had fallen among robbers, they passed by on the other side, the safe side.

The lawyer admitted that the Samaritan was neighbour to the man. Then, said Jesus, Go and do likewise, that is all. Mark the recurrence of the word "do" in the story. The man said, "What shall I *do?*" Jesus said, "This *do* and thou shalt live," what the law tells you, do it, and live; and then when the man had tried to evade the issue, and justify himself, He said. "Go, and *do* thou likewise."

There is life in keeping the law, but I have not kept it, and I cannot keep it in my own strength. Then He comes, and He gives me life. I am born anew, and now I can begin to do; and before He has done with me, I shall perfectly do all that the law demands. There are some old-fashioned statements which are very fine. My father often used to say, The difference between Law and Grace is this. The Law says, Do this, and live. Grace says, Live and do this. The new life is not intended to set us free from the moral requirement of law. It is to enable us to obey it.

Then follows the picture of the home at Bethany. Luke says, "In a certain village." John gives us the name, Bethany. Luke says that Martha received Him into her house, and she had a sister called Mary. Mary is quite secondary. When John writes, he says, "the village of Mary, and her sister Martha." Luke says that the house belonged to Martha. John says the village belonged to Mary! Evidently Martha was the householder. If you had called, she would have interviewed you!

Luke tells us of a day when Jesus came as Guest. What a day it was for them. Perhaps that was the first time they had entertained Him, but more likely He had often found His way to the home.

Now look at those two women. Of Martha, Luke tells us she "was cumbered about much serving;" a far better word for us today, with our modern method of speech, is the word *distracted*. She was distracted by much serving. What a great soul this Martha was. Jesus was the Guest, and the one thing of supreme importance in the heart of Martha was that He should have adequate welcome. I can see her. I have met her in this life, haven't you? Those hurrying feet, those swiftly moving fingers; love suddenly suggesting something else to make the welcome more perfect. Love always multiplies itself. She went to do something, and on her way, love suggested two other things, and she moved a little more quickly; and while she was going to do these, four were

suggested; and then she hurried after the four, and by the time she has begun those, the four are eight things crowding in; and by the time eight are begun, there are sixteen, and so she became distracted! God bless her; a great soul. But she was trying to express love in service, and it reacted. It was a sad reaction. She got so distracted, that the next thing we see her doing,—think of it,—this woman whose one concern was to make Jesus welcome;—we see her rushing in and complaining of His carelessness as well as her sister's. She said, "Dost Thou not care?"

Now look at Mary. What is she doing?

"She had a sister called Mary, who sat at the Lord's feet, and heard His word."

Is that right? It certainly is not right. There is a little word there, "also,"

"Who *also* sat at the Lord's feet, and heard His word."

What is the meaning of the "also"? It might mean that Martha sat at His feet, and Mary also sat at His feet; but if it means that, the story is gone, and there is no sense in it. It must therefore mean that Mary had taken her part in service, "who *also* sat at the Lord's feet." Martha goes on and on until she is distracted; but Mary *also* sat at His feet. That is a most vital distinction. Some people seem to imagine that all she did was to sit herself down, to have a good time. If she had done that, Christ would never have commended her. Mary knew the one deep secret that love cannot finally express itself in service. It must take the place of devotion, of discipleship.

That I am not imagining all this is found if we consider the Saviour's appraisement of the two women. Very tenderly but very definitely He rebuked Martha. He said:

"Martha, Martha, thou art anxious and troubled about many things; but one thing is needful."

He did not say the many things were wrong, but He said you have not added to the many, the one, which is the supreme necessity, the one thing of discipleship, of learning that in relationship to Me, you must not only give, you must take time to receive; you must sit at My feet, and learn of Me. So He commended Mary. He said, "One thing is needful," and Mary has it, has chosen it, the one supreme necessity. That is the way Mary's character was strengthened, by

sitting at those feet. "One thing needful." Mary had learned that secret.

God give us to know what it is to combine service with worship. That story is finished in the eleventh chapter of John; and in the twelfth of John. In them we see both those women again, and what the passing of time did for them.

LUKE XI. 1-32

WE now survey the paragraph found in Luke eleven, verses one to thirty-two. Let us first examine the method of Luke in this paragraph. Following the life of our Lord chronologically, there is a gap between chapters ten and eleven. John fills that gap in chapters nine and ten, so far as verse twenty-one. Between the things recorded in chapter ten of Luke, and the things which he is now about to record, Jesus went up to Jerusalem, and there opened the eyes of the man born blind.

The story in the first thirteen verses of Luke eleven is concerned with the matter of prayer. Then at verse fourteen, and to the end of the thirty-second verse, Luke goes back to something that had occurred at an earlier period. He begins, "And He was casting out a demon"—showing that he was looking back. Unquestionably he went back to those incidents to illustrate something, that we find in these first thirteen verses. In Matthew twelve, we find the story of the casting out of the demons in the synagogue, and of the critics of Jesus, and of His use of the parable of the tenantless house. Here again, however, in verses twenty-seven and twenty-eight, we have something peculiar to Luke. Matthew tells us, also, about the sign of Jonah.

Our next study will begin with verse thirty-three, where Luke continues the story begun in the first thirteen verses. Let me read verses thirteen and thirty in close connection:

"If ye then, being evil, know how to give good gifts unto your children, how much more shall your heavenly Father

give the Holy Spirit to them that ask Him? . . . No man, when he hath lighted a lamp, putteth it in a cellar, neither under the bushel, but on the stand, that they which enter in may see the light."

That is the connection in the discourse; but between, Luke records certain earlier events in illustration of a truth emerging in the first thirteen verses. So we may divide our paragraph thus: First, verses one to thirteen, instruction concerning prayer; and verses fourteen to thirty-two, an excursus in illustration.

The occasion of the particular instruction our Lord gave His disciples concerning prayer was that of a definite request. What called forth that request?

"It came to pass, as He was praying in a certain place, that when He ceased—."

They had watched Him at prayer. Nobody can tell whether it would be correct to say that they had heard Him pray. I do not know whether He was praying silently, or whether He was praying audibly; but quite evidently they had watched Him. I have no doubt, as was His wont, He was praying alone. In chapter nine, at verse eighteen, we read:

"It came to pass, as He was praying alone, or apart, the disciples were with Him."

They were still there, but He was praying apart. My own conviction is that He was doing that here, also.

"It came to pass as He was praying in a certain place, that when He ceased, one of His disciples said unto Him."

The occasion of His teaching, then, was a request preferred, when His disciples had watched; and I think possibly had listened to Him praying alone. They had seen Him, and they had possibly heard Him; and His praying inspired them with a passion to do the same thing.

Now, what was the request? They did not say, Lord, teach us *how* to pray. They said, "Lord, teach us to pray." They were not asking Him to teach them how to do it. He had done that, in the great Manifesto. I am convinced, as I ponder this narrative, that what they felt that day is exactly what we have all felt some time or other, not that we wanted to know *how* to do it, but that we wanted to be taught to *do* it. They did not want a philosophy of prayer, or the interpretation of a method. They wanted somehow to be able to pray like He prayed.

"Lord, teach us to pray, even as John also taught his disciples."

That is a little window throwing light on the ministry of John. It is evident that John had taught his disciples, that John's prayer-life had influenced his disciples. These disciples had seen Jesus enter into the region of prayer. They saw Jesus praying on some higher level than that in which John prayed. There was something more in the praying of Jesus than even the praying of John. They said in effect, John taught his disciples. They learned the lessons. Teach us to pray. Lift us on to Thy level of prayer.

He answered them; first, He gave them a model of prayer; and then He gave them a philosophy of prayer.

First, as to the model.

"And He said unto them, When ye pray, say, Father, Hallowed be Thy name. Thy Kingdom come. Give us day by day our daily bread. And forgive us our sins, for we ourselves also forgive every one that is indebted to us. And bring us not into temptation."

Now, as we read that, we all real-

ize that we have heard it in substance before, in the sequence of our Lord's ministry. They knew it, too. He took some of the petitions out of a prayer that He had already given them in a complete form, in the ethical Manifesto. I am insisting upon time notes, because if we are to get the value of the teaching, we must get back into their mind, and see the point at which He said these things to them. When they said, Teach us to pray, He said in effect: I have already taught you the form, and given you the field of it. He did not now repeat the whole prayer, but He gave sentences from it. Surely He was flinging them back upon the fact that He had already given them the perfect model.

The nature of prayer is revealed in the full model, and in the sentences from it which our Lord quoted here. What are the first things we are to say?

"Father, Hallowed be Thy name. Thy Kingdom come."

He has only taken two sentences, but we interpret them by the whole, and find that He said in effect: the first activity of prayer is not that of getting something for ourselves, but of getting something for God. Take it in its entirety.

"Our Father Who art in the heavens."

What are we to ask for? That His name may be hallowed on earth, that His Kingdom may come on earth, that His will may be done on earth. The first passion of prayer is a passion that God's will may be done, that God's heart may be satisfied, that God's purposes may be realized. That is the first realm in which prayer is to operate. Praying to God, on behalf of God.

"The Son of man came to seek and to save that which was lost."

When we say a man is lost, what do we mean by lost? We think immediately of the man's dereliction, and the man's punishment, and the man's condemnation. But we are not thinking in the right order. If we have lost something, and talk about it as being lost, the word lost reveals our loss; and it is not the thing we think about, but the *person* who has lost it. A very simple illustration may help us. I remember when my youngest boy was about six or seven years old. His mother and he were out in London, in a London fog. They were in a motor bus, and when it stopped, the mother got out, and waited for the laddie to get out. For some reason he was a bit slow, and on went the bus, into the fog, with the boy. He was lost. Who do you think suffered the most in the few minutes he was lost, the boy or the mother? The mother suffered most. I am not saying the boy did not suffer, but the agony of the mother's heart was the greater. When you think about a lost soul, think about God! All the passion of Calvary pulsates through the petitions of this prayer. "Thy name be hallowed." God's name has been blasphemed. "Thy Kingdom come." He is being robbed of His own possession.

"Thy will be done; on earth as in heaven."

First pray to God on behalf of God. That is the first realm of prayer.

Then what? Once more, a couple of sentences out of the complete prayer. First on behalf of God, then on behalf of man. When we get there, notice the limitations of prayer. Bread for a day, no more. Day by day. Forgiveness, yes, if we forgive, and not else. That is the petition in the prayer that most people want to dodge. Go back to the complete prayer:

"Forgive us our debts, as we also have forgiven our debtors."

We *have forgiven*, not *When we forgive* them. Someone says, That is not the ground of grace, and that does not belong to us. Let it be remembered that Jesus did not give that prayer to men outside the Kingdom. He gave that to men inside the Kingdom. If I go to a man outside, steeped in sin, I do not say to him, If you promise to forgive, you will be forgiven. The man outside gets his forgiveness with

no condition, when he believes; but once he is in the Kingdom of the Son of His love, he lives within the laws of that Kingdom. Then he does not get forgiveness unless he is ready to forgive, unless he has forgiven.

Take these sentences, or take the fuller prayer, and notice, we cannot pray the prayer alone. There is not a single pronoun in the singular number; they are all plural. When we pray this prayer, we must include other people, and pray with them, to " Our Father."

Another suggestive fact is that the personal pronouns which refer to us in the prayer are all of them either objective or possessive, except one. We love the nominative case. It is used when we are the subject of the sentence. We find it once in this prayer;—" We have forgiven." The only place in prayer in which we use the nominative case, and make self the subject of the sentence, is when we are telling God we have forgiven the people who have wronged us.

Having thus recalled them to the model of prayer, already given, He went on, and gave them a parable with an application. It is generally said that in this parable He was teaching them the necessity for importunity in prayer. I hold that He was teaching them the exact opposite. He certainly did not intend to liken God to a sleepy man in bed, who would not give to his friend, except under pressure. The value of the parable is that of contrast. He said in effect, Even a man who has gone to bed, and does not want to be disturbed because he is warm and comfortable, will rise and give his friend because he keeps on asking. God is no sleepy One in bed, wanting you to beg and pray, when you ask. When we are dealing with God, there is no need to beg and beseech. God is waiting. Quicker than the lightning's flash, when we ask, seek, knock, the answer comes. God is not asleep. Someone says, I have been knocking at heaven's gate a long time, and He has not answered. If that is true, you had better go away. God does not give you what you ask because it is better for you not to have it. His answer is, "No." This, then, is a parabolic contrast. All that the friend was, God is not; and the friend's answer stands in sharp contrast to the answer of God.

Having given them a parabolic contrast, He now gave them a parabolic comparison.

"And of which of you that is a father shall his son ask a loaf, and he shall give him a stone? or a fish, and he for a fish give him a serpent? Or if he shall ask an egg, will he give him a scorpion? If ye then, being evil, know how to give good gifts unto your children, how much more shall your heavenly Father give the Holy Spirit to them that ask Him?"

You, being evil, nevertheless know how to give good gifts to your children. If that is so, how much more your Father will give all things, nay, the best things, the Holy Spirit to them that ask Him. Thus His teaching on prayer ends on the declaration that the highest in prayer is that attitude that seeks and obtains from God, His Holy Spirit. That is initial, but it is continuous. That is where we begin, and when we receive the Holy Spirit at first we are born again; but the prayer-life is the life that is always seeking and always receiving; the filling, the infilling, the overflowing of the Spirit.

Now Luke goes back for illustration. The grammatical form of the statement shows that he was going back.

What, then, is the point of the illustration? "He was casting out a demon," and there were those who gave a false statement of the secret of His power. They said He had done it by Beelzebub. Mark carefully what He said to them:

"And if I by Beelzebub cast out demons, by whom do your sons cast them out? therefore shall they be your judges. But if I by the finger of God cast out demons, then is the Kingdom of God come upon you."

Matthew records Him as saying,

"If I by the Spirit of God cast out demons."

I have no doubt He said both of these things. Matthew reports Him as saying, He will give good gifts to His children, and by the Holy Spirit He cast out demons; and Luke records Him as saying, He gives you the Spirit, and by the finger of God demons are cast out. There is no contradiction. The phrase, "the finger of God," is synonymous with "the Spirit of God." He claimed, then, that their accounting for His power was false, when they said He was in league with the devil; declaring rather that He was in league with the Holy Spirit of God.

He then used another figure of speech. He said that the strong man guardeth his own court until a stronger than he comes and overcomes him. The strong man armed is the devil. Jesus is the Stronger than he; and that is how He cast the demon out. What was the secret of His superior power? The Spirit of God, the finger of God.

Link that up with the word in verse thirteen.

"If ye then, being evil, know how to give good gifts unto your children, how much more shall your heavenly Father give the Holy Spirit to them that ask Him?"

They had seen Him praying. They asked to be taught. He gave them His teaching, ending with this climacteric word:

"How much more shall your heavenly Father give the Holy Spirit to them that ask Him?"

Luke then records the incident which tells how He claimed that He cast out demons by the Spirit of God. It is as though He had said, You have seen Me praying. All I do, I do in the power of prayer; that is, I am ever looking to God, and receiving from God, receiving the fulness of the Spirit, and by that Spirit demons are cast out.

In connection with that incident, Luke records something Matthew does not.

"And it came to pass, as He said these things, a certain woman out of the multitude lifted up her voice, and said unto Him, Blessed is the womb that bare Thee, and the breasts which Thou didst suck. But He said, Yea rather, blessed are they that hear the word of God, and keep it" (verses twenty-seven and twenty-eight).

Matthew does tell us that this was the occasion when His Mother came, and wanted to persuade Him to go home, and He said, "Who is My Mother?" I am inclined to think that woman was somewhere there, and that Mary heard her say,

"Blessed is the womb that bare Thee."

He replied,

"Yea rather, blessed are they that hear the word of God, and keep it."

Thus a false idea of His relationship was corrected. Said the woman, Blessed is she that bare Thee and the paps that gave Thee suck. Yes, He said, but there is a higher relationship; it is relationship in the Spirit, which creates a closer tie than kinship in the flesh.

Continuing his illustration, Luke tells us that on that occasion our Lord rebuked those who were asking for a sign in the realm of the material, in the realm of the spectacular. He said that such seeking was the result of the fact that the generation was evil, and declared,

"And there shall no sign be given to it but the sign of Jonah."

In effect, He affirmed that the only sign powerful and prevailing would be that of His death and resurrection. In the presence of that affirmation we ask, when did the sign of His death and resurrection become powerful and prevailing? Never until Pentecost, never until the Spirit came. His resurrec-

tion gathered His disciples back again, who had been scattered by the Cross. It filled them with mingled feelings of fear and joy; but they never came to the place of complete apprehension, they did not understand His Cross, even after His resurrection, until the Holy Ghost came. It was after Pentecost that the sign became a powerful and prevailing sign.

"How much more shall your heavenly Father give the Holy Spirit to them that ask Him?"

and the Spirit is the One Who takes the ultimate sign, and makes it a definite proof of everything concerning Jesus Christ. He went on, and spoke of what they had as an immediate sign, through His wisdom and His preaching; Solomon and his wisdom, and Jonah and his preaching were not enough; a Greater than Solomon or Jonah was He; they had His words. The ultimate sign, however, would be His death and resurrection, interpreted by the Holy Spirit.

In every one of these three incidents the central element is that of the Spirit. The last words about prayer was that God gives the Spirit to them that ask Him. Then, in the illustrative incidents, the Spirit is declared to be the secret of His power; relationship with Him is that created by the Spirit; and the ultimate Sign is given by the interpretation of the Spirit.

Confessedly this is a remarkable paragraph. They saw Him praying, and desired the secret. He gave them the sentences from the model, and showed them that the ultimate in prayer is the reception of the Spirit initially and continuously. That is the secret of power over demons; that is the secret of kinship with God; and that is the secret of demonstration in witness.

LUKE XI. 33-52

CHRONOLOGICALLY, that is, in the sequence of our Lord's ministry, this paragraph is linked with the first thirteen verses in the chapter. By reading the thirteenth verse in im-

mediate connection with verse thirty-three, the sequence in the teaching of our Lord is maintained;

"If ye then, being evil, know how to give good gifts unto your children, how much more shall your heavenly Father give the Holy Spirit to them that ask Him? . . .

" No man, when he hath lighted a lamp, putteth it in a cellar, neither under the bushel, but on the stand, that they which enter in may see the light."

Whereas we dealt with verse thirteen in our previous study, we need to tarry with it now for brief comment, in order to see the connection of thought between it, and the teaching now to be considered. These, then, are the words of that verse:

" If ye then, being evil, know how to give good gifts unto your children, how much more shall your heavenly Father give the Holy Spirit to them that ask Him? "

Your heavenly Father shall give the Holy Spirit to them that ask Him, was the declaration of a great fact. For a moment think of it in its application to those men. What bearing had it in their case? How did it affect them? Now, let it be at once recognized that they did not ask for the Holy Spirit, and they did not receive the Holy Spirit until the day of Pentecost. They did not understand, nor could they. It was a tremendous declaration, but they could not grasp it; and He knew that they could not. Everything He said to them was stored in their memory, and never grasped until Pentecost. It is important that we should realize that.

Our Lord made the supreme declaration to these men about prayer, and through them to us for all time. If you ask the Father, He will give you the Spirit.

Let us go a little further on chronologically. Our Lord was talking to these men in the upper room, and He said:

" I will pray the Father, and He shall give you another Comforter that He may be with you for ever, even the Spirit of truth; Whom the world cannot receive " (John xiv.16).

Here, He said, Ask the Father, and He will give you the Holy Spirit. A little later on, He said, I will ask the

Father, and He shall give you the Holy Spirit.

Let us go still further. Our Lord had been to the Cross, and was alive from the dead, and He was talking to those same men. He said:

" Behold, I send forth the promise of My Father upon you; but tarry ye in the city, until ye be clothed with power from on high " (Luke xxiv.49).

This shows that they had not then received the Holy Spirit.

Following the sequence yet a step further, we come to the second chapter of the Acts of the Apostles, and we read something that Peter said:

" This Jesus did God raise up, whereof we all are witnesses. Being therefore by the right hand of God exalted, and having received of the Father the promise of the Holy Spirit, He hath poured forth this, which ye see and hear " (verses thirty-two and thirty-three).

Take these things in sequence. Jesus said, Your heavenly Father will give the Spirit to them that ask Him. I will ask the Father, and He shall give you the Holy Spirit. Tarry ye in Jerusalem, until ye be endued with power from on high. Then Peter declared, He, exalted to the right hand of God, hath shed forth this.

He told them the tremendous truth that God was willing, waiting, ready to give the Holy Spirit to them that asked, but they did not ask; they did not understand, and they did not receive the Spirit. It is true that John tells us that when the Lord was in the upper room, before His ascension, He said to that little group of men, breathing on them, " Receive ye the Holy Spirit." They did not then receive the Holy Ghost. It was a prophetic and symbolic breathing, because after that He said, Wait until you are endued with power. At Pentecost they received the Spirit, because He asked, and when He asked He represented them, and He represented us. God gives the Holy Spirit in answer to asking, but they could not ask, they did not ask; they were too blind; they did not understand. Then He said, I will

146

ask; and in the right of His Cross and resurrection and ascension to the right hand of the Father, representing all who believe in Him, He asked for the Spirit, and God gave the Spirit. Thus the Father gave the Spirit, through the Son, to all believing souls. Now we ask, and we receive, because He asks. That is the beginning of Christian life. What happens when a man becomes a Christian? He receives the Holy Ghost, and no man is a Christian until he does. When a soul comes to Christ empty-handed, trusting Him, what does he receive? The gift of the Holy Ghost. So he is born of the Spirit. After that, progress depends upon continued asking, and continued receiving. There is no need for us now to say we are waiting for the Spirit. That is not true. There is a little chorus I used to sing many years ago, and I sang it quite sincerely:

> "My all is on the altar,
> I'm waiting for the fire.
> Waiting, waiting, waiting,
> I'm waiting for the fire."

I never sing it, now. Why? Because it is not true. When my all is on the altar, God never keeps me waiting for the fire. The law of asking for the Spirit, is perpetual asking; that is the law of living in right relationship with Him. When that is done, the Spirit is always being given, so that He flows in, and overflows, and flows out.

Now, on the basis of that great declaration of the thirteenth verse, the Lord went straight on, and said,

"No man, when he hath lighted a lamp, putteth it in a cellar."

He gave them in verses thirty-three to thirty-six teaching about light; and then in verses thirty-seven to fifty-two we have something that in some ways is not connected, but in other ways is. A Pharisee asked Him to dinner, and He went, and things happened in the Pharisee's house. He denounced the false teachers. So that there is a spiritual sequence here. We have, therefore, two things to do; first to consider what He had to say about

light; and then to consider His denunciation of false teachers.

First, then, as to light.

"No man, when he hath lighted a lamp, putteth it in a cellar, neither under the bushel, but on the stand, that they which enter in may see the light" (verse thirty-three).

That is the figure of speech of which our Lord made use. A lamp, and a lamp that has been lighted. What is the function of a lighted lamp?

"That they which enter in may see the light."

That is why, when the lamp is lighted, we do not put it in the cellar, or put a bushel over it; but we put it on a stand. That is perfectly plain and simple.

Now, how did He apply it? First, remember that He had used this figure before;

"And no man, when he hath lighted a lamp, covereth it with a vessel, or putteth it under a bed; but putteth it on a stand, that they that enter in may see the light" (chapter eight, verse sixteen).

But then He had added,

"For nothing is hid, that shall not be made manifest; nor anything secret, that shall not be known and come to light."

Whereas the figure is the same in chapter eight, as in chapter eleven, the application is different. In chapter eight He was teaching them their responsibility as to what they had heard, in order to publish, for His next words were,

"Take heed therefore how ye hear."

This for the sake of others. There, He was speaking of responsibility concerning others. Here, He was speaking of responsibility concerning personal life. The lamp of the body is the eye. He did not say that the eye is the light of the body, but the lamp. Now, it is true that the eye is that which lights the body in a sense. We know where we are, because we have eyes. The body is under the dominion of eyes. The eye is the lamp of the body; and our actions are guided by that fact. But the eyes do not light the body, any more than a lamp lights a room. If we go into a dark room, we may have our eyes wide open, but we cannot see a thing. Eyes are no good for seeing unless there is light. It is equally true that light is no good for seeing, unless we have eyes. A blind man, though the light is all about him, cannot see. A man with eyes, and no light, cannot see. We must have light, and we must have lamps. The eye is the lamp, not the light; but it is the instrument of the light. Therefore the necessity for a single eye instead of an evil eye. The perfect eye, without astigmatism, no myopia the single eye is an eye that focusses properly, truly. The single eye is the lamp for the light. The evil eye is the eye which distorts things, so that light is no use.

Our Lord did not say that the eye is the lamp of personality. The eye is the lamp of the body. What, then, is the lamp of personality? The Light is the Spirit of God. What is the lamp? To answer that, we may go back to the Old Testament, and in those matchless Proverbs of Solomon, we find this significant declaration, chapter twenty, verse twenty-seven:

" The spirit of man is the lamp of
        Jehovah,
    Searching all his innermost parts."

The spirit of man, not the Spirit of God. The spirit of man is the lamp of Jehovah, not the light. It is the instrument through which light becomes effective.

Now we turn to the New Testament, I Corinthians, chapter two. I break in on Paul's argument at verse nine:

"As it is written,
    Things which eye saw not, and ear
        heard not,
    And which entered not into the
        heart of man,
    Whatsoever things God prepared
        for them that love Him.

But unto us God revealed them through the Spirit; for the Spirit searcheth all things; yea, the deep things of God."

This is not the spirit of a man, but the Spirit of God.

" For who among men knoweth the things of a man, save the spirit of the man, which is in him? Even so the things of God none knoweth, save the Spirit of God. But we received, not the spirit of the world, but the spirit which is from God; that we might know the things that were freely given to us of God."

We receive a spiritual nature from God, and we receive that nature that we may know the things freely given to us from God. The spirit of man is the lamp of Jehovah. My spirit life is the centre of my personality; but if there is no light, it is no good; and if the light beats about me, unless that eye is single, it is no good. The essential light comes with the coming of the Holy Spirit, and that is perfect light; but whether I apprehend it, whether I am able to conduct my life in accordance with the light, depends upon my own eye, the spirit life within me. If that is single, unified in devotion to God in Christ, then the Holy Ghost can illuminate all my way. If my own spirit life, the eye, the lamp of Jehovah, the spirit which is the lamp of Jehovah, the instrument of the light; if that is evil, the Holy Ghost cannot illuminate my life. A tremendous truth, this. Our Lord said,

" Look therefore whether the light that is in thee be not darkness. If therefore thy whole body be full of light, having no part dark, it shall be wholly full of light, as when the lamp with its bright shining doth give thee light."

If we are in darkness, what is the matter? Our eye is wrong. There is no question about God's light. There may be a great question about our eye. A man may say, My conscience does not condemn me. That is no proof that we are right. Sometimes we need to condemn our conscience. Our conscience may be out of order. If our eye is evil, that is why we are in darkness. Our first care must be to see to it that our spirit—the lamp of the Lord—is in order. Only do not let anybody else interfere with your eye. It is a matter for yourself and God. Jesus said something about a mote and a beam. We had better pay attention to that teaching, also. Here, then, is the connection of teaching. He will give, He has given the Spirit, the light is shining; it is shining now. Are we in darkness? Then there is something wrong in our eye, in our spirit life. It is not single; it is not unified in its devotion to the Lord. When there is breakdown in the instrument of vision, the light cannot shine.

Luke then continues,

" Now as He spake, a Pharisee asked Him to dine with him, and He went in, and sat down to meat. And when the Pharisee saw it, he marvelled that He had not first bathed Himself before dinner."

Luke is careful to show that this happened in close connection with this teaching. The Pharisee asked the Lord into his house, and the Lord accepted his invitation, and went in, and trampled tradition under foot, absolutely neglected the traditional ceremonial washings, upon which these men were insisting. He did not wash His hands ceremonially, and the Pharisee marvelled; and that led our Lord to these remarkable words in verses thirty-nine to forty-four. He first exposed the Pharisees for that which was their supreme fault and failure. What was it? Attention to externalism, with neglect of the internal condition of their life. He said, You are making clean the outside of the cup, and of the platter; and

" your inward part is full of extortion and wickedness."

Then He went on, and upon those men whose fault He had summarized, He pronounced three woes.

" But woe unto you, Pharisees! for ye tithe mint and rue and every herb, and pass over justice and the love of God."

Were they wrong in the tithing of

mint and rue and every herb? No, but they were wrong in what they neglected;

" These ought ye to have done, and not to leave the other undone."

He pronounced a woe upon them for an inversion of values. They were laying their emphasis upon the trivial, and neglecting the essential.

But again:

" Woe unto you, Pharisees! for ye love the chief seats in the synagogues, and the salutations in the marketplaces."

He was now denouncing their evil motives. That is what they loved, that is what they were seeking, the chief seats in the synagogues, and the salutations in the marketplaces. Their motive was self-centred.

And once more:

" Woe unto you! for ye are as the tombs which appear not, and the men that walk over them, know it not."

That is a terrifying word. He was denouncing them for the corrupting influence that they were exerting, all unconsciously, on the people. We must get back into the Eastern atmosphere, and into a medical atmosphere to understand that. Tombs, and men not knowing as they walk over them, are inhaling their pestilential vapours.

Then something happened in the house.

" One of the lawyers answering saith unto Him, Teacher, in saying this Thou reproachest us also."

The Lord immediately replied by pronouncing three woes on them, also;—

" Woe unto you lawyers also! for ye load men with burdens grievous to be borne, and ye yourselves touch not the burdens with one of your fingers."

That was denunciation of insincerity, which had become a tyranny to other men. These lawyers were superadding to the commandments of God the traditions of men; and they would not touch one of the burdens with their finger. They were not living by their code; insincerity.

But again:

" Woe unto you! for ye build the tombs of the prophets, and your fathers killed them."

That was satire. He intended it should be.

" Therefore also said the wisdom of God, I will send unto them prophets and apostles; and some of them they shall kill and persecute; that the blood of all the prophets, which was shed from the foundation of the world, may be required of this generation; from the blood of Abel unto the blood of Zachariah, who perished between the altar and the sanctuary; yea, I say unto you, it shall be required of this generation."

Their fathers killed the prophets, and they put monuments up to killed prophets, and went on with the same business of killing prophets. The second woe was against hypocrisy.

But He had not done with them;

" Woe unto you, lawyers; for ye took away the key of knowledge; ye entered not in yourselves, and them that were entering in ye hindered."

He was talking to lawyers, to scribes; and the insignia of the office of the scribe was the key. When He said to Peter, I will give you the keys, the office of the scribe was in His mind, the interpreter of the moral law. Now He said, You scribes who hold the key, what have you done? You have taken away the key of knowledge, and you have hindered those who were entering in. The key was the insignia

of their office; and He said, You have failed, you have prostituted your office.

Thus the denunciation of the Pharisees was for the inversion of values, for evil motives, for corrupting influence; the denunciation of the scribes was for insincerity, hypocrisy, and the prostitution of office.

The connection of spiritual values in all this is patent. All this happened, right there and then, in connection with His teaching on prayer; and what He had been saying about light. The twelve were there; His witnesses were there. They had asked to be taught to pray. He had told them the ultimate asking in prayer is that of asking for the Spirit. He had then told them of the value of right relation of their spirit in order to reception of the light of the Spirit of God. Then He had denounced the false teachers. When the eye is single, and not evil, when the Spirit is beating in upon that inward spirit-nature, then none of the things denounced is possible. There will be no inversion of values, no evil motives in service, we shall exert no corrupting influence. There will be no insincerity, no attempting to impose burdens, no hypocritical building of the tombs of the prophets, while we still kill them; and no prostitution of our office. The secret is the Spirit as light, and the spirit of my own life single in its devotion. When that is so, we fulfil the sacred function of teaching and prophesying, without any of the failures denounced in that memorable hour.

LUKE XI. 53–XII. 21

THE verse with which chapter twelve opens links that which is to follow with what has immediately preceded. The opening verse reads:

" In the mean time, when the many thousands of the multitude were gathered together, insomuch that they trod one upon another, He began to say unto His disciples first of all."

" In the mean time," en ois, literally, in which, that is, during which things.

What things? The last two verses of chapter eleven constitute the introduction to chapter twelve;

" And when He was come out from thence, the scribes and the Pharisees began to press upon Him vehemently, and to provoke Him to speak of many things; laying wait for Him, to catch something out of His mouth."

The connection is full of importance. The time is quite patent. He had been in the house of a Pharisee, and in that house had solemnly and terribly denounced the Pharisees in a threefold woe; and when challenged by a lawyer, had denounced them also in a threefold woe.

"When He was come out from thence, the scribes and the Pharisees began to press upon Him vehemently, and to provoke Him to speak of many things."

Two things are stated there. The first is physical, the second mental. They positively jostled Him as He went out. They were so angry, they got near to Him, and almost laid hands on Him. They pressed upon Him vehemently, is the physical declaration. Then they

"began to provoke Him to speak of many things, laying wait for Him, to catch something out of His mouth."

One writer has said of this, and I think that what he has said is warranted, that it was

"a scene of violence probably unique in the ministry of Jesus."

Then, while this was going on, the people were gathered together,

"insomuch that they trod one upon another."

The story which Luke thus begins runs on continuously to verse nine in chapter thirteen. Let us set out the movement. He began to teach His disciples; and this continues to verse twelve. Then there was an interruption by "one out of the multitude," and He answered him (verses thirteen to twenty-one). After this He resumed His teaching of His disciples (verses twenty-two to forty). Then Peter interrupted Him, and He answered him (verses forty-one to fifty-three). Then He addressed Himself to the multitudes (verses fifty-four to fifty-nine). There followed another interruption, to which He replied (xiii.1-9).

Our present study is concerned with this first teaching of our Lord, and the first interruption. The occasion, then, of this particular teaching of His disciples on the part of our Lord was a

tumult. The hour was characterized by the hostility of the ruling classes, the interest and excitement of the crowds, and the perplexity of His disciples. Speaking in the presence of the crowds, and certainly that they might hear Him, He addressed Himself to His disciples first of all. What did He say to them? He warned them, verses one to three; He guided them, verses four and five; He comforted them, verses six to twelve.

First, as to His warning (verses one to three):

"Beware ye of the leaven of the Pharisees, which is hypocrisy."

What did He mean by that? The history of the Pharisees is a wonderful history. They arose in the Maccabean period; and were to the Jewish people at that time, what the Puritans were to England in the period of their greatness. The Pharisees constituted an order, created to prevent the nation coming into contact with other nations, and losing its purity and its identity; and their influence was of the highest, and of the best. The Pharisaic movement arose out of the passion of men for the Divine ideal for the nation. In the days of Jesus, they had become utterly degenerate. They had lost their spiritual and moral influence; and in effect He said to His disciples, The leaven that has destroyed them is hypocrisy. In that warning our Lord was interpreting the failure of one of the most magnificent movements that had ever arisen in the history of God's ancient people. The leaven of hypocrisy had destroyed it. What is hypocrisy? Hypocrisy quite literally means wearing a mask. A hypocrite is a man who wears a mask, so that his features are not seen. Hypocrisy is dishonesty. These Pharisees were masquerading.

He said, Beware of this, for

"there is nothing covered up, that shall not be revealed."

The mask is coming off, sooner or later.

Then, in close connection, He said:

"Wherefore whatsoever ye have said in the darkness shall be heard in the light; and what ye have spoken in the ear in the inner chambers shall be proclaimed upon the housetops."

That was a very remarkable use of a figure of speech. Our Lord took the same idea, and used it in another application. These men had a message to deliver, and they had spoken it in the darkness, they had whispered it in the ear. It was a message of truth. This, also, would come into the open. It shall be heard in the light, though you whispered it in the darkness. It shall be proclaimed upon the housetops, although you said it in the ear in the inner chamber. Hypocrisy is the wearing of a mask. The mask is coming off. The truth may be hidden for the moment. It is coming into the light. Everything, whether evil or good, will be manifested. Therefore, Beware of the leaven of the Pharisees, which is hypocrisy. It has destroyed the witness of the Pharisaic movement, and it will destroy your witness, if once it works in you. But remember, on the other hand, that even though in fearfulness and trembling the words of truth are uttered, in the darkness, and the inner chambers, truth is coming out into victory and manifestation; and that, just as surely as hypocrisy is to be unmasked.

Then followed His words of guidance (verses four and five). Notice how tenderly He spoke. He began,

"And I say unto you My friends."

He was talking to His disciples, who had seen their Master jostled, and heard Him badgered. They had seen men round about Him, in whose eyes there gleamed the evil light of murder; and it was inevitable that they would be trembling and afraid. If that is the attitude taken up towards Him, what about them?

Therefore He said to them,

"I say unto you My friends, Be not afraid of them that kill the body, and after that have no more that they can do. But I will warn you whom ye shall fear, Fear Him, Who after He hath killed hath power to cast into hell; yea. I say unto you, Fear Him."

In that word He gave them guidance. He told them to be free from false fear, and filled with true fear. He said there was to be no fear of the man who kills the body. A philosophy of life is there. He did not say: Do not be afraid of those who kill you. He said, Do not be afraid of those who kill the body, and after that—. That little phrase, "after that," is arresting and revealing. Is there anything "after that"? If a man shall kill my body, am I not dead? Jesus said, Men can kill the body, but after that they have no more that they can do. In effect He said, If a man kills the body, he paralyses his own arm, so that he can do no further harm. Reverently, may we not say that is the tone, temper, and spirit of the attitude in which He went to His Cross. He knew they would kill His body, but could not touch Him. That is what made Him say on another occasion:

"No man taketh My life away from Me, I lay it down of Myself; I have power to lay it down, and I have power to take it again."

So He looked at that little group of men, and said to them, Do not be afraid of that. As a matter of fact, it came to all the twelve, save one, that men killed their bodies.

But there is a fear which is proper. It is the fear of Him Who is able to kill, and to fling into Gehenna, which outside Jerusalem was in the valley of Hinnom, the place where they cast the refuse from the city for burning. Lifting this into the spiritual realm, He said, There is One, that is God, Who is able to cast into hell; fear Him. Thus He gave them guidance.

Then He went on, and gave them comfort (verses six to twelve). The passage is full of beauty. Having warned them, having guided them, showing them the false principle of fear, which is to be banished, and the true principle of fear, which is to be preserved; He talked to them, and that in language of ineffable comfort.

"Are not five sparrows sold for two pence? and not one of them is forgotten in the sight of God. But the very hairs of your head are all numbered. Fear not; ye are of more value than many sparrows."

That was the outcome of what He had just said. Observe the movement there, the strangeness of it and the beauty of it. Fear not them that kill the body. Fear God. But because you know God, Fear not! Are not five sparrows sold for two pence, and not one of them is forgotten in the sight of God—not one of them. The very hairs of your head are all numbered. A man said to me one day, Do you believe, really, that God counts the hairs in your head? I said to him, The Bible never says so. It says He numbers them, and the Greek word means labels them! That is far more wonderful than counting them.

Then, continuing, He said;

"And I say unto you, Every one who shall confess Me before men, him shall the Son of man also confess before the angels of God; but he that denieth Me in the presence of men shall be denied in the presence of the angels of God."

And then, solemnly,

"And every one who shall speak a word against the Son of man, it shall be forgiven him; but unto him that blasphemeth against the Holy Spirit it shall not be forgiven."

To this He added,

"And when they bring you before the synagogues, and the rulers, and the authorities, be not anxious how or what ye shall answer, or what ye shall say; for the Holy Spirit shall teach you in that very hour what ye ought to say."

Now, through those verses there runs the note of intention. He intended to comfort the hearts of those disciples in the presence of manifested hostility. Not a sparrow forgotten in the sight of God. The hairs of the head numbered. They were of more value than many sparrows. If they confessed Him, He would confess them before the angels. If they were put in prison, the Holy Spirit would guide them.

Father, Son, and Holy Spirit are all committed to the disciples of Jesus; God, as Father, knows the falling of the sparrows, and cares for them; the Son is waiting for the day when He will confess their name; the Spirit is at their disposal to help them in every hour of difficulty.

Thus He warned them against hypocrisy. He guided them as to the principle of fear that was to master them, false fear to be banished, that of personal suffering and death, spiritual fear of God for ever to fill their souls. He comforted them by committing the Father, the Son, and the Spirit to them.

Then came an interruption.

"And one out of the multitude said unto Him, Teacher, bid my brother divide the inheritance with me."

A voice was heard in the crowd appealing to Him suddenly, breaking in on His conversation with His disciples, and apparently uttering a cry for justice; but, as we shall see presently, it was actually an expression of covetousness.

How did our Lord answer that? First, by a sharp, repressive question,

" Man, who made Me a Judge or a Divider over you? "

It is well to ponder it. Christ did not come into the world to do that kind of thing. He said, I am not here to judge or to divide. I am not here to deal with material substance and possessions in that way.

Then He stated a principle. "He said unto them." What is the meaning of "them" there? The disciples? No, I do not think so. Does it mean the crowd? It may; but I believe the "them" meant the man and his brother, the brother who wanted the inheritance divided, and the brother who was not doing it. What did He say?

" Take heed, and keep yourselves from all covetousness; for a man's life consisteth not in the abundance of the things which he possesseth."

Then I think He talked to the crowd.

"And He spake a parable unto them, saying, The ground of a certain rich man brought forth plentifully."

The parable follows upon what He said to the brothers.

His first statement uttered a principle. He warned against one thing; covetousness; and then gave a reason for the warning;

"A man's life consisteth not in the abundance of the things which he possesseth."

The Greek word for life there is *zoe*. It means the animal principle of life of any sort, whether it be in a flower, a butterfly, a beast, or a man. It is a very remarkable thing that the New Testament writers took hold of the word, the apparently lower word, *zoe*, and lifted it into the highest realm. Whenever we read of eternal life, the word used is *zoe*. This is the word Jesus used when He said that man's life consisteth not in the abundance of the things he possesseth.

This man said,

"Bid my brother divide the inheritance with me."

I want some of the *things;* my brother has got all the *things;* tell him to give me some *things*. The life of the world today, apart from godliness, is always conditioned by things! Men are relating their lives to things, instead of God. Jesus said a man's life does not consist in the abundance of the things he possesseth.

Then He gave them a story, that of the rich fool. Listen to Him:

"My fruits . . . my barns . . . my corn . . . my goods . . . my soul."

Then, like the crack of thunder,

"But God said unto him, Thou foolish one, this night is thy soul required of thee, and the things which thou hast prepared, whose shall they be?"

A man's life consisteth not in the abundance of the things!

"The things which thou hast prepared, whose shall they be?"

This was infinite satire, shot with eternal compassion, "Whose shall they be?"

Then, in closing words, the Lord summed up the whole situation:

"So is he that layeth up treasure for himself, and is not rich toward God."

LUKE XII. 22-53

AFTER the interruption by the man in the crowd concerning his inheritance, our Lord resumed the teaching of His disciples.

"And He said unto His disciples, Therefore I say unto you, Be not anxious for your life," and so on.

When the man had asked Him to bid his brother divide the inheritance with him, our Lord had replied,

"Who made Me a Judge or a Divider over you?"

"A man's *life* consisteth not in the abundance of the *things* which he possesseth."

Now the teaching runs on, and is coloured by that incident. He returned to the subject of *"things,"* and of *"life;"* but He was talking to His disciples. His first words were those of tender comfort, verses twenty-two to thirty-four; and then He called them to the fulfilment of responsibility in verses thirty-five to forty. At that point Peter interrupted Him, and from verse forty-one to forty-eight, we have the account of that interruption, and of our Lord's reply. That goes on, until it merges into one of the most marvellous passages in the whole of the story of the life of Christ, a great soliloquy, beginning at the forty-ninth verse, and ending at the end of our paragraph, verse fifty-three.

In His teaching here our Lord resumed subjects already dealt with. He went back first to the subject of God's care (verses twenty-two to thirty-four). He had spoken of the confession of some, that the Son of man would make at His coming. He went back to that subject (verses thirty-five to forty-eight). He had told them that they would have to face persecution. He returned to that subject, also (verses forty-nine to fifty-three).

In reading His words of comfort, notice the outstanding injunctions. Verse twenty-two, "Be not anxious." Verse thirty-one, "Fear not." Verse thirty-three, "Sell . . . give." These are the essential notes of what our Lord said.

"Be not anxious." Why not? Because of the value of life. The life is more than the food, and the body than the raiment. Therefore be not anxious for your life. But surely my life is dependent upon food? Oh, no, He said, it is not. You can starve to death so far as your body is concerned, but your life is still there. That was His perpetual outlook upon personality. It was revealed in the words:

"Fear not them that kill the body, and after that have no more that they can do."

Life is not finally dependent upon physical food. Man does not live by bread alone. So He said, Be not anxious. It is difficult not to be anxious. He knew it, and so called them to consider. Verse twenty-four, "Consider." Verse twenty-seven, "Consider." What were they to consider? The ravens, the birds; the lilies, the flowers. What are we to see when we do so? We are to see that the ravens do not sow, or reap. They have no store-chamber or barn;

"God feedeth them; of how much more value are ye than the birds!"

By which He did not mean to say that we are to sit down and expect God to feed us, as He feeds the birds. He said they sow not, they reap not, they have no store-chamber, nor barns, and yet God feeds them. But we can sow, and reap, and have barns; and we ought to sow, and reap, and have barns; and if God cares for the birds who have no forethought and rationality, how much more will He feed us, to whom He has given foresight and rationality.

Again, consider the lilies. They toil not, we can toil; they spin not, we

can spin; but Solomon was not arrayed like one of these, and if God so clothe the lilies which can neither toil nor spin, how much more shall He clothe us, to whom He has given the capacity for toiling, and the capacity for spinning. Therefore, do not be anxious. He Who has endowed us with the faculty of reason, is not going to leave us. Supposing the day comes when I cannot toil and spin, and I cannot sow and reap and gather into barns, then when I cannot, God can; and I am safe every way. That is what He was teaching. I am not to expect God to do anything for me that I ought to do for myself in the power that He has bestowed upon me in the rationality of my personality.

Then "Seek." Here there is a negative and a positive.

"Seek not ye what ye shall eat, and what ye shall drink, neither be ye of doubtful mind. . . . Yet seek ye His Kingdom."

Again our Lord is not saying that we are to take no thought for these things. He says we are to take no anxious thought. We are not to be anxious. We are not to make these things the supreme passion of life. The urge of life is not to be in order that we may eat and drink and be clothed; but rather His Kingdom. The supreme passion of all our days, in all our ways, is to be a passion for the Kingdom of God, and that not as some "far-off Divine event" only, but as something already existing, with which we are to seek right relationship. The passion of life is to be a passion for the Kingdom of God, and the measure in which we obey this injunction, is the measure in which we pass into the realm of unruffled peace and rest and calm.

Then we have His summarizing word in verse thirty-two.

"Fear not, little flock; for it is your Father's good pleasure to give you the Kingdom."

Observe an interesting and vital connection here. Seek ye the Kingdom. It is your Father's pleasure to give you the Kingdom. He will give us what we seek. He will give us all the benefits of the Kingdom, if the passion of our heart is that of seeking it; that Kingdom which His wisdom governs, His power sustains, His love encompasses.

What a comprehensive and revealing word of Jesus this is;

"Fear not, little flock; for it is your Father's good pleasure to give you the Kingdom."

Supposing, for the sake of argument, a purely and merely literary critic came across that sentence in some new brochure, I can imagine such a critic saying, The person who wrote this, or said this, broke down in his figures of speech. He begins,

"Fear not, little flock."

That is the figure of the shepherd and his sheep. Then He said,

"It is your Father's good pleasure."

There He has forgotten the shepherd and his flock, and has taken the figure of a father and family. And yet again,

"your Father's good pleasure to give you the Kingdom."

Now He has once more changed His figure to that of a Kingdom and a King.

As a matter of fact, if the metaphors merge, they do not mix. They constitute a perfect portrayal of the whole fact of the Kingdom of God. The whole statement is Eastern, and we know that in Eastern lands, the head of the tribe is at once the shepherd of the flock, the father of the family, and the king of the kingdom. Here God is seen in the threefold relationship. Fear not, little flock, the Lord is your Shepherd, you shall not want. It is your Father's good pleasure to give; Like as a Father pitieth His children. To give you the Kingdom; "The Lord reigneth." Our Lord was pledging God as Shepherd, Father, and King, to us, and to that which we seek in personal life and service.

"Fear not, little flock; it is your Father's good pleasure to give you the Kingdom."

Then followed that word that has application for those to whom it comes with power.

"Sell that which ye have, and give alms; make for yourselves purses which wax not old, a treasure in the heavens that faileth not, where no thief draweth near, neither moth destroyeth. For where your treasure is, there will your heart be also."

That calls to the true investment of treasure, the true investment of life. Sell that you have, and give. Sell and give. Traffic with what you have, in order to bless others, and not to bless yourself. That is the true investment. The dividends are postponed, but they are perfectly safe. In consonance with that, we call to mind another word of Jesus in the realm of money.

"Make to yourselves friends by means of the mammon of unrighteousness; that when it (the mammon) shall fail; they (the friends you make) may receive you into the eternal tabernacles."

Then, passing on, He referred to their responsibility (verses thirty-five to thirty-seven). That responsibility is revealed in the words,

"Loins girded about . . . lamps burning . . . looking for their Lord."

To such as fulfil it, He said He would come and make them sit down, while He served them. He will gird Himself and serve those who serve Him in this age and this generation. In this connection His last word was, "Be ready."

Then came the second interruption.

"And Peter said, Lord, speakest Thou this parable unto us, or even unto all?"

The question is interesting and arresting. It inquired whether the things the Lord had been saying were applicable to the crowd of people round about, or only to the disciples.

Mark well the Lord's answer. He said,

"Who then is the faithful and wise

steward, whom his lord shall set over his household, to give them their portion of food in due season?"

He answered the question by a question; which narrows and extends. Our Lord said in effect, Whether I am talking to you or the crowds, depends. I am talking to My stewards; and of course you are stewards, but the door is open. Other people may come if they will, into My Kingdom, and become My servants, and stewards.

"Who then is the faithful and wise steward?"

That is the question.

Having shown that His teaching here was for His stewards, and for none other; He made His special application.

"Blessed is that servant, whom his lord when he cometh shall find so doing. Of a truth I say unto you, that he will set him over all that he hath. But if that servant shall say in his heart, My lord delayeth his coming; and shall begin to beat the menservants and the maidservants, and to eat and drink, and to be drunken; the lord of that servant shall come in a day when he expecteth not, and in an hour when he knoweth not, and shall cut him asunder, and appoint his portion with the unfaithful. And that servant, who knew his lord's will, and made not ready, nor did according to his will, shall be beaten with many stripes; but he that knew not, and did things worthy of stripes, shall be beaten with few stripes."

What does this teach as to stewardship? That it is the duty of stewards to feed the flock, and not to tyrannize. It was Peter who raised that question, and later in his first letter I read:

"The elders therefore among you I exhort, who am a fellow-elder, and witness of the sufferings of Christ, who am also a partaker of the glory that shall be revealed; Tend the flock of God which is among you, exercising the oversight, not of constraint, but willingly, according to the will of God; nor yet for filthy lucre, but of a ready mind; neither as lording it over the charge allotted to you, but making yourselves ensamples to the flock."

He evidently had learned his lesson.

Then the Lord broke away into a great soliloquy.

"I came to cast fire upon the earth; and what do I desire, would that it were already kindled! But I have a baptism to be baptized with; and how am I straitened till it be accomplished."

That was a great heart-burst. Matthew does not give it; Mark does not give it; John does not give it. Only Luke records it. Do not forget the atmosphere; the hostility of the rulers, the excited crowds, the perplexed disciples.

In that heart-burst I discover first His sense of the purpose for which He was in the world.

"I came to cast fire upon the earth."

John had said:

"He shall baptize you in the Holy Spirit, and in fire" (Luke iii.16).

In Acts we read how the Spirit came, and the fire came (Acts ii.3).

Next I find revealed the passion of His life,

"What do I desire? would that it were already kindled."

His passion was that of fulfilling His purpose.

Then I learn His sense of the only method by which that fire could be cast;

"I have a baptism to be baptized with."

He was looking on to the whelming baptism of His death.

In view of all this, His sense of limitation is made manifest.

"How am I straitened till it be accomplished."

In effect, Christ was saying, There are things I cannot do today. I am straitened. I have come to cast fire. My supreme passion is that that fire should be cast. It cannot be cast until I have been baptized with My passion baptism; and until that is accomplished, I am straitened.

Then, again addressing Himself to

His disciples, He declared the process that would eventuate;

"Think ye that I am come to give peace in the earth? I tell you Nay."

My coming will be divisive. There will be those gathered to Me, and those who will reject Me.

Today we stand on the other side of that passion baptism; and He is no longer straitened.

"O Jesus, Lord, 'tis joy to know
Thy path is o'er of shame and woe
  For us so meekly trod.
All finished is Thy work Divine,
The throne of glory now is Thine,
  Exalted by Thy God."

He went to His passion baptism. He cast the fire, and His heart is already

seeing of the travail of His soul, and being satisfied.

Is there yet any sense in which He is still straitened? There was a time when Paul had to write to some believers and say,

"Ye are not straitened in us, but ye are straitened in your own affections."

Christ may sometimes still have to say that He is straitened; but if so, it is because His stewards, those within His Kingdom, responsible for His business, are doing something less than seeking God's Kingdom, and are sometimes found beating each other. May God save us from such failure, and enable us to be so devoted to His Kingdom and Himself, that He may be unstraitened in us.

LUKE XII. 54–XIII. 9

AFTER His great soliloquy, our Lord again addressed Himself to the multitudes. His address, beginning at verse fifty-four, runs to the end of verse fifty-nine. Then He was interrupted again (xiii.1).

There are two things, then, for us to examine; first, His address to the multitudes, as found in verses fifty-four to fifty-nine in chapter twelve; and then the interruption, as some of them, at that very season, brought Him a piece of news, and He heard it, and answered it.

"He said to the multitudes also."

That word, "also," shows He was not excluding the disciples. He had been talking to the disciples, the crowd listening. Now He began to talk to the multitudes, the disciples listening. Let us first inquire what was the reason of what He said to the crowd on that occasion. The answer to that question is to be found in a little phrase which occurs incidentally, but which is essential. He said,

"Ye know how to interpret the face of the earth and the heaven; but how is it that ye know not how to interpret *this time?*"

The phrase, "this time," reveals the

underlying reason of everything He said. In chapter ten, at verse twenty-three, it is recorded that He had said:

"Blessed are the eyes which see the things that ye see! for I say unto you, that many prophets and kings desired to see the things which ye see, and saw them not; and to hear the things which ye hear, and heard them not."

"This time," then, was the time that kings and prophets had desired to see, and had not seen, the time when things were being said that men had waited to hear, and had never before heard. In other words, He said what He said to the multitudes, upon this occasion, because of His own sense of the vital significance of His mission.

Think of the facts of that time; the world facts. The whole world was bludgeoned into submission to the Roman Empire, and the authority of the empire was centralized in an emperor, who was claiming Divine attributes. Then think of the significance of the presence of Jesus in the world at that time. There was none, not even among His own disciples, who understood the profound significance of that fact. But He knew it—"this time."

What, then, did He do, in view of His sense of the greatness of the time?

He rebuked them, and He appealed to them. His rebuke is found in the words,

"When ye see a cloud rising in the west, straightway ye say, There cometh a shower; and so it cometh to pass. And when ye see a south wind blowing, ye say, There will be a scorching heat; and it cometh to pass. Ye hypocrites, ye know how to interpret the face of the earth and the heaven; but how is it that ye know not how to interpret this time?"

He declared that they were weather-wise. He did not say it was wrong to be weather-wise. He told them that their general observation of Nature was perfectly correct. He said, You are right. When you are conscious of a cloud arising in the west, you say, There is a shower coming. You are quite right. That is the quarter from which you get your rain. Or, When you are conscious of a south wind, you say, It is going to be hot. He said, You are quite right, "it cometh to pass." You are weather-wise, but spiritually you are blind.

"How is it that you do not know how to interpret this time?"

You are correct about the wind, but you know nothing about the Spirit. Your observation of the sky is accurate, but you cannot see anything beyond the sky, you cannot see the heavens. That was their condition. Our Lord rebuked them in the form of a question. He said, "How is it?" How does it come to pass that you can be so correct in your observation of the sky, and so blind in the presence of the spiritual things that are happening about you?

He had said to His disciples:

"Blessed are the eyes which see the things which ye see . . . and hear the things which ye hear,"

and now He said to the multitude, You are blind, you do not understand the day of your visitation. You do not understand the time in which you are living. Weather-wise, and spiritually foolish, blind, insensate. How is it?

He answered His own question in the very form by which He addressed them: "Ye hypocrites." That is why They knew how to interpret the face of the earth and the heaven; but they did not know how to interpret the time. The reason for their blindness was 'heir hypocrisy. He had warned His disciples against this when He said,

"Beware ye of the leaven of the Pharisees, which is hypocrisy."

A hypocrite is a man who is attempting to appear what he is not, who is living a lie. There may be a hypocrisy of goodness, or of badness. I sometimes wonder which is the worse, the man who is going through life, pretending to be good, when he is not; or the man going through life, pretending to be bad, when he is not. That is a psychological problem not now to be debated.

Continuing, He asked another question.

"Why even of yourselves, judge ye not what is right?"

In that question there was recognition of the fact that every man has the faculty for discernment.

"The spirit of man is the lamp of Jehovah."

Every man's nature is spiritual, and through the spirit of man God deals with human personality. Men describe this faculty as conscience; but conscience is a human word, and a human idea, and men have difficulty in interpreting the nature of it. The Bible is explicit. It declares that the spirit of man is the lamp of the Lord. Jesus said to these men, Why don't you of yourselves know what is right? Have you lost all your power of spiritual observation? How is it that when you are weather-wise, you are so blind to the facts in the midst of which you live? The cloud that is rising big with mercies and blessings to fall upon your head, you do not discover. The breath of the wind now blowing upon you, speaks of scorching heat, and you do not understand.

Then, in close connection, He went on,

"For as thou art going with thine adversary before the magistrate, on the way give diligence to be quit of him; lest haply he drag thee unto the judge, and the judge deliver thee to the officer, and the officer shall cast thee into prison. I say unto thee, Thou shalt by no means come out thence, till thou have paid the very last mite."

Thus, after rebuking them, He made a great appeal to them to get right with God. The illustration is that of the law court. Four words reveal this; adversary, magistrate, judge, and exactor or officer. These were all officers of a court of law. The adversary was the legal opponent; the magistrate was the ruler, the first in rank. The judge was the one who made decisions. The officer, or the exactor, was the one who carried out the sentence of the judge. In the ultimate court of life, the adversary is God, the magistrate is God, the judge is God, and the exactor is God. Our first and last allegiance is to God; and in His Kingdom He is Magistrate; Adversary, of the lawbreaker; Judge, deciding; Exactor, carrying out the sentence.

God cannot be bribed. God cannot be caught out by a side issue. God cannot be hoodwinked. In Isaiah, the prophecy of the Kingship of God, as vested in His Servant, it says of the coming One,

"He shall not judge after the sight of His eyes, neither decide after the hearing of His ears; but with righteousness shall He judge the poor, and decide with equity for the meek of the earth."

That becomes arresting when we think of it by contrast. How do we judge today? We judge by the sight of the eye, and by the hearing of the ear; and we cannot help it. There is no other way for us to do. Go into any court of law in this land, and what do you find? A judge, and possibly a jury, and it is the business of the court to decide whether the criminal is guilty or not. The witnesses are called to speak; and there are only two things they can do; they can speak of what they saw, and what they heard. There is no other way. All verdicts are found by that method.

Now mark the contrast; He does not judge that way, not by the sight of the eyes, or the hearing of the ears; not by testimony given to Him. How, then, does He judge? With righteous judgment.

Here Christ reveals God as the Adversary against the criminal; as the Magistrate, the First, the Ruler; as the Judge, deciding, and that without a jury; as the Officer, carrying out the sentence. Taking that view of the spiritual Kingdom, in which they were so blind, He appealed to them, and said, .

"As thou art going with thine Adversary before the Magistrate, on the way give diligence to be quit of Him"—

to be delivered from Him—

"lest haply He drag thee unto the Judge, and the Judge shall deliver thee to the Officer, and the Officer shall cast thee into prison."

Thus Christ was saying to these men, "Get right with God." This appeal is arresting when considered thus in connection with the speech to the multitude. He said: You are blind, you are blind spiritually. What is the cause of your blindness? You are hypocrites. What is the reason of your hypocrisy? You are not right with God. No man was, or ever could be, a hypocrite if he were right with God. If a man is wrong with God, then he becomes a hypocrite, trying to deceive; he deceives himself; he becomes blind. He knows when there is going to be a shower of rain; he knows when it is likely to be hot; but he has no sense of the winds of God that are blowing across his life; no sense of the significance of the time in which he lives. From that parabolic and tenderly satirical rebuke of the weather-wise and the spiritually foolish, He made His appeal in terms of law, that they would get right with God.

Then follows the story of another interruption.

"Now there were some present at that very season."

Notice how careful Luke is to mark the time, "at that very season." Why did these men tell Jesus of that occurrence at that very season? They told Him of something Pilate had done. Some hot-headed Galileans had broken some Roman law. Pilate heard of it, and sent out a company of soldiers, a punitive expedition. The soldiers arrived as these Galileans were in the act of sacrifice and worship; and they slew them right there, and mingled their blood with their sacrifice. Now, I submit that we should never have known why they told this to Jesus, if He had not made it perfectly clear. What did He say?

"Think ye that these Galileans were sinners above all the Galileans, because they have suffered these things?"

In close connection He gave them another case. I always believe these men who told Him about the Galileans, were Judæans, and they had no sympathy with the Galileans. I think they told Him with pious satisfaction. He took the illustration of the Galileans; but added a reference to something which had happened in Jerusalem itself, at the heart of Judæa. There, the tower of Siloam had one day fallen, and killed eighteen people.

Look at this a little more closely. He had rebuked them for not being able to interpret the time; and they came to Him, and in effect they said, We are not so blind as Thou dost make us appear. We recognize the activity of judgment as suggested by the parable of the law-court. To show their understanding, they told Him this story of the Galileans and Pilate. They were standing up in smug self-satisfaction, and never more blind than then. And Jesus said to them, Is that it? Is that what you are thinking? Do you think that those Galileans were sinners above all the Galileans? Do you think calamity of that kind demonstrates extreme turpitude? I tell you, Nay, you are wrong. You are misinterpreting justice and judgment, and the ways of the Magistrate, the Adversary, the Judge, and the Officer.

"Except ye repent, ye shall all in like manner perish."

Or do you imagine that when the tower of Siloam fell and crushed eighteen, and they were killed, that that proves they were

"offenders above all the men that dwell in Jerusalem? I tell you, Nay; but, except ye repent, ye shall all likewise perish."

The proof of their blindness was in the illustration they gave. They did not understand God. That is not God's method. Catastrophe is no proof of special sin. The physical, which they treated as sacramental of the moral, is quite incidental. A man can perish though Pilate never slay him. He can perish though no tower crush him. He may die in his bed, with his friends all about him; and even have music while he dies; but he will be damned unless he repent. Perishing, said Jesus, cannot be interpreted in the terms of the physical. It lies deeper, in that spiritual realm where you are so blind.

Then He gave them a parable, revealing the true principles of the Divine government of human life. A man had a fig tree in his vineyard; it belonged to him, his were the rights of the proprietor. He came seeking fruit, his was the moral right of expectation. He found none, and he said, "Cut it down;" his was the right to destroy. But there was a vine-dresser, who said,

"Lord, let it alone this year also, till I shall dig about it, and dung it."

I am not asking you,—as though the vine-dresser said to the owner of the tree,—I am not asking you to pity it. I am not asking you to let it shun its moral obligation. I am asking for it a new chance to bear fruit, when I have provoked it, and fertilized it.

"If it bear fruit thenceforth, well; but if not, thou shalt cut it down."

Thus He showed that the judgments of God are rooted in righteousness, the rights of the proprietor; that the judgments of God are exercised always in infinite patience. Finally, however, if, in spite of the righteous demand, and the long patience, and His own ministry of mediation, there is no fruit, then He is at one with God in judgment; and the judgments of God are irrevocable.

LUKE XIII. 10-21

WE are still following our Lord in the last six months of His earthly ministry, and most likely this incident occurred on the other side Jordan, where He spent so much of that final period. Luke does not name the locality, nor state the exact time. The record of the incident is peculiar to him. The place was a synagogue. The time was a Sabbath day.

There are two movements in the narrative. First the action of Jesus when He came into the synagogue, which occupies verses ten to thirteen; and then the attack upon Jesus by the ruler, in verses fourteen to twenty-one. Simple though the incident is, it is full of light, full of colour, full of revelation.

Let us first look at the woman at the centre of the picture. Eighteen years, says Luke, she had been "bowed together." That is a medical term, and it is not found anywhere else in the New Testament. The Greek word might be translated quite accurately as, "bent double." We are told, moreover, that she "could in no wise lift herself up." "Lift herself up" is again a medical term. It occurs in one other place in the New Testament, in John eight, where it speaks of Jesus in the Temple, and the woman taken in the act of sin. There John says He lifted Himself up. She was quite unable to look up. If you had met her she could not have looked at you; bent double, her eyes were always on the ground, and she "could in no wise lift herself up."

Luke tells us in a very significant phrase, that she "had a spirit of infirmity," and therefore was bent double, and therefore could not raise herself.

The interpretation of that phrase, "a spirit of infirmity," is found in verse sixteen. Jesus said of her,

"Ought not this woman, being a daughter of Abraham, whom Satan had bound."

The spirit of infirmity was an evil spirit. This woman was held in the grip of a physical malady, described by this physician-evangelist and writer, as bent double, with no ability to straighten herself at all; and Jesus says, Satan had bound her.

Here, then, was a case in which an evil spirit had produced a physical malady that lasted eighteen years. There is no suggestion in this story, that there was anything of immorality in this woman's life. She was the victim of a demon activity, under what circumstances we do not know, producing a physical disability, and holding the woman in it for eighteen long years. There is no hint of this mastery having produced an immoral effect in her life. As a matter of fact, here she was in the synagogue. She had found her way to the place of worship, and when Jesus presently called her a daughter of Abraham, He did not merely mean she was a Jewess; that was patent. He was using the term in its full spiritual significance as revealing her faith in God. Here, then, was a case of physical suffering, that was directly produced by the power of Satan. I am not attempting to explain this. There may be many other such cases in the world. There are things we have not fathomed yet in life, concerning the mystery of suffering, and the power of evil. We take the facts as revealed, and proceed to consider the action of Jesus.

Jesus came into the synagogue, and we may tell the story in two or three very simple sentences. First He saw her. Of course He did. He always saw. As we go through these stories of His life, we find again and again that the persons He seems to have seen first, were those in direst need. On another occasion He entered a synagogue where was a man with a withered hand. In that story we are told that the rulers watched Him, to see what He would do. They, too, saw the man with the withered hand. They had probably seen him come and go often in the past. They had not taken very much notice of him; but the very day Jesus came, unconsciously they complimented the Lord by knowing that the one man that He would see, would be that man. It is always so. He saw this woman. If there is a man or a woman in any assembly of human beings, more in need than any other, that is the man or the woman that Jesus is after.

Then He spoke to her, He called her "Woman." There are other occasions when He used the term, and on His lips it was ever a word of infinite and beautiful tenderness. Then He touched her, as He said,

" Woman, thou art loosed from thine infirmity,"

and in a moment she was straight. A characteristic of the healing work of Jesus was that it was immediate, it was complete. There was no wondering whether the person was healed, when He healed. There was no hysterical delay. People may fling their crutches away, and have to pick them up again. They never picked them up again when He healed. The woman was healed, she was completely healed, ' immediately she was made straight." Look again, and observe the spiritual significance of the action of our Lord. This woman was bound by Satan; and Jesus, by a word and touch, set her free. Thus we see the power and authority of Jesus over Satan himself. Satan had bound her, and she could not loose herself, and no one could loose her. Christ loosed her. He snapped the bond in which Satan had held her, mastered the power of the evil one. He was stronger than the strong man armed, and dispossessed him there and then, in that soul who for eighteen years had been in the realm of suffering. There are mysteries in the story that baffle us, things we do not understand. Why was such a thing permitted? How did Satan gain that power over this woman? These and many other questions may remain unanswered. But the fact remains; a woman, not immoral, but a worshipper, a daughter of Abraham in the full spiritual sense of the word, is seen bound by Satan, and Christ, passing that way, coming into the synagogue, broke the power of the enemy, and liberated the woman from her disability.

Now let us listen to the ruler of the synagogue. He was angry. In the words of Scripture, " he was moved with indignation." The ruler of the synagogue, devoted to the worship of God, angry! Why? There was a woman who had entered the synagogue, a cripple, a derelict, a sufferer, now standing erect, and glorifying God.

And the religious ruler was angry! What a revelation. What is the meaning of this? He was the ruler of the synagogue, and he was angry in the presence of the suffering daughter of Abraham, rest red to health. What was the matter with him?

Let us listen to him. He addressed the people in the synagogue, but what he said was an oblique attack upon Jesus.

" He said to the multitude, There are six days in which men ought to work, in them therefore come and be healed, and not on the day of the Sabbath."

He was declaring that the procedure was irregular. It had broken in upon the correct order of things. Men *ought* to work six days a week, which means they ought not to do anything on the Sabbath. His objection was not to the fact that the woman was healed; indeed, that to him was so secondary that he did not seem to be touched by it. That was the calamity. His objection was to the violation of the ceremonial law of the Sabbath. He did not consider the healing of the woman, but rather that work had been done; and, according to him, work of any kind was wrong on the Sabbath. That is what he said. Men *ought*. "Ought" represents the thing that is necessary, the thing that is imperative, the thing that is a duty, the thing that is the true impulse of life, they ought not to be healed, or Jesus to heal on the Sabbath; because that is in the realm of work.

Thus, he was relegating a victory in the spiritual realm to the physical level. He only saw the physical act of the straightening of the woman. He was blind entirely to the fact that the physical was merely the result of a spiritual thing that had taken place in the synagogue. In that synagogue that day the power of evil in the spiritual world had been mastered. He did not see that at all. He saw the hands of Jesus touch the woman. That was work. He saw the woman a cripple, with her face to the ground, suddenly stand erect, as she straightened herself. That was work. It would be amusing, if it were not tragic! To him, ceremonial was more than humanity. In order that the ceremonial rite of the Sabbath might not be broken in upon in any way, he would gladly have left the woman to suffer until the first day of the week. So he is revealed.

Now turn from him, and look at, and listen to, Jesus. The first thing I notice is that He, also, was angry. This we know by the way He addressed him, "Ye hypocrites." That is the language of anger.

He then proceeded to justify His description.

"Doth not each one of you on the Sabbath *loose* his ox or his ass from the stall?"

That, in view of the ruler's anger in the presence of the loosed woman, is the evidence of hypocrisy. By this question, our Lord revealed the fact that, in the last analysis, this man's objection was not to the violation of the Sabbath. Christ said in effect, If loosing this woman from her bond by the touch of My hand, is work; what are you doing when you loose your ox or your ass from the stall, simply to take them away to watering? You do that, said Christ again in effect, and

it does not trouble you. But now you are angry.

Thus it is evident that while this man was professing to stand for the sanctities of the ceremonial law, there lurked in him hostility to Jesus, and that was the underlying reason of his objection. Thus the Lord unveiled his hypocrisy.

Then He took him on his own ground, and used his own word. This man said, "Ye *ought*." Jesus said,

"*Ought* not this woman, being a daughter of Abraham, whom Satan hath bound, lo, these eighteen years, to have been loosed from this bond on the day of the Sabbath?"

The ruler said, You *ought* not to do anything on the Sabbath. But, said Jesus, your "*ought*" does not apply if your ox or your ass is thirsty. *Ought* not this woman, who is a daughter of Abraham, who has been bound for eighteen years, to have been let loose? Why does your "*ought*" apply in the case of this woman, when it does not apply in the case of your ox or your ass? As He said on another occasion, Is not a man of more value than a sheep? These men were presumably careful of their animals. They would not have objected to loosing an ass or an ox on the Sabbath. Neither would Jesus. But He did object to their setting up one law when property was in danger, and another law for a human being, when enthralled in suffering and agony. Over against the *ought* of the ruler, He put another *ought*. There is a necessity deeper than the one the ruler has named. With Jesus, humanity is of far more importance than the ceremonial law.

"The Sabbath is made for man, and not man for the Sabbath."

In saying that, our Lord was not relegating the Sabbath to an unimportant position, but putting it in its right position. It is a minister to the well-being of men; and if this woman, a daughter of Abraham, needs to be freed from the power of Satan in the realm of the spiritual, then the mastery of the evil one shall be ended on a Sabbath day, and she admitted into the realm of freedom and realization.

As I look at the ruler, I see that a man who has lost his sense of the worth of humanity, has lost his sense of the truth about God. He did not know God. On the contrary, Jesus, knowing God, knew the value of humanity. A man who has lost his vision of God, and does not know God, has always lost his sense of the value of human life. But a man who knows God, knows the value of every human life, and knows that the tithing of mint and anise and rue and cummin are trivialities by comparison with the necessity for righteousness and truth and justice and mercy.

Luke says that His adversaries were put to shame. I do not know quite how to interpret that. I should like to think that it meant in the finest sense, they were ashamed of themselves. I am afraid it does not mean that. But it is true that the multitude rejoiced in the glorious things He was doing.

Then what? Now mark the "therefore." That introduces the next phase. He repeated in brief form two parables which He had uttered in an earlier part of His ministry. We find them in fulness in the thirteenth chapter of Matthew. They were, the parable of the tree which was a false growth, and that of the leaven which is always a disrupting force.

A grain of mustard seed never develops into a great tree, unless it becomes abnormal. The grain of mustard seed, developing into a great tree, is not the sign of the progress of Christianity, but that of an abnormal growth, so that there is room for birds to lodge in the branches. The birds are symbolic here of evil things.

We are familiar with the long-continued controversy about the parable of the leaven. The popular interpretation is that the leaven is a type of good. All expositors admit that everywhere else in Scripture leaven is a type of evil. I hold that this is no exception to the rule.

Why did He repeat these two parables? Because He saw and understood the attitude of this ruler of the synagogue, and of the people. He thus revealed His sense of the difficulties confronting His own work. He did not mean that His work was not coming to victory ultimately, but that in its process there would be admixture.

In the incident, taken as a whole, two kingdoms are seen, the kingdom of Satan and the Kingdom of God. The kingdom of Satan is there. Satan bound the woman, and blinded the ruler. The Kingdom of God is there. Jesus loosed the woman, and corrected the ruler. The kingdom of Satan binding and blinding; the Kingdom of God loosing and correcting.

Thus the Kingdom of God is seen mightier than the kingdom of Satan. God's anointed King is able to loose the captive that Satan binds, and He is at least willing to illuminate the blindness of their rulers. The victory was with the Kingdom of God as seen in the Person of His Son.

There is one little word in the narrative, which I have already emphasized. The compulsion that masters the kingdom of evil, and the compulsion that masters the Kingdom of God, are revealed in the word *"ought."* The ruler said what *ought* to be done, and in his *"ought"* there was utter disregard for humanity in its suffering. The devil must not be interfered with on the Sabbath. Nothing must be allowed to violate the conventionalities of ceremonial and ritual in religion. That is Satan completely unmasked! The *"ought"* which in the last analysis is callous in the presence of human suffering, is the spawn of hell.

Now listen to the other.

"Ought not this woman, who is a daughter of Abraham, be loosed?"

That is the compulsion of a compassion that sets man at his right valuation. What is his right valuation? It can best be stated in most familiar, but most sublime words:

" God so loved the world that He gave His only-begotten Son."

That is the compulsion of the *"ought"* of Jesus, the master-passion, the loosing of those that are bound, the straightening of the woman, the breaking of Satan's power, the giving of liberty to the captives.

In that little word *"ought"* hell and heaven are seen. It depends upon what our *"ought"* is, as to whether we are loyal to the kingdom of Satan, or to the Kingdom of God.

Thus in the incident the two kingdoms are clearly seen; and we can, without asking the opinion of friend or neighbour, discover to which Kingdom we belong. We shall find the answer, if we discover the meaning of the *"ought"* that compels us.

LUKE XIII. 22-35

IN this paragraph Luke records another incident in the same period of the Peræan ministry.

"And He went on His way through cities and villages, teaching, and journeying on unto Jerusalem."

This statement takes us back to the fifty-first verse of chapter nine,

"And it came to pass, when the days were well nigh come that He should be received up, He stedfastly set His face to go to Jerusalem;"

which introduces the story of the last six months, during which our Lord was all the time moving to Jerusalem.

The present story has two movements; first the account of a speculative question, and the Lord's answer; and then that of a threat that was reported to Him, and the Lord's reply. The account of the question and answer occupies verses twenty-three to thirty.

"And one said unto Him, Lord, are they few that are saved?"

The question, in all probability, was perfectly sincere. I see no reason to doubt the sincerity of it. As to the reason for the asking, who can tell? Possibly the person who asked the question was a very discerning questioner, wondering at the winnowing process that was going forward, and the deflection from Jesus of multitudes in those last months. Probably this watcher was wondering whether there would be any success at all to the ministry of Jesus by the time He had done His work. The crowds were still about Him, but, in understanding, were evidently gradually dropping away from Him. Christ's ministry was one that was constantly winning

men by His attractiveness, and winnowing the crowds, so that it was difficult to stay with Him; and by the time He had done, not one single human being stood by Him as a loyal disciple. One tragic sentence tells the story, not of the crowds only, but of the inner circle of the twelve,

"They all forsook Him and fled."

I cannot help wondering whether perhaps this was a discerning person. He saw the crowds and their attitude, and he saw they were gradually drawing away; and he said,

"Lord, are they few that are saved?"

On the other hand, it may have been the question of one anxious about himself, wondering, after all, in the presence of the teaching of Jesus, and the demands of Jesus, if it were possible that he could be saved. Jesus never suggested in the days of His flesh that it was going to be an easy thing to be a Christian. That heresy has been reserved for this soft age, in which we are more concerned about statistics than about spiritual power.

"If any man would come after Me, let him deny himself, and take up his cross daily, and follow Me."

No suggestion there of softness. Moreover, His ethical standard was so high that honest men must have trembled, as they tremble still, if they read the Sermon on the Mount. So it is possible that the question may have been asked by one who was conscious that the ideals of Jesus were impossible of realization,

"Lord, are they few that are saved?"

Now, how did Jesus answer? We may speculate about the question as long as we like, but about the answer of Jesus there is no room for doubt. First, let it be observed that He gave no answer to the question. Secondly, let it be recognized that He very definitely replied to the questioner. That is not a distinction without a difference. The question moved in the realm of speculation, and our Lord did not reply to it. That, in itself, is very suggestive. There are many things about which people would like a dogmatic answer; and there is a sense in which He does not answer that kind of inquiry. Some people always want to be *sure*. And there are certain things about which we must be sure; but speculative questions generally operate in the realm of the things not vitally important. Dr. John Hutton once said in my hearing:

" Some people are always looking for a dead certainty. Well, when they get it, the principal fact about it is that it is *dead!* "

What, then, did He say to him?

" Strive to enter in by the narrow door."

Observe the significance of that.

"Are they few that are saved?"

said the man. To which Jesus replied in effect: Don't waste your time debating that question; look to yourself; are you saved?

" Strive to enter in at the narrow door."

That was the first emphasis of the Lord's answer.

But He said more.

" For many, I say unto you, shall seek to enter in, and shall not be able when once the Master of the house is risen up, and hath shut to the door."

A technical word at this point. There should be no full stop at the word " able." The statement was not merely that many shall seek to enter in and shall not be able. It marks the limit of opportunity as being reached

" when once the Master of the house is risen up, and hath shut to the door."

Christ thus says that opportunity to enter the door is limited. There will come an hour when the Master of the house will close the door that is open today.

Then He went on and told this questioner what many will say in that day.

" Lord, open to us. . . . We did eat and drink in Thy presence, and Thou didst teach in our streets."

And He revealed what His answer would be;

" He shall say, I tell you, I know not whence ye are; depart from Me, all ye workers of iniquity."

The plea which many will offer in that day will be that of familiarity with Him. We know Thee, we sat down and drank in Thy presence. You came to our town, and taught in our streets. We know all about You. Yes, but Jesus will say, I do not know you. It is a dreadfully solemn word. The issue of individual salvation is not to be decided by familiarity with Him, but by a personal relationship, and such personal relationship as can only be expressed as He says, I know you. Paul once spoke of knowing God, or rather being known of God. It was a significant change; knowing God, or rather known of God. Christ said in effect, You may be familiar with Me, have sat down at My table, have stood and listened to My teaching, but all that is not enough. A man's salvation does not result from familiarity. It must be based on personal relationship.

To all this He added another statement;

" There shall be the weeping and the gnashing of teeth, when ye shall see Abraham, and Isaac, and Jacob, and all the prophets, in the Kingdom of God, and yourselves cast forth without. . . . And behold, there are last who shall be first, and there are first who shall be last."

In these words He revealed the fact that relationship with Him does not necessarily result from birth privilege. Men, then, were depending upon the fact that they were related to Abraham, to Isaac, and to Jacob. His declaration was significant, and far-reaching. Blood relationship means nothing. The thing that matters is spiritual kinship, which shares the faith of the fathers, and obeys the impulse which moved them.

Thus, as we listen to Jesus dealing with a speculative question, the motive of which we do not know, answering not the question, but the individual, we see that the one who asked the question was trembling on the very verge of hesitancy. Strive, said Jesus; quit your speculations on subjects that are not of vital importance. Strive to enter in, because there is a limit to opportunity. The day will come when the Master of the house will rise up, and shut the door. In that day familiarity with Me will be of no avail unless you have personal relationship with Me; and the fact of your descent from Abraham, and Isaac, and Jacob will be of no value. They will come from the distances, the outsiders, the aliens, people you hold in despite, and sit down, if they have personal relationship with the Master of the house, and you be cast out.

Let us never forget our Lord's answer to this question; and when we are inclined to wonder whether many are going to be saved, or few, let us hear His voice coming to us across the years, and coming as the living voice of the living Lord saying in effect; I have no answer to speculative questions which have no moral value in them. Strive to enter in. The one business of life is that of getting into right relationship. Strive to be among the number of the saved, whether there be few or many.

Now we pass to the second movement in the incident. "In that very hour." By that phrase Luke linked this story with the one we have been considering.

One can imagine that these Pharisees were standing by, listening to His answer; and in all probability specially angered by that part of it which made blood relationship with Abraham, Isaac, and Jacob unimportant. They came and said to Him,

"Get Thee out, and go hence; for Herod would fain kill Thee."

They told Him of a threat against His life. Now, undoubtedly what they told Him was true. Had they invented this story about Herod being bent on His destruction, He would not have replied as He did, by sending a message to Herod. Not for a moment, however, do I suggest that their telling Him was inspired by respect for Him. On the contrary, they told Him, inspired by hatred for Him, as all the story shows.

Surely this was on their part an attempt to get rid of Him, by an appeal to His fear. We laugh at the fatuous folly of imagining anything of the kind, but that would seem to have been their motive. They felt that they must get rid of Him somehow, and thought perhaps thus to secure His flight.

The supreme value of the story is that of the answer He gave. What was His reply?

"Go and say to that fox."

This was a term of uttermost contempt. As a matter of fact, we do not quite get the sarcasm of it in our translation. The Greek word there is feminine; and if we put it accurately into our speech, it would be,

"Go and tell that vixen."

He used the feminine name for Herod. We cannot find, in the story of Jesus, another occasion when He spoke contemptuously of a human being. I do not know a story more tragic than the story of Herod. It is the one story that gives me solemn pause, whenever I am considering our Lord's method with individuals. I would say, as a general rule, and I know of no exception to it except this, that there was no case hopeless in the presence of Jesus; and yet Herod seemed to have been so. He never saw Jesus till Pilate sent Jesus to him a little later on. Jesus avoided him. Jesus sent him a stinging message of contempt now. Presently Pilate sent Jesus to Herod, and we read that Herod "was exceeding glad" to see Him. Why?

"He hoped to see some miracle done by Him!"

Whenever a man wants to see Jesus merely to see Him work a miracle, he is wronging his own soul. Herod was. He wanted some new titillation of his enfeebled personality. When they did thus stand face to face, Jesus refused to speak to him, said never a word. Herod asked Him all manner of questions, and He never answered him. He had nothing to say to him. It is an appalling picture. Jesus evaded Herod; sent him a message of contempt; and when face to face with him, had nothing to say to him. It is a solemnizing story. A man may get into such a condition when he yields to the base, that even Christ has nothing to say to him.

They said,

"Herod would fain kill Thee."

He said,

"Go and tell that fox,"

what? In no part of the story of Jesus can we find anything more wonderful than this in its dignity, in its majesty, in its authority, in its supreme revelation of the fact that our Lord was walking a Divinely ordained pathway, carrying out a programme of high heaven and Almighty God, with which hell could not interfere.

Listen to Him.

"Go and say to that fox, Behold, I cast out demons and perform cures to-day and tomorrow, and the third day I am perfected."

That is the ultimate in His programme —perfected? What did He mean? His face was set to Jerusalem. He had made it distinctly clear that He was going to Jerusalem to die. This is how He now referred to that fact in the presence of the threat of Herod.

"The third day I am perfected."

That is the Divine aspect. Again,

"Nevertheless I must go on My way today and tomorrow and the day following; for it cannot be that a prophet perish out of Jerusalem."

That was the human aspect. He knew He was going to death, but when He spoke of going to death, He said in effect to the man who was reported as desiring to kill Him; You cannot kill Me, Herod. Go and tell that fox that My programme is arranged, and that nothing can interfere with it. Go and tell him I carry on, casting out demons, performing cures today and tomorrow; and the third day—that poetic way of referring to a consummation—the third day, the culminating day, I am perfected. I carry out to completion My programme, and that includes the Cross. This first movement rather described His programme on the Divine level; the second included the human element in it,

"for it cannot be that a prophet perish out of Jerusalem."

That is the end on the human level. I am going to Jerusalem to die by the hands of sinners; but I am going in that day to round out My mission, and neither Herod nor hell can interfere.

This attitude of our Lord towards His Cross is everywhere apparent. The fact cannot be over-emphasized that He never referred to His Cross without declaring its necessity, and its issue in resurrection. He did not go to the Cross a Victim. Let us get rid of the unholy word. He went as a Victor in a Divine programme. I cast out demons and perform cures today and tomorrow; and when the end comes the third day, I am perfected.

"Nevertheless I must go on My way today and tomorrow, and the day following; for it cannot be that a prophet perish out of Jerusalem."

All this became sun-clear to the consciousness of the disciples on the day of Pentecost. When Peter was speaking for the first time after the coming of the Holy Spirit, of Jesus and His Cross, how did he put it?

"Him, being delivered up by the determinate counsel and foreknowledge of God, ye by the hand of men without the law did crucify and slay."

Thus His enemies said to Him: You had better go; get hence; Herod is after You! There is no irreverence in what I now say. There is a holy merriment of a Man in the eternal counsels of God, as He laughs at Herod and says, Go and tell that fox he cannot interfere with Me. I march along the Divine pathway. I came to carry out the Divine programme, and in the very hour when by the hands of men I am slain, I am perfected. *Teleioo* is the verb; and on the Cross the great cry was cognate, *tetelestai,* It is accomplished, it is perfected.

But He had more to say. What next? There are no words in the Bible that I feel more inadequate to read or to interpret than those that follow. There is a heart-break in them, the heart-break of God. There is in them the threnody of the eternal pity,

"O Jerusalem, Jerusalem, that killeth the prophets, and stoneth them that are sent unto her! how often would I have gathered thy children together, even as a hen gathereth her own brood under her wings, and ye would not! Behold, your house is left unto you desolate; and I say unto you, Ye shall not see Me, until ye shall say, Blessed is He that cometh in the name of the Lord."

That was the revealing of His heart. We cannot read it without hearing the tears in His voice; the great Mother heart of God is there.

And yet, because Jerusalem would not, then the pity and the purpose could not prevent the punishment.

"Behold, your house is left unto you."

The word "desolate" is in italics. No man can be dogmatic as to whether the word desolate should be there or not, but the fact is there, even if the word is omitted.

"Behold, your house is left unto you."

We need not say desolate, for desolate indeed the house is, if abandoned by God. At the beginning of His public ministry He went into the Temple and He cleansed it, and then He spoke of it as " My Father's House." He is at the end, now, and He does not call it " My Father's House." He calls it " your house." It is left unto you. If the Temple of God be left to us, without the God of the Temple, it is desolation indeed!

But He did not end there. The very last words have in them a ray of hope, a revelation of the deepest thing in His heart. Your house is left unto you, but

"I say unto you, Ye shall not see Me until ye shall say, Blessed is He that cometh in the name of the Lord."

All these things reveal the august majesty of His conception of His own mission, the unfathomable pity and compassion of His heart, His strict adherence to the necessities of righteousness even in punishment, and finally, the certainty that the day of victory would come.

LUKE XIV. 1-24

IN this paragraph we begin a story, the whole of which includes the rest of the chapter, chapter fifteen, chapter sixteen, and the first ten verses of chapter seventeen. It is the story of the last Sabbath day in the ministry of Jesus, of which we have any record prior to His arrival in Jerusalem for the final things. In it we have the account of events in the house of a ruler; events that took place directly He had left that house; and His teaching in connection with those events.

These twenty-four verses give the account of the happenings in the house of the ruler, and the story is, in some senses, one of the most arresting, one of the most startling of all chronicled in this Gospel of Luke.

It breaks up into three parts. In verses one to six we have a dramatic incident. Immediately following it, we have the startling criticisms which Jesus uttered, in verses seven to fourteen. Finally, we have a story which Jesus told in that same house, in verses fifteen to twenty-four.

In verse seven we read,

"And He spake a parable unto those that were bidden."

From that phrase, "those that were bidden," we know that this was a formal occasion. That, in itself, is arresting. In it we have a sign of the degeneracy of the age in which Jesus exercised His ministry. Gradually they were encroaching upon hours which had ever been held to be sacred. There was a tendency to turn the closing hours of the Sabbath day into occasions for visitation and receptions. It was a sign, I say, of the degeneracy of the age. The same thing is being done by Christian people today. Many such go to church in the morning, often arriving late, and then in the afternoons they have visitations and social receptions. The whole thing is a sign of spiritual decadence.

At such a reception Jesus was one of the guests. It may at once be said that His going justifies the receptions. The reply is that it does justify our accepting such invitations, providing that when we arrive, we say the same sort of thing Jesus said when He was there, and do the sort of thing He did.

Now, what did He find in that ruler's house. A critical atmosphere. Luke says,

"There was before Him a certain man that had the dropsy."

What brought that man there? There is no doubt that he was there, having been invited, but he was not there because they desired his company. Why was he there? Let us read on;

"And Jesus answering spake."

Answering? But nobody had spoken. Nobody had raised any objection to Him. He had come in, unquestionably as one of the bidden guests, and when He entered, the first thing He saw, was the man put before Him, a man with the dropsy. Now I know the meaning of "answering." He answered their action in putting him there.

"He went into the house . . . on a Sabbath to eat bread, and they were watching Him. And behold, there was before Him a certain man that had the dropsy. And Jesus answering spake."

He knew why he was there. They had brought him there, and put him there, to see whether He would heal on the Sabbath. All through the ministry of Jesus that had been a point of difficulty between the rulers and Himself. Our Lord was constantly trampling under foot the conventions of men, and violating the false sanctions that they had built around the Sabbath in varied forms of ritual.

He answering them, said,

"Is it lawful to heal on the Sabbath, or not?"

I think I can catch His accent, and hear the emphasis. I believe He said that in such a way that they knew He intended to say to them what they were saying to Him. That is to say, He said in effect: "I know what you are thinking. I know why you put that man there. You are asking that question, or rather wanting Me to answer it."

"But they held their peace."

Every now and then, as I listen to the story of these men, I think they did have some lucid intervals, and this was one of them!

Then

"He took him, and healed him, and let him go."

That was the answer to the question; and then, with fine irony, He did the thing He was constantly doing, revealed the fact that their objection was not an honest one, that there was something deeper than their supposed antagonism to His breaking through upon rite and ritual and ceremonial. He said,

"Which of you shall have an ass or an ox fallen into a well, and will not straightway draw him up on a Sabbath day?"

Some of the old manuscripts—I see our revisers have made a note of it—read,

"Which of you shall have a *son* or an ox?"

He said, Which of you respects the attitude you are now taking up, when something that is dear to you is involved? If your son, or your ass; or your ox or your ass, were fallen into the pit, would you not get it out on the Sabbath day? Then they had another lucid interval. They did not speak.

This dramatic incident being over, the afternoon reception must go on. Luke says,

"And He spake a parable unto those that were bidden, when He *marked* how they chose out the chief seats."

In order to see what Jesus saw, we must understand the method of seating guests in these Eastern homes. That method was most often that of the triclinium. The triclinium was a table with seats for three. On an occasion like this, they would have a number of such tables, with seats for three. The centre seat at every table was the seat of honour. Supposing there were nine people, there would be three triclinia, and they would thus be seated in groups of three, numbering them from one to nine. In the first group, number two would be the guest of honour; in the second group, number five would be the guest of honour; and in the third group, number eight would be the guest of honour. In that case the host would be number nine, taking the lowest place; while the guest in the middle of the centre table was the chief guest of the occasion. Luke says,

"Jesus *marked* how they chose out the chief seats."

He watched them as they were choosing their seats; and He saw them endeavouring to obtain those centre seats.

Then, as He looked at them, He saw the sort of people who were there. He did not see a single one there who was poor or maimed or blind or lame. They simply were not there. They never are at that particular kind of function. He saw them all, a well-to-do, prosperous, smug, self-satisfied crowd, struggling for the chief seats.

Then He did perhaps the most unconventional thing He ever did. He criticized the guests for their bad manners; and the host for his false principle in hospitality.

To the guests He said:

"When thou art bidden of any man to a marriage feast, sit not down in the chief seat; *lest*"—let that word be underlined in your mind—"*lest* haply a more honourable man than thou be bidden of him."

Do not try for the chief seat. Why not? Because the place of honour is for the honourable man; and a man who struggles to sit in the place of honour proves thereby that he is not an honourable man. A truly honourable man is never an office-seeker.

"Lest haply a more honourable man than thou be bidden of him."

Then, addressing Himself to the host, He used that word "lest" again.

"He said to him also that had bidden Him, When thou makest a dinner or a supper, call not thy friends, nor thy brethren, nor thy kinsmen, nor rich neighbours; *lest*"—lest what? "Lest haply they also bid thee again."

This meant that the danger, if we ask these rich folks, is that they will ask us again. But that is why we do ask them, because we expect them to ask us again. Our Lord said that such an attitude towards life cuts the nerve of hospitality. That is never hospitality which is offered with the expectation of receiving again.

I submit by the standards of life today, that these are still revolutionary ideas. Our Lord was showing the relation between bad manners and bad motives, and good motives and good manners. If our motives are bad, our manners are bad. If we are seeking for self-exaltation, then we jostle to get the place of distinction. If our motive is good, if we are seeking nothing for ourselves, we shall never jostle for the place of distinction. If our motive in asking people is that we may be asked again; then all our hospitality is of the essence of rudeness; but if we offer hospitality and bring in the poor, and the maimed, and the blind, and the lame, who cannot recompense us because they have no means of doing so, then we are blessed. That is real hospitality.

It is arresting here to notice how our Lord saw the light of the eternal flashing upon the present. He said,

"Thou shalt be recompensed in the resurrection of the just."

Nearly all the dividends of Christian consecration are postponed. We shall be supplied with all necessary things in this world, but all the great returns will come in the life that lies beyond.

So we pass to the last stage in this story of events in the house of the ruler. Someone in the crowd said,

"Blessed is he that shall eat bread in the Kingdom of God."

I believe that it was a perfectly sincere ejaculation. Some commentators treat it as an ironic exclamation. I do not so understand it. To me, it seems evident that this man, whomsoever he was, one of the guests, saw through what Jesus had said, the gleaming glory of the Kingdom of God, saw the beauty of the ideal that Jesus was presenting, saw that a social order mastered by those principles, a social order in which there is no office-seeking, or jostling for position, a social order in which hospitality asks for no return or reward, but is reaching and going out towards the needy, was perfect; and so exclaimed,

"Blessed is he that shall eat bread in the Kingdom of God."

Now, once again we are arrested by our Lord's answer to that exclamation. His answer took the form of a story. Our Lord did not deny the blessedness of the Kingdom of God in the story He told. He did not deny the accuracy of what the man had said,

"Blessed is he that shall eat bread in the Kingdom of God."

But what He did, was to say in effect;

Yes, you admire the ideal, but you are not prepared to act upon it. Humanity may admire the ideal, but it is not prepared to enter into it.

A consideration of the story shows first that the Kingdom of God is a Kingdom of grace, into which men enter by receiving a gift from God. God provides the table. Men enter the Kingdom as they receive its gift as from God, as they become the guests of God.

Then it shows that the right to enter into that Kingdom of God is the right of invitation, that God is calling; that God says,

"Come, for all things are now ready."

Therefore, finally, it shows that if we are excluded from that Kingdom, it is because we refuse the invitation.

The chief value of the story is that it shows why men so refuse. One man said,

"I have bought a field, and I must needs go out and see it."

Another man said,

"I have bought oxen, and I go to prove them."

Yet another said,

"I have married a wife, and therefore I cannot come."

One word employed by our Lord here is arresting. It is the word "excuse." The Greek verb means to be left aside—to beg off, and the idea is well expressed by our word excuse. There is a great difference between a reason and an excuse. If a man learns something when he is about eleven or twelve years of age, he is never likely to forget it. I was about that age when I learned the difference between a reason and an excuse. I was in school at Cheltenham. My schoolmaster was Mr. J. L. Butler. For some reason I had not done my home work, and I took a note from Mother, which ran something like this: "Will you please excuse George's lessons today, Elizabeth Fawn Morgan." I gave it to Mr. Butler, and he was gracious, and he said, "Certainly, Morgan, all right." I went to my classes, until the time came to go home. As I was preparing to do so I heard Mr. Butler say, "Where are you going, Morgan?" "Home, sir." "Your home work before you go, if you please." "I brought a note, sir." "I know you brought a note; that was an excuse, not a reason; you will stay and do your work!" I have never forgotten it.

"They all began with one consent to make excuse."

Back of an excuse is lack of desire.

Now, examine the illustrations our Lord gave of excuses. One said he had bought land, and had to go and see it. That man was either a liar or a fool. You business men, would you buy land you have never seen? My previous remark applies to you, if you say you would.

The next man said he had bought oxen, and was going to try them. All I have said about the first man is true of the second. It may be perfectly true, that you do not look a gift horse in the mouth; but you do look at the horse you are buying. Imagine a man buying oxen he has not proved.

The last man said he had married a wife, and therefore he could not come. He was the most foolish of them all. Why didn't he take her with him? Just excuses.

What is the first man's excuse? Possessions; the realm of real estate. What is the second man's excuse? Oxen, labour, the realm of commerce. What is the third man's excuse? A wife, the realm of natural affection. Those are the three things that are keeping more men out of the Kingdom of God today than any other;—earthly possessions, commerce, and natural affection. They admire the ideal,

"Blessed is he that shall eat bread in the Kingdom of God."

Yes, said the Master, in pictorial and parabolic form, You admire it, but you won't come into it; and your excuses move in these realms. These are the things that possess the human heart, while God is excluded.

It was a remarkable Sabbath afternoon in that ruler's house; the dramatic incident of the healing of the man; the startling criticisms that Jesus uttered of guests and hosts; the exclamation of one illuminated mind, who saw the glory of the Kingdom; and the solemn story in which Jesus revealed the reluctance of the human heart to yield itself to the Kingship of God. When that was all over, He left the house, and the next part of the story tells what happened outside.

LUKE XIV. 25–XV. 2

AFTER telling the story which illustrates the reluctance of the human heart to enter into the Kingdom of God, Jesus left the house of the ruler. Luke then briefly but graphically describes the scene outside,

"Now there went with Him great multitudes; and He turned, and said unto them."

Try and visualize that scene. Luke emphasizes the fact of the crowd. He says, "great multitudes." By this time in His ministry, wherever Jesus went, He was followed by the crowds; all sorts and conditions of people followed Him, hanging upon His words, watching for His working of miracles, keenly interested in Him, attracted by Him, and evidently inclined towards Him, with some kind of desire to stay with Him, to be associated with Him.

We see Him, then, coming out of the house of the ruler, and quite evidently beginning to walk away. We watch Him in imagination, as He turned His back upon the house, and began to go on His way. The people who had been waiting for Him, at once started after Him. Then

"He turned, and said unto them,"

that is, He turned to address them. That is the scene.

In the rest of the chapter we have the record of what He said to these crowds; and then in the first two verses of chapter fifteen we find the account of the effect produced by His speech and action. Luke tells us of the effect produced upon two classes of people, Publicans and Sinners, and Pharisees and Scribes.

The things He said that day were among the most solemn and searching that ever fell from His lips. It is important that we keep in view that eager crowd, attracted by Him, inclined towards Him, all of them feeling they wanted to be with Him in some way, numbers of them feeling they would like to be enrolled as His followers. Jesus turned and faced them, and in what He said, we find perhaps the supreme instance of His statement of the terms of discipleship. In the course of His words there is a thrice-repeated phrase, " cannot be My disciple," " cannot be My disciple," " cannot be My disciple;" and in connection with it a revelation of the only terms upon which men may be His disciples.

Moreover, this was the one and only occasion upon which He very clearly explained the reason for the severity of His terms.

Consider first the terms of discipleship as here stated. I think I never read them without being filled with a certain sense of fear, without being inclined to say, Are those, indeed, the terms? Then I wonder whether I am a disciple. Did any one ever read that first statement about hating father and mother and child and brother and sister, and one's own life, without having in the mind a sense of fear? Yet He did say that, unless this were so, a man " cannot be My disciple." The next statement is not quite so startling at first. It is far more startling, however, when we face it;

" Whosoever doth not bear his own cross, and come after Me, cannot be My disciple."

That has a religious and theological and ecclesiastical sound about it, which we are inclined to accept on that account. But note it honestly;

" Whosoever doth not bear *his own* cross."

Jesus did not say My Cross, but "his own cross." That must finally be interpreted by His Cross, but the emphasis is on a personal cross;

" Whosoever doth not bear his own cross, and come after Me, cannot be My disciple."

Then presently our Lord used the phrase a third time, summing up what He had said in the first two;

" Whosoever he be of you that renounceth not all that he hath "—

father, mother, wife, children, brothers, sisters, and his own life;

" Whosoever he be of you that renounceth not all that he hath,"—and so takes up the cross,—" cannot be My disciple."

The Lord never said it would be easy to be Christian, never once! We are wronging our message, and failing to fulfil our mission when we declare that discipleship is easy. I am convinced that we are failing in our appeal to young life when we represent Christianity as the secret of having a good time. We shall get hold of young life more successfully when we represent Christianity as Jesus did, as a crusade. The Cross underlies it from beginning to end.

" If any man cometh unto Me, and hateth not."

That is the point that halts us. We must remember that here we have the Oriental idiom of sharp contrasts, and the word hate is used as the opposite of love. It is hardly necessary to say that our Lord was not claiming that in order to discipleship we should have a malicious attitude of heart towards our loved ones. He was facing the possibility of competition in loyalty with the things that He names. And, it is arresting that He did not name a low thing, an ignoble thing. He was facing the possibility, which often occurs, of a conflict between that which is beautiful in itself, and loyalty to Him. Nothing is fairer finer, more beautiful in human life, than love of father, and love of mother, love of wife, and love of children, love of brothers, and love of sisters; and yet these fair things may, and often do, challenge our loyalty to our Lord. Thus He was declaring that if ever an hour strikes when there is a conflict between the call of the highest earthly love and the call of Christ; then there is only one thing to be done, and that is to trample across our own hearts, and go after Him, without any compromise and any questionings.

This must be interpreted finally by the next thing;

" Whosoever doth not bear his own cross, and come after Me, cannot be My disciple."

The taking up of the cross always means the emptying of the life of everything that is merely selfish in motive, and high things may become that. If there shall come a moment when a man has to choose between the call of Christ to sacrificial life and service in the attitudes and activities of his life, and the appeal of high and beautiful earthly affection, there is only one thing to be done according to these terms of Jesus, and that is to follow Him.

All this, our Lord made superlative as He added,

" Yea, and his own life also."

Now, is there anything a man loves more than his own life? The devil and Jesus say the same thing very often, but from entirely different standards and with radically different meanings. It was the devil who first said to man,

" Ye shall be as gods."

And Jesus says to us,

" Ye therefore shall be perfect, as your heavenly Father is perfect."

They were both appealing to the capacity for being godlike. In the appeal there is the difference between heaven and hell, because the two conceptions of God are diametrically opposed. In connection with this statement of Jesus as to a man's attitude to his own life, I recall words Satan spoke to God about a man.

"All that a man hath will he give for his life."

And then I remember that Jesus asked,

" What shall a man be profited, if he shall gain the whole world, and forfeit his life? or what shall a man give in exchange for his life?"

These two things reveal a man's proper estimate of the value of his own life; and gives significance to the statement of Jesus that unless under conditions of His call, a man hate his life also, he cannot be His disciple.

The severity of these terms is self-evident; and yet is it not a little late in the day to complain of the severity of those terms? In 1914, that dire, dark, disastrous year when the War broke out, I hastened back to London from the country on that fateful August day, and day after day I watched the sons of Britain go. First there went that army of Britain which the Kaiser called " negligible." Close to my church in London were the headquarters of the Guards; to the right, close by, the headquarters of the London Scottish; and just beyond, the headquarters of Her Majesty The Queen's Westminster Rifles. They were the first to go, and others followed, until five million went—before conscription was applied. They marched, and they marched, often enough singing Tipperary! What agony can lie hidden under the flippancy of a song! With splendid heroism they went. I can hear them going yet, the tramp of their feet through the night and day, the finest of our young manhood. Didn't they love father? And mother? Didn't they love wife, the young wife they left? Didn't they love the bairns that waved them farewell? Didn't they love brothers and sisters? Didn't they love life? Of course they did; but an hour had struck when something higher than the earthly calls they loved the best, appealed to them, and they went in loyalty to the call that had come to them.

That is all that Jesus wants, but He needs that. When we talk about the severity of the first line of His terms, the question that arises is this; Is the Christ to have a loyalty lower than the loyalty of our boys and yours to their country's call? He calls for much; He calls for everything. He calls for the march that may have no return, and can have no compromise.

His next statement of terms interpreted the first.

"Whosoever doth not bear his own cross."

The Cross is the interpretation. He demands this loyalty, because His enterprise is a crusade. Its method is that of the Cross, and there is no other way. He says, therefore, that unless a man come after Him, and take up his own cross, he cannot be His disciple. Because He goes that way, His disciple must go that way.

What is this cross? What is the meaning of it? A good deal of unintelligent nonsense is talked about the cross in the experience of the believer. I have heard good people speak of some suffering of their own, some physical disability, some mental trouble, some loss in material things, some very real personal suffering, as being the cross. They say of such experiences: "Of course we have to bear the cross." That is not the cross. I am never sharing in the cross merely because I am suffering. While suffering is ego-centric, while it belongs entirely to me personally, it is suffering, and God knows I am not speaking unsympathetically of such suffering, but that is not the cross. We never touch the realm of the Cross until we are suffering vicariously; until our suffering is the suffering of sympathy with others, and strength is being poured out in order to help others. That is the cross. We can only interpret our cross by His Cross. I have found it an arresting and revealing thing to take the demands of Jesus as uttered at Cæsarea Philippi, and place them side by side with the greatest thing written under inspiration, by the apostle concerning the Lord Himself. Paul wrote,

"Have this mind in you which was also in Christ Jesus, Who, existing in the form of God, counted not the being on an equality with God a thing to be grasped, and held for Himself, but emptied Himself, taking the form of a Servant, being made in the likeness of men; and being found in fashion as a Man, He humbled Himself, becoming obedient even unto death, yea, the death of the Cross."

There is the cross. "He emptied Himself," "the death of the Cross."

"If any man would come after Me, let him deny himself, and take up his cross, and follow Me."

"He emptied Himself." If I am going after Him, I must deny myself. He went all the way to the Cross. If I am going to be His disciple, I must consent to accept that Cross as the principle of all life and service. That is what He meant here. He says, If men are coming after Me, they must enter into My enterprise, and they must go My way. Discipleship does not merely mean that it insures the salvation of the soul. It means fellowship with Him in the travail, and then in the triumph. Unless we are prepared for that, He says we cannot be His disciples.

Having thus declared the terms of discipleship, He gave the reason for the severity of His terms. He went right on, and said,

"For which of you, desiring to build a tower, doth not first sit down and count the cost."

Then He took another figure, that of a king going to war, taking counsel. Two illustrations; the illustration of the man desiring to build, and the illustration of a king going to battle.

Why did He employ these illustrations? Why, at that point, did He take these two figures of building and battle, and use them in that way?

I do not know any one passage of the New Testament that, I think, has suffered more in interpretation than this. The reason of this is probably to be found in one little word in the Authorized Version. In the Revised Version, both English and American, we read that after He gave the illustrations, He said, " So *therefore*." Now, the Authorized Version rendered that, " So likewise." That little word " likewise " has misled us in interpretation. If He then said, " So likewise," that must suggest that He meant, If you are coming after Me, you must count the cost, as the man who is going to build a tower must count the cost. Or as a king going to war, must take counsel whether he is able to meet him that comes with twenty thousand, with his ten thousand; so must you take counsel as to your ability to end the war victoriously. That would mean that after He had stated the severity of His terms, He said in effect: If you are thinking of coming with Me, you had better count the cost. He meant nothing of the kind. As a matter of fact, His very terms show that there must be no counting of cost, that if a man is to come after Him, there is to be no comparing, and bargaining between earthly loves and the call of Jesus, that a man hesitating in the call to fellowship with the Cross, cannot come. He was not telling men that they must count the cost. He was telling them that He had to count the cost. He is the Builder. He is the Warrior King. That is why He used these illustrations. He said, " So therefore," that is why the terms are severe. That is why you cannot be My disciple save on fulfilment of these conditions. It was as though He said: I am in the world for building and for battle, therefore I have to reckon upon the quality of My workmen and My soldiers.

All the Biblical revelation shines through this. He was nearly at the end of His ministry. Six months before, or nearly so, He had used the same two figures of speech about His work. At Cæsarea Philippi He had said: " On this rock I will build My Church "—building; " and the gates of Hades shall not prevail against it "—battle. On both occasions He revealed His own estimate of His work in the

world. He came into it for building; He came into it for battle. He came into it principally for construction; but in the process of construction He had to do destructive work. He is the Builder, but He is the Warrior. This harmonizes with the whole Biblical revelation. Its history is that of God's activity on behalf of a sinning race. It has ever been that of building, and of battle. The Bible opens in a garden. It closes in a city. Between the opening and closing is the story of God's operation through the ages towards the building of the city; and on the way, because of sin, the Lord is a Man of war.

When Charles Haddon Spurgeon issued a magazine, he called it, *The Sword and Trowel.* What made Spurgeon call the magazine that? He selected the title from the story of Nehemiah. But no one supposes that he named a Christian magazine because of the story only, save as he recognized its profounder significance. Nehemiah, and the men who built the walls of the city did so with the sword in one hand, and the trowel in the other. Thus our Lord's illustrations harmonized with the revealed activities of God.

Look again at that interested crowd, attracted, inclined towards Him. He turned and gave them the terms of discipleship, and I believe that He saw on the faces of that crowd revelations of its thinking. The thinking of the crowd was the thinking of the human heart, the thinking of my heart. They looked at Him, as though they would say, But why make Thy terms so severe. We are all interested, we are all attracted, we are all ready to make Thee King if Thou wilt only consent in a certain way. We would like to be enrolled.

Seeing that look, and knowing the human heart, He said in effect: I will tell you why My terms are severe. I am in the world for building and for battle. I want men and women who will stand by Me until the building is done, and the battle won. Jesus is far more concerned with quality than with quantity. If the Church of God could only discover that lesson today, what a sifting there would be in church rolls. How soon we should be cleansed from our unholy boasting that we have a large membership. The story of Gideon is still applicable. God can do more with three hundred men that lap, than with thirty-two thousand of a mixed multitude. The Lord needs men He can depend upon to stand by Him, laying brick on brick, though the bullets fly, until He has won His war, and built His city. That is why His terms are severe.

All this He finally emphasized by another "therefore."

"Salt therefore is good."

He changed His figure of speech, returning to one He had used to the disciples in an earlier period of His ministry;

"Ye are the salt of the earth."

"Salt therefore is good."

But what good is it when it has lost its savour? With a fine scorn He says,

"It is fit neither for the land nor for the dunghill; men cast it out."

It is no use. Men and women are no use to Me, said Jesus, unless they have the true property of salt. A Scotch version renders that, If it have lost its tang. "Tang" is a good biting word. People who look upon Christianity as something pleasant and easy, have no tang, no bite, no aseptic influence in the world, nothing to stop the spread of corruption.

"If the salt have lost its tang, wherewith shall it be seasoned? It is

fit neither for the land, nor for the dunghill; men cast it out."

Then He ended with a challenge:

"He that hath ears to hear, let him hear."

In conclusion, observe the results. He said,

"He that hath ears to hear, let him hear. Now all the publicans and sinners were drawing near unto Him to hear Him."

That is a very revealing connection. The publicans and sinners were drawing near to hear Him. The men and women who know their own need, are the men and women who will press close to the King and the Saviour, Who lifts a high standard. What follows?

"The Pharisees and scribes murmured."

The dilettante folk, quite satisfied with themselves, are not affected by what He said, but are repelled by what they see. They said,

"This Man receiveth sinners, and eateth with them."

This Man Who has declared terms so severe and imperative as to make the heart tremble down the centuries, nevertheless receives sinners, and sits down and eats with them. The effect produced on publicans and sinners was that they were attracted by what they heard, searching as it was. On the other hand, Pharisees and scribes were repelled by what they saw, because they had lost the vision of true values.

LUKE XV. 3-32

I SUPPOSE if we were selecting the great chapters of the Bible, it is certain that we should choose, among others, this fifteenth chapter of the Gospel according to Luke. I think that would be done by the most superficial student of the Scriptures. It would be done by such because of its matchless pictorial beauty. Among all the things that our Lord said, none is more wonderful in its light and its

shade, its colour and its glory, than this. I think, also, that those who have given longest time to the study of it, would still feel it to be one of the greatest chapters, and that because in a very remarkable way in this chapter we have focussed the great fact for which the Bible stands, and the great truths revealed through the process of the literature.

Now to consider it in its place in

the record. Chapter fifteen must be kept in close connection with chapter fourteen. In the first two verses of this chapter, fifteen, we are told the effect produced by what Jesus is reported to have said in chapter fourteen; and the effect produced upon other people by what they saw Him do. The chapter begins,

" Now all the publicans and sinners were drawing near unto Him to hear Him,"

which follows immediately upon the last words that our Lord is reported as having spoken to the crowd of people that He found waiting for Him when He left the house of the ruler;

" He that hath ears to hear, let him hear."

He had been saying perhaps the severest things He ever said as to the terms of discipleship, and He ended by challenging those who listened to Him,

" He that hath ears to hear, let him hear."

Luke runs straight on, and says,

" Now all the publicans and sinners were drawing near unto Him to hear Him."

The severe things attracted the people who knew their need.

But there was another company there, Pharisees and scribes; and they

" murmured, saying, This Man receiveth sinners, and eateth with them."

It would seem as though they had hardly listened to what He had been saying. They were impressed by what they saw, and what they saw is revealed in what they said;

" This Man receiveth sinners."

What did they mean? The word " receiveth " is a very strong word. I should do no violence to it if I read,

" This Man receiveth unto Himself."

What they saw was the attitude of Jesus towards that unwashed crowd, unwashed ceremonially, and very probably many of them unwashed physically, that promiscuous crowd. The rulers saw that He was receiving them, which means, to use a daring phrase, He was hail-fellow-well-met with them. There was nothing of aloofness about His attitude. He did not gather His garments about Him as the rulers did, that they might not be defiled by their touch. Moreover, He sat down and ate with them, possibly, on that very occasion, sitting down with a group, and sharing their lunch with them. He was making Himself one with the sinners, and positively eating with them. Their concern was that they believed that if He became the boon companion of sinning men, He would contract their defilement. They were quite right, if He had been such an one as they were. They could not have done it. That is the background.

" And He spake unto them this parable."

To whom? Unquestionably, especially to His critics, but with equal certainty, to all the multitudes. The first value of this chapter is that Jesus addressed it to religious people. In the parable He was expressing the reason of His attitude to that unwashed crowd; and He was explaining why He was not polluted by His contact with them.

We will take a general survey of the parable, and then examine its phases. It may be perfectly permissible to say that we have three parables; but if we do, we must remember that they constitute a triptych, they are linked up to each other, and I much prefer to treat Luke's word.

" He spake unto them this parable,"

as applying to the whole. The old Fathers declared emphatically that this is not three parables, but one parable in three movements.

If we take the first only, we have not all the teaching. If we take the second, we have not all the teaching. If we take the third, only, there is a good deal of the teaching that is missing. If we take the first and second, it is not yet complete. If we take the second and third, it is still incomplete. If we take the first and last, we have lost something very important. All that is only to say again, that it is a threefold parable.

What, then, is the theme of the parable? The grace of God. That is its theme from beginning to end. Grace is revealed as the explanation of what the rulers criticized; and grace is unveiled as what the crowd needed.

What, then, are the three phases? There is the story of the shepherd. There is the story of the woman. There is the story of the Father.

What do we see when we look at the shepherd? Suffering. What do we see when we look at the woman? Seeking. What do we see when we look at the father? Singing. Of course, each value is found in some measure in each story, but each has a special emphasis. The principal emphasis of the first is that of the shepherd who through suffering finds the sheep. The principal emphasis of the second is that of the persistent quest, or searching of the woman, until she find the lost drachma. The principal emphasis in the last is upon the gladness and the joy in the father's house, and the father's heart, when the boy comes home. Here, then, is a parable emphasizing suffering, seeking, singing.

Now, mark the unity of the three. They are all concerned with lost things,—lost sheep, lost silver, lost son. In every case the lost is found and restored. In each story the issue is joy, whether it is sheep, or silver, or son. The lost things are found, and they are restored, the sheep to his owner, and the flock; the drachma to circulation, and currency, and value; and the boy to the meaning of life in his father's home. They are all lost. They are all restored. Joy is the issue in every case.

In the first two, that which is lost, is sought. In the last one, that which is lost, seeks. The shepherd sought his sheep. The woman sought the silver. The father did not seek the son. The son sought the father. Thus within the sweep of the parable Cal-

vinists and Arminians find their place. Calvinists, in the fine sense of the word, will put their chief emphasis on the first two phases. They had to be sought. They are quite right. But the Arminians will insist that there was nothing done for the boy until he sought his father, and came home. They are quite right. It is all here. Someone says he cannot square these things. No, you cannot square a circle. The first movement is from God. That is perfectly true; but man will never get the value of that movement until he seek. Divine sovereignty and human free will. We cannot square them. No, we never shall. The arcs constitute a circle, and the Lord sitteth upon the circle of the earth, and upon the circle of every metaphysical problem we are facing.

Now, let us look a little more closely at the different phases. Take it as a whole, and we see God, whether in the first phase, or the second phase, or the third phase.

Why, then, the three phases? I cannot escape from the conviction that the Fathers of the Church were right in their interpretation of this. In it they saw the Son in the first, the Spirit in the second, and the Father in the third. In the first we have a revelation of the work of God the Son; in the second an unveiling of the activity of God the Holy Spirit; and in the last the unveiling of the heart of God the Father. That is why I said at the beginning, that if we take one phase, we have truth, or any two, we have truth, but not all the truth. All the truth about Divine grace, all the truth about the attitude of the eternal God towards sinning and sinful humanity, is revealed in the three phases of this matchless story.

As to the first. Our Lord here used a figure which He had used before. Indeed, this first phase of the parable is found in the eighteenth chapter of Matthew, not word for word, but certainly thought for thought. Then, however, He applied it to the attitude of the Father;

"Even so it is not the will of your

Father Who is in heaven, that one of these little ones should perish."

Now He used it again, and unquestionably it is still a revelation of the attitude of the Father, but the search for the lost sheep is revealed as the work of the Son.

What a reticent reference is here on the part of our blessed Lord, to that journey He took to find the lost sheep.

"But none of the ransomed ever knew,
How deep were the waters crossed;
Nor how dark was the night that the Lord passed through
Ere He found His sheep that was lost.
Out in the desert He heard its cry—
Sick and helpless, and ready to die.

"'Lord, whence are those blood drops all the way
That mark out the mountain's track?'
'They were shed for one who had gone astray,
Ere the Shepherd could bring him back.'
'Lord, whence are Thy hands so rent and torn?'
'They're pierced tonight by many a thorn.'"

God in His Son, suffering, the journey rough and rugged and steep. No words of interpretation can be sufficient. Let us not attempt to express the unutterable sorrows and sufferings.

But how does it end? With joy, and that was the joy that was set before Him, which made Him endure the Cross, despising the shame, the joy of finding that lost sheep, and bearing it on His shoulders back again. That is the Divine grace, revealed in God the Son.

That does not mean that God the Father does not suffer, and it does not mean that God the Holy Spirit does not suffer. Faber was right when he said,

"There is no place where earth's sorrows
Are more felt than up in heaven."

There is no aggregate of human sorrow in human experience. I may have my sorrow, and you may have yours. Mine is poignant, yours is poignant, but we cannot put them together and say that your sorrow and mine are twice as much as mine is. But all sorrow is centred in the heart of God. In the suffering of the Son we have the expression of that, and the activity of it. The way of humanity's return is the way of Divine compassion, which becomes passion in suffering. This, then, is the first phase of the revelation, the work of the Son, suffering.

We pass to the second. The woman is the type of the Spirit's operation through the Church. From the very first page of the Bible, and throughout, the Motherhood of God is a fact recognized; and the Spirit of God is always the revelation of the Motherhood of God. The first reference to the Holy Spirit in the Bible suggests Motherhood.

"The earth became waste and void; and darkness was upon the face of the deep, and the Spirit of God moved"

—What an inadequate word, "moved." The word is "brooded," the great word of motherhood,

"brooded over the face of the abyss."

The woman is typical of the Spirit here operating through the Church. She is the Bride of the Lamb. Here, then, we see God the Spirit, seeking, searching. The Church is the Bride, and the Spirit through the Church is revealed as seeking the lost silver. It is a piece of silver, a drachma, something of value. It still has on it the superscription of the king, it still has on it the mintage, but it is lost, it has no purchasing power. It is of no current value. That, in itself, is a view of humanity. Not only the lost sheep that has wandered away; but the lost coin that has no purchasing value; and the Spirit through the Church is seen seeking, always seeking until she find it.

Thus we come to the last phase. In it we see the Fatherhood of God. First of all we see him supplying his son with his substance. Everything he had, he had from his father. That is a philosophy of life. Whatever we spend in life of force, physical, mental, and spiritual, we obtain from God. All the forces of our life are His forces. The devil never made a human being. A human being! The devil never made a blade of grass. He has destroyed a good many.

Another fact about God is self-evident, although it is not specifically stated. The father is seen suffering the loss of his son.

" The Son of man is come to seek and save that which was lost."

A lost son. When a son is lost, who suffers most, the son who is lost, or the father who has lost him? Fathers and mothers can answer that question! We should be far more earnest in our missionary work if we could get into the suffering heart of God. We cannot over-emphasize the suffering of humanity. But humanity is suffering because it is away from God, and He is suffering more than humanity does, while humanity is away from Him.

Then, of course, the culminating and principal revelation of this story is that when the son gets back, the father is seen singing. This is an amazing picture of God. While he was yet a long way off, his father saw him. That is very beautiful. But the next thing is the startling thing,

" he ran, and fell on his neck, and kissed him,"

and the Greek word there is " kissed him ;" if we would have it in good, colloquial English, he " smothered him with kisses." That is a picture of God, an old man running, and so far losing his dignity as to fall on the neck of a besmirched lad, and smother him with kisses. What an apparent sacrifice of dignity! And yet we know that an old man is never more dignified than when he runs to meet his boy coming back. That is God. I dare not have drawn that picture, but Jesus did.

Look again. He smothered him with kisses. But he is not clean! That is what the Pharisees were saying about Jesus and the unwashed crowd. Would it not be well if he waited until he is washed? Would it not be well to

wait until those rags are removed, and he is decently clothed? Would it not be well to wait, and see how he does, put him on probation, and if he does well, perhaps his father may receive him? That is the vulgarity of our supposed respectability and accuracy that lack God's love. To all our cautious criticisms the Father would say ; —Let me get my arms about him, and his head pillowed on my breast, and then he will tell all the truth. That is God.

It has been said that if this is the Gospel, there is no need of sacrifice and a Cross. Thirty years ago, Professor Ives Curtiss, of Chicago, wrote a book about Semitic religions. Among other things, he described the sacrifice of the threshold. If a son, whether through rebellion or legitimately, left home for a season, it was the habit to offer a sacrifice upon the threshold on his return. The purpose of the sacrifice was twofold, first an atonement for possible sin, and secondly a feast to be spread when the threshold was crossed. I asked Professor Curtiss, " Have you ever applied the thing you have described there, to the story of the prodigal son ? " He looked at me, and said, " I never thought of it, but surely it may apply."

Now, I am not going to dogmatize about it, but I do say that the sacrifice was offered, and the feast was the outcome. This Eastern custom, which persists to this hour, is there also. I do not want to press that, but do not let us be in a hurry to say that there is no sacrifice there. But even if, in the phase of the parable that shows the attitude of the father, there is nothing said about the Cross, go back, and watch the Son on His journey across the mountains with blood tracks all the way. Love will welcome the boy, but not at the cost of purity.

Thus in the threefold parable we see God in the Son suffering, in the Spirit searching, and in the Father singing when the boy comes home.

But Jesus had not quite done. He had something else to say, and He went on, and said it.

" Now his elder son was in the field."

There is another son. What are we to do with this elder son? It is rather interesting, I nearly said amusing, how men have struggled to explain this. I have heard it said that this is the difference between the Jew and the Gentile. That is very absurd, because we cannot say of the Jew what the father said of this son. The difference is not between Jew and Gentile. The difference is between two sons, one self-righteous, and the other a sinner. But that is not all. Look at this elder son, what do we find? He was devoted to his father's law, and he was devoted to his father's service; but he was entirely out of sympathy with his father's heart; and therefore unable to set the true value upon his brother. The Pharisees and scribes were the men Jesus was looking at when He talked about the elder son. He was taking them at their own valuation, devoted to the law and service of God. To them He said, in effect; You cannot understand God, you cannot understand the heart of God; if you did, you could not look with contempt upon these men outside, with whom I am mixing. The elder son was out of sympathy with the heart of his father. How many sons of God are like that, even in the Church today!

Some years ago I heard my friend, Samuel Chadwick, say something about this story, with which I am going to close this meditation. When he rose to preach, he said, "I am going to preach on the third Son in the parable of the prodigal son." Then he showed the two, the younger breaking his father's heart, and the elder out of sympathy with his father's heart. Then he said: "Isn't there another Son? Yes, there is. He is the Man Who was uttering the parable. He was God's Son, His ideal Son on the human level. He never broke God's heart with His sin, but He was so in sympathy with God's heart that He died to save sinners." That is the third Son of the parable of the prodigal!

Where are we? Are we related to Him in very deed? Then the measure of our relationship is the measure in which we know what it is to suffer in order to serve and save; to seek diligently, and count no case hopeless; and, above all, to sing with the Father when the boy comes home.

LUKE XVI. 1-13

WE are still considering the story of one Sabbath afternoon in Peræa, in the last six months of our Lord's ministry,—and indeed, very close to the end of it. Having uttered the parable of lost things, His teaching went right on. Chapter sixteen begins,

"And He said also unto the disciples."

He had been speaking primarily, all through, to the Pharisees and scribes, the critics. Turning from them, He addressed His disciples, but the word "also" shows that He still had the Pharisees in view in all He said.

In what remains of the story of this Sabbath, that is, to the tenth verse of chapter seventeen, there are three distinct movements. First,

"He said also unto the disciples,"

and this runs on to the end of verse thirteen. At verse fourteen we read,

"And the Pharisees who were lovers of money, heard all these things; and they scoffed at Him. And He said unto them."

The first verse of the next chapter begins,

"And He said unto His disciples."

There He resumed His teaching of His disciples, and that takes us to the tenth verse, where the story of the Sabbath day ends.

We now take the first section, the things He said to His disciples. The Pharisees were men whose outlook on life had become completely materialized, notwithstanding the fact that they were claiming to be the spiritual and moral rulers of the people. In order to discover that, I go for a moment beyond the section we are now considering. The fourteenth verse says,

" The Pharisees who were lovers of money, heard all these things, and they scoffed at Him."

They were mastered by desire for material gain, while claiming to be the teachers of the moral law, and the interpreters of spiritual life to the people. Knowing this, our Lord followed the parable concerning lost things, with teaching which moved entirely in the realm of money. Indeed, this underlies all the teaching which follows to the end of this Sabbath day. In verse one of chapter sixteen, He said:

" There was a certain rich man."

Verse fourteen says:

" The Pharisees who were lovers of money."

In verse nineteen again He said:

" Now there was a certain rich man."

To His disciples He told a story, and followed it by certain clear and concise teaching about money.

The story is one revealing the acumen and cleverness of a rogue. He was a rogue to the end. What he did was wrong. He had no right to change those accounts. All he did was in order that when he was put out of his place as steward, the friends he had made would take him in. It was extremely clever. One man owed a hundred measures of oil, and he let him off with fifty; and the other man owed a hundred measures of wheat, and he made him pay eighty. I don't know why he made the difference between fifty percent and twenty percent. He had been robbing his master, and was about to be turned out of his office. What should he do? He decided to make himself safe by robbing his master again. He was an entire rascal. He said he had not strength to dig. Most probably a case of disinclination rather than disability. He

said to beg he was ashamed. That is the only decent thing recorded of him, and yet even that was an evidence of pride. I am emphasizing all this because it is important. Jesus ended the story by saying that his lord commended him. It seems at first sight a strange story for Jesus to have told. Notice, however, very carefully, that there is not a single syllable that suggests that our Lord was commending the man for what he did.

Why, then, did Jesus tell it? If we continue the reading, we shall see.

" For the sons of this age are for their own generation wiser than the sons of light."

Our Lord did not say the sons of this age are wiser than the sons of light; but

" The sons of this age are *for their own generation* wiser than the sons of light."

That is how He ends the story, and at once I see the value of it.

It is intended to institute a contrast between the sons of this age, and the sons of light. The Pharisees and scribes were listening, the sons of that age; and so also were His disciples, who were going out to represent Him, and carry on His work. He was talking to them, and by the story instituted a contrast in motive and in method, between the sons of this age, and the sons of light. He commended, not the action of dishonesty, but the acumen of the man. That is the whole point of the story. He was showing His disciples the astuteness, the acumen, of the sons of this age, and He said that they are wiser in their generation than the sons of light, more astute in carrying on their enterprises than the sons of light are in carrying out theirs.

Then immediately He applied His story;

"And I say unto you"—His disciples—" Make to yourselves friends by means of the mammon of unrighteousness; that when it shall fail, they may receive you into the eternal tabernacles."

This is a great verse, the rendering of which in the King James' Version has caused much perplexity. There it reads:

"Make to yourselves friends of the mammon of unrighteousness."

Our Lord did not suggest for a single moment that we were to make friends of the mammon of unrighteousness. There is a wide difference between "of" and "by means of." The mammon of unrighteousness is to be used, and used in this way. He was talking about money. He called it "the mammon of unrighteousness." Unrighteousness does not there mean wickedness. Money is not immoral. Money is non-moral. That is a very important distinction. Some people say money is the root of all evil. The Bible does not say so. Money is not the root of all evil. There is no evil in money, and there is no good in money. Money is entirely non-moral. It is the use of it which is good or evil. It may be used for good, or for bad. We can take our money, and so use it as to blast our own souls, and blast men and women round about us; or we can take that same money, and so use it as to bless our own souls, and bless men and women round about us. Some years ago there was a good deal of talk about tainted money. There is no such thing as tainted money. I think there is money I would refuse to receive from certain people. I think there are people in the world whose money I would decline to take if they offered it, not that the money is bad; but the people are bad; and if I took their money, I might be helping to damn their souls.

Our Lord tells us that we are to make friends by means of money. How am I going to make friends to myself by the means of it? In the way exactly opposite to what this man did. He robbed his master, to make friends for himself, so that they would take him into their houses. Now, said Jesus, You are to use money in order that you may make friends by the means of it, who shall receive you into the eternal tabernacles.

There is a man who does wrong, but he is clever, and his cleverness is operating for himself. The only admirable thing in him is his astuteness. Astuteness can be evil, but it remains astuteness. Now, said Jesus, the sons of this age are wiser for their own generation than are the sons of light. They are more astute and clever. But here is the way in which you are to be astute. You are to be astute in the use of your money, by making friends, that when *it* fails, what? When the mammon fails; *they,* who? The friends you make by its use, may receive you into the eternal tabernacles.

Money which, in itself, is a non-moral thing, can be used to blast or bless. In any case, there comes a day when it fails. Sixty seconds after a man is dead he cannot sign a check! All a man can do is to leave his money behind him, for other people to quarrel over, which they mostly do. Personally, I am a strong believer in the idea that it is a poor thing to hang on to money until we are dead. Make use of it, now. How? Make friends by means of it, and when it fails, in that very moment, when your hand is no longer able to sign any check, they, the friends you made, shall greet you in the eternal tabernacles. Put upon your money the measurement, not of your own generation, as these men are doing. It fails, when your generation ends. They are wiser "in their generation." Mark the limit of it. They are clever for today, and fools for ever. You make such use of your money, said Jesus, that when it fails, they shall receive you.

How many investments have we made of that kind? There was a hymn which we used to sing a good deal,

"Will any one then at the beautiful gate,
    Be waiting and watching for me?"

Are there any who have gone on, who are likely to want to see us when we arrive, because of the use we made on their behalf of our wealth? Thus the measurements of the undying ages are placed by Jesus upon the transactions of today, in the market-place, or with our banking account.

But He had not done. Let us, then, go on.

"He that is faithful in a very little is faithful also in much; and he that is unfaithful in a very little is unrighteous also in much. If therefore ye have not been faithful in the unrighteous mammon, who will commit to your trust the true riches? And if ye have not been faithful in that which is another's, who will give you that which is your own?"

Having told them the right use of money, He proceeded to show them the principle of fidelity. Here let us get our terms right, and go carefully, or we may miss our way. He says,

"He that is faithful in a very little is faithful also in much."

What does He mean by that? I think the general interpretation of that passage has been that it means if I am faithful in a little thing, then I shall be trusted with a big thing. That is not the real meaning of the statement. That is reversing cause and effect. He did not say, He that is faithful in a very little *will be* faithful in the much. He said, He *is*. He that is faithful in the little. Who is the man faithful in the little? The man who is faithful in the much. If a man is faithful in the much, he will be faithful in the little. That is the true order. What is the little, and what the much? The little is "the mammon of unrighteousness;" the much refers to the eternal verities, the things of the spirit life; right relationship with God. The man who is faithful in his relationship with the spiritual world will be faithful in his dealing with money. It does not mean that I am to climb to faithfulness in the big thing, by faithfulness in the little. It means rather that I must be right with the big, in order to be right with the little. Another word of Jesus, uttered long before this, reveals the same philosophy. He said to His disciples, when He gave them the ethical Manifesto, "Seek ye first the Kingdom of God, and His righteousness," the

much; "and all these things," the little, "shall be added unto you." He was calling men to a right view of life, to a right view of relative values. So here He said, If men are to be faithful in the little of mammon, they must be faithful in the much of the things of God. He that is faithful in the little is the man who is faithful in the much; and he who is unrighteous in the little thing, is the man who is unrighteous in the bigger thing. That is the principle of fidelity.

The man who is right with God will be punctillious about little things; and if we see a man who is not careful about little things, we may know he is not careful about the much, the eternal things. A man whose spirit, mind, and body, whose whole personality, is poised towards the eternities, will treat every flying moment as of value. That man will never talk about killing time! Was there ever a more abominable phrase than that? What right have we to murder time? But men will do it, unless they are related to eternity.

We sing,

"Give every flying moment, Something to keep in store."

And we are ever doing it, whether the thing we are keeping in store is what we want to find as harvest by and by, may be another question. The man, I repeat, whose life is poised to the ages, is the man who never trifles with the passing moment; and the man who is laying up treasure in the heavens is the man who will know how to use the mammon of unrighteousness.

What next?

"No servant can serve two masters; for either he will hate the one, and love the other"—

that is, if he is a vehement sort of man; or if he is a gentle sort of man;—

"he will hold to one, and despise the other."

The alternative is the same in either case, but two temperaments are in view. One man is very positive and elemental and vehement, the sort we usually call temperamental. What a multitude of sins this word is made to cover today! That man will hate one and love the other. I think I prefer him to the other fellow. The other man is cooler,

" He will hold to one, and despise the other."

In either case the fact remains—

" No servant can serve two masters."

What He meant was made clear at once as He said:

" Ye cannot *serve* God and mammon."

The emphasis there is on the word *serve*. You cannot *serve* God and mammon. You will either hate the one and love the other; or else you will hold to the one, and despise the other.

Which are we doing? Are we hating God and loving mammon? Or are we loving God and hating mammon? Are we holding to God and despising mammon? Or are we holding to mammon, and despising God? When money masters a man it blasts him. When God masters a man, He makes him. And if God masters a man, the man does not abandon his money, but he masters his money, and he makes his money lay up dividends for the eternal habitations; the non-moral money becomes a vehicle of blessing humanity, and glorifying God. On the other hand, the man mastered by money, will patronize God and make a convenience of Him. It cannot be done in the last analysis, but that is what a man will try to do.

In the whole of this teaching, our Lord was showing His disciples that there are two motives in life; love of money, or love of man. These Pharisees and scribes loved money. Jesus loved man. But if we go a little deeper, we find the principle. The love of money, in the last analysis, is love of self; and love of man, at its fountain head, is love of God. The Pharisees and scribes loved themselves, and therefore they loved money. He loved God, and therefore He loved man.

The contrast is self-evident, and, in the light of the story He told them, it is a call to exercise wisdom. The sons of this age are wiser for their generation than the sons of light, said Jesus. It was His judgment upon the sons of light. He did not say they were not sons of light. But they lacked ability to deal with their great enterprises. It is passing strange how this comparison of Jesus has run all down the centuries, and remains true today. Take the enterprises of the devil in this city, and the enterprises of God in this city, and you will see exactly what Jesus meant. The devil never goes on holiday. He never goes to sleep. The sons of this age are far wiser in the way they advertise their wares, in the way they illuminate their buildings, in the way they keep what they want to keep in front of the eyes of the crowd, than are the sons of light. Indeed, the sons of light seem sometimes to think that saintliness is a synonym for a dim religious light. The contrast is seen in the difference between the way in which sometimes a man who is a church member conducts his own business, and the way in which he attends to the affairs of his church. I often wish I could get some Christian men to bring into the Church of God half the enthusiasm they are putting into their Rotarian business. The sons of this age are more keen, and astute, are characterized by more acumen, than are the sons of light. I am not arguing for sensationalism, though I would rather have that, than stagnation. I am not arguing for anything irreverent, or merely spectacular. I am arguing for an understanding of what Jesus said, that the sons of light ought to bring to bear the measurements of the eternities, and the balances of God, upon the business of the Kingdom.

LUKE XVI. 14-31

THE connection of this paragraph with the one last considered is vital. It tells the story of the Pharisees' interruption, and mockery of our Lord, and His teaching resulting therefrom.

The account of the interruption is given in very few words;

"And the Pharisees, who were lovers of money, heard all these things; and they scoffed at Him."

That is the statement, and it reveals an open and positive interruption. Luke begins by giving us the facts concerning these men. They were "lovers of money," they were avaricious. The master passion of their lives was the love of material possession; and that was the subject concerning which our Lord had been talking to His disciples. When they heard this teaching "they scoffed at Him." The King James' Version rendered this, "they derided Him." Either translation is excellent, but it may help us if we look a little carefully at the word thus variously translated. *Ekmukterizo* is the word. Quite literally it means to turn up the nose, or to make mouths. The root of the word is a word meaning snout. It is an animal word; but it came to be used of the facial expression of people sneering, and holding others in contempt. It signifies preeminent disdain. *Mukterizo* means that; but the word here is *ekmukterizo,* and the prefix *ek* marks the fact that they did it openly. These men not only looked disdainfully, they openly laughed at Him, derided Him. They were filled with scorn for this poor Galilean peasant Who talked like that about money. To them, the teaching Jesus had been giving was so preposterous that they could not restrain their mockery. Do not forget that these were the moral and spiritual rulers of the people. There are still those who say that such teaching is characterized by other-worldliness, that it is not practical. What blasphemy there may be in the use of the word practical!

Their mockery was open, and ribald, and contemptuous. That mockery gave them away, for by it they revealed what Luke has recorded, "they were lovers of money." The master passion of their lives was money.

In reply to their mockery our Lord made certain statements, and then told them a story. The statements are found in verses fifteen to eighteen.

He first brought these men face to face with a contrast of motives, the sight of man, and God; the life that is lived, squaring itself with the opinions of men, and the life that always keeps God in view, and acts in accordance with that vision.

Then He uttered a revealing statement.

" That which is exalted among men is an abomination in the sight of God."

What did He mean by "that which is exalted among men"? In psalm forty-nine we have light on this. It deals with the subject of life conditioned by the passion for wealth. It is well worth careful study. In the course of it the psalmist says of the rich man:

" Though while he lived he blessed his soul
(And men praise thee, when thou doest well to thyself),
He shall go to the generation of his fathers."

Carefully observe that parenthetical line.

" Men praise thee, when thou doest well to thyself."

That is as true today as ever. We still praise men whom we call successful because they have done good to themselves in heaping up riches. Men will always praise their fellowmen for astute cleverness in amassing money.

Then, in a statement startling for its vivid scorn, He revealed God's attitude to this kind of thing as He said:

" That which is exalted among men is an abomination in the sight of God."

Quite literally, it is a stench in the nostrils of God.

Then He made a remarkable comment on the whole position.

"The law and the prophets were until John"—

that is, until the time of John's ministry,—

"from that time the Gospel of the Kingdom of God is preached."

The phrase, the Kingdom of God, connotes the Kingship of God, the authority of God, the sovereignty of God. Notice, that our Lord describes that as "good news." We are all liable to read that as though it referred to the Gospel of the grace of God. And so it does ultimately, but fundamentally it is the Gospel of the government of God.

Now, said Jesus, the law was from Moses until John. What then? Then the good news of the Kingship of God. Does the good news set the law aside? He was careful to deny that thought;

"It is easier for heaven and earth to pass away, than for one tittle of the law to fall."

The good news of the Kingship of God does not set aside the law, but it reveals its stern demands. That explains His next words;

"Every man entereth violently into it."

What did He mean by every man entering violently into the Kingdom of God? We shall find the explanation if we look again at the Pharisees. They were living by the standards of human opinion. Men were praising them because they were doing well to themselves. They were taking care of themselves, laying up treasure on the earth. Such men, in order to enter the Kingdom of God, would have to be violent, trampling under foot their prejudices. They were laughing at His idealism; they were deriding His contempt for gold upon the earthly level; they were mocking His view that the real value of money is to make friends who will receive us into the eternal habitations. To such He said in effect; You are quite right, in the opinion of men; you are justified in the sight of men; but God knows your hearts; and the thing exalted by men is a stench in the nostrils of God. The law functioned till John. Now there has come this new declaration, interpretation, manifestation of the Kingship of God; and if you are going to enter into that Kingdom, you will have to take yourselves violently. That was always His outlook on entrance to the Kingdom.

"If any man would come after Me, let him deny himself, and take up his cross, and follow Me."

If any man is coming into the Kingdom, he comes that way.

And then He suddenly made a statement about divorce. Expositors have felt the difficulty of the occurrence of these words at this point. Some have suggested that they constitute an interpolation by a later hand. I think there was a local reason for saying it there. The attitude of the rulers towards divorce at that time was very loose. Even Hillel had said that if a woman put too much salt in the broth, the husband had a sufficient ground for divorcing her! We seem to be going back to Hillel's idea today! Jesus knew these men, and He flung out for some reason, local and immediate in some sense perhaps,

"Every one that putteth away his wife, and marrieth another, committeth adultery; and he that marrieth one that is put away from a husband committeth adultery."

All the looseness had been permitted by men who had become lovers of money.

Then He told them a story. We call it the parable of the rich man and Lazarus. We have even given him a name, Dives. He is not named in the New Testament. Is it a parable? I am not going to answer the question dogmatically. Jesus did not call it a parable. Luke does not call it a parable. Moreover, the fact that, while the rich man is not named, the beggar is named, makes it probable that He was naming an actual case. It may be a parable. If so, at least it is striking that it is the only parable of Jesus in which a name is given to a person.

Whether parable or history, the story introduces us to two men, and their earthly condition is described. The rich man was clothed in purple and fine linen, faring sumptuously every day. The margin says,

" Or living in mirth and splendour every day."

As a matter of fact, the idea of mirth is not the word employed. It is quite a startling word. We have rendered it " sumptuously." The Greek word is *lampros,* which simply means brilliantly. That is to say, it comes from *lampo,* to radiate. The use of the word does not suggest a brilliance which is admirable, but merely the brilliance of display. I think the word which might best translate *lampros* for today would be the word flamboyantly. The very garbing of the man was that of luxury; and he was living flamboyantly. That is the one outstanding fact concerning him. We are not told this man was guilty of any sin which we should denounce as vulgar. His life was one of flamboyant display. He was a rich man, self-centred, displaying ostentatiously his wealth. Even the word Luke names for " gate," when he says the beggar was laid at his gate is a word that means a gate of beauty. It is important thus to see the sort of man he was. Neither then, nor now, would any earthly court of justice arrest or condemn that man. On the contrary, men would justify him, speak well of him; he was doing good to himself. In our Lord's presentation of him the emphasis is on his flamboyant ostentation.

Look at the other man. Our Lord has put the threnody of real pathos into His description of this man Lazarus.

" A certain beggar named Lazarus . . . full of sores."

We must go to Eastern lands to understand that.

" And desiring to be fed with the crumbs that fell from the rich man's table."

Don't put in there, " and no man gave unto him." That is from the parable of the prodigal son. I have heard those words positively added in that connection. He may have received the crumbs. We are not told he did not. We have simply a picture of abject poverty, of a pauper on life's highway, without question through certain social conditions, because the sequel proves that he was a godly man. And Jesus added:

" Yea, even the dogs came and licked his sores."

There was more kindness in the dogs than in the heart of the man who lived in the house, in purple and fine-twined linen. Even if we suppose that Lazarus did gain the scraps from the rich man's table, the rich man would not know about it. There was no generosity in letting him have the crumbs. We do not prove our care for any poor, wretched beggar by the wayside, when we give away the things we have already flung away, rummage sales notwithstanding!

That is our Lord's contrast. Now, the Pharisees would have spurned the beggar, and glorified the success of the wealthy man.

But the story of the two men is not ended. Our Lord went on with it. Something happened.

" It came to pass, that the beggar died."

" And the rich man also died."

They both died. The man with all his wealth could not bribe the grim rider upon the pale horse. He died. The beggar could not postpone the event. He died! They shared the common lot. They are both dead. That company of Pharisees, if there had been any sorrow, might have said of the beggar, " Poor wretch! what a blessing a man like that should have gone!" But of the other they would have said: " It is very sad this man has gone. We wonder what he was worth!" Indeed, they might have said: "What a successful man! Let us write his story for the encouragement of youth."

They both died! Is that all? No, said Jesus, that is not all. Death comes to all, but it does not end all. It does not end all for the rich man. It does not end all for the beggar. It does not end all for any mán.

Well, what was the difference? It does not say that Lazarus was buried at all. Indeed, the probability is that he never was buried, for at that time in Jerusalem, unknown and unclaimed beggars who died by the highway were carried to Tophet, Gehenna, and flung out where the fires were burning to destroy offal. The possibility is that the man whose business it was to clean things up, the scavenger, got the sore-infested body, and pitched it out to Tophet, the actual Gehenna, burning outside the city.

Well, what about the rich man? He "died, and was buried." Exactly. It would be interesting to know what the funeral cost!

Now, it is all over. They have got rid of one body in Tophet, and one body is buried. But, said Jesus, it was by no means over. Using the terminology of the theology of the Jews, He said, when the beggar died,

"he was carried away by the angels into Abraham's bosom."

Thus the Jews described the place "under the altar,"—another Jewish phrase,—where the souls in bliss were, after the earth life. Jesus said the angels carried him into the light where there was no more darkness; into the peace and rest of the bosom of Abraham, where there were no more sores, and no more hunger.

What, then, about this other man who was buried? He was "in Hades." Hades is the world of departed spirits. That is where Lazarus had gone. They were both in Hades. But in the world of departed spirits, the Master says one had reached Abraham's bosom, the place of rest and quietness and healing and peace; the other

"lifted up his eyes, being in tor-

ments, and seeth Abraham afar off, and Lazarus in his bosom. And he cried and said, Father Abraham, have mercy on me, and send Lazarus, that he may dip the tip of his finger in water, and cool my tongue; for I am in anguish in this flame. But Abraham said, Child, remember that thou in thy lifetime receivedst thy good things, and Lazarus in like manner evil things; but now he is comforted, and thou art in anguish. And besides all this, between us and you there is a great gulf fixed, that they that would pass from hence to you may not be able, and that none may cross over from thence to us. And he said, I pray thee therefore, father, that thou wouldest send him to my father's house; for I have five brethren; that he may testify unto them, lest they also come into this place of torment. But Abraham saith, They have Moses and the prophets; let them hear them. And he said, Nay, father Abraham; but if one go to them from the dead, they will repent. And he said unto him, If they hear not Moses and the prophets, neither will they be persuaded, if one rise from the dead."

What was the point of the narrative in its application to the men to whom our Lord was talking? First He was showing the importance of the right use of privilege in this life. Here was a man who made no friends by means of the mammon of unrighteousness.

He was showing, therefore, that the conditions beyond this life result from the facts of life here. The man who lives, doing good to himself, and the whole world justifies him and lauds him, is an abomination to God; and it is so because that man by that very self-centred life, is blasting his own soul. When he passes over, he passes over into the condition which he has created for himself.

Perhaps the most arresting thing is the final word. This man says, Send someone to my brethren; and the answer that comes to him from the bosom of Abraham is, They have Moses and the prophets; they would not hear if one rose from the dead.

That statement reveals the tremendous fact that life which is not affected by moral considerations will not be affected by the miraculous. A little later on another man named Lazarus died, and Jesus raised him from the dead. We are told distinctly that these same men tried to kill him! There came a day when they put Jesus to death, and He rose from the dead, but His resurrection from the dead made no appeal to men who lacked the moral sense which puts God first, and measures all life by the standards of eternity.

This is the one occasion in all the teaching of our blessed Lord when the curtain is drawn back, and we are permitted to look at life beyond the present. "He died." That does not end the story. Carried by the angels; buried and awake in anguish; which? It depends on whether life is adjusted to the Kingdom of God, or conformed to the false standards of men.

LUKE XVII. 1-10

IN these first ten verses we have the account of the last stage in Luke's wonderful story of a Sabbath afternoon in Peræa. Having rebuked the Pharisees for their scoffing, our Lord turned again to His disciples, and His teaching is a sequence and a sequel. In this paragraph we have His teaching on four distinct matters. First teaching on the subject of offences, (verses one and two); then teaching on the subject of forgiveness, (verses three and four); then teaching on faith, (verses five and six); and finally teaching concerning service, (verses seven to ten).

"It is impossible but that occasions of stumbling should come; but woe unto him, through whom they come! It were well for him if a millstone were hanged about his neck, and he were thrown into the sea, rather than he should cause one of these little ones to stumble."

These words were spoken in the interest of those whom our Lord described as "little ones." In Matthew, we find an occasion when He used the same figure of speech, "little ones" evidently referring to children. Here He was not speaking of children specifically. I do not mean that children are excluded. They were included in what He said; but He was speaking in the interest of the despised crowd that the Pharisees were holding in contempt, and criticizing Him for coming into close contact with them.

Notice His recognition of world conditions then, which conditions abide even until today. He said it is impossible but that occasions of stumbling

should come. All round about these little ones, all round about men and women everywhere, there are occasions of stumbling, causing them to stumble and fall and fail and sin. He recognized that these things are inevitable. While doing so, the solemnity of His next word,

"But woe unto him, through whom they come,"

is a revelation of the wrong of being the cause of such occasions.

These facts remain true today. Take the land as we know it today, our own land. Take the city as we know it today, our own city. Take the conditions of human life as we know them anywhere. Wherever we examine, whether in the slum areas, or on the boulevards, whether in the university, or the penitentiary, wherever life is being lived, we find occasions of stumbling. Here, then, is our Lord's word. The occasions of stumbling are there,

"But woe unto him, through whom they come."

The inevitability of stumbling-blocks in the way of men does not remove responsibility from those who put them there. A tremendous consideration, having the widest application. Here our Lord was tracing the fault, and the failure, and the sin, and the breakdown of men, to the reason for it, to those who create these stumbling-blocks, whomsoever they may be. He was going behind the fall of a little one, to find the man who put the stumbling-block in that little one's way.

Our Lord did not say that the stumbling may not be wrong in itself. He did not say that the sin of those who fall may not be a real sin; but for the moment He was considering causes, and He was saying in effect: The man who put the stumbling-block in the way of the little one is more guilty than the little one who fell over the stumbling-block.

There is a common consciousness abroad in the world today which recognizes the truth of that. Think of a situation in which we have been living for sixteen years all told. I am thinking of the War. I take this word of Jesus, and apply it there. It is a wide application, but it is justified. It is impossible but that occasions of stumbling should arise, but woe unto him through whom they arise. The last guilt of the War is upon those who caused it. Who were they? I have only referred to this in order to ask you to observe how extremely anxious all the nations involved in the War are to decline the blame for it. The common underlying human conscience is ringing true to the thing Jesus said, Offences will come, but woe unto the man through whom they come.

Whereas the principle applies nationally and racially, it applies also individually. Did that boy go wrong? He went wrong, and his wrong was sin. Was there someone who put a stumbling-block in his way? Then the man who did it, or the girl who did it, is supremely guilty before the High Court of Heaven. I need not labour the point. It is so self-evident.

Now notice the woe.

"Woe unto him, through whom they come."

The woe is not defined. Do not read this carelessly. Our Lord did not say that the woe upon such an one is that he shall have a millstone hanged about his neck, and be thrown into the sea. That is not the woe. That is the way of escaping the woe. "It were well for him." Christ was saying in effect; Rather than cause another to stumble, it were good for a man to be drowned in the depth of the sea. That might be a way of escape from the sin, and so from the woe that falls upon the man who is the occasion of the stumbling. Our Lord leaves the woe undescribed, leaves its nameless, unless we remember that He was now talking to His disciples, immediately after having given them a glimpse of life beyond death. If we read the story of "the little one," Lazarus, at the gate of Dives, and then see them in the life beyond, we may have some understanding of the woe.

The principle is one we do well to ponder, not only in its application, as we have said, to world affairs and conditions; but also to ourselves. These boys and these girls, these men, and these women, these simple, foolish souls, will find pitfalls everywhere, and they will fall over them; but the ultimate guilt of the man or the woman, or the society, for the condition that placed the stumbling-blocks is greater than that of the persons who fall over them.

So He passed to the second subject.

"Take heed to yourselves; if thy brother sin, rebuke him; and if he repent, forgive him. And if he sin against thee seven times in the day, and seven times turn again to thee, saying, I repent; thou shalt forgive him."

There was no break. Our Lord went straight on, and although there is a sudden and apparent change, He was really stating the case from the other side. Supposing some man does put a stumbling-block in my way, supposing he sins against me, what is to be my attitude towards him? I am to rebuke him. I am to point out the thing that he has done; and if he repent, I am to forgive him. And if in a day—mark it—if in one day that man put a stumbling-block in my way seven times, or seven different stumbling-blocks, and comes back and says, he repents, I am to forgive him seven times. It is not possible but that occasions of stumbling shall come; but woe unto the man through whom they come. It were well for him to escape from the woe if a millstone were hanged about his neck, and he should be thrown into the sea; but take heed to yourselves; if thy brother sin, rebuke him; and if he repent, forgive him.

If a man put a stumbling-block in my way, my first duty is to rebuke him. If he repent, I am to forgive him. If I do that, I am seeing to it that I am putting no stumbling-block in the way of the man who put the stumbling-block in my way.

Notice very carefully, that our Lord said if he repent, forgive him. We are not to forgive a man if there is no sign of repentance. If there is no sign of change of mind, if he persists in his sin, if he persists in doing the thing we have rebuked, we are not to forgive him. Forgiveness is based on his repentance. And yet, when our Lord repeated it, He said if he shall do this seven times, and *say* he repent, I am to forgive him. That sharply pulls me up. At first He said, If he repent, forgive him; and then, knowing the human heart, our Lord put the matter on another level, and said that if the man says he repents, I am to forgive him. Better to secure the sanctity and the beauty of our own character by being ready to forgive seven times, even though the man is not sincere, than by refusing forgiveness to a truly repentant soul, be in danger of putting a stumbling-block in his way.

Then we read:

"And the apostles said unto the Lord, Increase our faith."

That is arresting. I should not have been surprised if Simon Peter had said it, but Luke, the careful writer, says,

"The apostles said unto the Lord, Increase our faith."

There was unanimity in their sense of difficulty. They said, "Increase our faith." They never spoke more intelligently than they did in that moment. The appeal was the expression of their sense of the difficulties of life as He had thus presented it to them. Rather than cause a little one to stumble, it would be well to have a great millstone hanged about the neck, and be thrown

into the sea; and yet if your brother is causing you to offend, you are to rebuke him, and if he repents, you are to forgive him seven times a day. And the apostles said, Lord, "increase our faith." It was intelligent, because they did not say, Lord, increase our love. No, they said, Increase our faith, that which takes hold upon the unseen, and brings it to bear upon all life's activities.

"Faith is . . . the evidence of things not seen."

Increase our faith. Give us a larger, firmer grasp upon the eternal verities, or else we cannot live this way.

The reply of Jesus was significant and revealing.

"If ye had faith as a grain of mustard seed, ye would say unto this sycamine tree, Be thou rooted up, and be thou planted in the sea; and it would obey you."

I have spoken of their appeal as a highly intelligent one, and I think it was so, but notice His correction. They said, "Increase our faith." He said in effect: You do not want more faith. You do not want, if you are going to talk about bulk, anything bigger than a mustard seed. It is not bulk you want, it is not quantity of faith you need, it is faith of a certain quality.

What is there in a grain of mustard seed that is distinctive? Life. The life in a grain of mustard seed is enough in its operation finally and fully not merely to uproot a sycamine tree, but to uproot a mountain. Our Lord said "mountain" once on another occasion;

"Even if ye shall say unto this mountain, Be thou taken up and cast into the sea, it shall be done."

In Italy there is a remarkable tomb. An enormous block of granite was brought and placed there by order of the man who is buried underneath. Before he died he arranged that this great mass of granite should be laid over his tomb; and he did so, saying that he did it in order that if there ever was a resurrection, it might be

195

certain he should never rise! We smile at the folly of it. It is an interesting fact that this block of granite weighing tons is there, but split in two. Between the hour of his sepulture and the placing of that block over his grave, a bird flying across carrying an acorn, happened to drop the acorn right there. They put the granite slab in place, and if you see it now, that enormous slab of granite weighing tons, is split clean through the middle and the oak tree from the acorn is there, growing straight up through it! The living power in the acorn has split the granite. If you have faith as a grain of mustard seed, if your faith has but a living quality, if your faith is more than a dead orthodoxy, the acceptance of certain statements as true intellectually, if it is a living thing, which in your life is producing results that are in consonance with the things you profess to believe, then there is nothing impossible, said Jesus. You will be able to forgive your brother seven times. You will see to it you put no stumbling-blocks in the way of men.

Then He came to the last of these four matters, and again there is an apparent contrast, but He was going straight on;

" But who is there of you, having a servant plowing or keeping sheep."

The " but " shows connection. He knew that if men have faith as a grain of mustard seed, that if they have the faith which can remove mountains, there is a danger of pride. Therefore He said:

" When ye shall have done all the things that are commanded you, say, We are unprofitable servants."

This He introduced by a parable of contrast. He said:

" Who is there of you, having a servant "—and the word is *doulos,* it is a slave—" having a slave plowing or keeping sheep, that will say unto him, when he is come in from the field, Come straightway and sit down to meat," and I will wait on you.

Won't he rather say, Get ready for me, and when I have eaten, then you may eat?

" Doth he thank the servant because he did the things that were commanded? "

With that little parable in mind, let us go back for a moment in Luke's Gospel. In chapter twelve, we read,

" Let your loins be girded about, and your lamps burning; and be ye yourselves like unto men looking for their lord, when he shall return from the marriage feast; that, when he cometh and knocketh, they may straightway open unto him. Blessed are those servants "—that is the same word, *douloi* —" Blessed are those slaves, whom the lord when he cometh shall find watching; verily I say unto you, that he shall gird himself, and make them sit down to meat, and shall come and serve them."

There He was speaking of Himself, and He declared that when His servants' days' work is over, He will make them sit down, and He will wait on them. Here He said, Can you conceive a situation like that? Is that the ordinary thing? It was a parable in contrast. He was showing them the ways of the world. He had already told them what He would do with them. He was warning them against pride in spiritual power. He had just said, If you have faith as a grain of mustard seed you will see mighty things done. Now He said in effect: Don't forget when you see the mighty things done, because you have faith that is a living faith, you are not to take any credit for the things you have done. You are to be delivered from pride even in the hour of spiritual victory, for even at the best, we are unprofitable servants, and we have only done our duty. The marvel is that presently He will do for us what earthly lords never do for their slaves. But it will be wholly of grace, nothing we have a right to claim, nothing which ought to give us for one moment the lifted chin, or an air of braggadocia, or the strut of pride. I wonder if we believe that. Service that looks for reward is selfish. Yet how often we talk of the rewards that are coming. To serve for reward is not Christian, but anti-christian. He emptied Himself. He served for "the joy that was set before Him." Yes, but what was the joy? The joy of lifting other people, and blessing them.

And so the story of a wonderful Sabbath afternoon ends. For one moment, in conclusion look back on it. I watch Jesus all through these circumstances, and how radiant and wonderful He appears. The whole movement began in a criticism of Jesus for breaking the Sabbath day, when He healed the man. Then it continued in criticism of Him for making Himself the Companion of sinning men. It went on with laughter at Him for His otherworldliness of outlook. As through the day, the Sabbath day, the Sabbath afternoon, I watch Him, the first thing that arrests me is that for Him on the earthly level there was no Sabbath. Rest was

broken in upon everywhere. The social group in the house broke in upon His rest, by reason of the falseness of their living; the sinning crowds broke in upon His rest, by reason of their wounds and weariness and need. The scoffing rulers broke in upon His rest, by their ribaldry and their sneering. And the sincere but slow disciples also broke in upon His rest.

Yes, but look again. As we do so we see that on the eternal plane, far removed from all that which ruffled the surface of earthly experience, His was perpetual Sabbath. All the way through He was marked by a complete serenity, and an unfailing strength. In quietness and in confidence He took His way through. He is seen as the radiant Lord and Master of us all; giving up all thought of rest in the interest of humanity; and all the time resting in God, and held secure.

LUKE XVII. 11-37

IN Luke's narrative, considered from the standpoint of the historical or chronological sequence, there is a gap between verses ten and eleven in chapter seventeen. There is no doubt that our Lord was in Peræa when the message came to Him that Lazarus was sick; it was there that He tarried; and thence He went and raised Lazarus from the dead. The story is found in John eleven. In that same chapter we find that after He had raised Lazarus, He travelled north to Ephraim, where He tarried, for how long we are not told, but for some time apparently, in quietness, with His disciples.

The story as we have it here in Luke, takes up at that point, and we find Him travelling still further north than Ephraim, on the border line between Samaria and Galilee.

"And it came to pass, as they were on the way to Jerusalem, that He was passing along the borders of Samaria and Galilee."

That does not mean that He went into Samaria. It does not mean that He went into Galilee. He had already

left Galilee, not to go back, until after His Cross and resurrection. The opening phrase of this paragraph, "As they were on the way to Jerusalem," does not mean that at that time He was on His actual way to the city. The fifty-first verse of chapter nine marks the breaking point between Cæsarea Philippi and the final six months in the ministry of Jesus.

"It came to pass when the days were well nigh come that He should be received up, He stedfastly set His face to go to Jerusalem."

That was six months before the Cross, during which He was moving resolutely towards the ultimate. That is the fact which Luke had in mind when, at this point, he wrote,

"It came to pass, as they were on their way to Jerusalem."

In the next chapter, eighteen, at verse thirty-one, we read,

"He took unto Him the twelve, and said unto them, Behold, we go up to Jerusalem."

That is the record of the beginning of the final journey to Jerusalem.

In this section we have two things; an incident, that of the ten lepers; and following upon it, teaching which Jesus gave on the subject of the Kingdom, as the result of something said to Him.

I am almost inclined to say that the narrative of the ten lepers needs no interpretation. It is so explicit, and full of beauty. We may, however, tarry to emphasize two or three things. It is arresting to see these ten men, not daring to come near Jesus, standing away off, and reduced by leprosy, to the common consciousness of humanity. There were ten of them, and one of them was a Samaritan. " Jews had no dealings with the Samaritans," and it is equally true that Samaritans had no dealings with Jews. But we see them here united by common misery. They were reduced to the consciousness of their common humanity by that misery. Under such conditions men forget the things that hold them apart. It would almost seem as though there may be occasions when trouble and misery are beneficent, if they reduce men to the consciousness of their common humanity, and make them forget the things that divide. We passed through appalling experiences a few years ago. Oh, the misery of it, the agony of it; but for those four years and three months manhood was reduced to a common human consciousness. In that misery, men had no remembrance, no consciousness of the things over which they had quarrelled, and that had divided them, before the misery and the calamity came. The trouble is that when the misery passed, they remembered them all again.

Another arresting matter in this incident, is the method of Jesus with these men. In chapter five we had the story of Jesus and a leper, and there we were told ;—

"And it came to pass, while Jesus was in one of the cities, behold, a man full of leprosy; and when he saw Jesus, he fell on his face, and besought Him, saying, Lord, if Thou wilt, Thou canst make me clean. And He stretched forth His hand, and touched him, saying, I will; be thou made clean. And straightway the leprosy departed from him. And He charged him to tell no man; but go thy way, and show thyself to the priest."

Notice His method with that man. Here we have something different. When these men lifted up their voices,

" saying, Jesus, Master, have mercy on us, when He saw them, He said unto them, Go and show yourselves unto the priests."

He did not touch them, and did not say, I will, be thou made clean. He said, Go and show yourselves to the priests. In the earlier incident He cleansed first, and then sent the men to the priest. Here He sent them to the priests, and cleansed them on their way. I do not know why in one case He did one thing, and in another case another. The difference speaks of the variety in our Lord's dealings with men, even in the case of leprosy. And yet, less things than that, have sometimes divided the followers of Christ into sections. The pity of it!

It is noticeable, however, that in both cases He sent them to the priests. Why? The answer is found in the book of Leviticus, in chapters thirteen and fourteen, which contain the law of the leper. In the Divine economy the priest was appointed, to examine the leper and see whether he was suffering from true leprosy or false. Moreover, the priest was the one who was to pronounce him clean, if he were clean. So Jesus told these men to obey the Mosaic economy, in order that the priest might pronounce them clean.

His method with these ten was that of sending them to the priest, before they were cleansed. Therefore their going was the going of faith. Evidently they were cleansed as they journeyed.

Then the astonishing element in the narrative emerges. There were ten of them cleansed, and only one came back to thank God. Jesus said,

" Were not the ten cleansed? but where are the nine?"

What a revelation of the fact that Christ values gratitude, and misses it when it is not expressed. We had another illustration of it in chapter seven. When He went to the house of Simon He missed the common courtesy of the Eastern home. "You gave Me no water for My feet, you gave Me no kiss, My head with oil you did not anoint; you neglected the common courtesies." Are we not all in danger of being among the nine, rather than being represented by the one, forgetting and failing in our praising? We have almost lost the art of pure praise. Even our hymns of praise merge into thanksgiving, which is less than praise. Thanksgiving is the expression of our gladness that God is good to us. Praise is worship, adoration, the expression of our sense of the goodness and the glory of God. In praise we give to God. Let us never forget that in the Old Testament God has caused it to be written by inspiration,

"Whoso offereth praise glorifieth God."

And at least, we ought to give Him thanks for what He does for us. Were there not ten cleansed? Where are the nine?

Our next section contains teaching on the Kingdom, first to the Pharisees, about the immediate, verses twenty and twenty-one; and then to the disciples, about the ultimate, verses twenty-two to thirty-seven.

The Pharisees asked Him,

"When the Kingdom of God cometh?"

That question, as they asked it, was a satirical question. Let us glance on to the nineteenth chapter, and the eleventh verse;

"And as they heard these things, He added and spake a parable, because He was nigh to Jerusalem, and because they supposed that the Kingdom of God was immediately to appear."

That statement shows the attitude of the people towards Him. There was a widespread conviction that He was going to establish the Kingdom of God, as they understood the establishment of the Kingdom of God. All through our Lord's ministry, His difficulty with the rulers, as well as with the people, was that they had a mistaken idea of the Kingdom of God. They were looking merely for an earthly kingdom. They were expecting the power of Rome to be broken, the despotism of Rome ended, and that a kingdom would be established then and there, of a material nature. Against that false and materialistic conception Jesus flung Himself in all His teaching. These Pharisees knew that He was making His way to Jerusalem; and so they asked Him when the Kingdom of God was coming. The cynicism of the inquiry is self-evident.

When we understand the spirit of the question, we understand His answer. That answer consisted of two negatives, and a positive. The first negative;

"The Kingdom of God cometh not with observation."

The second negative;

"Neither shall they say, Lo, here! or, There!"

The positive;

"For lo, the Kingdom of God is among you."

He began by saying,

"The Kingdom of God cometh not with observation."

I do not know any passage which has suffered more at the hand of expositors than this. It has been interpreted to mean that the Kingdom of God comes so quietly, that its coming cannot be seen. That is not so. When the Kingdom of God comes, it is seen at once, whether in a man, or a nation.

Everything depends upon the meaning of the word "observation." Now, as a matter of fact, that is the only place in the New Testament where the abstract noun in the Greek, *parateresis,* which we have translated "observation," occurs. The verb, *paratereo,* from which it is derived, is also rare. It only occurs in Mark iii.2, Luke vi.7, Luke xiv.1; Luke xx.20, Acts ix.24 and in Galatians iv.10. An examination of these will show that the word is always sinister. It always means the watching of hostility.

Thus our Lord declared that the Kingdom of God is not manifested to eyes that are watching critically, inspired by hostility. Again, Neither, said Jesus, shall they say, Lo, here, or There. That is to say, it will never come with localized effect, so that men can say, Here is its centre, or there.

Then He made the positive declaration. He said,

"The Kingdom of God is among you."

Not *within* you, but *among* you. The word is *entos*, and its use with the plural always means in the midst, not within an individual, but in the midst of a group. Here again we are face to face with one of the common and popular misinterpretations of a great saying. It is affirmed that Jesus meant that the Kingdom of God is within every man. He certainly did not say that the Kingdom is within the man who is hostile to the Kingdom of God. The men to whom He was then speaking, He denounced presently as whited sepulchres, and hypocrites. The Kingdom was not within them. The Kingdom of God was among them then, because the King was there.

Then He turned to His disciples.

"And He said unto the disciples, The days will come, when ye shall desire to see one of the days of the Son of man, and ye shall not see it. And they shall say to you, Lo, there! Lo, here! go not away, nor follow after them."

He was speaking about the period that was then just ahead, when He would no longer be among them as He then was. In chapter ten, verses twenty-three and twenty-four, we read,

"Blessed are the eyes which see the things that ye see; for I say unto you, that many prophets and kings desired to see the things which ye see, and saw them not; and to hear the things which ye hear, and heard them not."

He was then referring to the days of His earthly ministry. Now He said to the disciples,

"The days will come when ye shall desire to see one of the days of the Son of man, and ye shall not see them."

That is to say, the days are coming when I shall not be here as I am with you now. The days are coming when the Kingdom will not be among men in the sense it is among you now, because I am here. He then charged them that during that period they were not to be seduced. Some would arise who, in His absence, would say Christ is here, or Christ is yonder. They will say, Lo, here, or Lo, there. They will localize the place for the Kingdom. Do not be seduced during that period. We are in that period now. While the spiritual presence of Christ abides, as to bodily presence, He is absent, and has been since His Ascension. Every now and then somebody has arisen, and said, Lo, here, or There; here is the Man, or here is the centre; and alas, many of the elect have been seduced on the way through the centuries. Against this peril our Lord was warning His disciples.

Having referred to the period immediately ahead in that way, He then tells them of the ultimate.

"For as the lightning, when it lighteneth out of the one part under the heaven, shineth unto the other part under heaven; so shall the Son of man be in His day."

The period of His absence will end with the manifestation of the Son of man, in a coming and an unveiling, which will be so patent that all men shall know that the day has come.

Then, in an aside, He said,

"But first must He suffer many things and be rejected of this generation."

Even His disciples were hoping He was going to set up the Kingdom then on a material basis. No, He said, I am on the way to the Cross. That must precede the final manifestation.

He then went on to show the conditions which will exist when He comes. He told them that in the day of His advent, in the day of His unveiling, in the day when the Son of man is revealed, after the period in which He is hidden, He will not find everybody ready and waiting for Him. Things will be going on just as they were in the days of Noah and Lot. All the ordinary avocations of life on the material plane, eating and drinking, giving in marriage, buying and selling, will be going on, when suddenly, crashing across the commonplaces of life, the Son of man will be manifested. The day of the unveiling of the Son of man will break upon all the world's affairs suddenly.

He said, moreover, that it will be a punitive breaking in. It will be a day of punishment and a day of discrimination,

"I say unto you, In that night there shall be two men in one bed; the one shall be taken, and the other shall be left."

The one taken is the one that is punished, not the one left. There is nothing here about the second coming of the Lord so far as the Church is concerned. That is not the subject. Our Lord here was dealing with world conditions; He was declaring the judgment of all that He will find contrary to Himself. When the Son of man comes, His coming will be so definite and positive, that men cannot miss it. There will be no need to announce it. It will be like the lightning's flash, illumining all the heavens. In that day He will find the world going on just as in the days of Noah and Lot; and He will find people true to Him as well as people submerged in their iniquities. Therefore His advent will be a coming in punishment, and yet of discrimination.

The disciples said to Him, "Where, Lord?" Is not that arresting? He was warning them against that idea

of locality, and yet they said, Where? Their "Where?" was geographical. Their "Where?" was materialistic. What did He say?

"Where the body is, thither will the eagles also be gathered together."

His "where" was universal and moral. They said, Where will this happen? Where will be the centre of Thy coming? And He said, Where the body is, the eagles are gathered. Where that is, which needs dealing with, there the coming will be. A universal thing, dealing with all life, and dealing with it completely.

All this teaching had to do with earthly conditions. The heaven beyond, to which the saints of God will be gathered, is not referred to at all. He was referring to the terms of the people expecting the Kingdom, and the terms of the Pharisaic criticism; and He said in effect; Yes, there will be a day when the earthly Kingdom shall be set up. That earthly Kingdom will be set up when the Son of man comes; and when He comes, there will be no need for any special announcement of His arrival, Lo, here, or There; all the earth will know.

Will He find all the earth waiting for Him? On a later day He said,

"When the Son of man cometh shall He find faith on the earth?"

This should read,

"Shall He find *the* faith on the earth?"

He did not answer the question, but the obvious inference is that in the day of His coming He will not find "the faith" triumphant on earth. There will be mixture. Here He reveals the same truth. The world will be going on just the same, eating and drinking, marrying, buying, selling. But when He comes, the whole process ends; and the ending will be the ending of everything that offends, and the true order will be established. Only the things that are in harmony with the Divine Kingship will remain.

LUKE XVIII. 1-30

IN these thirty verses we find the last things in the public ministry of our Lord, as recorded by Luke, prior to the final journey to Jerusalem. If for a moment we glance on to verse thirty-one, we find these words:

"And He took unto Him the twelve, and said unto them, Behold, we go up to Jerusalem."

That is where the story of the final journey begins.

Here, then, we find ourselves in the same general surroundings as those which have characterized our last few meditations. His disciples were still with Him. The critical rulers were still standing by. And all about Him was the general and promiscuous crowd.

In this paragraph there are two sections; first two parables that fell from the lips of our Lord; and then two incidents, which unquestionably took place in close connection.

The first parable was spoken to His disciples.

"And He spake a parable unto them,"

begins chapter eighteen, and the "them" must be interpreted by a glance back to the twenty-second verse of the previous chapter,

"He said unto the disciples."

As there, so here, He was speaking to His disciples. Then, in the same realm of ideas, Jesus addressed Himself to others;

"And He spake also this parable unto certain who trusted in themselves that they were righteous."

The first parable was spoken specifically to His disciples; the second quite evidently specifically to the critical crowd of rulers, who were trusting in themselves that they were righteous, and were setting all others at nought. The two parables moved in the same realm of thought, but had two entirely different emphases.

The first parable opens with a very arresting statement;

"And He spake a parable unto them to the end that they ought always to pray, and not to faint."

That tells us why this parable was uttered. I do not think any one would care to be dogmatic as to whether that statement is Luke's by inspiration, or a statement which Jesus made before He uttered the parable.

"He spake a parable to the end that they ought always to pray, and not to faint."

Possibly Luke introduced the parable by recording what Jesus had said before He uttered the parable. In any case, we have the reason for the parable. It was uttered by Jesus in order to emphasize the necessity for prayer, and the necessity for prayer as a constant activity.

"He spake this parable unto them to the end that they ought always to pray, and not to faint."

We must not forget the connection of the parable with teaching He had recently given. He had been speaking of the fact that in the day of His final Manifestation, things would be going on in the world just as they had been in the days of Noah, and in the days of Lot. Consequently, the age in which these men were called upon to live would be days of great difficulty. The parable, then, is a revelation of what is necessary for the life of faith, in an age which is not conducive to faith. In such an age, prayer is the very essence of life. Under such circumstances, our Lord says, in effect, there is one alternative offered to us, prayer or fainting. Our Lord's outlook upon the age, and of the life of His people through that age, is that unless men pray, they will faint.

It may be asked, How can people always pray? The answer is that we must understand what prayer is. Prayer is far more than uttering

202

words. I can pray when I do not think I am praying. We can pray without any words at all. Prayer, in the last analysis, is the urge of the life towards God, and spiritual things; the setting of the mind upon things above, as Paul has it. Every detail of every day can be mastered by that urge. Prayer literally means to wish forward. Prayer, then, is desiring towards the ultimate, the urge that for ever masters life for the coming of the Kingdom of God, and the victory of all things spiritual. Now, said Jesus, Unless your life is of that nature, you will faint.

"Men ought always to pray and not to faint."

Thus we learn the purpose of the parable. In the light of that statement, let us consider it.

"There was in a city a judge who feared not God, and regarded not man."

The fear of God was not in his heart, and consequently, he had no regard for man.

"And there was a widow in that city; and she came oft unto him, saying, Avenge me of mine adversary."

The word avenge means, not revenge, but exercise justice. This widow was not asking him to take vengeance on any one. What she said was, Do me justice as against my adversary. And he would not for a while, and

"Afterward he said within himself, Though I fear not God, nor regard man; yet because this widow troubleth me, I will avenge her, lest she wear me out,"

literally, "lest she bruise me." The picture is that of a judge, whose office it is to administer justice, who has no respect for authority, for the authority of God, or the opinion of man. He neither fears God nor regards man. To him a widow comes, and he has no time for her, he gives her no attention. But she keeps on coming. The parable is generally called the parable of the importunate widow. At last this judge says: In order that I may be free from her worrying, I

will do what she wants. His motive was not the fear of God. His motive was not respect for the woman. His motive was that he did not want to be bruised!

Nearly all expositors declare that the parable teaches us that we must be importunate in prayer. I hold, on the contrary, that it teaches that when we are dealing with God there is no need of importunity. It is a parable of contrast all through. Our Lord said,

"Hear what the unrighteous judge saith. And shall not God avenge the elect, that cry to Him day and night, and yet He is longsuffering over them? I say unto you, that He will avenge them speedily."

Whereas the widow was importunate, through the tardiness of an unjust judge, God will avenge the elect speedily, so that there is no need for importunity on their part.

Everyone recognizes the contrast between the unjust judge and God. He had no regard for God and man; and the only reason he did what the woman asked was that he did not want to be bruised! Everyone sees the difference between that man and God. God is under authority. He is eternally under the authority of righteousness. He cannot violate justice, and He acts under the highest sanctions of the universe. So Jesus said in effect: If that man, to save his own miserable life from bruising, gives in answer to importunity, is it not certain that the God Who is righteous, will act speedily? God does not require persuading; does not require—forgive the word—worrying. "Speedily" is the word. Quicker than the lightning's flash is the answer of God to the cry of His people. His answers do not always come in the form we hoped they would, but He answers. Because we have a God quick and ready to answer every cry of the oppressed in the right way, prayer can be maintained constantly. "Men ought always to pray," ought for ever to link their life to that of God, and His readiness; and to know that when the answer does not come as we thought that it would, the answer is still there, and is always best.

Our Lord ended the parable with a very remarkable question,

" When the Son of man cometh, shall He find faith on the earth? "

That must be interpreted by His previous discourse. When He comes, the world will be going on as it had been going on. His question is,

" Will He find *the* faith on the earth? "

He certainly will find the elect, He will find people who have lived by faith, who have been through the buffetting, the bruising, and have surmounted the difficulty. They have always prayed, in order not to faint. But He will not find *the* faith in its final victory. The whole earth will not be filled with faithful souls when He comes. He was again reverting to the fact of the difficulty of the age, as He gave them this illustration of prayer in its necessity and in its possibility, because God is not an unjust God.

So we pass on.

"And He spake also this parable unto certain who trusted in themselves that they were righteous, and set all others at nought."

Now, if the first parable had to do with prayer, we may say that the second parable has to do with self-righteousness, which is perfectly true, only it is interesting to ʳbserve that when our Lord came to deal with this self-righteous crowd, He still spoke in that same realm of prayer. He shows us that self-righteous man when he is praying.

The reason of the parable is revealed in the opening statement quite definitely.

" He spake also this parable unto certain who trusted in themselves that they were righteous, and set all others at nought."

The Greek there, quite literally, is,

" They trusted in themselves that they were righteous, and set *the rest* at nought."

There is contempt in the expression— " The rest." There stood a group of rulers, with their garments gathered around them lest they should contract the defilement of the unwashed crowds, " the rest "!

" Two men went up into the Temple to pray."

Two men. Each was a man; and only a man. Our Lord described them first by the term which revealed them as Heaven saw them. Two men! Whenever men cross the threshold of the Temple, that is how they are listed by high Heaven.

Moreover, they both went up to pray. And there, in their prayers, the difference was revealed.

" The Pharisee stood and prayed thus with himself."

Can you find anything in literature to surpass that for satire? Listen ᴛo him.

" God, I thank Thee, that I am not as the rest of men, extortioners, unjust, adulterers, or even as this publican."

Evidently he had seen the other man! I think he was glad he was there, although he held him in contempt He was a dark and despicable sinner revealing by contrast the brilliance of his own position !

" This publican. I fast twice in the week, I give tithes of all that I get."

That was all his prayer. Five times he used the personal pronoun in the nominative case. God is recognized. He was ostensibly talking to God, but as revealed in the infinite satire of Jesus, he was praying with himself. He could not get away from God, but he was not near God. He had an intellectual conviction, but that does not make contact with God. Hell is full of intellectual conviction. God? Oh, yes. But he was so occupied with himself he could not get away from himself. He never made another reference to God at all. " I . . . I . . . I . . . I . . . I . . . ! "

" But the publican, standing afar off,

would not lift up so much as his eyes
unto heaven, but smote his breast, saying, God."

He began with the same word, but his
conception and attitude are revealed in
what he said next;

" Be Thou merciful to me, a sinner."

One personal pronoun in the objective
case—" me," and a description of the
person referred to, "a sinner," and a
gasp flung out into eternity, " Be merciful." Two men, one God; and each
man began by addressing God. The
one was so occupied with himself as
righteous, that he never made another
reference to God; and the other was
so occupied with himself as a sinner,
that he flung himself upon the mercy
of God, not daring to lift his eyes to
heaven.
Then our Lord uttered the finding,
the verdict of Heaven.

" I say unto you, This man went
down to his house justified rather than
the other."

That was the particular application;
and then, sweeping the circle around
all humanity, He made the general
one,

" For every one that exalteth himself
shall be humbled; but he that humbleth
himself shall be exalted."

Two men at prayer. One, eloquently,
in phrases circling round his own personality with which he was pre-
eminently pleased. The other, hating
his sin, and grasping out after the
infinite and tender compassion of God
to operate for him. And Jesus said in
effect: These two men were in the
Temple seeking justification. The one
man was justifying himself before
God. The other man was not asking
for justification. He was asking for
mercy. The man who justified himself
remained unjustified. The man who
sought the compassion of God, went
back to his house justified.
We turn now to the two incidents
The first is that of the children.

"And they were bringing unto Him
also their babes."

Luke's narrative is not complete. Matthew and Mark tell us the bringing of
the children followed upon our Lord's
statements concerning divorce. It was
when they heard what Jesus had to
say about divorce, that they brought
the children to Him. To me, that connection is pregnant with suggestion.
Glance at the incident. Luke says,

" They were bringing unto Him their
babes."

To whom does he refer? We have
generally said the mothers. Are we
sure? There is a children's hymn
which begins:

" When mothers of Salem,
    Their children brought to Jesus,
    The stern disciples drove them back
    And bade them depart:
    But Jesus saw them ere they fled,
    And sweetly smiled, and kindly said,
    ' Suffer little children
        To come unto Me.' "

It is very beautiful, but is it quite
correct? Luke does not say so. Moreover, he does not say the fathers did.
But when he tells how the disciples
rebuked them, the " them " in the
Greek is masculine, *autois*. That is
also the neuter form, but of course in
application to people it was not neuter.
That may include mothers, for in the
Greek language, where there were men
and women, they used the masculine
form; but it certainly means that the
fathers were there, too. If the mothers
only had been there, the feminine form
would have been used. I stress this
because, under the Jewish economy, it
was the father who was responsible for
the training of the children religiously,
and the Christian Church is suffering
today because fathers are not doing
their duty in that regard.

" But when the disciples saw it, they
rebuked them."

Do not be angry with them. I think
I can understand them. They knew
perfectly well, and were full of anxiety about it, that Jesus was moving
towards Jerusalem and towards some
final mystery of suffering. Had He
not been telling them so for six
months? In any case, these men felt

that their Master must not be disturbed by children!

Here, again, Luke has not told us something which Mark does record. Mark says that Jesus, "being moved with indignation," said the thing He now said. When the disciples would have prevented the little ones getting to Jesus, Jesus was angry. He was moved with indignation that any man, even His own disciples, should try to keep the children from His touch. It is central to the very life of the Church that this should be understood. It was in that connection that He uttered words that constitute the charter of the child to the end of the age;

"Suffer the little children to come unto Me, and forbid them not."

It was as though He had said, Whoever else you keep away, don't keep the children away,

"Forbid them not; for to such belongeth the Kingdom of God,"

or if you like the old rendering,

"For of such is the Kingdom of God."

He did not say, Bring the children to Me. He said, Do not hinder them coming;

"Suffer the little children to come unto Me."

Get a child into the presence of Jesus, and the child will go straight to Him. I would rather trust a child's judgment, than some people's. I tell you frankly, if I find a man a dog does not like, I am suspicious of the man. But the test of the child is supreme. If a child will go to a man, I want to know that man. Jesus said in effect: If you will let them, they will all come to Me. Do not hinder them. Do not get in their way. If we find children today, even in supposedly Christian homes, who do not want to come to Jesus Christ, it is because we have put something in their way.

"Forbid them not; for to such belongeth the Kingdom of God."

Then He applied the truth to the crowd. He said: Unless you are all children, you will never get to Me, or into the Kingdom of God,

"Whosoever shall not receive the Kingdom of God as a little child, he shall in no wise enter therein."

Finally, let us glance at the next incident. It is certainly suggestive that Matthew, Mark, and Luke all tell us that it was when Jesus manifested indignation at people who tried to keep the children from Him, and when He received them, took them in His arms and laid His hands upon them, that this young ruler came to Him. My personal conviction is that this young ruler having heard Jesus say what He had to say about divorce, and then seen Him in His attitude toward children, was impelled to appeal to Him, saying,

"Good Teacher, what shall I do to inherit eternal life?"

I think the inspiration of his question was what he had heard Jesus say, and seen Jesus do. Have you ever examined this young man? What a fine fellow he was. A man of fine temperament, upright and honest, discerning and knowing goodness when he saw it in Jesus. Also confessing it, in spite of the fact that Jesus wore the garb of the peasant, and he in all probability wore the purple of wealth and was a ruler among his people. Moreover, when he saw goodness he was humble enough to kneel. And yet once more, he was engaged on the highest quest possible, he was seeking life in its fulness, the age-abiding life. For the moment he could not pay the price. Whether he ever did so, we are not told.

The chief interest of the story is that of our Lord's method with him. Jesus first said to him:

"Why callest thou Me good? none is good, save one, even God."

Why is it so many expositors and preachers dealing with this story miss that out very largely, or dismiss it with a passing reference? When He said, Why do you call Me good, none is good save One, and that is God?

He meant one of two things. He either meant, I am not good, or He meant, I am God! We cannot escape the alternative. Schmiedel, in his article on the person of Jesus in the *Encyclopedia .Biblica,* admitted that there were five things in the New Testament story of Jesus that might be true, and the five he admitted might be true, were such as he thought showed that Jesus was not all we believe Him to be. This was one of them, because he claimed that Jesus meant He was not God. At any rate, Schmiedel was logical. All the rest of the story proves how false his deduction was. It is possible to be logical—and wrong. The question as put to the young ruler precipitated a problem upon the answer to which his whole life depended.

Then He flung upon him in quick succession the six commandments on the last table of the Decalogue. He did not take him to the first four. He flashed upon him the six which have to do with man's relationship with his fellow-men. And the young man replied:

"All these things have I observed from my youth up."

He was telling the truth.
Then Jesus said to him,

" One thing thou lackest yet; sell all that thou hast, and distribute unto the poor . . . and come, follow Me."

What did he lack? Poverty? That is an entirely false and faulty interpretation. He lacked the element of control over his life that comes from outside.

"One thing thou lackest yet."

He called him to sweep aside the things that, in his case, were hindering him, his wealth. That was the negative preliminary command; the positive and ultimate followed,

"Come, follow Me."

He thus called him to submit his life to control.
Now link that with the first saying.

"Why callest thou Me good? None is good, save One, even God."

If you want life, put out everything that is ministering to your self-centred satisfaction; submit, surrender; follow Me; yield your life actually to the control of God as you have seen God when you have seen Me.

"But when he heard these things, he became exceeding sorrowful; for he was very rich."

That is where we leave the story. I wonder how many of you have seen Watts' picture of the young ruler. It is one of the greatest things I know in art. Watts had a genius as an artist for painting the back of a man. If you see Watts' picture of the young ruler you won't see his face. He has not painted his face. You don't even see a profile. You see his back. That back is turned on Jesus, and Watts has managed to paint in the droop of the shoulders and the languid and flaccid hand, all the dejection of the man. I do not know any more about him. The story is left there, and we had better leave it there. We have no right to say he was lost. The story reveals the alternative offered to him, and records his refusal at that time.

The last thing in the narrative is the record of a conversation which took place about him.

"Jesus seeing him," seeing that back, "said, How hardly shall they that have riches enter into the Kingdom of God," —that is, with what difficulty,—" For it is easier for a camel to enter in through a needle's eye, than for a rich man to enter into the Kingdom of God. And they that heard it said, Then who can be saved?"

Exactly. The popular opinion would be that if a rich man could not be saved, none could. To that inquiry He replied:

" The things which are impossible with men are possible with God."

It is possible even for a rich man to enter the Kingdom,—with God. When a man becomes linked up with God, all impossible things become possible.

And then Peter said,

"Lo, we have left our own, and followed Thee."

And He said,

"Verily I say unto you, There is no man that hath left house, or wife, or brethren, or parents, or children, for the Kingdom of God's sake, who shall not receive manifold more in this time, and in the age to come eternal life."

So the incident ended. Do not forget that the face of Jesus was still set towards Jerusalem.

LUKE XVIII. 31–XIX. 10

WE are now entering upon Luke's account of the final things in the ministry of "The Word," to use his own name for our Lord (see i.2). From here on, everything is shadowed, or coloured, by the coming Cross, until the days of deep darkness are reached and passed, as the darkness merges into the dawn and the glory of the resurrection.

It is more than interesting to pause here a moment, to notice how consistently Luke has kept us face to face with the fact of the persistent purpose of our Lord through all this period. In the thirty-first verse of chapter nine he tells us that there appeared in glory Moses and Elijah, speaking with Jesus of the "decease," or

"the exodus which He was about to accomplish at Jerusalem."

In that same chapter, at verse fifty-one, we are told,

"When the days were well-nigh come that He should be received up, He stedfastly set His face to go to Jerusalem."

Then, in chapter thirteen, at the twenty-second verse, we read,

"And He went on His way through cities and villages, teaching, and journeying on unto Jerusalem."

In the seventeenth chapter, the eleventh verse, we find,

"It came to pass, as they were on their way to Jerusalem, that He was passing along the borders of Samaria and Galilee."

Now we have reached this thirty-first verse of chapter eighteen;

"And He took unto Him the twelve, and said unto them, Behold, we go up to Jerusalem."

The sequence is continued in the next chapter, the eleventh verse,

"And as they heard these things, He added and spake a parable, because He was nigh to Jerusalem, and because they supposed that the Kingdom of God was immediately to appear."

And yet again, in verse twenty-eight,

"And when He had thus spoken, He went on before, going up to Jerusalem."

Thus, all the way He is seen moving toward Jerusalem.

In this section there are two movements; first in verses thirty-one to thirty-four, the programme of the last things; and then two incidents, both of them connected with the city of Jericho; one outside the city as He approached it, and the other inside the city, as He passed through it.

Let us look with some care at these first four verses. First of all, we must keep in mind the fact that He was talking to His disciples.

"He took unto Him the twelve."

It would seem, moreover, as though for this teaching, He left all His disciples outside, except these twelve. He took the twelve, those twelve men whom He had chosen, and appointed to be with Him, that presently He might send them forth; those twelve men who for two and a half years had been most closely associated with Him. Today they were walking amid the perplexing shadows caused by the thing He had told them, first at Cæsarea Philippi, that He must go to the Cross. From that time, they are seen, keeping near to Him, but frightened, amazed, perplexed. Six months have gone since that first foretelling of the Cross, and now Luke says,

"He took unto Him the twelve, and said unto them."

In what He said He gave them the programme of what was then immediately to follow.

"Behold, we go up to Jerusalem."

That is the first thing.

"And all the things that are written through the prophets shall be accomplished unto the Son of man."

That is the full statement. Then He exactly revealed the process.

"For He shall be delivered up unto the Gentiles, and shall be mocked, and shamefully treated, and spit upon; and they shall scourge and kill Him; and the third day He shall rise again."

Mark with what particularity of detail He told them all that was about to happen. From that moment Luke's story follows that programme. "Up to Jerusalem." The story of that journey begins in the thirty-fifth verse of chapter eighteen, and continues to chapter nineteen, and verse forty-four. "Be delivered up to the Gentiles." The story of that begins in the forty-fifth verse of chapter nineteen, and runs to the middle of verse fifty-four in chapter twenty-two. Then He said, but with details of description, that He would be "put to shame." The story of that begins in the middle of verse fifty-four in chapter twenty-two, and runs through to the twenty-fifth verse in chapter twenty-three. "They shall kill Him." That story is in chapter twenty-three, verses twenty-six to fifty-six. "He shall rise again." That story is in the first twelve verses of chapter twenty-four.

The first matter which arrests our attention in the programme is that Jesus said,

"We go up to Jerusalem, and all the things that are written through the prophets shall be accomplished unto the Son of man."

He thus declared that the pathway before Him had already been revealed in the prophetic writings; and that these prophetic foretellings would all be brought to fulfilment.

What, then, were the things that the prophets had foretold? First,

"He shall be delivered up unto the Gentiles."

His delivery to the Gentiles was Israel's ultimate sin. That sin ended her earthly career, and began the career of the heavenly people of God, fulfilling in themselves all that of which the earthly people had so signally and continuously failed.

Yet there is a deeper note in the statement than that.

"He shall be delivered up unto the Gentiles."

Whereas the delivery of Jesus by Israel to the Gentiles in order to put Him to death was of the nature of a base betrayal, it was more. On the Day of Pentecost one of these twelve, a man who did not understand the programme at the time, looked back; and when he referred to this fact, he did so thus:

"Him being delivered"—the same word—"Being delivered by the determinate counsel and foreknowledge of God, ye by the hands of men without the law"—Gentiles—"did crucify and slay."

Thus Peter recognized the betrayal of Jesus by Israel, but reserved the words "delivered up" as describing the act of "the determinate counsel and foreknowledge of God." When Jesus said He would be "Delivered up" to Gentiles, He was indicating Israel's sin, but He was also striking the deeper note of His consciousness that all that was coming to Him, was under the government of God.

Then in detail He described what would happen to Him;

"Shall be mocked, and shamefully treated, and spit upon; and they shall scourge and kill Him."

All that took place when He was in the hands of the Gentiles. It was the

Roman soldiery and the Roman power that did these things. That does not minimize the sin of Israel's betrayal, for it is a more dark and dastardly thing to hire a man to murder a man, than to murder the man yourself. But it does involve the Gentile world. That world, as represented in the Roman Empire, and in the procurator, was not without light. Roman jurisprudence proves that the Roman people had not been without light. They knew the difference between right and wrong between justice and injustice. Jesus was handed over to the Gentiles, at their highest level of law and government. They are seen in His case, violating every principle of law, and every element of justice. The procurator said he found no fault in Him, and yet He was buffeted and spit upon, and ill-treated in answer to the howling of a mob. That was humanity's sin. Israel sinned in handing Him over; and humanity, outside the circle of revelation that had come to the Hebrew people, violated justice, and He was shamefully treated.

Then softly, "And kill Him." That is the ultimate in sin. That is sin in its final manifestation in human history. They killed *Him*. There are many things recorded in human history, which are dreadful, but nothing quite so appalling and so terrible as the murder of Jesus. Then sin expressed itself ultimately and finally. It did its worst, and its uttermost. When I remember Who He is, and what manner of Man He was in all His life and conduct and speech and ministry, and see Him done to death on Calvary's Cross, then, unless there is some explanation of this thing which is deeper than the historical, and profounder than the happening, I declare that this universe is not governed by a good God, or He never would have permitted it. But presently, when the light of resurrection flashes back upon the Cross, and the Day of Pentecost comes, I see debased humanity, Jew and Roman alike, being born into a new spirit and a new manner of life, and the rivers of purity beginning to flow through human affairs, then I know there is something deeper in

that death than the murder, then I know that if that was the ultimate of sin, it was also the ultimate of grace. It is in the presence of that, I touch the deepest meaning of the lines we love to sing,

" I lay in dust life's glory dead,
    And from the ground there blossoms red,
    Life that shall endless be ! "

The final interpretation of those lines, whether George Matheson meant it so or not I cannot tell, is there in Calvary !

That, however, is not the last thing in the programme ! The final word is,

"And the third day He shall rise again."

We must not mutilate these records if we are considering the Cross, and we must not mutilate the records if we are considering Christ in relationship to His Cross. I repeat what is a commonplace of exposition, and yet cannot be too often repeated; there is not a single instance from Cæsarea Philippi to the end, when Jesus foretold His Cross, but that at the same time He foretold His resurrection.

The supreme value of that paragraph is that of its revelation of His perfect knowledge of all that lay before Him. *He* told His disciples, to the last detail, the things that were going to happen to Him. If we interpret the Cross by the records, we cannot speak of Jesus as a Victim. He was a Victor. To declare, that in fine heroism, He submitted to the inevitable on the human level is to miss the deepest truth. The fact as revealed is that He walked the pathway of a Divine ordination, with head erect, and dignity, even to the moment when, after the bitterness of His Cross He said,

" Father, into Thy hands I commend My Spirit."

Luke ends that account of the giving of the programme to the disciples by saying :

" They understood none of these things; and this saying was hid from them, and they perceived not the things that were said."

This was inevitable. Naturally, they could not follow Him. They understood Him as He said He was going to Jerusalem. They probably understood Him when He said He would be delivered to the Gentiles. That was a legal expression, showing what would be the action of the rulers. They understood Him when He said He would be mocked, and shamefully treated, and spit upon. They knew the kind of thing that would happen to Him when He got into the hands of His enemies. They understood Him when He said they would kill Him. But, when He said the third day rise, they could not understand, and they never grasped the significance of it. Therefore, neither did they understand the true significance of His suffering and death.

Let us now glance at the two incidents recorded as connected with the beginning of His final journey to Jerusalem. They are very beautiful, and very familiar.

"And it came to pass, as He drew nigh unto Jericho, a certain blind man sat by the wayside begging."

Jesus had now crossed the Jordan. He was again in Judæa, at a place about fifteen miles away from Jerusalem. As He entered Jericho, the incident of the blind man occurred. Don't confuse this man with Bartimæus. Matthew and Mark tell of two blind men, one says one man, and the other two men. One of them was Bartimæus. They both record the fact that He dealt with these men as He was leaving the city. Luke very distinctly says that this happened as He drew nigh to Jericho.

The blind man heard the tramp of the crowd. He asked what the noise meant, and they told him that Jesus of Nazareth was passing by. Then he cried, saying:

"Jesus, Thou Son of David, have mercy on me."

Quite evidently this man had heard about Him. His designation of Him is very significant. He had heard about Jesus, and for some reason, quite unexplained, he had not only heard about Him, he believed in Him, and he gave Him a full Messianic title,

"Jesus, Thou Son of David. Have mercy on me,"

was his cry.

"And they that went before rebuked him, that he should hold his peace, but he cried out the more a great deal."

As he went on clamouring, he dropped the name "Jesus," but retained the Messianic title, "Thou Son of David." What then?

"Jesus stood, and commanded him to be brought unto Him."

Now mark the rapidity of movement. He said,

"What wilt thou that I should do unto thee? And he said, Lord, that I may receive my sight. And Jesus said unto him, Receive thy sight; thy faith hath made thee whole."

It is a dramatic story. Without doing any violence in translation, we may put the conversation into poetic form;—

"Son of David, pity me.
What would'st thou I do for thee?
Lord, that I myself may see!
Then see, thy faith hath saved thee!"

What was the issue? When the blindness passed, he followed Jesus, glorifying God; and the people gave praise to God.

He was travelling towards His Cross. A blind man clamoured out of his faith in Him as the Son of David. Christ called him and gave him his sight. Thus the compassion and passion of the Cross are seen in action.

Then He arrived in the city. Jericho at that time was largely peopled by Roman tax-gatherers, and priests of Jerusalem; which is a very suggestive fact. It was an evil place. The highway between Jericho and Jerusalem was not safe. Our Lord's parable of the Good Samaritan had recognized that. His going through

that city is significant! It was a city
cursed from of old. He was on His
way to His Cross. He need not have
gone through Jericho. There were
other ways, but He went through Jericho, and the only incident recorded is
this story of Zacchæus, and I have no
doubt the reason of His going was the
finding of this man.

Zacchæus was a chief publican, and
he was rich; which, interpreted by
the facts of the time, means that he
had been a rogue. The Roman system
for gathering taxes never permitted a
man to become wealthy, except he ex-
torted more than was due. Rome
gave to a man a specified area, in
which he was responsible for raising
the taxes. Rome fixed the schedule of
taxation, and then this man must remit
to Rome what she had demanded.
Then Rome asked no more questions.
If he were a just man, his income was
sufficient for him. He had tremendous power, and so if he were a rogue
he might extort more than was due,
and so become rich. When some of
these publicans went to John the Baptist and said, " What shall we do? " he
knew them, and he said,

" Extort no more than that which is
appointed you."

Zacchæus was rich, and as a publican,
that means he was a rogue.

But he was a curious little man.
The crowd was going by. The blind
man heard it, Zacchæus saw it, but
he could not see the cause of it, and
could not understand what it meant,
and wanted to find out. And Luke
says—read it carefully,—

" He sought to see Jesus *who He
was.*"

He did not climb the sycamore tree to
see Jesus. He did not know who He
was, or who was there attracting the
crowd. Suffering from the disability
of shortness, he could not see over the
shoulders and heads of the crowd; and
he was very curious and resolute, and
so he climbed the tree to see who was
in the middle of the crowd, causing the
commotion.

When Jesus arrived under that syca-

more tree, He saw Zacchæus, and He
said,

" Zacchæus, make haste, and come
down; for today I must abide at thy
house."

He came down, and received Him
joyfully. I am inclined to think that
one reason why he was glad to receive Jesus was that he was pleased
to do anything that would annoy the
Pharisees!

Then the curtain falls for a little
while. Je   went   . Did you hear
the crowd outside, the group of Pharisees a. rulers when they saw Him
go into that house? They said,

" He is gone in to lodge with a man
that is a sinner."

To them it was shocking. He was
accepting hospitality of a rogue; more
than that, He had asked for it. And
that was Christ's first method with
this man. He asked him for his
hospitality.

I have often wondered what Jesus
said to him. I am sure He talked to
him courteously, but there was more
than courtesy. Presently the curtains
are drawn back, or the doors swing
back, as the case may have been in
that house, and they both come out
together. Luke says, "And Zacchæus
stood." That means he had come out,
and was about to say something in
public. He spoke to Jesus in the
presence of the crowd. Hear what
he said;—

" Behold, Lord, the half of my goods
I give to the poor."

That was his first statement. He was
not then describing his past life, but
his new decision. In all probability,
for long time he had been taking half
the goods of the poor. Now he would
give. Then, continuing, he said,—

" And if I have wrongfully exacted
aught of any man, I restore fourfold."

That, also, was his new decision. He
would make restitution.

Thus he came out from his interview with Jesus with two resolves; I give, I restore. He went in, mastered by the passion to get. He came out, swept by a compassion that gives. His life had been one in which he had made revenue the means of self-enrichment. Now he would make righteousness the method of self-abnegation. Something had happened inside the house. What had happened? I need not speculate, because Jesus answers the question. He said,

"Today is salvation come to this house."

Salvation, then, turns an essential nature from greed to graciousness; and turns the passion of a life from selfishness to righteousness. And Jesus added that he had become a son of Abraham because of the thing that had happened.

Then He interpreted the whole incident from the standpoint of His own action:

"For the Son of man came to seek and to save that which was lost."

In the house He sought him, and He found him, and He saved him. The saved man is seen with the essential note of his personality, I give; and the new passion of his activity, I restore.

Once more do not forget that all the time Jesus was moving towards His Cross; and whether it was the blind man, or Zacchæus, He was acting in the power of that Cross to which He was taking His way.

LUKE XIX. 11-28

THE opening words of this paragraph, "And as they heard these things," link it with that which has immediately preceded. Thus it gives us the occasion upon which our Lord uttered the parable of the pounds.

"And as they heard these things, He added and spake a parable."

What, then, are the things that are referred to?

They had heard Zacchæus, after the private interview in his home with Jesus, saying,

"Behold, Lord, the half of my goods I give to the poor; and if I have wrongfully exacted aught of any man, I restore fourfold."

Then they heard Jesus say,

"Today is salvation come to this house, forasmuch as he also is a son of Abraham. For the Son of man came to seek and to save that which was lost. As they heard these things, He added and spake a parable unto them."

That marks the connection quite clearly.

The rest of the verse, eleven, tells us why Jesus uttered the parable.

"Because He was nigh to Jerusalem, and because they supposed that the Kingdom of God was immediately to appear."

Now, whereas I have stressed the fact that this was the connection of the utterance, it is evident that He gave the parable, not so much because of what they had just heard Him say with regard to Zacchæus, but because of what was in their minds at the time then.

"They supposed that the Kingdom of God was immediately to appear."

It is possible that they had interpreted His declaration that He was come to seek and save the lost, in a material sense as pointing to a political emancipation. Be that as it may, they supposed that the Kingdom of God was immediately to appear because He was nigh to Jerusalem.

For three and a half years He had been going up and down that countryside. Now He was close to the end, and everything was becoming climacteric. Whether the "they" refers to His disciples or the crowds, we cannot decide definitely. Personally, I think it referred to the disciples, and to the crowds. The feeling was widespread.

He was nigh to the city, the centre of everything, and at that particular time of year, they knew perfectly well that Jerusalem would be more full than it ever was at any other time. The Passover feast was approaching. The crowds were coming from everywhere. Josephus tells us that at least two million people, beyond the ordinary population of the city, gathered to the city and its environs, for the Passover feast. The popular idea was that something was going to happen.

" They supposed that the Kingdom of God was immediately to appear."

They supposed, that is, it seemed to them. That was their conviction. For three and a half years He had been going about. He had moved the multitudes strangely; the Galileans are specially devoted to Him. The Judæans were suspicious still, under the influence of their rulers; but there was a general expectation that something was about to happen; and this is what they thought would happen, the Kingdom of God would immediately appear.

The word " appear " there is a strong word. It describes an intensive and positive appearance. They were expecting something climacteric, a crisis of manifestation. All of which simply means that they expected that now He would assert Himself as Messiah, as they understood Messiahship. They thought He would now proclaim Himself as King, and set up, there in Jerusalem, the Kingdom of God. They expected that the Kingdom of God would immediately appear as they understood the Kingdom of God, as they were interpreting the Kingdom of God, as they desired the Kingdom of God. His own disciples were among the number.

They interpreted the Kingdom of God as a setting up of the throne of David literally and materially in Jerusalem, the breaking of the Roman yoke, and the realization of what they supposed was the Messianic order. There were multitudes of them ready to get round Him, flocking to His banner. Because of that, He spoke this parable unto them.

The parable of the pounds, then, was one in which He intended to show them that they were entirely misunderstanding the Kingdom of God. They did not understand all that was necessary to the establishment of a world order, over which He should reign as King. He did not intend to say He never would so reign; but they were mistaken in their understanding of the nature of the Kingdom, and consequently they were mistaken in their understanding of the times. They did not understand the process; and because of that He gave them this parable. There are those who still think that a Jewish Kingdom will yet be established. There is no warrant in Scripture for such a view. The Kingdom is coming, and He is coming to reign; but His Kingdom will not be Jewish. A little later on He excommunicated the nation. They had no vision of the truly essential things in the Kingdom of God, apart from the realization of which the earthly order can never be established. George Macdonald wrote:

" They all were looking for a King,
    To slay their foes and lift them
        high.
He came a little baby thing,
    That made a woman cry."

It is an interesting fact that in this parable our Lord was employing something with which they were all familiar, which had actually happened more than once already in their neighbourhood. Archelaus, Herod the Great, and later Antipas, all did this very thing. They left their kingdom for a time being, or their tetrarchy as the case may be, and went up to Rome to receive a kingdom.

Take the case of Archelaus. He had built his great palace in Jericho, where Jesus was uttering this parable. It may be—this is pure imagination, and may be entirely wrong—but it may be that the house of Zacchæus was near the palace; very likely the palace was in view. From that palace in Jericho Archelaus made his pilgrimage to Rome; and he went to Rome to ask that he might be named king. He was tetrarch, but he was not satisfied with being a tetrarch. He wanted the name and privilege of kingship; but he had to receive it from Rome, and so he went there to ask for it. Moreover, when he went, he left a man, Philippus, in charge with money to maintain the revenue of the tetrarchy while he was away. And further, when he was gone to Rome, they sent a special deputation from his tetrarchy to Rome to inform the emperor that they did not want, and would not have him to be king. Now, taking that incident, He employed it, applying it to Himself in order to correct the false idea, that the Kingdom of God was immediately to appear.

In the parable, then, there are three things to be noted. First, the fact of postponement; secondly, the period of waiting between the going away and the return, and how it was to be filled up; and thirdly, the fact of His return in complete and absolute authority. In this last application the historic event was different. Archelaus failed. He went to Rome to receive a kingdom, and he did not obtain it. Jesus said, I am going away to receive a Kingdom, and I shall return in authority. I am going away; consequently, what you are expecting won't take place immediately; and between My going and My coming, you have responsibilities.

He first insisted upon the fact of postponement.

"A certain nobleman went into a far country, to receive for himself a kingdom, and to *return*. And he called ten servants of his, and gave them ten pounds and said unto them, Trade ye herewith till I come. But his citizens hated him, and sent an ambassage after him, saying, We will not that this man reign over us."

Here a very important question arises. What was postponed? His Kingship? By no means. What was postponed was the thing that they thought was immediately to happen, namely, the appearing, the manifestation of the fact of His Kingship. His Kingship was not postponed. He was going away to receive a Kingdom; and if we may speak of the mission of our Lord in the term of our calendars and

almanacs, He set His face to Jerusalem, and went to Jerusalem, and He went to the city, He went down into death; He arose from among the dead and He ascended on high. He received the Kingdom when He ascended. It is always a little difficult to speak of great spiritual matters in the terms of the temporal and the material; and yet, so far as we can do it, the coronation day of Jesus was the day of His ascension. When He ascended, He ascended to be crowned. That is what Paul means in the great Philippian passage, when he tells us, stressing the emptying, the coming from the far-flung splendour of eternal relationship, to live our human life,

"And being found in fashion as a Man, He humbled Himself, becoming obedient even unto death, yea, the death of the Cross."

What next?

"Wherefore also God highly exalted Him, and gave unto Him the name which is above every name; that in the name of Jesus every knee should bow."

That happened when, the earthly work completed, He went away to receive His Kingdom; and He received it at His ascension. So that which was postponed was not His crowning, but the manifestation of it, the appearing of the Kingdom of God on earth. And that is postponed still in its fulness, in its finality. It is only postponed. It is coming!

"Li't up the hands that hang down, and confirm the feeble knees!"

There is a terrible danger of letting the hands hang, and the knees waver. It is a wrong attitude. The King will appear, and the Kingdom will appear, and this earth literally, actually, will yet know the beneficence of the beneficent autocracy of Jesus. He is coming! But He is King now.

"And he called ten servants of his, and gave them ten pounds."

Here let us be careful not to confuse the parable of the pounds with the parable of the talents. They are entirely different. In the parable of the talents, the Lord gave to one ten, and another five, and to one one. That was a parable dealing with variety of gifts. This is not that, and that is not this. In this case every servant had a like amount. If that was a parable showing variety of gifts, this is a parable stressing equal opportunity, during the Lord's absence. He has given to every one of H's bondservants a pound. This marks common opportunity, and common responsibility. In Ephesians, in the fifth chapter, Paul said,

" Look therefore carefully how ye walk, not as unwise, but as wise, redeeming the time, because the days are evil."

There is a marginal note against that word " redeeming," which suggests the rendering, " Buying up the opportunity." The word " time " is not the usual word for time; it rather suggests a special moment, that is, an opportunity. And the Greek word for redeeming is not the ordinary word. It has as its base the marketplace, it is a commercial word. In it we have the picture of Greek merchantmen, chaffering over their wares, watching for the right moment to buy or sell. The idea is that of successful business ; " Trade till I come."

Our Lord did not define the pound, but we know what it is. It is undoubtedly the witness to Him which is committed to every one of us. The Lord is hidden from the eyes of the world. There is no definite, clear manifestation of the Kingdom of God in all its majesty on earth, and never has been in nineteen hundred years, but He is King. Until He come again, it is our business to prosecute His enterprise in the world. To every man a pound, to everyone a deposit, for which that one is responsible, so that it will bring results that hasten the realization of the Divine purpose. There is not a single one of the bondslaves of Jesus Christ who is not, in his or her measure, responsible in this world for trafficking for Jesus, with the great deposit of truth, of the Gospel, of the ethic of Jesus, of all that

He came into the world to accomplish. Everyone is responsible for the prosecution of the commerce of heaven in the interests of the absent King.

To the servants was committed this responsibility.

" But his citizens hated him."

It is remarkable He referred to them all as his citizens. All men are His citizens. He claims Kingship over all.

His citizens hated him, and sent an ambassage after him, saying, We will not that this man reign over us."

I need not apply that. That is exactly what the world said then, and is saying still. Every subject of the King possesses a pound. What are we supposed to do with it ? To win these people from the attitude of antagonism, to that of allegiance to Him. That is our one business.

"And it came to pass, when he was come back, having received the kingdom."

That is arresting. He was drawing a distinction. Archelaus never received a kingdom, but this King has done so, and is coming back to establish it in outward manifestation. He describes what will happen when He comes.

"And he commanded these servants, unto whom he had given the money, to be called to him, that he might know what they had gained by trading. And the first came before him, saying, Lord, thy pound hath made ten pounds more."

He was taking no credit to himself. He had been trading with the pound, and it had gained what he put into it.

"And he said unto him, Well done, thou good servant ; because thou wast found faithful in a very little, have thou authority over ten cities."

"And the second came, saying, Thy pound, Lord, hath made five pounds. And he said unto him also, Be thou also over five cities. And another came, saying, Lord, behold, here is thy pound, which I kept laid up in a napkin ; for I feared thee, because thou art an austere man."

Our Lord did not admit the truth of that statement concerning Himself, but taking the man's estimation,

"He said unto him, Out of thine own mouth will I judge thee, thou wicked servant. Thou knewest that I am an austere man, taking up that which I laid not down, and reaping that which I did not sow; then wherefore gavest thou not my money into the bank, and I at my coming should have required it with interest? And he said to them that stood by, Take away from him the pound, and give it unto him that hath the ten pounds."

Thus at our Lord's return, He will deal with His servants, concerning what they have been doing with His interests while He has been away. In the story, one man had made full use of his deposit,—ten; one man had made partial use of his deposit,—he might have done better,—five; one man had made no use of it at all. He had preserved it. He did not spend it. He did not fling it away. He wrapped it up in a napkin. Oh, the napkins that are wrapping up the pounds of Jesus in the world today! He refused the responsibility.

Thus we see that when He does come, the Kingdom will appear, it will be manifest, it will appear as an established fact, an absolute and final fact. The first manifestation of His authority will thus be in His dealing with His servants. To the first He will say:

"Thy pound hath made ten pounds more . . . have thou authority over ten cities."

Thus the Lord rewarded him by giving him fuller responsibility, ten cities; and to the man who had gained five pounds, He gave five cities. From the man who had done nothing, He took away his pound.

To this hour Paul referred when he wrote,

"We must all be made manifest before the judgment seat of Christ."

"The judgment seat" is not the great white throne to the judgment seat of Christ we come, not to be judged as to our personal relationship to Him,

but as to our work. Paul, in another epistle, said that "each man's work shall be made manifest." Our work will be tried as by fire. If we have been building on the foundation gold, silver, costly stones, wood, hay, stubble, "the day shall declare it." As He tries our work by fire, the gold and silver and precious stones will be clarified to new beauty, while the wood, the hay, the stubble will be destroyed.

"If any man's work shall be burned, he shall suffer loss; but he himself shall be saved; yet so as through fire."

We shall be left with nothing but our own personal salvation. There is a note of sadness in it; a little mysterious, but there it is, saved as through fire. So with this failing servant in the parable. He was still a servant, but he had neglected his opportunity. For a time all he had to do was nothing. If I may dream my dreams, and go a little further, I imagine that presently he might go to the King, and say, Oh, let me do something! But we had better leave it, where our Lord left it.

Then the King is seen in this investigation, dealing with His enemies. They have rejected Him, and in the interest of the finally established Kingdom there can be nothing for them but swift judgment;

"These mine enemies, that would not that I should reign over them, bring hither, and slay them before me."

Thus all who refuse His Kingship are excluded for ever from His Kingdom.

In our paragraph there is one more verse.

"And when He had thus spoken, He went on before, going up to Jerusalem."

He was going towards His Throne. He was going to receive His Kingdom, and He gained it. He is still absent from the world as to manifestation. He is reigning. He is coming back. He has given every one of us a pound to prosecute His interests in the meantime. What are we doing with it?

LUKE XIX. 29-48

IN our last meditation we saw our Lord proceeding on the uphill road from Jericho to Jerusalem, with His face still stedfastly set towards that city. That is how the paragraph we considered last ended,

"And when He had thus spoken, He went on before, going up to Jerusalem."

We now come to the story of His arrival in the city, which we commonly call the triumphal entry. As we come to it, it may be well to point out that neither Matthew, Mark, Luke, nor John, gives us a complete account. To gain that we must combine these narratives. If we do so, we shall find that, whereas on what is commonly known as Palm Sunday, the Sunday before Easter, we celebrate His entry to the city; as a matter of historic fact, there were three entries on three successive days. His first entry was on the Sabbath. That is the day on which He rode into the city, and proceeding straight to the Temple, looked round about upon all things, without saying a word, and then left the Temple, and left the city. He went back again on the next day, that is on Sunday as we now say, and on that day, on His way to the city, occurred the pathetic and wonderful incident recorded by Luke, when on the Mount of Olives, as He reached the place where the whole city broke into view, He wept. He went back there again for a third time on the second day of the week, that is, on Monday. Three times over our Lord thus came with more or less of public notice into the city of Jerusalem.

In the case of the first entry to the city, that on the Sabbath, Luke only tells of the approach. Matthew and Mark tell us that He went into the city, and Mark adds the statement that He went into the Temple, and "looked round about upon all things," and then left the Temple. On that day, being the Sabbath, the Temple would probably be free from all traffickers, the tables of the money-changers would

not be there, when all the ceremonial worship of the Temple would be going forward. Thus we see Jesus entering, and going into the Temple, disturbing nothing. He "looked round about upon all things," and then turning His back on the Temple, He left the city.

The next day He came again, and it was on that next day, our Sunday, the first day of the week, when the Temple traffickers would be back in their places, that He cleansed the Temple of the whole of them. That, Luke tells us about very briefly. Then on the third day, Monday, He came again, and Luke gives us some account of the happenings that day, which was the day of conflict with the rulers.

That is a mechanical statement, but I commend it for careful consideration, for there was significance in that three-fold entry. The first entry was Kingly; on the second day, He went in as Priest; and on the third day as Prophet.

The first day's entry was distinctly Kingly. He entered the city of the King, and proceeded to the House of God, which was the very centre of the national life. Looking round about upon all things, He turned His back on it, and left, a most sad and ominous action.

He came on the next day as Priest, and finding the House of God desecrated, He cleansed it, driving out the money-changers, overturning their tables, and advancing upon them with majesty and dignity, not so much as King, but as God's High Priest, holding the House of God sacred to the worship of God. One of the evangelists tells us that on that day there gathered into the Temple court the sick, and He healed them, to the accompaniment of the singing of children. Thus He restored the Temple for a brief while to its first purpose.

On the third day He entered again, and was at once challenged as to the authority upon which He had done these things. On that day, His teaching was the supreme matter. In answer to their quibbles, in answer to their objections, with regal authority, as the ultimate Voice of God, He dealt with every situation as it arose, and every problem as it was suggested; thus functioning as the great Prophet of God.

Thus we are able to consider Luke's story in relation to the whole majestic movement of those three days. It was indeed a majestic movement. We have been following Him from Cæsarea Philippi when Luke says, He " stedfastly set His face to go to Jerusalem." All the way Jerusalem had been the goal of His journeying. Now He had come to the final things, the last hours, come to that which was ever before Him as the deepest passion of His life. He arrived in the city, majestic, and magnificent, no Victim this, but a Victor.

In this paragraph there are three things to be considered: preparation for the King's entry, verses twenty-nine to thirty-five; the procession on the road to the city, verses thirty-six to forty; and the approach and the entry on the next day, verses forty-one to forty-eight.

First, then, in verses twenty-nine to thirty-five, the account of the preparation for entry. Luke tells the beautiful story of the colt sought and found. Let us remind ourselves that this was a regal mount. We must not interpret these stories by the customs of the Western world. A colt was a regal mount in the Eastern lands, and in those times kings rode, not upon steeds, but upon asses kept especially for the purpose.

At this point in his narrative, Luke does not do what Matthew does. Matthew draws attention to the relation of the mount chosen by Jesus to prophetic utterances. In Zechariah, chapter nine, verse nine, we read:

" Rejoice greatly, O daughter of Zion; shout, O daughter of Jerusalem; behold, thy King cometh unto thee; He is just, and having salvation; lowly, and riding upon an ass, even upon a colt the foal of an ass."

It is important that we should understand this. Zechariah was not saying that when the King came He would prove His lowliness by riding on a colt the foal of an ass. He was rather saying that when the King came He would come in regal majesty, mounted as kings are mounted, upon an ass, even upon a colt the foal of an ass. I have seen it written, and I have heard it said that this was a great exhibition of the humility of Jesus, that He was willing to ride upon an ass. That is not so. It was for a sign and symbol of His Kingship, that He chose so to ride into the city.

This action of Jesus was, on His part, a definite provocation of demonstration. He decided to enter the city, on this arrival for the last time, in a way that must draw attention to Himself. The climacteric hour had come, and thus He elected to enter the city. This was something He had never done before. He had never done anything to provoke a demonstration. Over and over again we see Him withdrawing from the crowds, when the majority of the crowd seemed to be in favour of Him. Once they tried to make Him King. He sent them away, declining Kingship when they offered it to Him. But now He deliberately chose and arranged to enter the city thus as a King.

It was a regal mount, but there was nothing else on the human level, to suggest the King. Imaginatively, sometimes I have tried to look at that entry through the gates into the city from the standpoint of people who may have been watching at the moment. Jerusalem at that time was in charge of the Roman power. Pilate was there, and those in attendance upon his court were there; and the soldiers of Herod were all touched with the passion for Roman government and love of the Roman purple. I have no doubt, too, that among those surrounding Pilate, among the courtiers or the soldiers in charge, there would be Roman citizens from Rome itself. I have sometimes tried to imagine some proud, patrician Roman, at some coign of safe vantage, watching that entry of Jesus. Such would certainly have laughed at it. A procession of old clothes and broken trees! The patrician Roman would have called it distinctly plebeian, and so have dismissed it as unimportant. Jesus came to teach men that the plebeian is the patrician in the Kingdom of God.

And then I watch the entry from the standpoint of the Hebrew rulers, and I do not think their attitude was that of contempt for it. I think rather that they were strangely perturbed. They knew enough of their Scriptures to remember certain things like those I read from Zechariah; they knew some popular movement was on foot; they were afraid they were losing their authority, and they were making up their mind that before the week was over, they would deal with this situation. I have no doubt His method of entry on the human level precipitated their action, the action that ended from their standpoint in His murder.

Now look at it once more, not from the standpoint of the Roman, or the Hebrew rulers, but from the standpoint of its actuality. It was full of majesty. Go back to Zechariah again.

" Rejoice greatly, O daughter of Zion; shout, O daughter of Jerusalem; behold, thy King cometh unto thee."

How?

" He is just, and having salvation; lowly, and riding upon an ass, even upon a colt the foal of an ass."

The riding upon the ass did not prove the lowliness, but stood in contrast to it. Lowly, and yet riding as a King.

Then carefully mark the descriptive words: " just — having salvation — lowly." Compare this with what the proud patrician Roman had seen, passing along the streets of the imperial city in one of those triumphal processions of Rome, famous through the world. Mark them, those military imperators, who had bludgeoned some part of the world into submission; and then look at Jesus; " just, having salvation, lowly." That is true majesty. Contrast it with the tawdry tinselled stupidity of shining armour and mailed fists. The King, " just, having salvation; lowly."

To return to Luke's actual story. I do not think that much need be said about that procession. The poetic beauty of Luke's language carries the effect to our minds. But notice particularly that He was surrounded by His disciples, and it was they who raised the song.

" The whole multitude of the disciples began to rejoice and praise God."

That means far more than the twelve. Jesus had hundreds of disciples before He left this world, none of them perfectly instructed until after Pentecost. There were one hundred and twenty gathered in Jerusalem at Pentecost, and before that He had met five hundred brethren at once in Galilee, after His resurrection. Jerusalem at this time was filled with people from the whole region round about, and among them would be many of His disciples. They raised the song of jubilation as He approached the city.

Now, there is something very significant in what they said. I confess, the more I ponder it, the more I am surprised; because it seems to me to indicate a spiritual apprehension which I should be inclined to say they had not gained at the time. But perhaps they sang better than they knew.

" Blessed is the King that cometh in the name of the Lord, peace in heaven, and glory in the highest."

They did not say, Peace on earth. One's mind goes back immediately to the beginning of Luke, to the second chapter, and to the fourteenth verse. In that verse we hear the song of the angels,

" Glory to God in the highest, peace among men in whom He is well pleased."

Now, here the disciples were singing round Him on His way to Jerusalem for the last time, and they did not say a word about peace on earth. They sang rather of

" Peace in heaven, and glory in the highest."

Swept by the emotion of a real devotion to Jesus, they sang, " Peace in heaven." At His birth angels sang,

" Peace on earth among men in whom He is well pleased."

As He went to death men sang,

" Peace in heaven, and glory in the highest."

There can be no peace on earth that does not result from peace in heaven. It is when there is peace with God, that man finds peace on earth.

Then Luke tells us that the hostile Pharisees and rulers were angry with these men. Why were they angry at what they were saying? Because it would only mean one thing, the complete recognition of the Messiahship of Jesus.

" Blessed is the King that cometh in the name of the Lord."

To sing that on the highways leading to Jerusalem was approaching high treason against the Roman power; and so they said to Jesus,

" Teacher, rebuke Thy disciples."

Now notice it very carefully. Our Lord accepted the homage, and refused to silence the voices of His loyal subjects. He even went so far as to say,

" I tell you, that if these shall hold their peace, the stones will cry out."

Thus is evident His recognition of the significance of that hour; the tremendous issues of it, the eternal necessity for it, the vastness of it. Jesus said in effect, Rebuke them? The thing happening is so great that if there are no human voices, the stones will become vocal, the stones will cry out. What a wonderful movement it was towards the city.

Then omitting the story of the actual going into the city on that day, Luke tells of the approach on the next day.

I feel that perhaps the most powerful exposition of the first part of this story would be a solemn and reverent silence. There are three things to

consider. His tears, His lamentation, and His prediction.

" When He drew nigh . . . He wept over it."

The word for weeping there does not mean merely that tears forced themselves up and fell down His face. It suggests rather the heaving of the bosom, and the sob and the cry of a soul in agony. We could have no stronger word than the word that is used there.

" The Son of God in tears,
The wondering angels see.
Be thou astonished, O my soul,
He shed those tears for thee."

For while He wept over the city, the city was merely the crystallized centre of human attitude towards Him, and of human sin; and in the presence of it He wept.

Then there broke from Him that sad lament. Luke does not give it in fulness, but he gives it in its essence.

" If thou hadst known in this day,"

and some of the old manuscripts render that,

" This thy day, even thou, the things which belong unto peace."

The things that but yesterday His disciples, a multitude of them, were singing about " peace in heaven," and so peace on earth.

" If thou hadst known in this thy day, even thou, the things which belong unto peace! but now they are hid from thine eyes."

And then, He Who wept, and He Who lamented and sighed, pronounced the doom, for His is not a pity that violates justice.

" Thy King cometh unto thee, just and having salvation,"

lowly, and riding as a King.

" The days shall come upon thee, when thine enemies shall cast up a bank about thee, and compass thee round, and keep thee in on every side, and shall dash thee to the ground, and thy children within thee; and they shall not leave in thee one stone upon another, because thou knewest not the time of thy visitation."

Every detail of this was fulfilled literally within a generation.

We need not tarry with His action as on that second day He entered the Temple.

" He entered into the Temple, began to cast out them that sold."

The two things He said are significant.

" It is written, And My house shall be a house of prayer."

Where do we find that? In Isaiah.

" But ye have made it a den of robbers."

Where do we find that? In Jeremiah. He was quoting from their own prophetic writings. As He cleansed the Temple He ejected those who had turned the House of God into the place of traffic for personal enrichment, and so protesting against the profanation of the Holy Place, He restored it, for a brief hour at least, to its original purpose.

So ends the story, except for a summary of those last days.

"And He was teaching daily in the Temple. But the chief priests and the scribes and the principal men of the people sought to destroy Him; and they could not find what they might do; for the people all hung upon Him, listening."

At the end of chapter twenty-one we read,

" Every day He was teaching in the Temple; and every night He went out, and lodged in the mount that is called Olivet."

He never slept in Jerusalem during that last week, never stayed there a night. He went out to the mount called Olivet. I have no words to speak of it. We need hearts that feel it. The city had rejected Him. Presently He rejected the city. He came in as King, came in as Priest, came in as Prophet. There was no place for Him in Jerusalem. He left the Temple, and passed through the streets, and went out through the gates, and somewhere on Olivet, with the paschal moon rising, He spent the last nights of that week. In the city there was a conflicting condition. The rulers were hostile, the people popularizing Him.

" The people all hung on Him, listening."

The goodwill of the crowd, and the hostility of the rulers, and they were worth as much as each other. Thus we have seen Him arriving in Jerusalem.

LUKE XX. 1-18

OUR time note for this paragraph is found in the opening part of the first verse.

"And it came to pass, on one of the days, as He was teaching the people in the Temple."

The day referred to was the third day, that on which our Lord came to the city and Temple, not so much in the character of His Kingship, not so much in the sorrowful and heartbreaking character of His Priesthood, but as the Prophet, in the full sense of the word, the Interpreter of the way and will of God.

From the crowded events of this third day of entry, Luke gives us some incidents, the story of which occupies the whole of chapters twenty and twenty-one, and the first six verses of chapter twenty-two. It certainly was one of the most wonderful days on record in human history in very many ways, as we see Jesus, at the end of three and a half years of public ministry, knowing perfectly well that within a few hours comparatively, they will take Him and put Him on His bitter Cross.

On this day we see Him engaged in the last stage of His long spiritual and mental conflict with the rulers. Their opposition began at the very beginning. It had grown in strength. In those rulers our Lord had to do with the cleverest and the most astute men, and on the human level, the most learned men of His age, in that whole region. They were not illiterate men; but clever, with a cleverness almost amazing. In this story we see these men and Jesus face to face. It was the last clash between them. And, taking it thus as a whole, it does look, on the human level, as though they won, because the end of it was His Cross. And yet they did not win in a single encounter. From the standpoint of mere mental power, our Lord towered over them in the majesty of His illuminated intellect, and in the splendour of His method.

In these eighteen verses, there are two movements. In the first we see these authorities challenging Him definitely, authoritatively challenging Him, as to His authority. In the second movement we watch Jesus, having dealt with these authorities, turning to the crowd, and talking to them, undoubtedly in the presence of the men whom He had so signally silenced, and doing so in the terms of gravest solemnity.

The first thing that arrests me in the story is what Jesus was doing when they interrupted Him. He was teaching the people in the Temple, and preaching the Gospel. The Gospel was that which He had proclaimed all through His ministry, that of the Kingship of God, and the availability of God to the human soul, and that, in a new sense, because He was present. That was His good news. He was ever affirming the truth about God and man, found in the beginning of Genesis, that man is the offspring of God, and that he has the right of access to God, the story that God walked with man in a garden in the spirit of the day. God had been distanced from men by their sin, and by their degradation of religion. Jesus came and said,

" The Kingdom of heaven is at hand."

which does not mean it is coming presently, but it is here now. One day He said,

" The Kingdom of heaven is among you,"

because He was there. He was telling them that good news; He was evangelizing.

It was while He was doing this, that the rulers came upon Him. It is important to notice who these men were, because Luke is careful to tell us.

" There came upon Him the chief priests and the scribes with the elders."

At Cæsarea Philippi, six months before this time,

" Jesus began to show unto His disciples, that He must go to Jerusalem, and suffer many things of the elders and chief priests and scribes."

Luke tells us that these were the men who now came to Jesus in the Temple.

The names indicate the offices that were held by the men who constituted the Sanhedrim. The chief authority in Jerusalem was the Sanhedrim, and those who sat upon the Sanhedrim were the spiritual rulers, the priests; the moral rulers, the scribes; the civil rulers, the elders. This, therefore, was an official coming. They came to Jesus and they said, " Tell us," and that " Tell us " was an authoritative demand. They said in effect: We are the duly recognized and definitely appointed authorities in this city, spiritual, moral, and civil; and we come to You, with a demand, " Tell us."

They asked Him two questions:

" By what authority doest Thou these things ? "

and

" Who is he that gave Thee this authority ? "

In the Temple precincts they said

" Tell us: By what authority doest Thou these things ? "

By what authority did You come in yesterday and disturb the regular order of events by overturning the tables of the money-changers, and breaking in upon the securely vested interests of those operating here?

"Who is he that gave Thee this authority?"

Thus they asked the nature of His authority, and the derivation of His authority.

It should be recognized that in themselves these were perfectly proper questions. They moved in the realm of authority; and whenever any man claims to do anything, or to say anything with authority, other men have a right to ask him what is the nature of his authority, and whence he derives it.

This being recognized, we turn to the story again. These men had been watching Jesus for three and a half years, and at the back of their question was the conviction He had no authority at all; and on the human level they were quite right. He was not a priest, He was not a scribe, He was not an elder. He had no seat on the Sanhedrim. The propriety of their questions makes the fact that Jesus refused to answer them the more arresting.

The method of His reply is significant. Said He:

"I also will ask you a question; and tell Me."

They said, "Tell us." He said, "Tell Me." Their "Tell us" was the assumption of their authority. His "Tell Me" was the assumption of His. Thus while they challenged His authority, in the very manner of His reply He exercised authority. Said He,

"I also will ask you a question; and tell Me; The baptism of John, was it from heaven, or from men?"

The question in itself led towards a discovery of His authority. If these men had been perfectly honest, they would themselves, in answering His question, have answered their own. They said,

"If we shall say, From heaven; He

will say, Why did ye not believe him? But if we shall say, From men; all the people will stone us; for they are persuaded that John was a prophet."

Now, the first thing I observe here is that while they were extremely clever, they were wrong. If they had said, "From heaven," I do not believe He would have said what they supposed. I think He would have said, If you believe he was from heaven, consult what he said concerning Me. Consult the hour when, of Me, he said, he was not worthy to stoop down and unloose the latchet of My shoes; consult the hour when he declared that I had come with fan and fire and axe, the Messiah of God; consult the hour when he said,

"Behold the Lamb of God, Who taketh away the sin of the world."

If you will consult John, whose ministry you say was from heaven, you will have the answer to your question as to My authority, and from Whom I received it. I am convinced that is what He would have said.

Their consultation led them to an answer. They dare not say, "From men," for the people were persuaded that John was a prophet. They would not say, "From heaven," because they thought that would involve them in a dilemma. So they said, they did not know! They knew perfectly well, and they knew perfectly well when they had rejected John's ministry. That was the trouble with them. God never condemns men for ignorance. God's judgments are upon men who, having the light, disobey it.

Therefore, it was because of their dishonesty that He said,

"Neither tell I you by what authority I do these things."

Mark the dramatic movement of the incident. "Tell us," said they. "Tell Me," said He. We will not, said they. I will not, said He. Their refusal was that of dishonesty. His was that of stern necessity. They were not honest with John. They could not be honest with Him. He would not declare the profound secrets of His authority to men incapable of honesty.

After that interruption, He resumed His work. He was teaching the people, and preaching to the people the Gospel. He now resumed that work. Luke distinctly says,

"He began to speak unto the people."

What He now said, however, was the direct result of the interruption. He told them a story. Remember, the rulers were still listening. The story was about a vine. That was not new to them. They were familiar with their own literature, and therefore the figure of a vine and a vineyard was well known. In the Biblical literature it is first found in Psalm eighty, where Asaph sings of a vine God brought out of Egypt and planted. It is found also in Isaiah, in a song,

"Let me sing for my well-beloved a song of my beloved touching his vineyard. My well-beloved had a vineyard in a very fruitful hill."

Ezekiel four or five times used the figure. Jeremiah refers to it. Hosea says, "Israel is a luxuriant vine." Thus they would be perfectly familiar with it. At the time, the vine was the symbol of the Jewish people. On the great and beautiful gate of the Temple there was the figure of a vine, known as the golden vine. Thus He told them a story in the realm of their religious literature, using the symbol of their national life. As He did so, He sketched the history of the rulers down the ages. The vine of God had failed to bring forth the fruit that God was looking for. God looked that it should bring forth grapes, and it brought forth wild grapes;

"He looked for justice, but, behold, oppression; for righteousness, but, behold, a cry."

They had killed the servants of the Lord, and failed to bring forth fruit. Then He told them this startling thing; this story.

"The lord of the vineyard said, What shall I do? I will send my beloved son."

I can imagine one among the rulers saying; He was talking about John just now, and I remember that the day He was baptized somebody said that God spoke and said, "Thou art My beloved Son." Continuing His story, He told them that these husbandmen not only slew the servants, but when the son came they killed him,—"That the inheritance may be ours." That is exactly what these rulers were doing. Underneath their hostility to Him was their fear that they were losing their own authority. John tells us of a special meeting of the Sanhedrim, when they had said, What shall we do? We are in danger of losing our authority. They were intrigued by the story, and Luke tells us that He said at that point,

"What therefore will the lord of the vineyard do unto them? He will come and destroy these husbandmen."

Matthew tells us in this connection that they answered the question, and He ratified their finding. They said,

"He will miserably destroy those miserable men."

Thus He had appealed to their own conscience in the realm of what is right and proper, and He brought from them a sentence, the only possible sentence in such a case. The inevitable issue is that of the destruction of the husbandmen, and the transference of the vineyard to other husbandmen

Here, again, there is something Luke does not tell us that Matthew does. He excommunicated the nation. He said,

"The Kingdom of God shall be taken away from you, and shall be given to a nation bringing forth the fruits thereof."

Luke records them as saying: "God forbid,"—quite literally, "Be it not so."

Then He looked upon them, and said,

"What, then, is this that is written,
The stone which the builders rejected,
The same was made the head of the corner?"

He was quoting from the great Hallel, and from its closing sentences. The great Hallel consists of Psalms one hundred and thirteen to one hundred and eighteen. That group of psalms they sang either in part or in whole at nearly all the Jewish feasts. It would be sounding within that Temple, within a few hours when the Passover was observed.

"The stone which the builders rejected
Is become the head of the corner.
This is Jehovah's doing;
It is marvellous in our eyes.

"This is the day which Jehovah hath made;
We will rejoice and be glad in it,"

"Save now, we beseech Thee, O Jehovah;
O Jehovah, we beseech Thee, send now prosperity.
Blessed be He that cometh in the name of Jehovah;"

Those last three lines His disciples and the children had been singing the day before. Just beyond those words occur:

"Bind the sacrifice with cords, even unto the horns of the altar."

Just a few hours later, Mark tells us:

"When they had sung a hymn, they went out unto the mount of Olives."

There is no doubt that the hymn they sang was the great Hallel, or part of it. Probably Jesus sang with them, just before He went out to Gethsemane,

"Bind the sacrifice with cords, even unto the horns of the altar."

From that great hymn He quoted to them:

"The stone which the builders rejected,
The same was made head of the corner,"

and with dread solemnity added:

"Every one that falleth on that stone shall be broken to pieces; but on whomsoever it shall fall, it will scatter him as dust."

We are still teaching our children the song, and how I love it,

"Gentle Jesus, meek and mild."

That is beautifully true, but it is not all the truth. In the presence of wilful hypocrisy, and stubborn rebellion against God, Jesus becomes no longer meek and mild and gentle; but the wrath of the Lamb flames out; and here it was revealed, under the shadow of His Cross.

LUKE XX. 19-40

IN our last meditation we saw the authorities, chief priests, scribes, and elders, challenging our Lord's authority by asking Him two questions, first as to the nature of His authority, and secondly, as to its derivation. We considered, moreover, His reply to them, and His subsequent address to the people with the parable of the vineyard and the husbandmen. Now, this parable stirred the anger of the moral and spiritual rulers, the scribes and the chief priests, and they became active in their hostility.

"And the scribes and the chief priests sought to lay hands on Him in that very hour; and they feared the people; for they perceived that He spake this parable against them."

In the section now under consideration Luke tells us of this anger and activity, and gives an account of two of the methods they employed in their attack upon Him. The background of hostility is revealed in the words:

"And they watched Him, and sent forth spies, who feigned themselves to be righteous, that they might take hold of His speech, so as to deliver Him up to the rule and to the authority of the governor."

The reason of this is revealed in the previous verse;

"They perceived that He spake this parable against them."

That is what stirred their anger. They had apprehended the meaning of that parable. Matthew and Mark tell us the same thing in slightly different form.

Because of this, they

"sought in that very hour to lay hands on Him;"

that is, they decided to do violence to Him personally. John tells us that before this there had been a meeting of the Sanhedrim, when practically that decision was arrived at through the very plausible and clever speech of the high priest Caiaphas. They had a special meeting, and said, What are we going to do? When they had discussed the situation, Caiaphas said,

"Ye know nothing at all, nor do ye take account that it is expedient for you that one man should die for the people, and that the whole nation perish not."

That was the language of the refined politician, who was a murderer at heart, but who would cloak his murderous intention under the language of expediency. Now came the hour when they determined to carry out Caiaphas' suggestion. However, they dared not do it in that very hour. They were restrained. They feared the people. Being thus, for the moment, afraid to carry out their intention, they watched Him, and sent forth spies who feigned themselves to be righteous. The reason for this was that the power of life and death had been taken from them by the Roman authority. They could not condemn any one to death, even by their own laws, without the seal of the procurator upon the death warrant, and the sentence must be passed by Rome. Therefore they attempted to find in His speech some reason for delivering Him up to the rule and authority of the governor. Later on they lied about this very thing, in that when He was arraigned before Pilate, they charged Him with having preached sedition against the rule of Cæsar, and having declared it was illegal to pay tribute.

The two attacks were quite different. The first was purely political. The second was wholly religious, or doctrinal. The political attack is recorded in verses twenty-one to twenty-six; and the religious in verses twenty-seven to forty.

Now, whereas I have said they were attempting to involve Him in some lapse of speech in order to bring Him before the Roman authority, only the first part was likely to do that; and they were so completely routed in their political attempt, that they turned to religion, though it is difficult to see how this could have involved Him in any speech making Him liable to the Roman power.

First, then, let us examine the political attack. Approaching Him, they said:

"Teacher, we know that Thou sayest and teachest rightly, and acceptest not the person of any, but of a truth teachest the way of God."

Were they lying, or were they telling the truth? Did they really mean that? I cannot say. They certainly told the truth. Everything they said was so. He said and taught truly. He did not accept the person of any, and of a truth He taught the way of God. It was all true; and one wonders whether they really believed it. If so, the greater their condemnation. Then they asked Him this question:

"Is it lawful for us to give tribute unto Cæsar, or not?"

It was a distinctly political question. At that period there were two great political parties in Jewry, and that was a divisive question. The Pharisaic party always paid tribute under protest, affirming that the people of God had no right to be paying tribute to a pagan authority. The Sadducean party were in favour of paying tribute. They came to Jesus with this question, which, in their judgment, must involve Him in difficulty with one party or the other. If He had said it was not lawful to pay tribute to Cæsar, then at once the Pharisees would have agreed with Him, and the Sadducees would have been able to report Him to Rome as preaching sedition. If He had said, Yes, it is lawful, then the Pharisees could have said, Where, then, are Your Messianic claims? They were hoping thus to deflect public favour from Him. If once He admitted that it was lawful to pay tribute to Rome, in such admission, in their opinion, He would have discredited His Messianic claim with the listening crowds. The extreme cleverness and the astuteness of these men is evident.

How did He repulse their attack?

" He perceived their craftiness,"

and the first thing He said to them was,

" Show Me a denarius."

He compelled them to produce the coin. I think in all probability He had no denarius about His Person. I do not think He ever carried money. In that little fellowship Judas had the bag; and He was supported by a little group of wealthy women. Their names are given to us by Luke, of whom he says,

" Who ministered unto Him of their substance."

That may be the reason why He asked them to show Him a denarius. But it is remarkable that He did not ask His disciples to produce the coin. Judas might have found one. But they produced it. Look at it. It may be that you have seen a denarius of that period, as I have done, one that was actually current then. On the front of it was the embossed face of Tiberius Cæsar. From the standpoint of human opinion, it is a face characterized by strength and magnificence. Tiberius Cæsar in his youth was a man of singular physical beauty, very much debauched as time went on. On the other side there were two words, or two letters, as a monogram, Pontifex Maximus. Tiberius Cæsar on one side, and his title on the other, the greatest potentate. Jesus took the coin, and said,

" Whose image and superscription hath it ? "

At once they answered, " Cæsar's." I think there was a great hush everywhere. The people were all watching as they produced that coin. It lay there on the hand of Jesus for a moment, and He looked at it. This is one of the pictures I would like to see some artist paint, that scene, when Jesus had that coin lying on His hand. Very soon that hand was to be pierced by a nail under the authority of the man whose portrait He looked at. Such a picture should be so poised that that coin may be seen, with the image of Cæsar uppermost. The brutal animal strength of Tiberius Cæsar; let that be seen. And then Jesus looking at it. He said, Whose image and superscription is this? Cæsar, Pontifex Maximus?

Now mark the implicate of what He had done. Where did the coin come from? They had produced it. What were they doing with it Using it, trading with it; and trading with a coinage means that you are in debt to the State whose coinage you are using. He implicated them, when He asked them to produce the coin. It was their coin. They had it. They were trading with it.

Then, when in answer to His question,

" Whose image and superscription hath it ? "

they said, " Cæsar's," observe the futility of their coalition. Every merely political party is forgotten when He brings to bear upon questions of time the principles of eternity. Still holding it in His hand, perhaps handing it back as He said it, He uttered the words:

" Then render unto Cæsar the things that are Cæsar's, and unto God the things that are God's."

He passed behind all policies and all parties and all differing human opinions on the question of administration, or the question of statecraft, and declared a principle that applied then, and all down human history, and today;

" Render to Cæsar the things that

are Cæsar's, and unto God the things that are God's."

That means, first, that if men live under Cæsar's rule, if they are protected by the legions of Cæsar, if they are trafficking with Cæsar's money, they are in debt for the privileges created for them, to the government under which they live.

"Render to Cæsar the things that are Cæsar's."

Yes, but He said more.

"Render to God the things that are God's."

When He held the coin on His hand, He said,

"Whose image and superscription hath it?"

and they told Him. In what He now said to them, another question is implicated, and He might have asked them, Whose image and superscription is upon you? If that coin has stamped upon it the image of Cæsar, and the superscription that declares him to be pontifex maximus, the greatest potentate, on every human face is the image of God, for man is made in the image and the likeness of God; and the superscription on every human life is that God alone is "Pontifex Maximus." Thus He said in effect, As is the coin to Cæsar, so are you to God. Render to Cæsar the things that are Cæsar's; but do not forget that you are to render to God the things that are God's.

The inter-relationship of these statements is self-evident. Render to Cæsar the things that are Cæsar's. That is first in statement; but it is for ever qualified by that which follows. Render to God the things that are God's. Which does not mean we are to have a secular side to life and a sacred; which does not mean that we may be one thing politically, and another thing religiously. Paul, the apostle of Jesus Christ, in his Roman letter, said,

"For he"—the authority—"is a minister of God, an avenger for wrath to him that doeth evil. . . . For this cause ye pay tribute also. . . . Render to all their dues; tribute to whom tribute is due; custom to whom custom; fear to whom fear; honour to whom honour. Owe no man anything, save to love one another."

Paul was very emphatic that all authority is derived from God. As though Paul had said to the Romans, God is the Pontifex Maximus, and all other authority is delegated authority. Then he went on to show that it was given for the punishment of the evildoer and the rewarding of the good. Now, supposing the authority, whether imperator, or procurator, or any other, is not functioning according to Divine authority, is not punishing evil, but condoning it, is not rewarding the good, but penalizing it; then what am I to do? Disobey the authority, as I obey the authority of God. There are times when rendering to God the things that are God's, make necessary the breaking of human laws. There was a moment in the history of the American Colonists of Britain, when they broke with the authority of England; and they did it because they were true to God. Thus our Lord gave a complete philosophy of statecraft, and of the relation of His own people to the State.

It is interesting to notice that the word they used about paying tribute was not the word that Jesus used. They said, "Is it lawful to give tribute," *didomi*, to donate it. He said, *apo-didomi*. They said, Shall we give tribute. He said, Give back. The *apo* recognizes debt to Cæsar for privileges, and to God for everything. Luke says,

"And they were not able to take hold of the saying before the people."

There was nothing for them to take hold of.

"And they marvelled at His answer, and held their peace."

He was coming to the Cross, these were the last days in the Temple, and this the final clash with the authorities. They thus tried to involve Him with earth's political power, to procure

His death, and He completely routed them; and that not by the clever trickery of a master politician, but by a voice that revealed principles that abide for all time.

We pass on to the next attack.

"And there came to Him certain of the Sadducees."

The coalition was over. It had broken down. Luke reminds us that the Sadducees

"Say that there is no resurrection."

He defined them more fully in his second treatise;

"The Sadducees say that there is no resurrection, neither angel, nor spirit" (Acts xxiii.8).

Here he only refers to that which is pertinent to the story. Thus it is evident that these men came to Him with a foregone conclusion. They did not believe in resurrection. That is to say, they were naturalists in philosophy and in theology.

They told Him the story of a woman who had been the wife of seven brothers in succession, and asked Him,

"In the resurrection therefore whose wife of them shall she be?"

I do not hesitate to say that they intended that to be a grotesque illustration. They were endeavouring by the grotesqueness of their illustration to show the difficulties which the doctrine of resurrection created. Here is a woman, and she has had seven husbands; and presently when they meet on the other side, whose wife shall she be? The question really revealed the fact that in their thinking they were saturated with carnalism. They were thinking of the life beyond in the terms of the carnal. As a matter of fact, these men were not thinking about the life beyond, because they did not believe in it; but they were supposing, if there was a life beyond, that there would be carnal difficulties. Jesus knew what underlay their question. It was not finally of resurrection. It was a question of immortality, and that is seen in the way in which our

Lord answered them. He went behind the supposed difficulty, to the real naturalistic unbelief, which degraded humanity by thinking of it, as they were thinking of it.

"Jesus said unto them, The sons of this age marry, and are given in marriage; but they that are accounted worthy to attain to that age, and the resurrection from the dead, neither marry, nor are given in marriage; for neither can they die any more; for they are equal unto the angels; and are sons of God, being sons of the resurrection."

That was the first line of His answer. Very briefly, and yet very solemnly, and finally, He corrected their suggestion as to conditions in the life beyond. He did it by sharply dividing between "this age," and "that age." In this age certain things are, which will no longer be in that age. Thus He corrected the carnality of their view. He said those who have attained to that age, those who have crossed over, are equal unto the angels, that is, in that matter; He does not say they are angels, but they are equal to the angels, "being sons of the resurrection," and they "neither marry, nor are given in marriage." Marriage is a condition of this age. It is a part of the life that now is. It does not continue beyond. Every such relationship ends here.

Shall we know each other in heaven, someone asks? That is another subject. The friendships of earth will continue in heaven, the highest friendships here will run on there, but not in that way or in that realm. We shall certainly know each other, but conditions will be entirely different.

But He had not done with them. Continuing, He said,

"But that the dead are raised, even Moses showed in the place concerning the Bush, when he called the Lord the God of Abraham, and the God of Isaac, and the God of Jacob."

When Moses had communion with God in the Bush, in the language of men, Abraham and Isaac and Jacob had been dead quite a good while. They were dead. Yes, but, said Jesus, what

Moses said then, what came to Moses from God then is true,

" God is not the God of the dead, but of the living."

God said,

" I am the God of Abraham, and the God of Isaac, and the God of Jacob."

That means that they were not dead, even then.

" God is not the God of the dead, but of the living."

These naturalistic Sadducees, denying resurrection, were denying the persistence of personality beyond death. He said, you are wrong. These men you call dead are not dead. God is not the God of the dead, but of the living, and the persistence of personality beyond death makes at any rate credible the doctrine and the fact of resurrection.

And so their question was answered. Their naturalism was denied, their philosophy was contradicted, their trivial question was laughed out of court, as He affirmed the immortality of man, and the fact that men who died, so far as we may use the word, do not die, because God is for evermore the God of the living.

Luke ends the story by the statement,

" Certain of the scribes answering said, Teacher, Thou hast well said."

I never read that without wondering. Probably these scribes were of the Pharisees, agreeing with His philosophy; or possibly their agreement was again a feigned agreement. Be that as it may, Luke says,

" For they durst not any more ask Him any question."

They were completely routed. Thus we have seen the collapse of two attempts to catch Him in His speech, either in the realm of politics, or in the realm of religion. He was on His way to His Cross; but the Kingliness and the majesty of Him were shining brightly.

LUKE XX. 41–XXI. 4

FOLLOWING on, we are still with our Lord in the third day of His Temple experiences in that last week in Jerusalem.

Having repulsed the two attacks made upon Him; the political attack, concerning the paying of tribute; and the religious attack, concerning the doctrine of resurrection and immortality; our Lord propounded a question to them, and left it without any answer. Matthew tells us by that question propounded, He finally and fully silenced His foes. Mark tells us that His answer satisfied the multitude, " the common people heard Him gladly," that is, the mixed and promiscuous crowd, as distinguished from the rulers. Then, after that question had been propounded and had found no answer from them, He turned, as Luke tells us, and addressed His disciples in the hearing of all the people. Following this, the incident is given of the treasury and the widow.

First, then, as to our Lord's question to the rulers. Concerning this, Matthew tells us something which Luke does not, namely, that before He asked the question recorded by Luke, He had asked another,

" What think ye of the Christ? "

He was not asking their opinion of Himself. He was rather asking them a question in the realm of their own beliefs and their own expectation. If for a moment we change the Greek form of the word which is Christ, to the Hebrew, then I think we may get a clearer understanding of what our Lord meant. He said in effect, What is your opinion of the Messiah, Whose Son is He? They were familiar with their own Scriptures. They knew the prophetic foretellings, and those found in their matchless psalmody. They were familiar with the Messianic hope, so radiant, yet so misunderstood, so misinterpreted; it was the subject of theological discussions among them, some of their Rabbis declaring there must be one Messiah, and others that there must be two, one triumphant, and one suffering. These men were confused in their interpretation; but they all held, in common with the nation in its long history, the hope of the coming of a Messiah. In their literature He had been variously described, as the Daystar, the Daysman, Shiloh, Emmanuel, and in many other ways, but the word covering all the rest was Messiah, the Anointed He asked them, What do you think about Messiah? What is your idea about Him? Whose Son is He? Matthew tells us that they answered, showing their knowledge of their Scriptures, with perfect accuracy, David's.

Then came the great question that Jesus propounded to them. He said, How can Christ be David's Son, for David himself said in the book of Psalms,

" The LORD said unto my Lord, Sit Thou on My right hand, till I make Thine enemies the footstool of Thy feet. David therefore calleth Him Lord, and how is He his Son?"

How can a man's son be that man's lord? To the Eastern mind that presented a real problem. It was a peculiarly Eastern question. They had answered correctly that Messiah was to be Son of David; but David, whose Son He is, spake of Him as Lord. How can He be his Son, if He is his Lord?

Now, if we turn to the Psalm quoted (Psalm cx), we find in the King James Version it begins thus:

" The LORD said unto my Lord, Sit Thou at My right hand, until I make Thine enemies Thy footstool."

In the American Revision it reads,

" Jehovah saith unto my Lord."

That rendering draws a distinction between two names, both of them referring to God. In the King James Version the first " LORD " is printed all in capital letters, and the second " Lord " with an initial capital only, thus drawing the attention of the

reader to a distinction. The distinc tion is between Yahweh—or Jehovah as we now print it, and Adonai. " Je hovah saith unto my Adonai." Adona means Sovereign Lord. This singer o the olden times said, " Jehovah saith unto my Adonai." David was refer ring to Messiah, and he there calls Messiah his Lord. This, then, was the problem propounded—If Messiah is indeed the Son of David, how can He be David's Lord? They did not an swer Him. The answer is not given, but it is implicit.

Some years after, a Jew, who was also a member of the Sanhedrim, before he was apprehended by Jesus; and a pure-blooded Jew withal, as he said he was " a Hebrew of Hebrews," which means there was no mixture in his blood, his father and mother were both Hebrews; he of the tribe of Benjamin, was writing about Jesus, and he said:

" Concerning His Son, Who was born of the seed of David according to the flesh, Who was declared to be the Son of God with power, according to the Spirit of holiness, by the resurrection from the dead; even Christ Jesus our Lord."

Jesus was asking these men what they thought of the Messiah, and how He could be Lord as well as Son. Paul had no difficulty about it. He called Jesus, " Christ Jesus our Lord," and declared that He was Son of David according to the flesh, but that He was Son of God, and that He was declared so to be by the resurrection from among the dead.

In asking them this question, our Lord really went back to a question they had asked Him at the beginning of that day. They had said to Him,

" By what authority doest Thou these things? or Who is he that gave Thee this authority?"

He would not reply, because of their dishonesty. He then gave them a problem,

" The baptism of John, was it from heaven, or from men?"

They were dishonest; they would not answer; consequently He said,

"Neither tell I you by what authority I do these things."

Now He gave them another problem, a problem of the interpretation of their own Scriptures and Messiah. If they had only been able to see, if they had only been able to understand, the answer was simple. His authority rested in His Lordship. David calls his Son his Lord because He was only his Son after the flesh; but in the deep mystery of His being, He was God manifest in flesh. I cannot read that story without feeling that He was endeavouring to bring these very rulers to reconsideration. Up to the very last He was attempting to make them think, to save them from their carelessness, to compel them to consider. Our Lord was not going through these days rejoicing in the destruction of these enemies. Those weeping eyes over Jerusalem tell a different story. The wail of that broken heart we have already listened to,

"O Jerusalem, Jerusalem, that killeth the prophets, and stoneth them that are sent unto her how often would I have gathered thy children together, even as a hen gathereth her chickens under her wings, and ye would not,"

tells a different story. The common people heard Him gladly, the mixed massed multitudes of all sorts and conditions of men were even then swayed by Him; but it was the rulers He was trying to reach. But there was no answer, no investigation. They did not face the problem. Had they done so, they would have had to face His claims anew, but they did not do it. They were withdrawn and hostile, and set upon His death.

Then follows Luke's statement:

"And in the hearing of all the people," who Mark says were listening gladly, "He said unto His disciples, Beware of the scribes, who desire to walk in long robes, and love salutations in the marketplaces, and chief seats in the synagogues, and chief places at feasts; who devour widows' houses and for a pretence make long

prayers; these shall receive greater condemnation."

In those words of Jesus the deep and underlying reason of their maintained hostility is revealed; they were so blind they could not see, and so deaf that they could not hear. Notice His exposure of them. Their inspiration, they "desire," they "love." Their action, they "devour," "and for a pretence make long prayers." Inspiration and action. Desire and love what? They desire to walk in long robes, the evidence of their position as scribes. They loved the uniform, because it indicated the office wherever they went. They loved the salutations in the marketplaces and chief seats in the synagogues, and chief places at feasts; commerce, and religion, and society; they loved pre-eminence everywhere. They went through the marketplaces, and loved the salutations that came to them. They loved the chief seats in the places of religion, in the synagogues. They loved the chief places in social life, at the feasts. The inspiration of all their activity was self-centred. Anything that ministered to their pride, and anything that ministered to their lust—using the word in the highest sense, their own personal desires,—was the inspiration of all they were doing. As to their actions, They "devoured widows' houses," terrible indictment, all the significance of which perhaps is hardly manifest. He had cleansed the Temple at the beginning of His ministry as well as at the close. When He did it at the beginning, and again at the close, He overturned the tables of the moneychangers. What were they doing? Changing money at interest. The Roman historian declared that when at last Jerusalem was sacked by the Roman legions, they found in the vaults in the Temple no less than two and a half million sterling. "They devour widows' houses." "Graft" may be a new word, but it is not a new fact. Then mark the satire of the words; "For a pretence make long prayers." A long prayer is not necessarily an evil thing; but after all is said and done, the greatest prayers are often the briefest. I once heard my friend Samuel Chadwick say, when he went away from his home, he wrote every day to his wife, and when he was going a short journey the letters were short; and the further away he went, the longer his letters were; and that reminded him of some people. He thought some people must be a long way from God because their prayers were so long! "For a pretence," that is the point; masquerading as religious, while oppressing the poor, and loving only the things that ministered to themselves. Beware of them, said He to His disciples. That is the word of warning.

And the sentence He passed upon them was simply this. They "shall receive greater condemnation."

And so we come to the first four verses of the next chapter;

"And He looked up and saw the rich men that were casting their gifts into the treasury. And He saw a certain poor widow casting in thither two mites. And He said, Of a truth I say unto you, This poor widow cast in more than they all; for all these did of their superfluity cast in unto the gifts; but she of her want did cast in all the living that she had."

The old version used the word "abundance," but there is far more force in the word "superfluity." It gets nearer to the genius of the character of the offerings. All these had of their superfluity cast into the coffers, but she of her want did cast in all the living that she had.

This always seems to me to have been a sort of breaking forth upon the dark, dreary dulness of that day for Jesus, of a ray of light, of glory, and of beauty. That poor widow brought to Him a ray of brightness that gave Him soul satisfaction. His enemies had ceased questioning Him. They were routed completely by the calm dignity and finality of everything He had said to them. They had no more to say to Him. There was a hush, a lull in the storm that had been breaking across Him. And He looked up and watched.

This happened in the court of the women. We know that, because in the court of the women there were thirteen boxes, or vessels, into which gifts were flung; they were called *shopharoth*. Into these vessels the people were casting their gifts. Mark says Jesus watched *how* they gave. He saw what they gave, but He watched *how* they gave. Of course, the *how* includes the *what*. He was far more concerned with the motive, than the amount. He watched them give, and as His eyes watched, He saw the wealthy passing the coffers, flinging in their gifts into the vessels, great gifts. Then He saw one pauper woman, for that is the meaning of the word, poorest of the poor, and she came up and dropped in two mites.

Now, the two mites in value were about one-ninety-sixth of a denarius, and if we are to trust the computation of men today, and we have no reason to doubt it, a denarius was worth about seventeen cents. Now, if you are mathematician enough to find the value of one-ninety-sixth part of seventeen cents, you will see how much she put it. It speaks of abject poverty; and do not forget it was all she had. She had no more.

I cannot help watching, too, but I am watching Jesus. Jesus, who rode in as King; Jesus, Who came in as Priest; Jesus, Who had been there all day as Prophet; the Messiah, long looked for, hoped for; the Son of God. He was watching them as they crowded through the court of the women, and flung in their lavish gifts, munificent gifts, by all the calculations of men. And then those watching eyes saw this woman coming. He knew all about her. The two mites were all she possessed, and her very life depended upon them. But she was a daughter of Abraham. She believed in the God of Abraham. She saw the magnificence of the Temple; and by all human calculations she knew very well that her two mites were of no value to the Temple; but she was giving to her God, and she put in all that she had. Jesus was watching.

He was not only watching, He was appraising, and we have His appraisement of these gifts. What did He say? "Of a truth;" notice His emphasizing of the accuracy of His judgment by that formula of introduction;

"Of a truth I say unto you, This poor widow cast in more than they all."

He did not say she has cast in more than any one of them. He said, She has cast in more than the whole of them. Figuratively, He was emptying the thirteen vessels, and calculating and counting up all the shekels that were there, gold and silver, the munificent gifts, and He had the complete count of all that day contributed, and He held in His hands the balances of eternity. He put all the gifts of the rich into one hand, and the two mites into the other, and He said, Those two mites weigh more than all, she hath given more than they all. In the economy of God, said Jesus, for real value in the enterprise of the Kingdom the two mites of that woman are worth more than all the munificent gifts of the rich.

And then He gave His reasons. He said,

"All these did of their abundance, of their superfluity, cast in unto the gifts; but she of her want did cast in all the living that she had."

Two ways of giving, Jesus saw in the Temple courts that day; giving out of superfluity; giving all, out of want. The word rendered superfluity, or abundance; quite literally means giving out of that which was over and above, that is, giving out of the margin, out of that which they did not really need, out of what was not necessary to themselves. That is what they had given to God,—superfluity! Large gifts, totaling a large amount I have no doubt, but nobody had missed what was given. There had been no red streak of blood in the giving of these wealthy men. Superfluity! Then there was the giving of sacrifice, she out of her want. Want is penury, want is lack. Want is need, and yet out of that, she had given all her living, that is, her livelihood, all she was depending upon for the next twenty-four hours, to maintain life. She had poured it out, she had given it to God.

What does this story do for us? At any rate it reveals two ways of giving; giving out of superfluity, giving what we do not want and never miss; and giving with the red blood of sacrifice, streaked in the gift. Jesus said that woman has given more than they all. He had said that the scribes devoured widows' houses, and the next thing He saw was a lone widow putting two mites into the treasury. I wonder if her house had been devoured by a scribe!

Dr. Parker, of the City Temple, once said,

"The gold of affluence which is given because it is not needed, God hurls to the bottomless pit; but the copper tinged with blood He lifts and kisses into the gold of eternity."

LUKE XXI. 5-38

THIS section ends Luke's account of the third day in the final week in Jerusalem. Visualize the scene. Our Lord is seen, with His disciples about Him, and undoubtedly the crowds, also. He had a lull, a rest, so far as the hostility of His enemies was concerned, because

"they durst not any more ask Him any question."

Then watching, He had seen the giving of the rich, and the giving of the poor woman; and had uttered those words in which He had distinguished between two methods of giving.

Then Luke says, "some spake of the Temple." That is a very brief statement. Matthew and Mark tell us that it was His own disciples who spoke about the Temple, who drew His attention to it. Matthew says, "to the buildings," and Mark says, "to the buildings," and the "stones" of the Temple. I never read that without some sense of surprise and wistful wonder, as to what made the disciples draw His attention to the Temple that day. I have sometimes wondered if they had watched Him as He had come up again and again, and had seen Him so apparently absorbed with His message, and the importance of it, that to them it appeared as though He had never noticed the Temple. Be that as it may, the fact remains that the disciples drew His attention to the buildings, and the stones, and their doing so called forth His prediction about it. When He had made that prediction, they asked Him two questions, and He answered those questions.

Let us first consider His prediction.

"As for these things which ye behold, the days will come, in which there shall not be left here one stone upon another, that shall not be thrown down."

Thus, in an hour in which they were greatly impressed with the glory of the Temple, with the massiveness of the structure, with the gorgeousness of the decorations, and the beauty of it all,—to all of which they had drawn His attention,—they heard Him distinctly say that the days were coming when not one of those stones should be left upon another.

The prediction was perfectly clear. There was nothing veiled about it. There was no perplexing figure of speech. His language referred to the actual building and the stones. It was clear, definite, and, above everything else, startling. Nevertheless, in forty years the prediction was absolutely fulfilled. The city was razed, the Temple was destroyed by fire, and with a ruthlessness almost unmatched in history, the Romans saw to it that the thing was completely levelled and devastated.

A prediction so startling naturally led to the inquiry of the disciples;

"And they asked Him, saying, Teacher, when therefore shall these things be? and what shall be the sign when these things are about to come to pass?"

The first thing that impresses me as I read this is that they believed Him. This is a wonderful evidence of the confidence of these men in their Mas-

ter. It is quite a habit among expositors and preachers to criticize these disciples, and say they were blunderers. Yes, they made nearly as many blunders as I have, to say nothing of you! But do not forget that Jesus later said to those men, You have been with Me in all My temptations. In spite of their blundering, they were great souls. They did not doubt the possibility. They were sure He was right. They wanted to know when, and what should be the sign. These were their questions. And He answered them.

Here let us pause for a critical note. Is this the Olivet prophecy? In Matthew twenty-four and twenty-five we have the Olivet prophecy. Is this the same? The great majority of expositors think that it is. I will not be over-dogmatic, but I am quite convinced that this is not the Olivet prophecy. Matthew gives us the full Olivet prophecy. Mark gives us parts of it. There are some very clearly marked distinctions between that prophecy, and what Luke has recorded. He said many of the same things on Olivet, but He said much more. On Olivet, as I believe, they brought their questions again, in a more formal manner, and He gave a fuller answer. We shall therefore consider the answer as here recorded, without further reference to the fuller prophecy.

In verses eight to eleven we have the direct answer of Jesus to the two questions that were asked.

"And He said, Take heed that ye be not led astray; for many shall come in My name, saying, I am he; and, The time is at hand; go ye not after them. And when ye shall hear of wars and tumults, be not terrified; for these things must needs come to pass first; but the end is not immediately."

That was His answer to their first question, "When therefore shall these things be?" He said, Be careful. That is the meaning of, "Take heed," "Go ye not after them;" and distinctly He told them, "the end is not immediately." He had said that the day was coming when not one stone of the Temple should be left upon another, that should not be thrown down. They said, Lord, when? His answer was very careful. Do not be deceived. False Christs will arise, and men will say, Here He is, or The time is at hand. Don't believe them. Don't go after them. Don't be led away by them. The end is not yet.

Then they had asked Him another question, What shall be the sign when it is near, and in verses ten and eleven we find His answer to that.

" Nation shall rise against nation, and kingdom against kingdom; and there shall be great earthquakes, and in divers places famines and pestilences; and there shall be terrors and great signs from heaven."

Thus our Lord told them that there would be national upheaval, that there would be natural disturbances, wars and rumours of wars, earthquakes, famines, pestilences; but He said, Do not be deceived, the time is not yet. That is His answer so far.

Now watch carefully what follows, from verses twelve to nineteen.

" But before all these, they shall lay their hands on you, and shall persecute you, delivering you up to the synagogues and prisons, bringing you before kings and governors for My name's sake. It shall turn out unto you for a testimony. Settle it therefore in your hearts, not to meditate beforehand how to answer; for I will give you a mouth and wisdom, which all your adversaries shall not be able to withstand or to gainsay. But ye shall be delivered up even by parents, and brethren, and kinsfolk, and friends; and some of you shall they cause to be put to death. And ye shall be hated of all men for My name's sake. And not a hair of your head shall perish. In your patience ye shall win your souls."

Now, all that has nothing to do with us, nothing to do with the Church down the ages. It had to do with these men, between the hour when His prediction was uttered about the destruction of the Temple and the time of the fulfilment of that prediction. There would be for His witnesses a period of persecution. And this was so. The years between the crucifixion of our Lord and A. D. 70, when the

city fell and the Temple was destroyed, were terrible years for the witnesses of Jesus. We get a glimpse of it in the Acts. Almost immediately persecution broke out. Saul was one instrument, "breathing out threatening and slaughter." The witnesses were scattered from Jerusalem, and they went everywhere, preaching the Word. This is what He was foretelling. He said to them, Some of you " shall be put to death," and " not a hair of your head shall perish." In those words, incidentally, we have our Lord's outlook on personality. He had said once before to them, during the course of His public ministry:

" I say unto you, My friends, Be not afraid of them that kill the body, and after that have no more that they can do."

" Some of you shall they cause to be put to death . . . and not a hair of your head shall perish."

Now, what is next? Verse twenty, mark it carefully.

" But when ye see Jerusalem compassed with armies, then know that her desolation is at hand."

He said, That will be the sign. They had asked Him when, and what would be the sign. He warned them. Don't be deceived by false claimants that shall arise. Don't be deceived when people tell you the time is at hand. Do not be deceived by signs and wonders and wars and rumours of wars, famine and pestilence, national upheavals and natural disturbances. None of these is a sign.

" But when ye see Jerusalem compassed with armies, then know that her desolation is at hand."

Now, again He had come into the realm of the actual and the material. This was a prediction, as definite as His prediction that the stones of the Temple should be flung down. The city would be invested by armies, and it all happened. Forty years after, they came. Of this He said, When you see those armies outside, when you see the city invested, then that is the sign, the sign of what? The sign that My prediction is about to be fulfilled, and the Temple stones flung down.

Let us go on. What did He say next?

"Then let them that are in Judæa flee unto the mountains; and let them that are in the midst of her depart out; and let not them that are in the country enter therein. For these are days of vengeance, that all things which are written may be fulfilled. Woe unto them that are with child, and to them that give suck in those days! for there shall be great distress upon the land, and wrath unto this people. And they shall fall by the edge of the sword, and shall be led captive into all the nations; and Jerusalem shall be trodden down of the Gentiles."

He was predicting the very things that happened at the fall of Jerusalem. That was the hour when His prediction concerning the Temple was fulfilled; and He said the result of it should be that the people there should go out, and be scattered into all the nations, and Jerusalem should be trodden down of the Gentiles. It all happened literally in the year 70, Anno Domini.

Notice how careful He was to say that these would be the days of vengeance, that all things which are written may be fulfilled.

Let us now resume our reading, because we broke off in the midst of a sentence.

"Jerusalem shall be trodden down of the Gentiles, until the times of the Gentiles be fulfilled."

That is only a phrase, but it covers a long period. The times of the Gentiles are not fulfilled yet. Jesus said that these people should be driven out into all the nations. Can you find any nation in the world where they are not found today?

"And Jerusalem shall be trodden down of the Gentiles,"

and it has been trodden down of the Gentiles ever since. It shall be trodden down of the Gentiles until the times of the Gentiles be fulfilled, and it is still trodden down of the Gen-

tiles. Mohammedanism took possession of it four hundred years ago, but that was only one movement in the continuity. Some are saying that it is free now, under the protection of Britain. But Britain cannot give Jerusalem to the Jew, any more than she can give it to the Arab. Even to this hour Jerusalem is trodden down by the Gentiles. I know there is a Zionist movement in the world, and it is a very interesting movement, but it means nothing in the economy of God. Any return, that is a return in unbelief in Jesus is doomed.

But He had not done.

"And there shall be signs in sun and moon and stars; and upon the earth distress of nations, in perplexity for the roaring of the sea and the billows; men fainting for fear, and for expectation of the things which are coming on the world; for the powers of the heavens shall be shaken."

These are not the signs of the end. They are continuous facts. "There shall be signs," and the language is figurative, employed to describe the condition of earthly affairs running through the period. "Men fainting for fear, and for expectation of the things which are coming," not on the world, nor on the age, but on the "economy;" "the powers of the heavens," that is, "the powers that be ordained of God," all the ruling powers shall be shaken. Is not that a picture of the very hour in which we are living? That has all been happening within the last fifteen years. These things do not prove the end to be near. Can you find me any period since our Lord uttered the word, of which they would not have been true? The signs, as He gave them here, are continuous signs. The language is undoubtedly figurative, and describes conditions political and governmental, failure and unrest and upheaval. The signs are continuous. Therefore the only attitude of His people is that of continuous readiness for the consummation. There never has been an hour in the history of the Christian Church, when the signs have not pointed to the possibility of a consummation.

Well, how is it all going to end? He had not finished. Let us read on.

"Then shall they see the Son of man coming in a cloud with power and great glory. But when these things begin to come to pass, look up, and lift up your heads; because your redemption draweth nigh."

What things? All the things He has been talking about, signs in heaven, and distress of nations. The attitude of the Christian should ever be that of the lifted head, and a light upon the face, knowing that at any moment He may come. We cannot enter into the counsels of God beyond revelation; and if I am inclined to ask sometimes, Why has He not come? or, Why does He not come? then I am rebuked in my own soul because I have to answer, He knows; and I have to leave it there. Of that day and that hour knoweth no man, no, not even the Son, but the Father; one of the most mysterious and yet clear words that ever fell from the lips of Jesus.

Having thus given the formal reply to their question, He used another illustration and gave them a warning.

"And He spake to them a parable; Behold the fig tree."

Now, some student of prophecy says, That is the Jewish nation. But, in order that no one might imagine that He was merely speaking of the Jewish nation, He said more than that;

"Behold the fig tree, and all the trees."

He was not merely using the fig tree as the symbol of the nation, and therefore He added, "And all the trees." What He was about to say was true of any tree.

"When they now shoot forth, ye see it, and know of your own selves that the summer is now nigh."

Thus He was using a natural phenomenon to illustrate something He was about to say. His illustration meant that an effect is produced by a cause. When you see the trees shooting, you know that summer is nigh. The effect of the budding tree is demonstration of the cause, the rising of the sap, because summer is coming. Now, some people see signs today that the Jewish tree is budding anew. If so, it is putting forth a very dead stick. There is no sign of spiritual or moral renewal in that people. There is a revival of thinking about a Jewish Kingdom in the terms of the material.

"Even so ye also, when ye see these things coming to pass know ye that the Kingdom of God is nigh."

That does not mean that the Advent is imminent, but that the Kingdom of God is present, that God is reigning. As He said once, The Kingdom of God is among you. The Kingdom of God is at hand. Watch everything, and watching it, see God, and know that the Kingdom of God is ever nigh.

Then reverting to that hour that was immediate to them, He said,

"Verily I say unto you, this generation shall not pass away, till all things be accomplished."

Link that with their question. "These things" shall "all be accomplished" before the generation pass away. He had gone back to their question as to the destruction of the Temple.

Then mark it well, it was right there and then that there fell from His lips that august and majestic declaration,

"Heaven and earth shall pass away; but My words shall not pass away."

Then He continued;

"But take heed to yourselves, lest haply your hearts be overcharged with surfeiting, and drunkenness, and cares of this life, and that day come on you suddenly as a snare; for so shall it come upon all them that dwell on the face of all the earth. But watch ye at every season, making supplication, that ye may prevail to escape all these things that shall come to pass, and to stand before the Son of man."

Do not forget the circumstances under which all this was uttered. In a few hours they put Him on His

Cross; and yet with calm majesty and clear vision He surveyed the situation from the moment when He spoke, and away on until this hour in which we are living, and beyond. How far beyond, none can tell. His word to His people was a threefold one, "Take heed," "watch," "pray."

LUKE XXII. 1-23

THE last two verses of chapter twenty-one contain an interesting statement by Luke. He says,

"And every day He was teaching in the Temple; and every night He went out and lodged in the mount that is called Olivet. And all the people came early in the morning to Him in the Temple, to hear Him."

He did not sleep in Jerusalem on those nights. Sometimes one wonders whether He slept anywhere. I do not know. Yet the probability is that He did, for He was resting in His God, even in those critical and crucial hours. Of Him it surely would be true; "He giveth His Beloved sleep." He spent the days teaching in the Temple, and the eagerness of the crowd to hear Him even then, at the end, is manifested by that simple statement that the people came early in the morning to Him in the Temple to hear Him.

The present paragraph begins the story of events on the day preceding the crucifixion. The events recorded took place principally in the evening, and far into the night. It was a crowded day in many ways. From his narrative, Luke has omitted many things. He does not tell us anything about the washing of the feet, and those wonderful discourses that our Lord uttered in connection with the feet-washing. Only John has given us these. He does give us something of that conversation, which John has omitted, to which we shall come presently. He does not tell us anything about the singing of the Great Hallel. Neither does he tell us anything of the final prediction of suffering and glory. All these things took place on that day.

Here we may observe that in this narrative Luke has recorded two matters out of sequence as to their actual happening. Over and over again in Luke we find the record of an incident which took place at one point, put in another place, because it illustrates a matter then under consideration. The two things out of order here are, the exclusion of Judas which took place before the institution of the Feast; and the denial of Peter, which took place after the buffeting. These are not vital matters, I only refer to them in passing.

In the first thirteen verses of this chapter we have the story of the preparation for all that followed, and it is very arresting. It is quite evident that the whole atmosphere was one of crisis, and everything was moving towards a climax; and in these verses we see earth, and hell, and heaven, all preparing for that climax.

The preparation of earth;

"Now the feast of unleavened bread drew nigh, which is called the Passover. And the chief priests and the scribes sought how they might put Him to death; for they feared the people."

The preparation of hell;

"And Satan entered into Judas who was called Iscariot, being of the number of the twelve. And he went away, and communed with the chief priests and captains, how he might deliver Him unto them. And they were glad, and covenanted to give him money. And he consented, and sought opportunity to deliver Him unto them in the absence of the multitude."

The preparation of heaven;

"And the day of unleavened bread came, on which the passover must be sacrificed. And He sent Peter and John, saying, Go and make ready for us the passover, that we may eat. And they said unto Him, Where wilt Thou that we make ready? And He said unto them, Behold, when ye are entered into the city, there shall ye meet a man

240

bearing a pitcher of water; follow him into the house, whereinto he goeth. And ye shall say unto the master of the house, The Teacher saith unto thee, Where is the guest-chamber, where I shall eat the passover with My disciples? And he shall show you a large upper room furnished; there make ready. And they went, and found as He had said unto them; and they made ready the passover."

As to the earthly preparation. Luke names the chief priests and the scribes; Matthew names the elders and the chief priests; Mark names the three orders of the rulers, elders, scribes, and priests. The hostility of those rulers was now coming to definite action, and was set upon securing the death of Jesus. Luke says they "sought how they might put Him to death." This statement reveals the fact that there was a difficulty in their way. What was it? Why not go on and do it? "They feared the people." Thus it is seen that all the way, right to the climax, the great mass of the people were sympathetic towards Jesus. Presently they allowed themselves to be swept from their moorings, and clamoured with the rulers for His blood. Nevertheless, it is most interesting to notice in these last hours how the rulers feared them. Jerusalem was crowded. It was the passover season, and people were gathered there from all parts. The popular sympathy was with Jesus up to a certain point. This leads us to the preparation of hell. "And Satan entered into Judas." At the beginning of His ministry, directly Jesus had come to Jordan and been baptized of John, and attested Messiah, and anointed of the Holy Spirit, Luke tells us, " full of the Holy Spirit," He "was led in the Spirit in the wilderness during forty days, being tempted of the devil." That story ended with this statement:

"And when the devil had completed every temptation, he departed from Him for a season."

The Greek word there, which we have rendered " for a season," might be rendered " until." He " departed from Him until." It leaves a hiatus, a gap.

Our translators, feeling it was necessary to make it euphemistic, rendered the Greek word, " For a season." I am not saying this is inaccurate, but I often feel that when the translators are feeling after smoothness and rhetorical euphemism they may rob us of something somewhat startling, and I think it is so in this case. Luke says the devil had completed every temptation, that is, he had no other avenue along which he could approach the personality of Jesus, and so he left Him until! Until when? From that moment of perfect victory in the wilderness until this time, there is no reference to Jesus being attacked directly by Satan. The victory in the wilderness was an absolute victory. Satan was definitely and completely routed until! Here we see him coming back, and he is not coming straight to Jesus. Did he ever again do so? Yes, I think he did. Where? In Gethsemane he was drawing very near, but I do not think he came there. I think that if we could have seen things as they were seen by High Heaven, and low hell, on Calvary, we should have seen him there in person. I think that is something of what Paul meant when he said of Jesus,

" Putting off from Himself the principalities and powers, He made a show of them openly, triumphing over them in it."

The principalities and powers were surely led by the prince of them all. Here Satan is seen in his final approach, and he is attempting to reach Jesus, not with the seductions that he offered Him in the wilderness, and by definite attack upon Him, but through a disciple he hopes to reach Him, and get Him into his power for death. Satan is not omniscient. Even he did not grasp the significance of the dying that was coming. On the human level he won; he gained his instrument in gaining Judas; he brought about His betrayal, and put Him on the Cross; and then he found that:

" He, death by dying, slew,
He hell in hell laid low."

The hour of Satan's apparent victory in the dying of Jesus, was the hour in which the woman's seed bruised the serpent's head.

Judas went away, and communed—yes, it is the same word that we use when we talk of communion. There is a communion that is hell-inspired. There is a fellowship that is unutterably evil.

"He went away and communed with the chief priests and captains."

That is the fellowship of hell.

And what do we read next? "They were glad"! That is the merriment of hell, with torture at its heart. And then, they "covenanted" with him. That is the pact of hell. Luke does not tell us the amount. We know it. The price of a slave, thirty pieces of silver! And still it was not done. He "sought opportunity to deliver Him unto them." Well, why didn't he do it at once? The next phrase supplies the answer;

"In the absence of the multitude."

The sympathy of the people was still with Jesus all the way up to this point; and even Judas felt his life would not be worth a moment's purchase if he were found arresting Jesus, or leading others to arrest Him. Thus we see hell's preparation, and hell's hesitation, and hell's futilities, and hell's follies, and hell's malice!

Then we come to heaven's preparation, about which much need not be said. It is tender and very beautiful. Jesus said to His disciples, Go and make ready for us the passover that we may eat. Their question was revealing.

"Where wilt Thou that we make ready?"

That means that they had no place in which to eat the passover, which was strictly a family feast. Quite evidently the Lord had arranged this matter beforehand with some disciple who remains nameless. He told them where to go. He knew just the hour when they would see the serving man carrying the water. He said, Follow him into the house, and when you arrive, say

"to the master of the house, The Teacher saith unto thee, Where is the guest-chamber, where I shall eat the passover with My disciples?"

Unquestionably it was a password, and the man was waiting for it. He showed them into the room, and there they prepared.

We now begin the story of the things that took place when they passed into that upper room, that *kataluma,* that is, guest-chamber. As we have said, the paschal feast was a family feast, at which the head of the family presided. Here, then, was something strange, something different; a group of men all away from their own homes. They were guests in the home of another man, and that man was not presiding; he had lent him room. Yet this was a family gathering, but it was a new family! Jesus was the Head. He took charge. He presided, as the father of the household always presided at the paschal feast. Here was a new kinship. Away back in His ministry, He had said one day, Who is My mother, who are My brethren, and My sisters? They that do the will of God. Here they were, that little group with Him, the new family.

So they observed the paschal feast;

"He sat down, and the apostles with Him. And He said unto them: With desire I have desired to eat this passover with you before I suffer; for I say unto you, I shall not eat it, until it be fulfilled in the Kingdom of God. And He received a cup, and when He had given thanks, He said, Take this, and divide it among yourselves; for I say unto you, I shall not drink from henceforth of the fruit of the vine, until the Kingdom of God shall come."

There ends the story of the observance of the passover feast. Luke has omitted everything except the final thing. During the passover feast the cup was circulated four times, each time having a symbolic value. The last cup was always the cup of joy. That is the only one to which Luke refers. There can be no question that our Lord participated in the feast up to this point, up to that last cup, the cup of joy. This He distributed to them.

Very arresting are the words He uttered as they sat down;

"With desire I have desired to eat this passover with you."

The form of expression describes an intensity of desire. I think the emphasis should be placed on the words, *"this passover."* Why this passover? He had been at passovers before. "This passover," however, was the final passover recognized by God. We remember that dark night in Egypt so long ago, when the first passover lamb was sacrificed. Through all the intervening years the feast had been observed with more or less of regularity; sometimes with great ceremonial beauty, sometimes carelessly. It had ever been intended to remind them of the beginning of their life as the people of God, of their ransom and redemption out of slavery. Now Jesus said,

"With desire I have desired to eat this passover with you."

As I read that I cannot escape from the conviction that what He meant was this, I have moved towards this hour, desiring it all the way, this climacteric and final hour on the earthly level, when the real meaning of My mission shall be accomplished. In the twelfth chapter of Luke we have the record of how one day He broke out into a great heart-burst or soliloquy;

"I came to cast fire upon the earth; and what do I desire? Would that it were already kindled? But I have a baptism to be baptized with; and how am I straitened till it be accomplished."

He was then looking on to this hour. He said in effect, My mission in the world is to cast fire. It cannot be kindled yet; I have a baptism to be baptized with, and until the baptism is an accomplished fact I am straitened. Now He was in Jerusalem, and the passover had come, and He was

observing the paschal feast with that little group of men; and as they sat at the board, He said,

"With desire I have desired to eat this passover with you."

He partook of the feast until He came to the last cup, and then He said:

"Take this, and divide it among yourselves; for I say unto you, I shall not drink from henceforth of the fruit of the vine, until the Kingdom of God shall come."

What did He mean? Well, I admit that it is not easy of interpretation. My own is a very literal one. Do we find at any point, afterwards in the story, that He did drink of the fruit of the vine? Yes, John tells us that they gave Him vinegar, that is, sour wine, to drink, and He took it.

"Jesus, knowing that all things are now finished . . . saith, I thirst."

And they brought Him sour wine to drink, and He took it, and He drank it. He drank the fruit of the vine there on the Cross, sour wine. He drank wine, when? When He knew that the Kingdom of God had come, because all things were accomplished.

Now, observing the true sequence of events, we go on to verses twenty-one, twenty-two and twenty-three, coming back to verses nineteen and twenty afterwards. In these verses (twenty-one to twenty-three), we have the fact of the exclusion of Judas. Jesus said:

"Behold, the hand of him that betrayeth Me is with Me on the table."

If we compare that with the other stories, we find that it was the passover table.

"For the Son of man indeed goeth, as it has been determined; but woe unto that man through whom He is betrayed! And they began to question among themselves, which of them it was that should do this thing."

I know that it is a subject of long-continued controversy as to whether Judas sat down to the new feast or not. So far as I am concerned, I am absolutely certain he did not. He was excluded before the institution of the Christian feast. I recognize the difficulty. The story as found in Matthew and Mark does not help very much. John tells us very distinctly that when he had received the sop, and that was part of the passover feast, " He went out straightway."

But, be that as it may, notice how our Lord referred to it.

" The Son of man indeed goeth, as it has been determined."

Determined by whom? Was Jesus saying: "I am going to die. They have determined that "? Certainly not. If we want to know what He meant by that word " determined," we may turn on to the Acts. When Peter was preaching about this very thing, he said,

" Ye men of Israel, hear these words: Jesus of Nazareth, a Man approved of God unto you by powers, and wonders, and signs, which God did by Him in the midst of you, even as ye yourselves know; Him, being delivered up by the determinate counsel and foreknowledge of God, ye by the hand of men without the law did crucify and slay."

Jesus said,

" The Son of man goeth, as it hath been determined."

Peter, speaking by the Holy Spirit, said,

" delivered up by the determinate counsel and foreknowledge of God."

That is what Jesus meant. My going is in the Divine economy. My going is within the Divine programme. But that does not remove responsibility from human hearts.

" Woe unto that man through whom He is delivered up."

Now we ' have the account of the institution of the New Feast, and exposition is very little needed here. The passover feast being over, the cup of joy having been distributed, Judas having been dismissed, what then?

" And He took a loaf and when He had given thanks, He brake it, and gave to them, saying."

What do we see? A loaf in the hand of Jesus, and as He looked at it, He saw it as the symbol of His own body; and as His hand broke it He saw the breaking as the symbol of His own breaking. All that which was coming, was symbolized in the bread. What did He do with the broken bread? He passed it to these men who were round about Him, and He said,

" This do in remembrance of Me."

Then, taking a cup from the passover board, He gave it to them and said,

" This cup is the new covenant in My blood, even that which is poured out for you."

As I see Him take that loaf and look at it, and see in it a symbol of His body, then break it, and see that as the symbol of that through which He was about to pass; so I see Him take the cup, and see in its red colour, the symbol of His blood. He gave it to them. He did not participate. He did not eat the bread; He did not drink the cup. He dispensed it. He said, That bread broken is the symbol of My body. Eat it, partake of it. That fruit of the vine in that cup is the symbol of My blood poured out. Drink of it. I wonder if they remembered something He had said to them before, that except they should eat His flesh and drink His blood, there was no life in them. That was a strange saying. John says a hard saying, and when He said it, many of His disciples went back and stayed no more with Him. Whether they understood or not, here they were approaching the interpretation of that mystic saying.

Let us close with His earlier statement on this solemn occasion;

" With desire I have desired to eat this passover with you."

Why? Because this is the last; and

beyond it is that which shall be a fulfilment of everything that it typified and suggested through the running centuries. Thus, ere He passed to the actual Cross, and became our Passover, sacrificed for us, He instituted this Feast sublime in its simplicity of Bread and Wine, till He come.

"And thus that dark betrayal night,
  With the last advent we unite,
By one long chain of living rite,
    Until He come."

LUKE XXII. 24-38

THE Passover Feast having come to a conclusion, Judas was excluded, and the new Passover Feast was instituted. Then Luke records some things which Jesus said to His disciples, ere they left the room and the city.

First, corrective teaching which He gave them in view of the fact of contention among themselves (verses twenty-four to thirty). Then a personal word to Simon (verses thirty-one to thirty-four). Finally instructions concerning the new campaign which was before them (verses thirty-five to thirty-eight).

First, then, the corrective teaching, as found in verses twenty-four to thirty. Let us carefully recall the occasion upon which this teaching was given. A little word gives the key to the situation; it is the word "also." It is a link with what has gone before. Jesus had just told them that one of their number should betray Him. Then,

" they began to question among themselves which of them it was that should do this thing; and there arose also a contention among them, which of them was accounted to be greatest."

"A contention." What is the meaning of the word? The Greek word is derived from one which means a lover of quarrels. A contention was an activity among those who loved quarrelling. The word suggests that the activity was the outcome of a condition of mind. It was not something that happened then for the first time.

That it should break out there was an amazing thing. It was the solemn hour in which He took the bread in His hand, and looking at it, broke it, and saw in it the symbol of His body; and in which He took the cup in His hand, and saw the red fruit of the vine, and said, It is My blood poured out for you. The solemnity of that hour can hardly be overstated, and yet right there and then, they were quarrelling as to which was the greater. Now, as we have said, the word suggests continuousness, that it was the result of a disposition or state of mind. We have clear evidence in the New Testament records that it had been going on for at least six months. It is very significant that from Cæsarea Philippi, when our Lord began to show His disciples that He must go to Jerusalem and suffer, and be killed, and the third day be raised, continuously they broke in upon what He thus told them about His Cross, with this selfsame question, Who was the greatest amongst them?

While the fact thus stated is a sad one, there is an element in it of which we ought not to lose sight. The very fact that they were concerned about positions in His Kingdom proves their continued confidence in Him. He had told them He was going to the Cross. They did not understand Him. Peter was the spokesman of the mental attitude of the group, when he said, God help you, not that, Lord, that be far from Thee. They could not understand the Cross, they did not believe He was right in His determination to go to Jerusalem and suffer and die, and they sought to dissuade Him. Yet they still believed that somehow He was coming into a Kingdom. They knew perfectly well that He was in the toils of His enemies, but they believed still, that somehow He was coming into His Kingdom. Their very contention as to their relative positions of importance in His Kingdom is a proof of their unwavering confidence in Him. In all this I am not drawing on my imagination, Jesus said:

"Ye are they that have continued with Me in My trials."

But while it reveals their confidence, it also reveals their absolute ignorance of the meaning of His mission in the world. They never did understand until the Day of Pentecost. They had no conception of the meaning of Messiahship in the counsels and purposes of God. They were still thinking of the Kingdom of God in the realm of the material. They came to Him after the resurrection, and said,

"Dost Thou at this time restore the kingdom to Israel?"

They had not grasped the significance of His mission even when they were convinced that He was risen. Understanding came to them with the coming of the Holy Spirit. All their witness after shows that this was so.

That is all background, revealing the occasion of this corrective teaching. Now, what did our Lord say to them? His instructions constituted a revelation of the new order. He contrasted earthly ideas, with heavenly ideas; the methods of the world, with the methods of His Kingdom.

He began by saying:

"The kings of the nations have lordship over them; and they that have authority over them are called Benefactors."

I cannot read that without feeling that there was a tender yet satirical humour in the very voice of Jesus. He was looking out over the world order. The kings of the nations, what are they doing? Exercising lordship, and because they exercise lordship, they are called Benefactors. Earthly ideas of greatness are those of mastery. The king with the mailed fist subdues men, and they call him a benefactor. The kings of the nations exercise lordship. They are masters, they command, and those mastered call them Benefactors.

Then our Lord, for the revelation of a contrast, uttered a sharp impera-tive negative: "But ye not so." Our translators, in order to smoothness in reading, have introduced the implied verb "to be;" "Ye shall not be so;" but I prefer the more blunt form of the Greek, which summarily dismisses the earthly conception.

The negative dismissal was followed by the positive interpretation.

"He that is the greater among you, let him become as the younger."

To the Eastern mind this was revolutionary. It was unknown that the younger be counted more important than the elder.

"And he that is chief, as he that doth serve."

Then, in order to new emphasis, our Lord returned to the world order. He said:

"Which is greater, he that sitteth at meat, or he that serveth? is not he that sitteth at meat?"

To that there could have been but one answer by the standards of the world order.

"He that sitteth at meat."

Then came the sharp revelation of difference.

"I am in the midst of you as He that serveth."

Would they be prepared to say He was less than they were? By that standard the man who sits down to be waited on is the less, and the greater is the man who waits on him. The general conception today is that if you go to an hotel, and sit down, you are the great man, and the waiter is the menial. Christ said, "But I am among you as" the waiter! All this was and is a complete revolution in intellectual conceptions of social order.

And He had not done. He had something more to say.

"But ye are they that have continued with Me in My temptations; and I appoint unto you a Kingdom even as My Father appointed unto Me."

How did His Father appoint Him a Kingdom?

"I am in the midst of you as One that serveth."

The Divine way to the throne is the way of self-emptying and sacrificial service. That is what He meant. In effect He said; I appoint unto you a Kingdom of that sort. You are quarrelling as to who is the greater among you. You will never enter into kingly power and authority until you have learned that lesson. In the Kingdom of His appointment, men have two privileges. They eat and drink at His table, that is fellowship; and they sit on thrones judging the twelve tribes of Israel, that is authority. Greatness in His Kingdom consists of service. Thus the Kingdom of God is contrasted with all the world orders. The distinction between earthly conceptions of greatness and heavenly, is that between men in authority, who lord it, and are called Benefactors; and the Kingdom in which the man who waits at table is greater than the man that he waits upon. Do not forget that this teaching was given under the shadow of the Cross, the supreme hour of self-emptying, sacrificial service, and so of ultimate sovereignty.

Having said these things, He turned to Simon, and said:

"Simon, Simon, behold, Satan asked to have you, that he might sift you as wheat; but I made supplication for thee, that thy faith fail not; and do thou, when once thou hast turned again, establish thy brethren. And he said unto Him, Lord, with Thee I am ready to go both to prison and to death. And He said, I tell thee, Peter, the cock shall not crow this day, until thou shalt deny that thou knowest Me."

While speaking directly to Simon our Lord declared that a sifting process was upon them all. What He said about this is most arresting.

"Satan hath obtained you by asking."

That is the real force of the Greek verb. It is not merely that Satan had asked; he had obtained them by asking. What for? That he might sift them as wheat. Notice the plural pronouns. Satan had obtained them, all of them, that he might sift all of them as wheat. Then He dropped into the singular, by which we are not to imagine He had not prayed for the others, but He singled out the man who was in special danger, and in dire need of His help.

In this general statement we have a remarkable revelation of Satan. His purpose is revealed. It is a tremendous word that " sift you as wheat." It describes a winnowing process. Satan desired to take that group of men and sift them. An old Puritan commentator, Trapp, said, Jesus uses a fan, and sifts to get rid of the chaff; but the devil uses a fan and sifts to get rid of the wheat.

Satan is thus seen in his malice, but he is also seen as under God's authority. He cannot sift until he has had permission. He is the enemy of God, and the enemy of all, especially of those who put their trust in God. He is for ever considering them. God said,

"Hast thou considered My servant Job?"

It is a terrible word, revealing the malignant watching eyes of Satan, for ever searching the saint of God, and looking for the weak link in the chain, the weak door in the citadel to break in. Yes, but he cannot touch a hair upon the back of a camel that Job owns, until he has God's permission to do it.

"Satan hath obtained you by asking,"

but he had to ask. So, whatever the sifting that is coming, it is by Divine permission. That is the first thing that emerges in this wonderful word to all the group.

Then He says,

"I have prayed for thee."

The word that is used of Satan's asking is one that has a significance, suggesting the request to put to the test. Jesus said, "I have prayed," but that is not the same word as the one used of Satan's asking. This is a word that has as its root a thought of binding; and I have asked for you, committing

Myself for you as your Bondman, your Surety.

What startling and amazing matters are here revealed. A man, Simon, and the devil and Christ both praying for him. Satan asking to have him and sift him and destroy him. Christ standing his Bondman, asking that his faith shall not fail.

"I have prayed for thee, that thy faith fail not."

And let it be said at once his faith did not fail. His faith did not fail when he was denying his Master. Neither did his love fail. What did fail? His hope, and therefore his courage. When Peter came to write a letter long after, he broke out into a doxology;

"Blessed be the God and Father of our Lord Jesus Christ, Who according to His great mercy begat us again unto a living hope by the resurrection of Jesus Christ from the dead."

Hope was dead, and when hope is gone, courage fails, and man becomes a coward. Jesus knew his faith would not fail. He knew how deep he was going, but listen to this:

"But when once thou hast turned again, establish thy brethren."

That was our Lord's confidence in his restoration.

And Peter said, and he never said a finer thing,

"I am ready to go both to prison and to death."

He meant it. But Christ quietly said,

"I tell thee, Peter, the cock shall not crow this day, until thou shalt deny that thou knowest Me."

That second word of Jesus did not negative the first word;

"Simon, Simon, behold, Satan hath obtained you by asking, that he might sift you as wheat; but I made supplication for thee, that thy faith fail not; and do thou, when once thou hast turned again, establish thy brethren."

In effect our Lord said, "I know you will deny Me before the morning breaks. I know you as you do not know yourself, Simon. I know the weakness and the cowardice incipient in you; and I know where it will lead you in the dark hours ahead; but I have prayed for you, and you are coming back; and when you are come back, establish your brethren."

And so we pass to the last section in this teaching. He now turned back to the group,

"And He said unto them, When I sent you forth without purse, and wallet and shoes, lacked ye anything? And they said, Nothing. And He said unto them, But now, he that hath a purse, let him take it, and likewise a wallet; and he that hath none, let him sell his cloak, and buy a sword. For I say unto you, that this which is written must be fulfilled in Me, And He was reckoned with transgressors; for that which concerneth Me hath fulfilment."

That is all. He had finished.

"And they said, Lord, behold, here are two swords. And He said unto them, It is enough."

In view of the new order of life which He had come to establish, and which He had revealed, the new order, in which the secret of their greatness was to be the measure of their lowliness, and their willingness to serve; in view of the new order, in which they were going out into the world to serve, not to command, He now gave them new instructions different from the instructions He had given them when they went out while He was still amongst them. He looked back for a moment, and asked them, "When I sent you forth without purse," which carries money; "and wallet," which carries food; "and shoes, did you lack anything? and they said, Nothing. Now He said, under the changed conditions, when you go out, take your purse, you will need money; take your wallet, you will need to carry your food; and carry a sword, not for offence but for defense. Having told them that, He said,

"I say unto you, that this which is written must be fulfilled in Me."

In other words, He said, I am coming to the climax. My work on earth is about to end, and it will end in accomplishment. My work is now to be rounded out to completion. The implicate is that their work lay ahead. Thus He was interpreting the reason for the purse and the wallet, and the sword. They would be necessary because of all that lay before them. Now, it is arresting that He told them to take the purse, and the wallet, and the sword, but the only thing that seems to have impressed them, was the sword. They said, we have two. Jesus said, "It is enough." He was not referring to the two swords, but to the conversation. It was an abrupt dismissal. He dismissed the subject, and immediately left the city, and went to Olivet.

LUKE XXII. 39-65

IN this paragraph we have the record of the last things of the day before that of the crucifixion of our Lord. All of them happened in the night.

As reverently we follow Him, we are with Him in two places; first on the Mount that is called Olivet, in verses thirty-nine to fifty-three; and then in the high priest's house, verses fifty-four to sixty-five.

Luke does not name Gethsemane. He speaks of going to the Mount of Olives. Neither does Luke tell us whose house it was, save that it was the high priest's house. From other Gospel narratives we know that it was to Gethsemane that He went; and to the house of Annas that He was taken. To the house of Caiaphas He was taken presently, when the Sanhedrim gathered after day had broken. Luke says,

"And He came out, and went, as His custom was, unto the mount of Olives, and the disciples also followed Him."

In the thirty-seventh verse of chapter twenty-one, we read,

"And every day He was teaching in the temple; and every night He went out, and lodged in the mount that is called Olivet."

In the Gospel according to John, in the eighteenth chapter, John says (verses one and two),

"When Jesus had spoken these words, He went forth with His disciples over the brook Kidron, where was a garden, into which He entered, Himself and His disciples. Now Judas also, who betrayed Him, knew the place; for Jesus ofttimes resorted thither with His disciples."

If we put these two statements together, we get the surroundings. Luke says He did not stay in Jerusalem a night during that last period, but that He spent all those nights on Olivet. Then he says that after the Passover and the institution of the Feast, He left the city, and went to Olivet as His custom was. It is evident that Luke meant more than the custom of a week, although that was included, for John tells us, in that pathetic and poignant statement, that Judas knew where he would find Him, because He often went to that garden. He had often been to the garden of Gethsemane, across the little brook Kidron; and now again, the Passover feast being over, the new feast being instituted, night having fallen, He came to the Garden of Olives, Gethsemane.

In the story of the Garden, there are two movements; the agony of Jesus in communion; and the arrest of Jesus.

The agony of Jesus in communion.

"And when He was at the place, He said unto them, Pray that ye enter not into temptation. And He was parted from them about a stone's cast; and He kneeled down and prayed, saying, Father, if Thou be willing, remove this cup from Me; nevertheless, not My will, but Thine be done. And there appeared unto Him an angel from heaven, strengthening Him. And being in an agony He prayed more earnestly; and His sweat became as it were great drops of blood falling down upon the

ground. And when He rose up from
His prayer, He came unto the disciples,
and found them sleeping for sorrow,
and said unto them, Why sleep ye?
rise and pray, that ye enter not into
temptation."

That story is almost too sacred to
explore by the methods of exegesis or
exposition. And moreover, there are
things in it which have defied all exposition, and have baffled every exe-
gete. There are dim and darkling
mysteries hanging round that story,
into which we cannot finally penetrate.
Therefore let it be understood that
with profound reverence, and becoming reticence, we draw near.

Notice, first, that the account of the
experience of our Lord is surrounded
by something He said to His disciples;
said to them before it began, said to
them again when it was over. In
verse forty,

"Pray, that ye enter not into
temptation;"

and in verse forty-six,

"Pray, that ye enter not into
temptation."

The sympathy of His heart was with
them, His profound understanding. If
we translate with a little more blunt-
ness, being a little less careful about
the English idiom, and allowing it to
remain in the idiom of the Greek, then
this is how it reads,

"Pray not to enter into temptation."

In other words, He said to them,
When you are at prayer, you will be
safe from temptation. "Pray," and it
is the full word. We should do no
violence to it if we rendered it Worship. Prayer is more than petition.
Our Lord said to these men in effect:
If you are in prayer, you will be delivered from the force of temptation.
A whole philosophy of life blazes out
in that twice-repeated word of the
Lord to His disciples in that dark and
trying hour.

Think what an hour that was for
those three, and what an hour for the
others left outside. Remember those
six months that were now at an end,

to which we have made so many references in the course of our studies,
those six months since Cæsarea Philippi, with the strange foreboding that
filled them. They knew the attitude
of the rulers towards Him, and they
knew that now He was practically
within the toils of His enemies. It
was a trying hour for them, so trying
that they went to sleep. Luke is the
only one who tells us that it was from
sorrow that they fell asleep.

Undoubtedly, understanding the strain
they were under, He thus twice said
to them:

"Pray, that ye enter not into
temptation."

Maintain the life of fellowship with
God, however dark the day, however
rough the way, for the soul at worship, is the soul who is ever guarded
against temptation.

Now, reverently, let us see Him
alone with God. All the world was
left behind. All His friends were
outside, and He passed into the place
of communion with God. It was an
hour of "agony," but it was "agony"
in communion. Not for a single moment did He lose the sense of God,
or of the nearness of God, or of the
care of God in Gethsemane. Gethsemane is not Calvary. He said,
"Father," the word expressing His
sense of relationship, not in the Divine
alone, but in the human also.

Pondering the story carefully, we
ask what was uppermost in His mind
at the time? The answer is found in
the words, "This cup;"

"If Thou be willing, remove this cup
from Me; nevertheless not My will, but
Thine, be done."

Some of the most devout Bible students are not in agreement as to what
this really means. I am not going to
argue the case, but allow a little light
to fall upon it from other Scriptures.
In Matthew's Gospel, in chapter
twenty, we have the story of the coming to Him of the mother of the sons
of Zebedee, that is, James and John,
and the sons were with her, and she
said,

"Command that these my two sons may sit, one on Thy right hand, and one on Thy left hand, in Thy Kingdom,"

and Jesus said,

"Ye know not what ye ask. Are ye able to drink the cup that I am about to drink?"

What was in His mind when then He referred to His cup?

Again we have seen Him at that Passover board, where He took a cup in His hand, and said,

"This cup is the new covenant in My blood." "Drink ye all of it."

What, then, was in His mind?

Once more, in the eighteenth of John, where he records these garden experiences, we read, in verse ten,

"Simon Peter therefore having a sword drew it, and struck the high priest's servant, and struck off his right ear. Now the servant's name was Malchus. Jesus therefore said unto Peter, Put up thy sword into the sheath; the cup which the Father hath given Me, shall I not drink it?"

Now, if we group these references to a cup, I think there can be no escape from the conviction that the cup referred to was the passion that was ahead of Him, the mystery of Calvary's Cross. It has been said that He feared He would die physically, before the Cross, and was praying against it; but there is neither meaning in that, nor warrant for it. That is assuming that the only kind of death of value was that of the Roman gibbet. That is not so. He might have been put to death by the hands of lawless men by some other means than that of the Roman gibbet. He was not asking to escape physical death before the deep dying of the Cross. John tells us also in the last hours of His public life, when the Greeks came to see Him, He said,

"Except a grain of wheat fall into the earth and die, it abideth by itself alone; but if it die, it beareth much fruit. . . . Now is My soul troubled; and what shall I say? Father save Me from this hour? But for this cause came I unto this hour."

Here is the place where our exploration has to be reverent, and perhaps cease. He was in the garden, and now He did say,

"Father, if Thou be willing, remove this cup from Me; nevertheless, not My will, but Thine, be done."

All I can say is that as I ponder it, through that darkened window there is a mystic light shining, showing me the terrors of the Cross more clearly than I see them even when I come to Calvary.

But let us never lose sight of the fact that not for a moment was there any departure from the will of God.

"Father, if Thou be willing, remove this cup from Me; nevertheless not My will, but Thine, be done."

The communion was unbroken, even when the agony was expressed.

The thing is too sacred for the exploration finally of any human mind, but we are brought face to face with what that hour meant to Him, as He prayed on the margin of it, by the side of the unfathomable sea of sorrows, the sighing and the moaning of which come to us like the voices of perdition. We see Him in an unbroken communion, never ruffled, never faltering, with completely poised will, to the will of His God. So He prayed that prayer. Luke tells us that an angel came and strengthened Him, ministered unto Him. He was thus strengthened physically, mentally, spiritually, in the realm of His human nature, in that supreme hour.

The last thing is not to be explained, but to be read, the physical, sacramental sign of the abysmal spiritual anguish,

"He sweat as it were great drops of blood."

"All ye that pass by,
To Jesus draw nigh,
Come see if there ever
Was sorrow like His."

And so we pass on.

" While He yet spake, behold, a multitude, and he that was called Judas, one of the twelve, went before them; and he drew near unto Jesus to kiss Him. But Jesus said unto him, Judas, betrayest thou the Son of man with a kiss? And when they that were about Him saw what would follow, they said, Lord, shall we smite with the sword? And a certain one of them smote the servant of the high priest, and struck off his right ear. But Jesus answered and said, Suffer ye them thus far. And He touched his ear, and healed him. And Jesus said unto the chief priests, and captains of the Temple, and elders, that were come against Him, Are ye come out, as against a robber, with swords and staves? When I was daily with you in the Temple, ye stretched not forth your hands against Me; but this is your hour, and the power of darkness."

That story is equally, in quite another way, beyond exposition. The reading of it is enough. Jesus and Judas; a kiss, and the rebuke. Nothing I can say in denunciation of Judas would begin to approach the realm of words sufficient to denounce the dark and dastardly act. No brilliant essayist, or clever novelist, has ever been able to redeem Judas in the thinking of upright men from the evil of that betrayal and that kiss.

Then Simon Peter drew his sword, in blundering zeal, but far finer than Judas' kiss. Nevertheless, it is always to me a suggestive thing, holding my soul in awe, that the last act of Divine surgery performed by the tender fingers of Jesus, was made necessary by the blundering zeal of a disciple. I think sometimes He has been busy ever since healing the wounds made by the blundering zeal of disciples.

We stand in awe in the presence of the august majesty and dignity of Christ's attitude towards the rulers. How they had tracked Him through the years; how we have watched them, their growing hostility, their attempt again and again to catch Him in His words and bring Him under the authority of the civil power, that they might encompass His death. Now they were closing round Him, and Christ addressed Himself to them first. The only protest He made was against their method of arresting Him.

"Are ye come out as against a robber, with swords and staves?"

Then, with a satire that proved how high He was above all their machinations, and that He was not in their hands as much as in the hands of God, with Whom He had been in agonized communion in the garden, He said:

" When I was daily with you in the Temple ye stretched not forth your hands against Me."

Then the final august words:

" But this is your hour, and the power of darkness."

Mark it carefully, "your hour," you priests, you captains of the temple, you rulers, your hour! Yes, but behind it is the authority of darkness. Thus, while admitting it to be the rulers' hour, He showed what was the inspiration of their evil intent, they were acting under the authority and dominion of darkness.

Again we read on. Verse fifty-four,

"And they seized Him, and led Him away, and brought Him into the high priest's house."

In connection with that, let us read at verse sixty-three,

"And the men that held Jesus mocked Him, and beat Him. And they blindfolded Him, and asked Him, saying. Prophesy; who is he that struck Thee? And many other things spake they against Him, reviling Him."

Verse fifty-four tells us how they arrested Him, led Him away, and brought Him to the high priest's house. Verses sixty-three to sixty-five tell us how they treated Him there. Luke has inserted there the story of Peter's denial, though it took place later in the palace of Caiaphas.

It was illegal, under Jewish law, to arrest any man and take him to a place of detention, unless there was some specific charge preferred against him. In the case of Jesus there was no such charge. They attempted to formulate one when the irregular meeting of the Sanhedrim assembled at daybreak. The fact that they took Him to the house of Annas is arresting. There is an anomaly here in the fact that there were two high priests, Annas and Caiaphas. That was not the Mosaic order. That was not the Divine order. The facts were that Annas was the high priest, but he became unacceptable to Rome, and by the order of the Emperor he was set aside, but allowed to retain his title, and Caiaphas was appointed. Annas was content to have the title without the office, because he was able to carry on those nefarious practices, by which he was impoverishing the people, by means of temple tribute. He was wealthy by extortion and robbery. When they arrested Jesus, they took Him to the house of Annas. It was nearer to Gethsemane than the palace of Caiaphas. They could hold Him there until the morning, when He could be arraigned before the Sanhedrim.

" There they mocked Him, they beat Him, they blindfolded Him, and smote Him, saying, Prophesy; who is he that struck Thee? "

Can anything more dastardly be imagined?

" This is your hour, and the power of darkness."

Luke tells the story of Peter very simply (verses fifty-four to sixty). In Mark, which is, in a sense, Peter's own Gospel, we have the blunt truth about it all. When they arrested Him, Peter followed Him. Thank God for that. He followed Him afar off. Yes, that was the sad part of it; and yet are you surprised? I think not, if you know your own heart. They made a fire in the chill hour of the morning, in the court of Caiaphas' palace, and he went and sat among the crowd, and warmed himself. And, quite casually, with perhaps a little gloating malice in their minds, there came first a saucy servant maid who said,

" This man also was with Him."

Said Peter,

" Woman, I know Him not."

Presently another came, a man, and he said,

" Thou also art one of them."

And Peter answered,

" Man, I am not."

And then, an hour passed. Then another man said,

" Of a truth this man also was with Him; for he is a Galilean."

Peter said,

" Man, I know not what thou sayest."

What next?

"And the Lord turned and looked upon Peter. And Peter remembered the word of the Lord, how that He said unto him, Before the cock crow this day thou shalt deny Me thrice. And he went out, and wept bitterly."

There was a time in the younger years of my ministry when I should have enjoyed fifteen minutes, scoring Simon. But not now. I am not exonerating him from blame; but if I investigate my own heart, I am not surprised. Moreover, I have ceased criticizing him because there has dawned on me the fact that Jesus did not do so. He understood. He never gave him up.

" I have prayed for thee that thy faith fail not."

His faith did not fail. What is the meaning of that heaving bosom, and that breaking heart, as going out into the cold of the morning he wept bitterly? He still believed in Jesus, and he still loved Him, but his courage had failed because his hope had gone. He was down in the depths. The Lord turned and looked at him. What sort of a look was it He gave him that night? There was nothing reproachful in the look of Jesus. It was undoubtedly a look all full of love ineffable, and of infinite compassion; a look that had in it the light of assurance, even though he was denying Him. It was a saving look, a restoring look, a glance of the eye that said, I am here.

Let me conclude with a reminiscence. It was on an August Sunday, a good many years ago now. I happened to have nothing to do in London on that Sunday. I went in the morning to hear Father Stanton. He was an Anglican, with much in his service which did not appeal to me at all. He preached on that Sunday morning from the text,

"He looked round about upon all things, and went out."

Something he said at the close gripped me. He was talking about the eyes of Jesus, of how He looked about upon the Temple, of how He looked at many things; and he came to this, He looked at Peter and broke his heart. Then, leaning over his desk, he said,

"Don't ever forget that the look of Jesus, however wonderful, would have been no good, if at the moment Simon had not been looking His way."

Did you ever think of that? It is perfectly true. It reveals Simon to me again, vulgar, profane swearer, base denier, and yet underneath, loving Jesus, keeping his eye on Him; and so the watching eyes of Simon saw the love glance in the eyes of Jesus.

LUKE XXII. 66-71

LUKE has given a condensed account of the arraignment of Jesus before the Sanhedrim, in which he has emphasized the salient points. Other details are found in other Gospels, and perhaps we may, by way of introduction, fill in one or two of them, so as to have our background.

In our last meditation we saw Jesus arrested in the garden, and taken to the house of Annas, and there submitted to indignity, while they waited for the breaking of the day. With the breaking of the day there was a gathering, as Luke described it, an

"Assembly of the elders—both chief priests and scribes."

This gathering he calls the Council;

"and they led Him away into their council,"

the word rendered council being *Sunedrion*, that is, Sanhedrim.

From other narratives we know that this gathering was held in the palace of Caiaphas, not in the house of Annas; and we know, too, that Caiaphas had a semi-private interview with Jesus before He appeared before the Sanhedrim.

It was an official gathering, hastily called together in the early hours of the morning. From the standpoint of Jewish law, it was illegal. The place of gathering was illegal. There were three Jewish courts operating through Jewry at the time; a court in towns numbering less than 120, some authorities say 240, which consisted of three judges. Then there was another court for larger areas, consisting of twenty-three members. The final court was the Sanhedrim, in which there were seventy-one members; and the place of the meeting of the Sanhedrim legally was within the Temple courts. They had the right to gather together in a private capacity somewhere else; but such a gathering had no power to deal with Jesus at all. As a matter of fact, they did not deal with Him. That is to say, they passed no sentence on Him. They kept within the narrow limits of the law so far, but they investigated, and prepared for His death with great determination in this gathering. They found Him guilty of blasphemy, and for that reason they decided on His death. But before Pilate, that charge would have been of no avail, for the Roman Empire did not take any account of a charge of blasphemy in the Jewish sense.

Luke, in this condensed report, has recorded the two things that happened, which were then, and are for evermore, of profound significance. We see Jesus arrested and arraigned before the religious tribunal. In our next study we shall see Him before the civil tribunal. Luke has recorded the two questions which they put to Him, and the two answers which He gave.

Their first question was,

"If Thou art the Christ, tell us;"

and the second grew out of His answer to the first,

"Art Thou, then, the Son of God?"

Those are the two supreme questions about Jesus. They were then, and they are today. Is He the Christ? Is He the Son of God? When we have answered them, our answer will have revealed our attitude towards Christianity. They were two great central questions, mattering then supremely to that crowd in the Sanhedrim, mattering far more to the nation, mattering most of all to the whole human race. Is He the Christ? Is He the Son of God?

The first question was a strictly legal one, that is to say, it was put in a legal form,

"If Thou art the Christ, tell us."

Once before these authorities had come to Him with that same formula, "Tell us." Jesus said to them at that time,

"I will ask you a question, Tell Me."

There was a sharp and intended contrast between their "Tell us" and His "Tell Me." Here we find them using the same formula. It was a definite legal formula. As a matter of fact, they put Him on His oath. It was the method of administering the oath to the arrested person, demanding that He answer truthfully. They now put to Jesus, in concrete, clear-cut form, the one question of importance in view of all His life and all His ministry. Throughout His ministry He had claimed Messiahship. His followers had confessed Him Messiah. That is what discipleship meant to them. At the very beginning His very first disciple, Andrew, said, "We have found the Messiah," and all the way the numbers had grown who had ac-

cepted Him as Messiah. To those religious rulers it was a tremendous claim. The one undying hope in the hearts of devout Israel had been the coming of their Messiah. Now, that was the point of the question. Had He come? John had announced Him as Messiah, and then even John, in an hour of great mental perplexity, had wondered whether he was right, and so had sent the question,

"Art Thou He that cometh, or look we for another?"

This was the question which the religious rulers claimed that they would have settled by His statement. We know enough of these men to know, as we shall see presently, that whatever He had said, they would not have believed Him. Nevertheless, it was the question they asked. What will He say? Before the national representatives He was called upon to be explicit. Was He the Messiah?

Even from their standpoint, it was the question as to whether they had reached the focal point in their history. All the symbolism of their religion had pointed to One Who should fulfil all the ancient ritual, all the prophets' witness, those wonderful and marvellous names, Messiah, Shiloh, Daystar, Daysman, Immanuel, and many others, pointed to the crisis of Messiah's advent. Therefore they asked Him the question, which they had a perfect right to ask,

"If Thou art the Christ, tell us."

Now observe His answer. It was first a rebuking refusal, and secondly a revealing affirmation. He refused to answer their question in the form in which they had put it; but He gave them an answer that could leave no doubt in the mind of any one on that Sanhedrim of His claim.

He first said,

"If I tell you, ye will not believe; and if I ask you, ye will not answer."

This was a refusal to give them an explicit answer, and He gave them the reason for His refusal.

This answer takes us back to something which had happened in the Temple on the day when they were bringing all sorts of questions to Him, and at last He had asked them,

"How say they that the Christ is David's son? For David himself saith in the book of Psalms,
The Lord said unto My Lord,
Sit Thou on My right hand,
Till I make Thine enemies the
footstool of Thy feet.
David therefore calleth Him Lord, and how is He his son?"

Then they did not answer Him. Now they say,

"If Thou art the Christ, tell us,"

and He replied,

"If I tell you, ye will not believe; and if I ask you, ye will not answer."

To go a little further back. When they had demanded from Him, on an earlier occasion, an authoritative statement, He had said,

"I also will ask you a question; and tell Me, the baptism of John, was it from heaven, or from men?"

Then they had held a consultation, and had decided they would not answer Him. They said,

"If we shall say, From heaven, He will say, Why did ye not believe him? But if we shall say, From men; all the people will stone us; for they are persuaded that John was a prophet."

Jesus was thus reminding them of their attitude, as revealed before. Thus, in effect, our Lord said to that assembly of the Sanhedrim; You are not a fit body to investigate Me on this subject. You are dishonest. You ask Me for an affirmation, which if I make, you won't believe. What is the use of My making a statement to people with foregone conclusions, if after all I have said, and all I have done, you won't tell Me what your opinion is?

But He had not finished. He also said,

"But from henceforth shall the Son of man be seated at the right hand of the power of God."

"From henceforth," that is, from this point, from the point where you reject Me, from there, "From henceforth," when you hand Me over to death, when you give Me the Cross, from this point,

"From henceforth shall the Son of man be seated at the right hand of the power of God."

What did He mean by the Son of man being seated at the right hand of the power of God? He was taking them back to the very psalm He had quoted to them on that earlier occasion when He had said David called the Messiah his Lord, and asked them how could He be his Son? That psalm opens thus:

"Jehovah saith unto My Lord, Sit Thou at My right hand,
Until I make Thine enemies Thy footstool."

Now, said Jesus,

"From henceforth shall the Son of man be seated at the right hand of the power of God."

Those men knew the psalm. They knew its Messianic value. He now employed its terminology, and declared it would be fulfilled in Him.

"If Thou art the Christ, tell us."

"If I tell you, ye will not believe; and if I ask you, ye will not answer. But from henceforth shall the Son of man be seated at the right hand of the power of God."

No language could have been to those men a more definite and clear-cut and final claim to Messiahship than this. Thus He claimed Messiahship in the terms of their own Scriptures, with a clarity that could leave no room for misunderstanding on the part of the men to whom He spoke.

This fact has its value for all time. There, on that day, in that dark hour, after the betrayal of the night; there, before that illegal assembly, when they challenged Him in terms of law, while yet doing an illicit thing; Art Thou the Christ? He claimed definitely and positively that He was the One referred to, Who should sit at the right hand of the power of God.

When they heard Him say that, they put to Him what was not a studied and prepared question; but one arising out of His answer. They all said,

"Art Thou then the Son of God?"

The "then" in the question is significant, showing that what He had now said had led them to the conclusion that He was claiming to be the Son of God. How did they know that? He had not called Himself the Son of God. He called Himself the Son of man. He had quoted concerning Himself, as we have seen, words found in Psalm one hundred and ten. He said,

"From henceforth shall the Son of man sit on the right hand of the power of God."

What, then, does the psalm say about that?

"Jehovah saith unto my Lord."

Well, Who is that? David's Son. Now, here was the very question He had asked them previously, and they had not answered. Evidently they knew. The fact comes out now. Thus they understood that when He claimed fulfilment in Himself of the Messianic prophecy of Psalm one hundred and ten, He was claiming to be Son of God, and as the result of that understanding they asked Him their second question;

"Art Thou then the Son of God?"

How did He answer them? Simply, clearly, and explicitly this time? "Ye say that I am," which meant, What you say is so, that is what I am.

Thus, before the Sanhedrim, Jesus claimed to be the Messiah, and the Son of God. Now, if the second claim were false, He was a blasphemer; and if the first claim were false, He was fraud. This is what made them exclaim,

"What further need have we of witness? for we ourselves have heard from His own mouth."

Another of the evangelists tells us that when He made that claim, Caiaphas rent his robes. That was a legal act. It was provided that in the presence of definite blasphemy the high priest should rend his garments as indication of terror thereat.

For us, the supreme value of all this is that thus, practically on oath, our Lord claimed, before the Sanhedrim, that He was the Messiah, and the Son of God. In other words, He ratified the accuracy of Simon Peter's confession at Cæsarea Philippi. In passing, one wonders how much of this Simon Peter heard. I cannot tell. If he did hear it, it may have helped to break his heart when Jesus looked at him. In those days, six months earlier, Peter had said,

"Thou art the Messiah, the Son of the living God."

This confession Jesus now ratified. His enemies asked Him,

"Art Thou then the Christ?"

He claimed that He was. They asked Him then,

"Art Thou the Son of the living God?"

He claimed that He was.

It is interesting to remember that there were two of the disciples who went further in the trial than any, one was Peter, who had made the confession, and the other was John. Long years after, there came a day when John wrote the story of Jesus differently from the way in which the others had written it. Why did he write it? He himself tells us;

"These things are written, that ye may believe that Jesus is the Christ, the Son of God."

Thus John says in effect, I have written this book to show that Peter was right when he made his confession at Cæsarea Philippi; I have written this book to show that the claims that Jesus made that day before the Sanhedrim were true claims; He is the Christ, He is the Son of the living God.

LUKE XXIII. 1-12

IN answer to the challenge of the
Sanhedrim, Jesus had definitely
made the double claim, first that He
was the Messiah; and secondly that
He was the Son of God.

The first claim did not involve Him
in any danger, for others had claimed
Messiahship. Of course, such claim
was almost bound to stir hostility.
But the second claim, the inevitable
result of the first, that He was indeed
the Son of God, brought Him under
the serious charge of blasphemy, and
blasphemy merited death. But, as we
have seen, the Jewish authorities were
not able to inflict the death penalty.
They had lost the right to do that years
before this time. In order, therefore, to bring about His death, it was
necessary to put Him within the jurisdiction of the Roman power. It was
no use coming to Pilate charging Him
with blasphemy. He would have
laughed them out of the Prætorium,
for the Roman Empire was willing to
put any god into its Parthenon.

This fact accounts for what we see
them doing in the paragraph now
under consideration. There are two
movements. We see Jesus first before
Pilate, and then before Herod. In
other words, we see Him, to use His
own phrase, "delivered up unto the
Gentiles." It may be objected that
Herod was not a Gentile. Herod was
an Idumean. The Herods were all of
Idumean blood. Moreover His sending
to Herod was a secondary thing. It
was a part of the action of the Gentile world. Pilate sent Him to Herod,
and Herod sent Him back to Pilate.
So again we say, that we see Him
"delivered up unto the Gentiles."
When we think of that in the terms
of Pilate, as representing the Roman
Empire, it becomes arresting. What
will the Gentile world, which lived
outside the light of the revelation
which had been given to the Jewish
people, do with Jesus? That became
Pilate's own question presently. Angry
with the high priests, and mad with
the people, he said,

"What then shall I do with Jesus?"

Here, again, Luke omits much of
detail, and in a severely condensed
form gives us the salient facts. Evidently he resolutely omitted certain
things, in order that the great climacteric things might stand out clearly
and sharply. As in the story of the
arraignment before the Sanhedrim in
the early morning, he records the bare
and central facts of their legal challenge, and their consequent religious
challenge, and His answers; so here,
the same method is evident. There are
many details not given. First let us
read the seven verses, in which we see
Him before Pilate.

"And the whole company of them
rose up, and brought Him before Pilate.
And they began to accuse Him, saying,
We found this Man, perverting our nation, and forbidding to give tribute to
Cæsar, and saying that He Himself is
Christ a King. And Pilate asked Him,
saying, Art Thou the King of the Jews?
And He answered him and said, Thou
sayest. And Pilate said unto the chief
priests and the multitudes, I find no
fault in this Man. But they were the
more urgent, saying, He stirreth up the
people, teaching throughout all Judæa,
and beginning from Galilee even unto
this place. But when Pilate heard it,
he asked whether the Man were a Galilean. And when he knew that He was
of Herod's jurisdiction, he sent Him
unto Herod, who himself was also at
Jerusalem in these days."

"The whole company of them." Of
whom? The gathering of the elders,
and the Sanhedrim. The whole company, not "the whole multitude," as
it reads in the King James Version.
The word is *plethos*, that is, the complete number, the whole of those before whom He had been arraigned.
They rose up, and brought Him before
Pilate.

The story of Pilate is an interesting one. It is probable that the world
would never have heard much about
Pilate if it had not been for his connection with Jesus. But having this
notoriety, he has been a personality
full of interest to the student. We
know that he was hated by the Jews.

and that he hated the Jews. Almost immediately upon his arrival, he had committed an act that had incensed them beyond measure. He had brought the Roman ensigns, which bore the image of the Emperor, into the Holy City. To the Jew, this was an unpardonable sacrilegious act. He had to move them; but the people were incensed. He was cold, hard, dispassionate, cruel in his government. During four years he had been procurator, he had already clashed with the Judæans, with the Galileans, and with the Samaritans. That is the man to whom they brought Jesus. They had to do it if they wanted to get Him under Roman power, because he was a *procurator cum potestate*, that is, he possessed civil, military, and criminal jurisdiction, and so there was in him the power of life and death. When he said to Jesus, as one of the evangelists tells us,

" Knowest Thou not that I have power to release Thee, and power to crucify Thee? "

he was telling the literal truth on the human level. Trampling on all their pride, and prejudice, in order to get Jesus into the place of condemnation, they came to Pilate. The whole of them

" rose up, and brought Him before Pilate."

There was unanimity among them, in their hatred of Jesus, and in their determination to bring about His death.

Before Pilate, they preferred their accusation. It was impossible to bring a prisoner before the governor without formulating a clear-cut and definite accusation. They said, " We found." That was an official formula. In the English language, it may mean anything or nothing. There it expressed a judicial act, they were giving Pilate their findings, after His arraignment before the Sanhedrim.

" We found this Man perverting our nation, and forbidding to give tribute to Cæsar, and saying that He Himself is Christ, a King."

In introducing those words, "A King," they intended to interpret the word Christ for Pilate, and they did it in such wise as to be able to formulate the charge into one of treason. It may be that these men had become as materialized as all the rulers of the time seemed to have been; and thought only of Messiah in the terms of Kingship. The Old Testament Scriptures, in their prophetic writings, and in their psalmody, represent Messiah as having two offices. He was to be a King, and a Priest. The Messianic foretelling showed Him as One Whose crown is a mitre, and Whose ephod is purple. The priestly function of Messiahship had largely dropped out of sight among the interpreters of the time; and that may have caused the little word "A King;" but they were afraid to use it commonly, because to claim Kingship would be a treason in the Roman Empire. I think there can be no doubt that was why the phrase was used. They did not say a word to Pilate about His blasphemy. As we have said, Pilate would have paid no attention to that. They charged Him with perverting the nation, a distinct lie, from any standpoint, whether politically, or economically, or socially, or morally. They charged Him with forbidding to give tribute to Cæsar, a second lie, the twisting of something He had said a few hours before,

" Render to Cæsar the things that are Cæsar's, and to God the things that are God's."

They then told a partial truth,

" Saying that He Himself is Christ, a King,"

thus interpreting the claim in the terms of Kingship only. Thus we see these rulers truckling to Rome, lying, and interpreting Messiahship in the terms of Kingship only. What a revelation, of their own spiritual inability to understand their prophetic writings, and of their malice against Him.

Then Luke records Pilate's question;

" And Pilate asked Him, saying, Art Thou the King of the Jews? "

Here, again, much had happened to which Luke does not refer. He brings us to the point where Pilate, having had a private conversation with Jesus, put the direct question to Him, on the basis of the charge,

"Art Thou the King of the Jews?"

I cannot read it without thinking there was something of satire in it on the part of Pilate, and that the satire was for the Jews more than for Jesus. As Jesus stood there before him, He was bruised, battered, and bloody from the brutal treatment He had received in the earlier hours in the house of Annas, before they had brought Him to Caiaphas' palace. I seem to see that proud Roman looking at Him, strangely arrested, strangely perplexed, and then saying to Him,

"Art Thou the King of the Jews?"

Nevertheless, it was the question growing out of the charge? Do you claim Kingship?

Then came the answer. Here, again, we have an archaic form of speech, which does not carry to the English mind all the force of what was said. It really is a clear-cut affirmation of agreement, " Thou sayest." Christ said in effect, Yes, that is what I am. I am King of the Jews.

Here, again, we have Luke's severe brevity. His story reads on,

"And Pilate said unto the chief priests and the multitudes."

But that did not happen immediately. He was taken into the Prætorium, and the priests were left outside, and there was a very remarkable interview between Pilate and this Prisoner. Pilate investigated Him, and that remarkable conversation took place, which John records, in which Jesus said,

" My Kingdom is not of this world."

Luke has not given us the details. Pilate is here reported as asking Him the central question; Jesus is recorded as affirming the accuracy of the thing said; and then Pilate's finding is given,

" I find no fault in this Man."

It is important here that we should recognize that this was not an expression of a pious opinion. It was a legal finding, in the very terminology of the law-court of the time; just as in an English court of justice, the verdict would be, " Not guilty." To recognize this is to see the point at which Pilate's breakdown occurred. According to Roman law there was only one thing to do. Take His bonds off, and set Him free. Why did not Pilate do it?

" But they were the more urgent, saying, He stirreth up the people, teaching throughout all Judæa, and beginning from Galilee even unto this place."

Now Pilate found himself on the horns of a dilemma. Justice demanded that the Prisoner be released. Why the hesitation? Why halt a moment? He had found a verdict, he had uttered it—Not Guilty. The charge is not sustained, said the Roman procurator. I have investigated Him. He is not guilty. Why, then, were not the bonds taken off? Because in a moment there arose the clamour of the priests, their angry passions were stirred, and they declared to Pilate anew, changing their terminology, that Jesus was pestilent to the nation. Again Luke has not given all the particulars. Another evangelist tells us that they said,

" If thou release this Man, thou art not Cæsar's friend."

Now I understand why Pilate halted. He was calculating between policy and justice. It was a clear-cut issue. Justice demanded that the not guilty Man should be set free. Why not set Him free? Pilate was thinking: If I set Him free, these angry priests, whom I hate with all my soul, will start a riot, and they will report me to Rome; and I shall probably lose my position, and God knows how many I may have to slay if a tumult breaks out! What shall I do? Shall I be politic and sacrifice Him to them, to save the situation, for the sake of saving my own position; or shall I do justice even though the heavens fall? That was Pilate's problem. He went wrong where many a man goes wrong, when he sold his conscience for convenience and safety, when he spat in the face of justice, and adopted the way of policy.

But suddenly he thought of a possible way out of his dilemma. " Beginning from Galilee "? Did you say this Man is a Galilean? Then, I will wipe my hands of the whole affair. I will send Him to Herod. Let Herod deal with the case. I have not been talking to Herod lately. We have no love for each other, Herod and I. I may take this as a good opportunity to bridge over the difficulty, a difficulty created possibly when I mingled the blood of the Galileans with their sacrifices.

" Now when Herod saw Jesus, he was exceeding glad; for he was of a long time desirous to see Him, because he had heard concerning Him; and he hoped to see some miracle done by Him. And he questioned Him in many words; but He answered him nothing. And the chief priests and the scribes stood, vehemently accusing Him. And Herod with his soldiers set Him at nought, and mocked Him, and arraying Him in gorgeous apparel sent Him back to Pilate. And Herod and Pilate became friends with each other that very day; for before they were at enmity between themselves."

Here, again, we have strictly legal terminology;

"And when he (Pilate) knew that Jesus was of Herod's jurisdiction, he sent Him unto Herod."

The word there translated " sent " is the technical word, which indicated the remitting of a case from one court to another; and almost invariably in jurisprudence it meant remitting a case to a higher court. Pilate would not have admitted that Herod's court was the higher, but yet in the fact of sending Him, he apparently courteously said: Let Herod settle this; I will remit the case to him. I appeal the case from my court to his.

The story is one of the most tragic in the New Testament in many ways. The first tragic note is that of Herod's reception of Jesus, "He was exceeding glad." Why? He had long wanted to see Him. Why? He had heard about Him, and he hoped He would do some miracle! He expected some thrill for his degenerate, burnt-out life. In this spirit he put all sorts of questions to Jesus, and Christ never answered him. This is the one man in all the New Testament story, to whom Jesus had nothing to say! He had a good deal to say to Pilate. Jesus did everything He could to help Pilate; but He had nothing to say to this man. Go back in Herod's history for a moment. There was a day when he had come close to the Kingdom of God. There was a day when, mark the significance of the pregnant phrase, he "heard John gladly." Then came a day when, giving way to drink and lust, he found himself in difficulty, and John stood up against him, and forbade the incestuous union of the profligate. Even then Herod tried to take care of John. He put him in prison, not with the intention of killing him, but to keep him safe from the anger of Herodias. Then there came the day of drunken debauch when he made a promise to a dancing wanton; and to keep his word, beheaded John! He has gone down, and down, and down! Jesus never saw him, he never saw Jesus till then. Jesus had one day sent a message to him, "Go and tell that fox," and the Greek word is feminine, "Go and tell that vixen." Now, at last, he and Jesus were face to face. The vehement accusers were clamouring that Herod would do something.

Now watch the action of Herod. He refused entirely to treat Jesus as a criminal. He did not investigate the case at all. That is the meaning of this clamouring of the priests. As though they said, You are amusing yourself with Him. You are asking questions. You want to see Him work a miracle, but we want Him condemned. They vehemently accused Him, but he seems to have taken no notice of them. As a matter of fact, the priests were far more afraid of Herod than Pilate. They were afraid Herod would not hand Him over to death. They knew Herod. They knew he had no conscience at all. He did not care about anything. That is why they were so vehement; and he ignored the priests. He did not take any notice of them. Herod was not careful about any charge against Him. He treated Him not as a criminal, but as a buffoon. Mark the degeneracy of the man, who had in the time of John the Baptist's ministry heard him gladly. The hour had come in which he was not capable of looking at a case from a judicial standpoint.

Jesus is seen standing there, arrayed in mockery; bearing the taunts and gibes of the vulgar, debased soldiery, creatures of a coward named Herod. He never said a word. It is very appalling that He had nothing to say to Herod. In another way the silence was beautiful. He had nothing to say in protest against all the indignity that was heaped upon Him. He was as a lamb

" led to the slaughter, and as a sheep that before its shearers is dumb, so He opened not His mouth."

What a travesty of justice was all this! Observe the strange joining together of antagonisms, in opposition to Jesus. Pilate hated the priests. The priests hated Pilate. Pilate and Herod were at enmity with each other. Yet here they were all getting together. The Gentile world, and the Jewish world, and the hybrid world, the Idumean, all joined in hostility to Jesus. The rulers, hating Him, consistent all the way through. Pilate, indifferent at first, but anxious, because of the political situation that was being created, anxious about his own position, and violating justice. Herod, degenerate and amused!

LUKE XXIII. 13-25

HERE we see Jesus, back from Herod, and again arraigned before Pilate. Pilate referred to Him three times over by the same expression, "This Man," "this Man," "this Man." His enemies once used the same expression. Not a word is recorded here, as passing the lips of Jesus. Thus while necessarily and properly our thought is upon Him, by the method of the story, we are more occupied with those who are round Him, and especially with one man, Pilate.

Pilate had gained an advantage as the result of these happenings. What was it? The friendship of Herod. He and Herod had been at enmity, and it was not desirable to have Herod antagonistic to him, any more than it was for Herod to have Pilate antagonistic to him. This was now over. They had made friends. But as I look at him in this scene, I am more impressed with the disadvantage in which he found himself. He was in exactly the same dilemma as when, hoping to find a way of escape, he had remitted the case from his own court to the court of Herod. Herod had not treated

the case seriously at all. He had gladly received Jesus, hoping to see Him work some miracle that should give him a thrill, and when Christ had said nothing to him, he had mocked Him, and joined with his soldiers in heaping insults upon Him, and then sent Him back to Pilate. So that Pilate was exactly where he was.

In this paragraph we have the account of a threefold attempt on the part of Pilate to release Jesus. It is a confused story, for it was an hour of utter confusion. All judicial order had ceased. There was some judicial proceeding when He was first arraigned before Pilate, but here the judge is seen arguing with a mob. The Roman procurator, having all power over human life, on the human level, in that whole area, having the power to release Jesus, as he himself claimed, or to hand Him over to execution, is seen arguing with a mob, and at last the mob won, and Pilate was defeated.

Let us consider these three attempts. The story of the first opens significantly ;—

"Pilate called together the chief priests and the rulers and the people."

That was not so in the earlier proceeding. In that case it was purely a legal assembly. Pilate was now careful to see to it that not the rulers and the priests alone, but the people also were admitted. He called the people with the priests and rulers. He intended to make this effort to release Jesus, in public. He had first dealt with the priests, and dealt with them quite skilfully, until he found he was in their grip. Then he had tried to escape responsibility by sending Jesus to Herod. That having broken down, now he was going to appeal to democracy, attempting to sway the people to the side of Jesus. If he could do that, he might defy the priests. He

"called the chief priests and the rulers and the people together."

He then declared openly, in the presence of those rulers, those priests and leaders, and all the people, his judicial finding, and in doing so, employed the language of the law-courts. He said:

"Ye brought unto me this Man, as One that perverteth the people."

That was the charge they had brought against Him.

"And behold, I, having examined Him before you, found no fault in this Man touching those things whereof ye accuse Him."

He had already declared that on the previous occasion, "I find no fault in this Man." He now repeated it, and it was a strictly judicial sentence, "Not guilty." And he went further, as he said:

"No, nor yet Herod, for he sent Him back unto us."

Thus he declared that neither his court nor Herod's, had found Jesus worthy of death.

Then he made an amazing suggestion;

"I will therefore chastise Him, and release Him."

His judicial decision demanded the release of the Prisoner, but he said that before releasing Him, he would "Chastise Him"! There was Pilate's first declared decision to do that which was unjust. It was an absolutely unjust and unwarranted thing to chastise one declared innocent of the charges preferred against him. He was attempting to settle the matter by compromise. That very remarkable English statesman, John Morley, has an essay in one of his volumes on Compromise. In it he says that,

"under certain circumstances compromise is the most immoral word in the English language."

He was quite right. Compromise may be permitted if nothing of principle is involved; but the moment a man begins to compromise in the matter of principle, he is already damned. Pilate was saying in effect: This Man is guiltless. I am not going to hand Him over to crucifixion. I intend to release Him. Perhaps these men, whom I very much hate, will be satisfied if He suffers. I will chastise Him and release Him. Thus Pilate made an unjust proposal in the realm of compromise.

Now listen to their answer. Here, again, Luke gives us a condensed narrative.

"But they cried out all together."

Mark the unanimity of it. The people under the influence of chief priests and rulers,

"cried out all together, saying, Away with this Man, and release unto us Barabbas."

The Revised Version here omits a verse found in the King James Version, verse seventeen, which reads:

"For of necessity he must release one man unto them at the Feast."

That is found in some of the old manuscripts. Possibly our scholars are correct in believing that it was a glossary in Luke. Nevertheless, it has its bearing on the story, and perhaps that is why some copyist introduced it.

From other evangelists we know that Pilate had offered them their choice between Jesus and Barabbas. In reading that story in the other Gospels, I think we sometimes fail to see what happened. The general opinion seems to be that Pilate followed his usual course when he offered them a choice between Barabbas and Jesus. As a matter of fact, he did nothing of the kind. He departed from his usual course. We are told that it was Pilate's habit, at the feast to release a prisoner, and one of the evangelists adds "whom they would." On this occasion he did not allow them freedom of choice, but shut them up to a sharp alternative between two. He said, in effect: Now, it is usual and customary that any one of your prisoners, whom you choose, should be released to you at the Feast; but this year I will give you a choice between two. You can have Barabbas, or you can have Jesus. I am certain that he felt there could be no hesitation, because Barabbas, as we are told, had been arrested for "a certain insurrection—and for murder." No charge of murder had been preferred against Jesus. They had charged Him with inciting to insurrection, but not to violence.

Here let us pause, and carefully consider the story of Barabbas. He was arrested for insurrection and murder. That is to say, somebody had been killed as the result of his insurrection. He had raised an insurrection, right there in Jerusalem, which had resulted in loss of life. Thus he had been arrested, as guilty of insurrection, and of murder. I think we have made a mistake in talking about Barabbas as a common robber. There is little doubt that he was a political leader, guilty of insurrection. His name is suggestive; Bar Abbas, son of the father. That is a title, rather than a name. We may not know his name. Personally, I think we do. There are one or two of the old manuscripts, which Origen accepted as authentic, and they give his name as Jesus Barabbas, the very name and title of our Lord. That perhaps cannot be proven, but personally I have no doubt

at all that it was so, and that Barabbas was a false Messiah. During a generation in the history of the Jewish people, many false messiahs had arisen. This man had made the Messianic claim, and had taken the title Barabbas. Whether his first name was Jesus I am not prepared to be dogmatic, but the name by which we do know him is really a title suggesting Messiahship. He, in Jerusalem, had provoked a rising, an insurrection, with the intention of dethroning the Roman power, and setting up his own. That is Barabbas. He was not a common bandit. The very form in which Pilate asked his central question suggests that his first name was Jesus. He said:

"What then shall I do unto Jesus Who is called Christ?"

What made him say, "Who is called Christ"? My own conviction is that he was putting Him into contrast with the other Jesus who was called Barabbas. You are choosing Jesus called Barabbas, what shall I do with Jesus that is called the Christ?

To me, this is the key to the situation. If this were so, that he was a false Messiah, their choice was even more significant. Those rulers did not believe in his claim; but if they were to choose between a man who raised an insurrection, and imbued his hands with blood, and the Man against Whom no charge of violence could be made, they would rather have Barabbas than Jesus. At the back of their choice I see their own false understanding of the Messianic claim and mission and purpose of God Almighty. I see their materialized thinking about the Kingdom, the one thing that Jesus had swept away in all His teaching, and in a private interview with Pilate had said:

"My Kingdom is not of this world; if My Kingdom were of this world, then would My servants fight."

Barabbas had intended to set up a kingdom of the world, and had fought, and blood had been shed. Jesus had said, No, that is not the way of the Kingdom. Thus they made choice between two ideas of the Kingdom. They brought Jesus to Pilate on the charge that He was raising insurrection; and they chose, instead of Him, a man who was in prison because he had done that very thing, and had led to blood shedding. The inconsistency of it all is appalling!

Pilate, having heard their choice, made his second attempt to release Jesus. He had made his first by suggesting that he would chastise and release. Now we read,

"And Pilate spake unto them again, desiring to release Jesus; but they shouted, saying, Crucify, crucify Him."

That is very brief, and it was brief in fact. It was dramatic. " Pilate spake unto them again," and the Greek verb means that he exclaimed. Their answer was as sudden, and as brief. They " cried," said the Old Version; " shouted," says the New. Quite literally, " they *screamed,* Crucify, Crucify ! " It was short, and sharp, that second attempt. Pilate exclaimed, and they drowned him with their screaming, " Crucify, Crucify ! "

But he had not done. He made a third attempt, evidently waiting a moment until the clamouring and screaming of the crowd had subsided. Then he appealed once more to them. He said,

"Why, what evil hath this Man done? I have found no cause of death in Him."

Then he repeated his iniquitous and unjust proposal,

" I will therefore chastise Him and release Him."

You shall have your way so far. I will make Him suffer, I will chastise Him, though He is guiltless; and then I will let Him go, I will release Him. Then, what followed?

" But they were urgent with loud voices, asking that He might be crucified."

One can hear it across the centuries, the clamour of men who had lost their reason because of their hatred, and the wildness of their passion. They clamoured for His blood, and so Pilate finally decided to give Jesus of Nazareth to the Cross as the result of the howling of a half-mad mob, and we have his sentence. I wonder is there anything more tragic in history.

"And their voices prevailed."

Pilate had all day been listening to two voices; perhaps others, but two at least. One was the voice of his wife, who had sent him a message; and the other, the more insistent, was the voice of his conscience, which all day had been saying, Do the right, man, though the heavens fall, and though hell is moved, though Rome dismiss you, do the right. Stand square with your own conscience. But

" Their voices prevailed. And Pilate gave sentence that what they ask should be done. And he released him that for insurrection and murder had been cast into prison, whom they asked for; but Jesus he delivered up to their will."

As I said at the beginning, the central figure here is Pilate. We see him again in the story of Jesus once. When the deed was done, they came back to him, and asked for a guard for His tomb, there was mockery in his answer,

" Ye have a guard; go, make it as sure as ye can."

From extra Biblical history we know that what he grasped that day, when he sacrificed his conscience, he lost very soon. He was recalled, and disgraced. Then suddenly the history stops. One often wonders what happened to him afterwards. There is much legendary lore concerning him, which is of little value.

Yet the question is legitimate. No dogmatic answer can be given, but an alternative may be considered. Anatole France, in his book *Mother of Pearl,* has a story around Pilate. I do not know anything in literature in some ways more terrible than Anatole France's suggestion. It is called " The

Procurator of Judæa." France imagines him in the days after his dismissal, having secured enough wealth to be quite independent, going down to his own lands in Sicily, and living there in luxury, a dilletante. The story tells of his meeting there with an old friend of former days, and they talk together about the Jews, and the old days in Judæa, and at last his friend says to him:

" ' There was a young Galilean thamaturgist. His name was Jesus; he came from Nazareth, and he was crucified for some crime, I don't quite know what. Pontius, do you remember anything about the man?'

" Pontius Pilate contracted his brows, and his hand rose to his forehead in the attitude of one who probes the deeps of memory. Then after a silence of some seconds—' Jesus?' he murmured, ' Jesus—of Nazareth?' I cannot call him to mind.' "

There Anatole France's story ends. I think he wrote everything to lead to that point, the revelation of the possibility of a man becoming so deadened as really to have forgotten his hand in that affair. It is a tragic suggestion, and quite possible.

Here is another suggestion. The Coptic Church,—and nobody can be dogmatic in saying they were wrong, has a legend or a tradition, that Pilate became a Christian, under the influence of his wife, and that he was received into the Church. His wife was canonized by the Coptic Church, and the day of St. Claudia Procula, the wife of Pilate, in their calendar, is October 27th.

There is yet another story of his coming back to Rome, and being found in the catacombs, attending the meetings of the Christians, yielding himself to the Nazarene, confessing his sin.

I don't know. You do not know. But I do know that Anatole France's suggestion is possible. I have seen men who have lost all moral sense, and all conscience, and have forgotten Jesus of Nazareth, and who say in effect: "I don't seem to remember Him." It is an awful possibility. And I know another thing, that if there ever came a moment when, under the influence of his wife, or any other, Pilate somewhere knelt down and said, " O Nazarene, I sinned, I sinned, have mercy upon me," then I shall meet him in heaven, for Jesus died for Pontius Pilate, as well as for all other men.

We must leave it there, but do not let us miss the warning of the story. It is that of a man wanting to do right, living through a day tragic with the conflict within his own soul between conscience and convenience, and at last letting the voices of a mad mob prevail, and committing the sin against justice, and against God.

LUKE XXIII. 26-38

SO Luke tells the story of the crucifixion. In common with the other evangelists, he states the central fact with reverent reticence. It is dismissed in the simplest sentence that could be written; " There they crucified Him." Matthew, Mark, and John, each recorded the fact of the crucifixion in equally brief and reticent language. Matthew puts it thus: " When they had crucified Him." He thus only refers to it, as a fact accomplished. Mark puts the thing into two words, in our language three; " They crucified Him." John adopted exactly the same method, " They crucified Him."

I emphasize that because I am more and more convinced of the danger of allowing the physical fact to deflect our thought from the spiritual. I have often wished that no one had ever painted a picture of the crucifixion. I am not denying the tragedy of the physical, but I often feel that in connection with our children, we are in danger if we talk too much with them of the nails and the thorns and the spear. These were merely the incidentals, all of them necessary, I grant you, to work out into visibility before these poor human eyes of ours, something of the unfathomable sorrows of God in Christ in the Cross. Yet there is always a danger lest for very pity of heart, we become more occupied with the physical suffering, than with the spiritual agony.

In this paragraph, there are two movements; first the procession to the Cross; and then the crucifying, and the things that happened immediately in connection with that crucifying.

First, then, as to the procession to the Cross. Let us bear in mind the facts about our Lord as He was then on the physical level. Since He sat with His disciples at the Paschal Feast, no food or drink had passed His lips. He had been to Gethsemane, with its unfathomable mystery of spiritual anguish and mental agony and bodily strain, where the spiritual anguish was such that it had its sacramental symbol in that He sweat as it were great drops of blood. He had been to the house of Annas and had endured the brutal buffetting before His trial. He had been carried from there to the palace of Caiaphas, to that first meeting of the Sanhedrim. They had taken Him from there to the Prætorium, and He had appeared before Pilate. He had been carried thence to the palace of Herod, and there had been mocked. He had been brought back again to the Prætorium. indignity upon indignity had been heaped upon His head. That is how we see Him, on His way to the Cross.

John tells us in his story that He went out, bearing the Cross for Himself. Luke tells us about Simon of Cyrene. There is no contradiction. From the Prætorium to the gates of the city, Jesus carried His own Cross; and art has certainly represented the truth about this, when it has portrayed Him as sinking under its burden, after the strain of those terrific and tremendous hours. It was when they came to the gates of the city that they found this man, Simon of Cyrene. I am not going to enter into the discussion as to who the man was. There are two possibilities. Quite possibly he was a Jew; far more probably a negro.

There is no proof either way. There are those who hold one view, and others the other. He was a native of Cyrene, and he did not volunteer to carry the Cross of Jesus. "They laid hold" on him, says Luke. Matthew and Mark say they "compelled him," and the Greek word so translated is a military word, which means they impressed him. Whether it was out of some pang of pity in the heart of the soldiers, or whether it was that they were afraid lest He would die before they could wreak their brutality on Him on the Cross, I do not know; but they did the unusual thing of impressing this man, and making him carry the Cross of Jesus.

When Mark tells this story of Simon, he says that he was the father of Rufus and Alexander, evidently disciples of Jesus. Although Simon did not offer to carry that Cross, although they laid hold of him, and impressed him into the service, I think that as the result of carrying it, he became a follower of Jesus. It is at least an interesting fact that Mark names his two boys as having become disciples.

Then Luke tells us that:

"There followed Him a great multitude of the people."

Among them there were,

"Women who bewailed and lamented Him."

The wailing and lamenting are connected with the women, not with the crowd. These women were not Galileans. When Jesus turned to them, His method of address showed that they belonged to Judæa, and belonged to the city. He called them "Daughters of Jerusalem." These women were wailing and lamenting out of pure pity for Him. There are wells of sympathy in the heart of womanhood that always break out in the presence of suffering. As they saw Him, that Man of sorrows, with all the marks of brutality on Him, with face more marred than that of any other man, they broke out into wailing and lamentation.

Then Jesus turned, and uttered the

only words recorded as falling from His lips between His condemnation and the hours when He hung upon His Cross. Therefore they are significant words. What did He say?

"Daughters of Jerusalem, weep not for Me, but weep for yourselves, and for your children."

Then He repeated what He had already announced in the Temple courts and to His own disciples, the prediction of the doom that would fall upon the nation, and which did fall upon it within a generation after His crucifixion. He said,

"For behold, the days are coming, in which they shall say, Blessed are the barren, and the wombs that never bare, and the breasts that never gave suck."

Jesus declared that days were coming in which they would curse their motherhood, and declare it to be a blessed thing to have no children; days in which they would

"begin to say to the mountains, Fall on us; and to the hills, Cover us. For if they have done these things"—that is, the things of His suffering—"if they do these things in the green tree"—where life still existed, because the Kingdom of God had been brought so near—"what shall be done in the dry?"

That is, what would they do when the tree became dry, and handed over to the nemesis of iniquity?

They were strangely solemn words. In them there was pity, pity for those who were to suffer; and yet a reaffirmation of the sentence of doom upon the nation that had rejected Him. Ponder those words with care;

"Weep not for Me, but weep for yourselves."

Why did those women wail and lament? Because they saw His weakness, and that was all they saw. What do you and I see as we watch Him tread the *via dolorosa?* Weakness? If that is all we see, we are blind. Not weakness only, but power is manifest. We see Him going in a strength

that is not human, a strength that humanity cannot understand, a strength that defies the interpretations of philosophy and theology; it is the strength of the Divine compassion. I think Paul had this in his mind when, one day, he wrote that strange thing, that the weakness of God is stronger than man.

Pity for His weakness may result in disloyalty to Him. Pity for His weakness may be the result of blindness to His power. Is that not the story all the way through? Is not that the truth about His enemies, and rulers, and all those in authority? Is not that the truth about the people generally? They saw nothing of power. They saw only His weakness. On the way He turned to the lamenting and bewailing women, and He said, Do not weep for Me. But that is what we are all inclined to do. God help us, how can we help it? Yet He said, Don't weep for Me, and in that very word there was the evidence of His sense that He was proceeding in a might and a majesty which was demonstrated in the fact that He consented to death. On the human level, He need not have died at all. He might have escaped when His disciples in Peræa and elsewhere tried to persuade Him from going back to Judæa. What carried Him back? Might, power, strength, the might of redeeming love. So He said, Do not weep for Me.

In the twelfth chapter of the letter to the Hebrews I read:

"Consider Him that hath endured such gainsaying of sinners against Himself."

When, in 1881, the English Revision was published, I was startled to read the passage thus:

"Consider Him that hath endured such gainsaying of sinners against *themselves.*"

The American revisers restored the old rendering, but put this new one in the margin as an alternative reading. The question is, of course, one of manuscripts. Some of the manuscripts read "Himself," and some "themselves." No man can decide on the basis of manuscripts which word the writer employed. So far as I am concerned, I am quite convinced that it ought to be rendered as the English revisers have it. He endured the contradiction of sinners. Yes, but the fact that it was against Himself was not the deepest element in His pain. It was rather that their contradiction of Him reacted upon them for their destruction. That is what He said to these women,

"Weep not for Me, but for yourselves."

The very principle of the Cross flames out in these words of Jesus on the way to His Cross. "Daughters of Jerusalem," tender and beautiful word of address, Do not weep for Me, weep for yourselves and for your children. If we stand by the Cross, and pity His physical suffering, we have not really grasped the deepest truth concerning His sorrow. Let our sorrow reach the realm of His deepest sorrow. If it do, we shall find that when He was, on the human level, an object of human pity because of weakness, He was operating in the eternal power of redeeming love. In the last analysis, Jesus is never an object of pity on the part of sinful, condemned humanity. He is the Object of wonder and of true worship, as He is seen moving in regal splendour towards His Cross. His two closest comrades as He trod that sorrowful and Sovereign way, were two malefactors. He was "numbered with the transgressors."

And so we come to the crucifixion.

"And when they came unto the place that is called The skull, there they crucified Him."

"The place that is called The skull;" I do not know whether we have gained much by translating there. The King James Version reads, "which is called Calvary." The Greek word is *Kranion*, of which *Calvaria* is the Latin equivalent, and *Golgotha* the Hebrew. Whether the Greek word *Kranion*, or the Latin *Calvaria*, or the Hebrew *Golgotha*, each means the place of a skull. The word Calvary has taken a very definite place in the language of the Church. It only occurs once in the Bible, and now it has gone in the Revised. The actual place so named is not positively known. I personally believe that the traditional hill is not the place at all, and that General Gordon found the true site. It was evidently at the time the place of execution, outside the city wall, a hillock, in the shape of a skull. There "they crucified Him."

Now listen to the voices. The first that we hear is the voice of Jesus,

"Father, forgive them; for they know not what they do."

That is humanity at its greatest. Men have their conceptions of human nature, and of what things make for greatness therein. These conceptions are very many and very varied. I submit that humanity has never been seen greater than in the Man Jesus, when He said,

"Father, forgive them; for they know not what they do."

In the soul of Jesus there was no resentment, no anger, no lurking desire for punishment upon the men who were maltreating Him. Men have spoken in admiration of the mailed fist. When I hear Jesus thus pray I know that the only place for the mailed fist is in hell.

If that is humanity at its greatest, it is also an unveiling of the deepest fact in God.

"God willeth not the death of a sinner, but rather that all should turn to Him, and repent."

What does the Cross mean?

"Father, forgive them; for they know not what they do."

As I read that story I ask myself this question, Was that prayer answered? There can be but one answer, they were forgiven unquestionably. That does not mean necessarily that the forgiven men entered into right relationship with God, but it does mean that there was forgiveness for every man, in answer to that cry of Jesus Christ. Legendary lore has been busy with this matter. We cannot depend upon legendary lore, except that we know that at the back of every legend there is some element of truth struggling to express itself; often failing to do it by over-emphasis and grotesque emphases. I do not know, I have no evidence; but nothing would surprise me less when I reach the Land beyond, than to meet the men who drove the nails into the hands of Jesus, those who brought about His death. At any rate, the prayer was heard. Forgiveness was provided. I cannot listen to that first cry coming out of the perfected humanity of Jesus, and therefore revealing the deepest will and purpose and passion of God, without being perfectly certain that it was heard, that it was answered, and that there was forgiveness for all men.

Now let me read on, and we shall hear other voices;

"And the rulers also scoffed at Him, saying, He saved others; let Him save Himself, if this is the Christ of God, His Chosen."

What I hear in the scoffing mockery of these rulers is their test of Messiahship. What was their test? What did they say? If He is really the Messiah, if He is really the Chosen of God, let Him save Himself. It did not enter into their minds for a moment that the meaning of Messiahship was not the saving of Himself, but the saving of others. Their whole conception of Messiahship had become blunted, materialized, blasted; and when they saw Him on the Cross they said: That ends it, He is no Messiah, or He would never be there; He would save Himself. But still He hung there, and so right before their eyes was the supreme evidence of Messiahship. The thing they said was true. He saved others, Himself He could not save. That is Messiahship. He could not save Himself. Why not? Because He would save others. He can save others. Why? Because He would not save Himself.

Again;

"And the soldiers also mocked Him."

They did not say anything about Messiahship. They did not know anything about Messiahship. They did not care anything about Christ as the Chosen of God. That is not the point with the soldiers. That is not the concern of empire. They said,

"If Thou art the King of the Jews, save Thyself."

Here we see their test of Kingship. Ability to take care of Himself. They did not see that the true function of the king was to take care of his kingdom and all those who were members of it. How could they? They were soldiers of Rome. What did they know of an emperor who had no power to take care of Himself. If a Roman Cæsar failed to take care of himself they had no more use for him as Imperator. The qualification for a king was his ability to break men, and rule over them, and subdue them. So the soldiers mocked Him, and said: If You are the King of the Jews, save Yourself.

Thus, whether it is the voice of the religious rulers, or the voice of Empire represented in the soldiers, we see human life hell-inspired, with its one motto, "Look after yourself," and mastered by that conception of greatness, whether for Messiahship or Kingship. And yet, by the suffering, dying Saviour, Messiahship is demonstrated, in the fact that He will not save Himself, but that He will save others; and Kingship is assured for ever, by that selfsame fact of determination still to empty and humble Himself, that He may exalt and fill humanity.

And the last thing is the superscription.

"There was also a superscription over Him, THIS IS THE KING OF THE JEWS."

Observe the truth of it, and the limitation of it. He was the King of the Jews. He told Pilate that He was. When Pilate put that question to Him, He said, "Thou sayest." He was the glory and the crown of God's purpose in Israel. Through all the process of their history, at last, here is the One Who fulfilled the Divine purpose, and Whose right it is to reign, King of the Jews in very deed.

And yet how limited the superscription, and how it fails. That is chapter twenty-three. Go back to chapter one. Among other things there recorded is the announcement which the angel made to the Virgin Mother concerning the coming of Jesus;

"Thou shalt call His name JESUS. He shall be great, and shall be called the Son of the Most High; and the Lord God shall give unto Him the throne of His father David; and He shall reign over the house of Jacob for ever."

All that was said, but more;

"And of His Kingdom there shall be no end."

No end, *telos*, that is, no limit. It describes the uncircumscribed Kingdom of Jesus. King of the Jews. Yes, verily, and more, God's King, God's Anointed and Appointed King over all; and so that Cross is seen as the throne of imperial and eternal Empire!

LUKE XXIII. 39-56

WE now come to the final things which Luke has recorded concerning the Cross itself, and to the burial of the dead body of Jesus. There are three things to consider; the story of the malefactor; the final things on the Cross; and the burial.

First, then, Luke's story of the malefactor. As we have seen all through, and especially in these final movements, Luke's method is that of almost severe condensation. There are many things he does not tell us. On the other hand, there are things he does tell us, which apart from his narrative, we should never have known. It is well always to bear in mind Luke's method as he states it in his preface, where he says that, having received from eye-witnesses and ministers of the Word, the facts, he "traced the course of all things accurately from above," or "from the beginning;" and having done so, he set them "in order." Now, when he investigated this story, he discovered that one of the malefactors crucified with Jesus turned to Him in repentance and faith. Matthew, Mark and John tell us of the two crucified with Him. Only Luke tells us of the turning to Jesus of one of them. Matthew and Mark, however, tell us something Luke does not, namely, that at first both those men joined in the reproaches heaped upon the head of Jesus by rulers and soldiers.

There are senses in which it seems to me the story of the faith of the dying malefactor is the most remarkable in all the ministry of Jesus Christ. When we carefully consider what he said, first for Jesus, to the man on the cross on the other side, and then to Jesus, out of his own great sense of the necessity for release, I do not know any manifestation of faith quite so wonderful.

First, consider what sort of men those two were, who were crucified with Jesus. Matthew and Mark describe them by a word which today might be rendered brigands, or bandits. Luke uses another word, which means criminals, of the criminal class.

Now, with Luke, we fasten our attention upon one of them, not forgetting what Matthew and Mark tell us, that at first they both reproached Jesus. So far as we know, the only contact this man ever had with Jesus was the contact made there at the Cross. Of course, that cannot be positively affirmed. He may have seen Him. He may have come down from some mountain fastness and heard His teaching. We have no means of knowing, but so far as the narrative is concerned, it would appear that his only contact with Jesus was that made with Him at the Cross.

What, then, had he seen and heard? He had first seen the amazing sight of a Man submitting Himself to the brutality of crucifixion without any protest, without any whimper;

"He was led as a lamb to the slaughter, and as a sheep that before its shearers is dumb, so He opened not His mouth."

Then he had heard Jesus pray,

"Father, forgive them; for they know not what they do."

He had also heard the voices of the rulers, laughing at His Messianic claims, and the voices of the soldiers mocking at His Kingship.

Then this remarkable thing happened. Suddenly, in the midst of the gloom, in the midst of the tragedy, in the midst of the ribald mockery of these priests and soldiers, a voice was heard speaking on one of the crosses. One of the malefactors was speaking across the body of Jesus to the other malefactor, and reproving him. Now mark carefully the terms in which he did this. He said,

"Dost thou not even fear God, seeing thou art in the same condemnation? And we indeed justly; for we receive the due reward of our deeds; but this Man hath done nothing amiss."

Those words reveal the fact that an amazing revolution had taken place in the soul of this man. Luke describes him as a malefactor, that is, a criminal, a lawless man. That means a man who had put God out of count, and one who had no respect for his fellowmen, save to exploit them in his own interest, and if necessary to kill them. Yet now we hear him, recognizing God, "Dost thou not even fear God;" and recognizing the rights of his fellowmen; and owning that his punishment is just. That is repentance.

Then we hear him speaking to Jesus;

"Jesus, remember me when Thou comest in Thy Kingdom."

This is an amazing thing. Jesus was nailed to His Cross; He was dying. The dying malefactor was himself in

extremis, and he knew that Jesus was. But, he had heard Jesus talk to One out and beyond, and call Him Father, and he had heard Him pray, that the men who were wronging Him might be forgiven. He now made his appeal to Jesus, convinced that He was coming into His Kingdom, into a spiritual Kingdom of power and authority. Thus, in extremis, when Roman power had done all it could do with Him, had impaled Him upon this bitter tree, when there was no other earthly tribunal to which he could appeal, he had suddenly discovered that there was another Throne, higher than the throne of the Cæsars, another realm where there was a Father, Who could extend mercy. He saw in Jesus the One Who had the right of appeal to that Throne, to that Father, and he flung himself out into that wider area, into that higher reach of being,

"Jesus, remember me, when Thou comest in Thy Kingdom."

That was faith.

The answer of the Lord was the reply of Authority to that appeal;

"Today shalt thou be with Me in Paradise;"

Paradise, the region of Sheol or of Hades, where are the spirits of the just made perfect.

Has it ever occurred to you what that meant for Jesus? Reverently attempt to get back into the mind and heart of Jesus. Forsaken of His disciples, the butt of brutal mockery on the part of the rulers of His people, spit upon, cast out, all the howling mob round about Him, and suddenly this blaze of glory, this flame of light, one man recognizing His redeeming Kingship, and flinging himself out upon His mercy. Right there and then in measure, He saw of the travail of His soul, and was satisfied. As He swung the gates of the Kingdom of heaven open to the dying malefactor, He entered into the joy that was set before Him, for which even then He was enduring the Cross.

Miriam LeFevre Crouse has written an arresting poem on this incident,

" Three men shared death upon a hill,
 But only one man died ;
The other two—
A thief and God Himself—
Made rendezvous.

" Three crosses still
 Are borne up Calvary's Hill,
Where Sin still lifts them high ;
Upon the one, sag broken men
Who, cursing, die ;
Another holds the praying thief,
Or those who, penitent as he,
Still find the Christ
Beside them on the tree."

How beautifully all is gathered up in that couplet,

"A thief and God Himself—
Made rendezvous."

Following on, we read :

"And it ٬as now about the sixth hour, and a darkness came over the whole land until the ninth hour."

Three hours of darkness, and no record of what happened in those three hours. Three hours of silence, as well as three hours of darkness. As the three hours were ending, " at the ninth hour," says Matthew, Jesus spoke ;

" My God, My God, why hast Thou forsaken Me ? "

That is all we know about those three hours. That which transpired in those three hours, by the rising and the setting of the sun that marks time for this little world of ours, was so tremendous that it cannot be described, it cannot be told.

" None of the ransomed ever knew,
 How deep were the waters crossed,
Nor how dark was the night that the Lord passed through,
Ere He found His sheep that was lost."

And yet in the stream of human history, from its beginning to its close, hours, days, weeks, months, years, decades, centuries, millenniums,—from heaven's standpoint, the most tremendous period in all the running millenniums were those three hours of darkness and of silence.

" Well might the sun in darkness hide,
 And shut his glories in,
When Christ the mighty Maker died
For man, the creature's sin."

Luke now says,

"And Jesus, crying with a loud voice."

What did He say when He cried with a loud voice ? Luke does not record what He said—he simply tells you it was with a loud voice, but from other evangelists we know that He said, " It is finished." Having said it, He then said,

" Father, into Thy hands I commend My Spirit."

Then, as Matthew and Mark make clear, it was when He bowed His head, that the veil of the Temple was rent in twain from the top to the bottom. All this is a story to think about, and to think about until thought is drowned, and the heart is touched, and the will subdued. Those three hours, so appalling, so wonderful, the only light on which is the cry of desolation—

" My God—My God—why hast Thou forsaken Me ? "

Then the loud voice, mark it well, not the weak trailing voice of a defeated One, but the strong voice of a Victor. " It is finished." Then the quiet, calm, confident voice,

" Father, into Thy hands I commend My Spirit."

Go back to the first recorded words of Jesus ;

" I must be in the things of My Father."

Now listen,

" It is finished, Father, into Thy hands I commend My Spirit."

Whatever it was, was done, and it was done in the darkness, and the silence of those three hours.

Then Luke records some of the effects produced immediately. The centurion said,

"Certainly this was a righteous Man."

The dying malefactor had said three hours before,

"This Man hath done nothing amiss."

Then follows a statement peculiar to Luke.

"The multitude that came together to this sight, when they beheld the things that were done, returned smiting their breasts."

That was not the effect usually produced upon the crowd by a public crucifixion. They had seen strange things that day. They had heard strange voices speak. The terror of the darkness had certainly impressed them. They scattered, smiting on their breasts, with the sense of tragedy; may we not hope in the case of many of them, the sense of sin. As I read it, it would suggest a preparation for the day of Pentecost.

Luke tells us also that His kinsfolk were watching from afar. I have no doubt James and Jude were there, His two brothers after the flesh, and I believe that this was the hour when they were constrained to yield to His mastery. I do not know that. At any rate, it is an arresting fact that they were in the upper room with the disciples, when they were waiting for the coming of the Spirit, and they were there with the disciples in the Temple when the Spirit came.

The narrative ends on a note of exquisite beauty, the account of the burial of Jesus. No hand but the hand of love ever touched the dead body of Jesus. They were lovers who took Him down from the Cross. They were lovers who provided the grave, and carried Him there. Here appears Joseph of Arimathæa. Luke is careful to describe him; "a councillor," that is, a member of the Sanhedrim; "a good and righteous man;" "he had not consented to their counsel and deed"—that is, he did not vote for the death of Jesus; "looking for the Kingdom of God." John tells us that he was "a disciple . . . but secretly

for fear of the Jews." It is an interesting fact that on that day, when He was dead, those who cared for His final burial were secret disciples, Joseph of Arimathæa, and Nicodemus. In the hour of crisis, it is often some loud-voiced Peter who says, Though all forget Thee, yet will not I, who fails, while the secret disciples suddenly gain courage. Joseph's action was that of his love, even in the hour of keen disappointment. That was the feeling of all the disciples. Love is stronger than death, and they were loving hands.

The same thing is seen in the women.

"The women, who had come with Him out of Galilee, followed after, and beheld the tomb, and how His body was laid."

How they loved Him, those disappointed women.

There is where we now leave Him, the dead Christ. Think of it. If that is all, you and I are of all men most pitiable! William Newman wrote about that grave,

"'Twas night! Still night!
A solemn silence hung upon the scene;
The keen, bright stars shone with unclouded light,
Calm and serene.
Hushed was the Tomb!
The heavy stone before its entrance lay;
No light broke in upon its silent gloom
No starry ray.
The moonlight beamed;
It hung upon that garden soft and clear,
Around the watchful guard its radiance gleamed
From helm to spear.
The Tomb was sealed!
The watch patrolled before its entrance lone;
The bright night every passing step revealed;
None neared the stone!"

The dead Christ!

But He was not dead. He was not dead, even then. He had descended into Hades. He had gone into the world of spirits. What for? All I know is that in that world of departed spirits He proclaimed His victory. I know no more than that, except that

He welcomed the malefactor, and led him into Paradise,

"Today shalt thou be with Me in Paradise."

LUKE XXIV. 1-32

OUR last study left the dead body of the Christ in the rock-hewn tomb. Now we come to chapter twenty-four, which opens with a very significant word; "But!" When I was a boy they taught me that BUT was a disjunctive conjunction. That is very correct. It is disjunctive, but it is also conjunctive. Whenever we find a But, we know that the thing we are about to read is linked to something already read, and yet we know that we are now going off into an entirely different realm. Our chapter opens with a "But," a glorious disjunctive conjunction, linking the things already recorded, to those about to be recorded, but suggesting a change.

As we have said, we left the body of our Lord in Joseph's tomb. The women had taken their last look. The story resumes with these women;

"But on the first day of the week, at early dawn, they came unto the tomb, bringing the spices which they had prepared. And they found the stone rolled away from the tomb. And they entered in, and found not the body of the Lord Jesus."

Here, again, Luke gives a very condensed account of the first day of resurrection; and having done that, omitting all intervening days, he tells of the ascension.

From the first day, he selects incidents that took place in the early morning, in the afternoon, and in the evening. In this study we consider his record of the things which happened in the morning, verses one to twelve; and the things which happened in the afternoon, verses thirteen to thirty-two.

The story of the morning begins with the women, and ends with Peter. In the first seven verses, the women and the angels; in verses eight to

eleven, the women and the disciples; and, in one verse, twelve, Peter.

First, then, the women and the angels, verses one to seven.

"But on the first day of the week, at early dawn, they came unto the tomb, bringing the spices which they had prepared. And they found the stone rolled away from the tomb. And they entered in, and found not the body of the Lord Jesus. And it came to pass, while they were perplexed thereabout, behold, two men stood by them in dazzling apparel; and as they were affrighted and bowed down their faces to the earth, they said unto them, Why seek ye the living among the dead? He is not here, but is risen; remember how He spake unto you when He was yet in Galilee, saying that the Son of man must be delivered up into the hands of sinful men, and be crucified, and the third day rise again."

We see the women engaged in a great ministry of love, but a ministry all filled with sorrow and hopelessness. Very beautiful it is to see them coming, bringing their spices. They brought them to show their love for a dead Master. They thought of Him as dead. They loved Him with a great love. Love is stronger than death. Their love for Him had not ceased. Their faith in Him had not failed. But the things they had hoped for had not been realized. He was mastered, beaten, put to death, but still they loved Him, and they came to find a dead body, and honour it.

And then they found the angels there. Luke describes them as men.

"Two men stood by them in dazzling apparel."

Let us assume that they were angels. How interested the angels had been in that span of a generation in the process of earthly history, when the Son of God had ceased to appear to them

275

in the form with which they had been familiar from the day of their own creation. When He came to earth He did not empty Himself of Deity, but of a form of manifestation. He emptied Himself of the form of Sovereignty, and took that of a Servant. While on earth, heaven could only see Him as they watched Him on earth. And there is no doubt that they did watch Him. Angels desired to look into these things. An angel announced His coming; and when He arrived, an angel choir sang about it. In the course of His ministry they waited on Him in the wilderness, and in Gethsemane. Now they have come from the heavenly places, and they have something to say to these women. Their first comment was one of rebuke, very tender, very beautiful, but still rebuke.

"Why seek ye the living among the dead?"

But they thought He was dead. Yes, and that angel rebuke showed that they ought to have known that He would rise;

"He is not here, but is risen; remember how He spake unto you when He was yet in Galilee, saying that the Son of man must be delivered up into the hands of sinful men, and be crucified, and the third day rise again."

Does that not take us back to what Matthew and Mark tell us, He

"began to show unto His disciples, that He must go to Jerusalem, and suffer many things of the elders and chief priests and scribes, and be killed, and the third day be raised up."

And He had told them that same thing repeatedly, never once referring to His Cross without declaring that He would rise again.

Now heaven was talking to earth. Angels who had kept their first estate, clothed in dazzling glory, talked to these women, and they said, Why are you seeking the living among the dead? Quite evidently heaven was familiar with what He had been saying to the disciples, for the angel repeated it almost exactly. Don't you

remember when in Galilee He told you He must be delivered up into the hands of sinful men, and be crucified, and the third day rise again? That is the first movement in the early morning. Women, with loving hearts seeking the dead body to honour it, and heaven talking to them very gently, but with rebuke.

What followed immediately?

"And they remembered His words."

Suddenly illuminated by the heavenly messengers, the whole thing came back to them. The misty picture became focussed and sharp and clear. Yes, He had said He would rise again. They remembered. In spite of the fact that our Lord always told them He would rise again, I believe they had never really heard it. Literally, of course, they had heard it, but they never caught the significance of it. To me there is no other explanation of the fact that the whole crowd of them were not waiting around the grave to see the risen Jesus. They had heard, but they had never understood. I think, personally, that their orthodoxy prevented them understanding Jesus. Let me illustrate from another story. At the raising of Lazarus, Jesus said to Martha:

"Thy brother shall rise again."

To which Martha replied,

"I know that he shall rise again in the resurrection at the last day."

She believed in resurrection ultimately, but did not think for a moment that our Lord referred to an immediate raising of the dead. So with these men, when they heard Him say that He should rise again, they thought He referred to resurrection "at the last day," and so failed to catch the real significance of what He said. Luke says here,

"And they remembered His words."

I think that then for the first time the meaning of His teaching dawned on them.

Thus remembering, they

"Returned from the tomb, and told all these things to the eleven, and to all the rest. Now they were Mary Magdalene, and Joanna, and Mary the mother of James; and the other women with them told these things unto the apostles."

Mary Magdalene, said Augustine, was *"Apostola Apostolorum,"* the apostle to the apostles on that matter of the resurrection.

"And these words appeared in their sight as idle talk; and they disbelieved them."

Is that all? No, something else happened in the morning.

"But Peter arose, and ran unto the tomb."

Peter, the man who had denied Him with oaths and curses. Where had Peter been from that awful hour when he went out with a broken heart from the judgment hall? He had been with John. Luke does not tell us that, but we know from the other Gospels that the women went to John, and Peter was with him. Blessed be John for evermore. He took Peter in, before the resurrection, and before his restoration. He was with John when the women found them.

"But Peter arose, and ran unto the tomb."

Can't you see him running? Yes, John went with him, and John was the younger man, and arrived first. Luke does not tell us that. He keeps our attention on Peter. He

"ran unto the tomb; and stooping and looking in, he seeth the linen cloths by themselves,"

that is, just as they had been wrapped round the dead body of Jesus, undisturbed grave-clothes. He saw the linen cloths by themselves, only the cerements and not the body there, he saw them,

"and he departed to his home, wondering at that which was come to pass."

Then Luke tells us something about the afternoon.

"And behold, two of them were going that very day to a village named Emmaus, which was threescore furlongs from Jerusalem. And they communed with each other of all these things which had happened. And it came to pass, while they communed and questioned together, that Jesus Himself drew near, and went with them. But their eyes were holden that they should not know Him."

One of the remarkable characteristics of those forty days between the resurrection and the ascension is that it was possible for Jesus to be with disciples and they not know Who He was, until He desired to make Himself known. Here we see Him walking with them, and they did not know Him.

There is no story of the postresurrection period more full of fascination to me than this. If any one can read this story, and not believe that there is even in that resurrection life the manifestations of the humour of God, I do not understand that person. There is a tender and beautiful playfulness in the way He dealt with these men. Humour is as divine as pathos, and I cannot study the life of Jesus without finding humour there. He, the risen Lord, the Lord of life and glory, having triumphed over death and sin, joined these two desolate travellers who were thinking of Him as dead, and said to them:

"What communications are these that ye have one with another, as ye walk?"

In other words He said, What are you two talking about?

"And they stood still, looking sad. And one of them, named Cleopas, answering said unto Him, Dost Thou alone sojourn in Jerusalem, and not know the things which are come to pass in these days?"

By which he meant: Are You the only man in Jerusalem ignorant of what has been going on?

"He said unto them, What things?"

Just imagine *Him* asking them, "What

things?" He was drawing them out.
He wanted them to talk, and they did;

"And they said unto Him, The things
concerning Jesus the Nazarene Who
was a Prophet mighty in deed and word
before God and all the people."

They still believed in Him. They still
loved Him. That was the language of
perfect faith. They had seen Him die.
In certain ways they knew He was
defeated. Even though He were defeated, they were still saying that He
was mighty in deed and word before
God. But they had not done; there
was more to say;

"And how the chief priests and our
rulers delivered Him up to be condemned to death, and crucified Him.
But we hoped that it was He Who
should redeem Israel."

Thus we see their attitude, and in
it a wonderful revelation of what the
Cross had done for the disciples of
Jesus. It had not destroyed their love
for Him, nor their belief in Him, and
His intention, but it had slain their
hope. In the Cross they saw failure.
" We hoped," past tense !

Yes, but they had not quite done;

" Yea, and besides all this, it is now
the third day since these things came
to pass. Moreover certain women of
our company amazed us, having been
early at the tomb; and when they
found not His body, they came, saying,
that they had also seen a vision of
angels, who said that He was alive.
And certain of them that were with us
went to the tomb, and found it even as
the women had said; but Him they
saw not."

That is where the whole Christian
movement would have ended, had there
been no resurrection. The final proof
of the resurrection is in the Christian
Church.

Now Jesus began to talk to them;

"And He said unto them, O foolish
men, and slow of heart to believe in all
that the prophets have spoken!"

Mark well His method. He took them
back to their own writings, their sacred
literature, to the things most familiar
to them,

" Behooved it not the Christ to suffer

these things, and to enter into His
glory?"

His first word for these men was a
rebuke, as the first word of the angels
to the women was a rebuke, a little
sterner than the angels,

" O foolish men, and slow of heart
to believe in all that the prophets have
spoken! And beginning from Moses
and from all the prophets, He interpreted to them in all the Scriptures the
things concerning Himself."

I never read this without having the
feeling that I would have given anything to travel that road, and hear
what He had to say. One could almost
imaginatively follow some of the things
as one thinks of the Old Testament.
They listened to this Stranger as He
took their own sacred writings, and
interpreted to them their deepest meaning. They listened to Him as He revealed to them the profoundest depths
in the suggestive ritual of the Mosaic
economy, as He breathed in their ears
the secret of the love which lay at the
heart of the ancient law. They listened
to Him as He traced the Messianic
note in the music of all the prophets;
showing that He was David's King,
" fairer than the children of men," and
in the days of Solomon's well-doing,
He was "the altogether lovely " One.
He was Isaiah's Child-King with a
shoulder strong enough to bear the
government; and the name Emanuel,
gathering within itself all the excel-
lencies. He was Jeremiah's " Branch
of Righteousness, executing justice and
righteousness in the land." He was
Ezekiel's " Plant of renown," giving
shade and giving fragrance. He was
Daniel's stone cut without hands, smiting the image, becoming a mountain,
and filling the whole earth. He was
the ideal Israel of Hosea, " growing
as the lily," " casting out His roots as
Lebanon." To Joel, the Hope of the
people, and the Strength of the children of Israel; and the Usherer in of
the vision of Amos, of the " Plowman
overtaking the reaper, and the treader
of grapes him that soweth seed;" and
of Obadiah the " Deliverance upon
Mount Zion and holiness;" the Fulfilment of that of which Jonah was but

a sign. He was the "turning again" to God, of which Micah spoke. He was the One Nahum saw upon the mountains publishing peace. He was the Anointed of Whom Habakkuk sang as "going forth for salvation." He was the One Who brought to the people the pure language of Zephaniah's message, the true Zerubbabel of Haggai's word, for ever rebuilding the house of God; Himself the dawn of the day when "Holiness—shall be upon the bells of the horses," as Zechariah foretold; and He the "Refiner," sitting over the fire, "the Sun of Righteousness" of Malachi's dream.

"In all the Scriptures the things concerning Himself."

And then they arrived.

"And they drew nigh unto the village, whither they were going; and He made as though He would go further. And they constrained Him, saying, Abide with us; for it is toward evening, and the day is now far spent. And He went in to abide with them. And it came to pass, when He had sat down with them to meat, He took the bread and blessed; and breaking it He gave to them. And their eyes were opened, and they knew Him; and He vanished out of their sight. And they said one to another, Was not our heart burning within us, while He spake to us in the way, while He opened to us the Scriptures?"

They offered Him hospitality, and He accepted it; and then He gave them hospitality. There are two movements. We have a hymn, one of the most popular: "Abide with me, fast falls the eventide." It is a great hymn of Lyte's. He wrote it when the shadows were lengthening about him. I am not objecting to a line in it. I am not objecting to a thought in it. Nevertheless the whole idea of the hymn is this: Come in, and take care of me, come in, and look after me;

"Abide with me, fast falls the eventide;
The darkness deepens; Lord, with me abide;
When other helpers fail and comforts flee,
Help of the helpless, on, abide with me!"

But that is not what these men meant. They did not ask Him to stay there, to take care of them. They asked Him to stay, that they might take care of Him. That road was a dangerous way, and they said, The day is far spent; come and stay with us. And He went in. He did not need the love that was willing to take care of Him. I love Lyte's hymn. But do not forget the other side. I said something like that in my own Church in London some years ago, and a woman named Evelyn Davies heard me, and so she wrote another hymn, which correctly interprets what these men meant;

"Abide with us, the nightly shadows fall,
The road is lone and rough for one and all;
But Thou, a Stranger here, wilt lose Thy way,
So come and be our Guest until 'tis day.

"'Abide with us! Oh, do I hear aright
That you will give Me shelter for the night,
And welcome Me, as Guest, within your home?
Oh, happiness, I'll bring you to My throne!'

"Come in! we fain would entertain Thee now,
And chase that look of sadness from Thy brow;
Footsore and weary, Thou with Thy long walk,
Abide with us, and let us freely talk.

"'I will come in and gladly stay with you;
You know not yet, My children, what you do.
My heart is always yearning for that word
"Abide with us"—which I have just now heard.'

"So in the calm of that blest evening hour
Those two disciples learnt the secret power
Of close communion with their unknown Lord,
Whom they before had seen—but now adored.

279

" O Jesus, come, and likewise with us
  stay,
We'll give Thee welcome on Thy
  lonely way;
Our lives at Thy disposal we will
  place,
With acts of love, Thy sorrow deep
  to chase.

"Abide with us, and treat us as Thy
  friends;
Thus may we for past coldness make
  amends;
Our door to Thee be always open
  wide;
Come in, and ever with us now
  abide!

" Thus may we know Thee really as
  Thou art,
As friend with friend learns each the
  other's heart.
Within our doors reveal Thyself the
  way;
Lead us to heaven, at eventide, one
  day."

Don't give up Lyte's hymn, but remember that the risen Master, victorious over sin and death and hell, the crowned Lord of all the universe, when offered hospitality, accepted it. I think He still loves to hear us say:

" Oh, come to my heart, Lord Jesus,
  There is room in my heart for
   Thee."

LUKE XXIV. 33-53

IN our last meditation we left two disciples in Emmaus; but we left them completely changed in all their outlook; not yet perfectly apprehending the wonder of the thing that had transpired, and yet face to face with the fact that the Master, Whom they had spoken of so tenderly, yet mourned as dead, and Whom they had conceived of as having failed to accomplish His purpose, was not dead, but alive. Had they not walked with Him? Had they not listened while He talked to them? Had they not seen Him taking His place at the simple meal at eventide, and turning it into a veritable sacrament as He broke the bread, and then vanished? Strangely perplexed, but as Peter said long after, writing of his experience, they were

" born again unto a living hope by the resurrection of Jesus from the dead."

They at once started back to Jerusalem to join the group of disciples there, and to tell them the news. But when they came, before they had a chance to tell them, the disciples had something to tell the two, and they did so. Then while they were all in that upper room talking of these things, Jesus stood in the midst of them.

They had not intended to go back to Jerusalem that night; they had travelled that sixty furlongs to Emmaus; unquestionably intending to stay there the night, but they could not stay; they had to get back; and Luke points out very clearly that they did not wait at all;

" They rose up that very hour, and returned to Jerusalem, and found the eleven gathered together, and them that were with them."

Before the two could tell their story, they were greeted by the eleven with news;

" The Lord is risen indeed, and hath appeared to Simon."

Then the two told their story;

" They rehearsed the things that happened in the way, and how He was known of them in the breaking of the bread."

The greeting of the eleven was significant; they were now sure that the Lord was indeed risen, because He had " appeared unto Simon." As though that settled it! As we saw before, there had been a rumour, before the two had started to Emmaus. They had said,

" Certain women of our company amazed us . . . saying they had also seen a vision of angels, who said that He was alive."

But now there was proof positive. A man had seen Him!

And it was a wonderful fact undoubtedly to all of those men. "He hath appeared to Simon." Simon! The man who had openly denied Him! Of that appearance we have no account except that it certainly was a very definite one, so definite and so striking, that when Paul, in the fifteenth chapter of the first letter to the Corinthians, massed the evidences of the resurrection by the testimony of those who saw Jesus, he mentioned it, "Then to Cephas."

It is quite legitimate for us to wait with wistful wonder. I wonder where He found him. I cannot tell you. We do know, however, that when Mary took the news in the early morning it was to Peter and John she went. John had a house in Jerusalem, and evidently Simon had been found by John on that dark and bitter night, when with broken heart he had gone from the judgment hall, and taken him there. I wonder if Jesus went to that home, and if so, who was there, because John had taken the Mother of the Lord to his house. I am inclined to think if Jesus went to the house, He did not see John, nor His Mother. It was a private interview. In that interview all the sin and the shame of the denial were dealt with and settled and put away for ever. I can imagine that Jesus might have said to him somewhat like this: Simon, do you remember how, six months ago, I told you I must die and rise? And, Simon, you were so terrified at the dying that you never heard about the rising. Simon, do you remember that I warned you, because you did not perfectly trust Me, you would go down into the depths! But I prayed for you, that your faith should not fail, and it never failed. Now, Simon, do you understand why I went to the Cross? I am the living Lord, and your sins are forgiven. All that is imagination, but I do not think it misses the mark very much. This, however, is certain, He did appear to Simon! That is the glory of the story.

Then the two told their story, and how He was known to them in the breaking of the bread.

Then something happened, strange, and enough to terrify them, as it did terrify them. Quite suddenly, without the opening of a door, or the shooting of a bolt, for they were assembled with doors shut, for fear of the Jews, Jesus was among them;

"And as they spake these things, He Himself stood in the midst, and saith unto them, Peace unto you."

"He Himself," notice the emphasis. "He Himself," no phantom, no mere ghost, no phantasy of the imagination, no vision flung up out of their own mind. No, "He Himself" stood in the midst of them!

"Peace unto you." That is how He greeted them. It was the ordinary greeting of the East, just as common as the greeting with which we are familiar when we say to each other, "Good morning." But on His lips the ordinary had become extraordinary. They had never heard it said with the same authority before. There must have been a mystic marvel and majesty in the words as He then uttered them. The commonplace became suffused with light and glory, and meant something it had never meant before— "Peace unto you."

Then we read:

"But they were terrified and affrighted, and supposed that they beheld a spirit."

And what wonder? The door was shut, they were wondering at the news that Jesus was risen, had appeared to Simon, and had walked with two of them along the highway to Emmaus. Then, suddenly they saw Him standing among them, and they heard Him greet them, as naturally as He so often used to do. Of course they were terrified. It was the closed door that created the difficulty. They "supposed that they beheld a spirit."

Now let us read on, and there is something more wonderful than this. It is wonderful because there is no final explanation of it.

"And He said unto them, Why are

ye troubled? and wherefore do questionings arise in your heart? See My hands and My feet, that it is I Myself; handle Me, and see; for a spirit hath not flesh and bones, as ye behold Me having. And when He had said this, He showed them His hands and His feet. And while they still disbelieved for joy, and wondered, He said unto them, Have ye here anything to eat? And they gave Him a piece of a broiled fish. And He took it, and ate before them."

What was He doing? He was demonstrating to them the reality of the resurrection. He was there, the same hands, the same feet. There were wound-prints in them. Thus they saw that it was actually their Master, Whom they had seen done to death on a Roman gibbet. Then, determined to make them realize it, He said, Is there anything here to eat? They found a piece of a broiled fish, and He ate it. Thus He was demonstrating the reality of His Personality, and the corporeal reality of His resurrection.

Now, there are senses in which all this is utterly inexplicable. But that does not say it was not actual. Moreover, there is a Scriptural explanation of it. Paul, under the guidance of the Holy Spirit, has given us the explanation. In the fifteenth chapter of First Corinthians we read:

" But some one will say, How are the dead raised? and with what manner of body do they come?"

The idea that there can be a resurrection which is not corporeal is absurd. Paul is careful to state the difficulty; and it is a difficulty;

" With what manner of body do they come?"

Then he replies:

" Thou foolish one, that which thou thyself sowest is not quickened except it die; and that which thou sowest, thou sowest not the body that shall be, but a bare grain, it may chance of wheat, or of some other kind; but God giveth it a body even as it pleased Him, and to each seed a body of its own."

He goes to Nature, and he says, You put a seed into the ground. It dies, but it comes again; but what comes again is not that which you planted; but that which comes again would never come again except for that which you did plant. That is a phenomenon of Nature, which is just as inexplicable as the resurrection.

Then he says:

"All flesh is not the same flesh; but there is one flesh of men, and another flesh of beasts, and another flesh of birds, and another of fishes. There are also celestial bodies, and bodies terrestrial; but the glory of the celestial is one, and the glory of the terrestrial is another. There is one glory of the sun, and another glory of the moon, and another glory of the stars."

All of which means, there are diversities of corporeal substance. The statement of central value is that there are celestial bodies, and bodies terrestrial. Moreover, there are other bodies. Sun, moon, and stars are neither celestial, nor terrestrial. One is solar, another lunar, others stellar. The word celestial, *Epouraneos,* above the sky, is purely relative, and in that sense may be applied to sun, moon, and stars. Here, however, Paul was using it to differentiate between bodies fitted for the terrestrial, or earthly sphere, and bodies fitted for a life that is super-terrestrial. But in either case there is corporeal reality. There is a body that belongs to the heavenly, and there is a body that is fitted for the earthly.

This, he then applies to the resurrection:

" So also is the resurrection of the dead. It is sown in corruption; it is raised in incorruption; it is sown in dishonour; it is raised in glory; it is sown in weakness; it is raised in power; it is sown a natural body; (*Soma psuchikon;*) it is raised a spiritual body (*Soma pneumatikon*). If there is a psychical body, there is also a spiritual body."

Jesus, before He died, had a psychical body, the earthly, the terrestrial. After His resurrection He had a spiritual body, the heavenly; the celestial. His resurrection body was no longer limited by the laws that limit the terrestrial body. He was the same. Look at His hands; look at His feet. He was capable of eating. But He was not the same. Personality is not dependent upon identity of material dwelling. None of us has the same body that we had seven years ago. There is not a particle of us here now that was us then. We are always fashioning the material dwelling-place. In resurrection there is not merely a change in the body, within the same material, there is a change in the character of the material, a body fitted for the higher reaches, but still a body.

That is the explanation of what these disciples saw in the upper room. All the appearings and disappearings of Jesus during those forty days are full of wonder. He appeared and He vanished, He appeared and He vanished, He appeared and He vanished. What was He doing? He was getting them accustomed to the fact, that even when He was not visible to the eyes of the earthly body, He was still present and available, and He might appear anywhere. His body was now changed, so that at His will, He could talk to a woman in the garden the first thing in the morning, or He could talk to two for several miles on a walk, and they not know Him; and yet when He desired, there was no mistaking Him. "Mary." "Rabonni!" and she knew Him. He broke the bread, and they knew Him. Strange and wonderful mystery; but the fact that it is inexplicable by what we now know, does not mean that it is not actual. One day we shall perfectly understand, for that is the kind of body we shall have in resurrection life. So He presenced Himself amongst them.

Now let us go on. He began to teach them.

"And He said unto them, These are My words which I spake unto you, while I was yet with you, that all things must needs be fulfilled, which are written in the law of Moses, and the prophets, and the psalms, concerning Me."

Thus He did with the whole company in the upper room, in some senses, what He had done with the two walking to Emmaus.

"Beginning from Moses and from all the prophets," He had "interpreted to the two in all the Scriptures the things concerning Himself."

We are not told He gave interpretation to the group, but He did declare that all the Old Testament witnessed to Him. He named the whole of the Old Testament in its three great divisions, the *Torah*, which means the Law, which is often called "Moses;" the *Nebiim*, the Hebrew word for Prophets; and the *Kethubim*, or in the Greek, *Hagiographa;* and that third section was constantly called the Psalms, because the Psalms were placed first in it. All things, He said, must needs be fulfilled which are written therein concerning Him.

Luke tells us that, having made this declaration;

"Then opened He their mind, that they might understand the Scriptures."

He opened their minds. That word "opened" is a very remarkable one. The Greek word *dianoigo* means to thoroughly open up. I do not know that there is any word in our language that may help us more than the word disentangled. That is what He did for their minds, freed them from all prejudice, from all pride, somehow dealt with their mentality so that the picture blurred, indistinct, out of focus, came sharply into focus, and they saw the whole thing, not in detail, but in sequence.

Then He summarized;

"Thus it is written, that the Messiah should suffer, and rise again from the dead the third day; and that repentance and remission of sins should be preached in His name unto all the nations, beginning from Jerusalem."

That is our Lord's summary of the teaching of the Old Testament, as proven true by His presence in the midst of that group in the upper room. The great fact, the Christ, suffering and dying. The result, repentance and remission of sins, man's attitude, and

God's act. That is the whole meaning of His mission.

The responsibility of His disciples is created by these things;

" Ye are witnesses of these things."

That was to be the whole business of those disciples. That remains the whole business of the Christian Church.

Finally, for this work they were to be equipped;

"And behold, I send forth the promise of My Father upon you; but tarry ye in the city, until ye be clothed with power from on high."

Thus Luke's story is indeed condensed, but it covers all the ground. He came into their midst. He demonstrated the reality of His Personality. He set the seal of Divine authority upon the whole of the Old Testament. He summarized its teaching; it pointed to a Christ Who should suffer and rise; with the result that repentance and remission of sins should be preached, beginning at Jerusalem, but not ending there. He told that band in the upper room that they were to witness to these things, to be His credentials, His evidences, His witnesses,—to transliterate,—His martyrs, that is, His confessors.

Then Luke, omitting all intervening days and incidents, records the ascension;

"And He led them out until they were over against Bethany; and He lifted up His hands, and blessed them. And it came to pass, while He blessed them, He parted from them, and was carried up into heaven. And they worshipped Him, and returned to Jerusalem with great joy; and were continually in the Temple, blessing God."

That is the story of the ascension. " He led them out." From where? From the city, from the Temple, from all the old order which was effete, and being done away. The last attitude in which they saw Him was with hands lifted up. They were the lifted hands of priestly benediction; and as they saw Him so, He parted from them. It was an act. He began to walk away, and then He was carried, *anaphero*, that is, was borne up into heaven. Thus He passed away from their sight; and they worshipped and returned, and were continually in the Temple. Mark that very carefully. That is where they were, in the Temple, when the Spirit came.

The best place to end a study of Luke is in the first chapter of Acts;

" The former treatise I made, O Theophilus, concerning all that Jesus began both to do and to teach."

That reference was to this treatise which we have been studying. Luke does not call it a record of all that Jesus did and taught, but of

"All that Jesus *began* both to do and to teach."

The story of all He *began* to do and teach. In the Acts we have the story of His continued doing and teaching. We are linked with the living Christ by the Spirit Who came in fulfilment of the promise of the Father, and we are called to be witnesses of all these things. So the matchless story from the pen of Luke comes to its conclusion.

Printed in the United States of America